SUNDAY MISSAL

2026-2027

Living with Christ
500 Salisbury St.
Worcester, MA 01609
1-800-321-0411
www.livingwithchrist.us

bayard

Design and Layout: Jessica Llewellyn

Illustrations and photo credits: page 8, Michael Connors

ISBN 978-1-62785-876-2

Printed in the U.S.A.

To order more copies:
Tel: 1-800-321-0411
Website: www.livingwithchrist.us

CONTENTS

How to Use This Missal

YOUR COMPANION FOR PRAYING AND LIVING THE EUCHARIST

Over the years, the use of personal missals has changed. Before Vatican Council II (1962-65), when the Mass was said in Latin, most people needed a missal during the Mass to understand the priest's words.

Vatican II made important changes in the Mass because it recognized that the celebration of Mass was lacking several important things. First, it needed to be in language the people could understand. Second, the people were to be truly involved as "full, conscious, and active" participants in the many prayers, songs, and ritual actions of the celebration.

The Mass is not to be something that just the priest does, but something that the whole community or assembly does together—singing, listening to God's word, praying for the needs of the Church and world, thanking God, sharing the consecrated bread and wine, and finally being sent back to their homes, schools, and workplaces to live what they celebrated: God present with us to change our lives and gather us into God's own community of justice, love, and peace.

As a result, after Vatican II many parishes encouraged more participation and discouraged using missals during Mass, except perhaps by those who could not hear the readings. The focus was on listening when the Scriptures were proclaimed aloud—a reminder that God was present and speaking to us in that word.

USING THE MISSAL TO PREPARE FOR SUNDAY

So, if we are not encouraged to use our missal at Mass, is there still a use for a Sunday missal? The answer is yes. But we should now use our missal at home to help us prepare to celebrate the Sunday Eucharist more fully.

The Mass celebrates God's presence with us in word and sacrament. Through Scripture we learn how God has been present with us and what we must do to live rightly in relation to God and others. But making Scripture's message our own is not always easy. In order to get more out of our Sunday listening, we should preview the readings at home during the week.

This Sunday Missal offers resources for you, your family, and your friends to prepare for a richer celebration each Sunday. Different from other Sunday missals, this missal includes not only all the prayers and Scripture readings for the Sunday Masses, but also a variety of other helps to use at home so you can participate at Mass more "fully, consciously, actively, and as befits a community," as Vatican II desired.

WEEKLY RESOURCES FOR PREPARING FOR SUNDAY

This Sunday Missal helps you to pray and live the Eucharist by preparing each week for a richer celebration of Mass. For each Sunday throughout the year, you will find:

- **A brief reflection** inspired by the readings to consider how God's message might resonate with everyday life
- **The complete text of all of the Mass prayers and Scripture readings** chosen by the Church. Also included are these other major feast days: Mary's Immaculate Conception, Ash Wednesday, the sacred three days of Holy Week, i.e., the Triduum (Holy Thursday, Good Friday, and Holy Saturday), Mary's Assumption into Heaven, and All Saints
- At the end of each Sunday, there are helps for deepening your appreciation of both the Scripture readings and the Mass prayers from the Roman Missal:

- **Responding to the word**: questions that help you pray about and discuss the meaning and application of the Scripture readings
- **Taking a closer look**: information and reflections on biblical words and themes from the Scripture texts (indicated in bold and followed by a + in the text)

GENERAL HELPS FOR PRAYING AND LIVING THE EUCHARIST

In addition to the weekly helps, this missal contains several features that you will find helpful for deepening both your understanding of the Church's liturgical year and your prayer, including:

- **Seasonal backgrounds** at the start of each liturgical season, together with suggestions for praying and living each liturgical season (e.g., pages 65-66)
- **Basic questions for exploring Scripture** (see page 598) that you can use to discover the meaning and application to your life of any Scripture reading
- **Explanations of the Church's liturgical year,** including the Church's liturgical calendar (see page 601) and the lectionary (see page 603)
- **A brief overview of Mark's gospel** (see page 605), the primary gospel proclaimed on Sundays this year
- **The differences between liturgical and devotional prayer** (see page 609), both of which help us grow in our life as disciples
- **A treasury of prayers** (see page 615) taken from Scripture, the saints, and the Christian tradition; and also a simple ritual for receiving Communion outside of Mass
- **A pronunciation guide for biblical words** (see page 648) for words indicated by an asterisk (*) in the Scripture readings

Our Eucharistic

Liturgy *The Order of Mass*

WE ARE A EUCHARISTIC PEOPLE

The celebration of the Eucharist or Mass is the central action that defines us as Catholics and directs our efforts to realize God's kingdom community today.

Our celebration is a ritual action that is repeated over and over so that by participating in it we can bring to consciousness, through word and sacrament, the deepest meaning of our lives.

Our celebration is *eucharist*, Greek for "thanksgiving," to remind us that our basic human relationship to God is a response to God's gifts. Everything that we have is God's gift. In our ritual, we celebrate the gift of God's own presence in the assembly that gathers, in God's word that we hear, in the consecrated bread and wine that are Christ's body and blood, and in the person of the priest who presides during the celebration.

Our celebration is also Mass, from the final Latin words of sending, *Ite missa est*, meaning "Go, you are sent." As we finish our prayer, we are reminded that we are sent to discover and proclaim God's presence in all the situations of our daily lives.

As Christians, we not only *pray* the Eucharist, but we are also called upon to *live* "eucharistic" lives. Just as Jesus took the bread, his body, and blessed and broke it to share with others, so we ask God to *take* us, *bless* us, *break* us, and *share* us with others so that "through him, and with him, and in him" we may also become sources of God's new life for the world.

Introductory Rites

ENTRANCE ANTIPHON (Turn to the appropriate day)

GREETING

In the name of the Father, and of the Son,
and of the Holy Spirit. ***Amen.***

1. The grace of our Lord Jesus Christ,
and the love of God,
and the communion of the Holy Spirit
be with you all.
And with your spirit.

2. Grace to you and peace from God our Father
and the Lord Jesus Christ.
And with your spirit.

3. The Lord be with you.
And with your spirit.

PENITENTIAL ACT

Brethren (brothers and sisters), let us acknowledge our sins, and so prepare ourselves to celebrate the sacred mysteries.

After a brief pause for silence, one of the following forms is used:

1. ***I confess to almighty God***
and to you, my brothers and sisters,
that I have greatly sinned,
in my thoughts and in my words,
in what I have done and in what I have failed to do,
(And, striking their breast, they say:)

through my fault, through my fault,
through my most grievous fault;
therefore I ask blessed Mary ever-Virgin,
all the Angels and Saints,
and you, my brothers and sisters,
to pray for me to the Lord our God.

May almighty God have mercy on us,
forgive us our sins,
and bring us to everlasting life.
Amen.

2 Have mercy on us, O Lord.
For we have sinned against you.

Show us, O Lord, your mercy.
And grant us your salvation.

May almighty God have mercy on us,
forgive us our sins,
and bring us to everlasting life.
Amen.

3 **The celebrant makes the following or other invocations:**

You were sent to heal the contrite of heart:
Lord, have mercy. **Or** Kyrie, eleison.
Lord, have mercy. **Or** ***Kyrie, eleison.***

You came to call sinners:
Christ, have mercy. **Or** Christe, eleison.
Christ, have mercy. **Or** ***Christe, eleison.***

You are seated at the right hand of the Father
to intercede for us:

Lord, have mercy. Or Kyrie, eleison.
Lord, have mercy. Or ***Kyrie, eleison.***

May almighty God have mercy on us,
forgive us our sins,
and bring us to everlasting life.
Amen.

The following invocations in either English or the ancient Greek are said, unless they have just occurred in a formula of the Penitential Act:

Lord, have mercy.	Or	Kyrie, eleison.
Lord, have mercy.		***Kyrie, eleison.***
Christ, have mercy.		Christe, eleison.
Christ, have mercy.		***Christe, eleison.***
Lord, have mercy.		Kyrie, eleison.
Lord, have mercy.		***Kyrie, eleison.***

GLORY TO GOD

Glory to God in the highest,
and on earth peace to people of good will.

We praise you,
we bless you,
we adore you,
we glorify you,
we give you thanks for your great glory,
Lord God, heavenly King,
O God, almighty Father.

Lord Jesus Christ, Only Begotten Son,
Lord God, Lamb of God, Son of the Father,
you take away the sins of the world,
have mercy on us;
you take away the sins of the world,
receive our prayer;
you are seated at the right hand of the Father:
have mercy on us.

For you alone are the Holy One,
you alone are the Lord,
you alone are the Most High,
Jesus Christ,
with the Holy Spirit,
in the glory of God the Father. Amen.

COLLECT (Turn to the appropriate day)

Liturgy of the Word

READINGS (Turn to the appropriate day)

HOMILY

PROFESSION OF FAITH: NICENE CREED
I believe in one God,
the Father almighty,
maker of heaven and earth,
of all things visible and invisible.
I believe in one Lord Jesus Christ,

the Only Begotten Son of God,
born of the Father before all ages.
God from God, Light from Light,
true God from true God,
begotten, not made, consubstantial with the Father;
through him all things were made.
For us men and for our salvation
he came down from heaven,
(At the words that follow, up to and including *and became man*, all bow.)
and by the Holy Spirit was incarnate of the Virgin Mary,
and became man.

For our sake he was crucified under Pontius Pilate,
he suffered death and was buried,
and rose again on the third day
in accordance with the Scriptures.
He ascended into heaven
and is seated at the right hand of the Father.
He will come again in glory
to judge the living and the dead
and his kingdom will have no end.

I believe in the Holy Spirit, the Lord, the giver of life,
who proceeds from the Father and the Son,
who with the Father and the Son is adored and glorified,
who has spoken through the prophets.

I believe in one, holy, catholic and apostolic Church.
I confess one Baptism for the forgiveness of sins
and I look forward to the resurrection of the dead
and the life of the world to come. Amen.

OR

APOSTLES' CREED

The Apostles' Creed may be used instead of the Nicene Creed, especially during Lent and Easter Time:

I believe in God,
the Father almighty,
Creator of heaven and earth,
and in Jesus Christ, his only Son, our Lord,
(At the words that follow, up to and including the Virgin Mary, all bow.)
who was conceived by the Holy Spirit,
born of the Virgin Mary,
suffered under Pontius Pilate,
was crucified, died and was buried;
he descended into hell;
on the third day he rose again from the dead;
he ascended into heaven,
and is seated at the right hand of God the Father almighty;
from there he will come to judge the living and the dead.

I believe in the Holy Spirit,
the holy catholic Church,
the communion of saints,
the forgiveness of sins,
the resurrection of the body,
and life everlasting. Amen.

PRAYER OF THE FAITHFUL

After each intention is announced, the people respond with this or another invocation:

Lord, hear our prayer.

Liturgy of the Eucharist

OFFERTORY CHANT

PREPARATION OF GIFTS

Blessed are you, Lord God of all creation,
for through your goodness we have received
the bread we offer you:
fruit of the earth and work of human hands,
it will become for us the bread of life.
Blessed be God for ever.

By the mystery of this water and wine
may we come to share in the divinity of Christ
who humbled himself to share in our humanity.

Blessed are you, Lord God of all creation,
for through your goodness we have received
the wine we offer you:
fruit of the vine and work of human hands,
it will become our spiritual drink.
Blessed be God for ever.

With humble spirit and contrite heart
may we be accepted by you, O Lord,
and may our sacrifice in your sight this day
be pleasing to you, Lord God.

Wash me, O Lord, from my iniquity
and cleanse me from my sin.

Pray, brethren (brothers and sisters),
that my sacrifice and yours

may be acceptable to God,
the almighty Father.

May the Lord accept the sacrifice at your hands
for the praise and glory of his name,
for our good
and the good of all his holy Church.

PRAYER OVER THE OFFERINGS (Turn to the appropriate day)

EUCHARISTIC PRAYER

The Lord be with you.
And with your spirit.
Lift up your hearts.
We lift them up to the Lord.
Let us give thanks to the Lord our God.
It is right and just.

PREFACE

The celebrant chooses from among the possible prefaces corresponding to liturgical seasons and feasts. These prefaces are for use with Eucharistic Prayers 1-3. Eucharistic Prayer 4 has its own fixed preface.

PREFACE 1 OF ADVENT

It is truly right and just, our duty and our salvation,
always and everywhere to give you thanks,
Lord, holy Father, almighty and eternal God,
through Christ our Lord.

For he assumed at his first coming
the lowliness of human flesh,
and so fulfilled the design you formed long ago,
and opened for us the way to eternal salvation,

that, when he comes again in glory and majesty
and all is at last made manifest,
we who watch for that day
may inherit the great promise
in which now we dare to hope.

And so, with Angels and Archangels,
with Thrones and Dominions,
and with all the hosts and Powers of heaven,
we sing the hymn of your glory,
as without end we acclaim:
Holy, Holy, Holy Lord God of hosts... *(page 35)*

PREFACE 2 OF ADVENT

It is truly right and just, our duty and our salvation,
always and everywhere to give you thanks,
Lord, holy Father, almighty and eternal God,
through Christ our Lord.

For all the oracles of the prophets foretold him,
the Virgin Mother longed for him
with love beyond all telling,
John the Baptist sang of his coming
and proclaimed his presence when he came.

It is by his gift that already we rejoice
at the mystery of his Nativity,
so that he may find us watchful in prayer
and exultant in his praise.

And so, with Angels and Archangels,
with Thrones and Dominions,
and with all the hosts and Powers of heaven,

we sing the hymn of your glory,
as without end we acclaim:
Holy, Holy, Holy Lord God of hosts... *(page 35)*

PREFACE 1 OF THE NATIVITY OF THE LORD

It is truly right and just, our duty and our salvation,
always and everywhere to give you thanks,
Lord, holy Father, almighty and eternal God.

For in the mystery of the Word made flesh
a new light of your glory has shone upon the eyes of our mind,
so that, as we recognize in him God made visible,
we may be caught up through him in love of things invisible.

And so, with Angels and Archangels,
with Thrones and Dominions,
and with all the hosts and Powers of heaven,
we sing the hymn of your glory,
as without end we acclaim:
Holy, Holy, Holy Lord God of hosts... *(page 35)*

PREFACE 2 OF THE NATIVITY OF THE LORD

It is truly right and just, our duty and our salvation,
always and everywhere to give you thanks,
Lord, holy Father, almighty and eternal God,
through Christ our Lord.

For on the feast of this awe-filled mystery,
though invisible in his own divine nature,
he has appeared visibly in ours;
and begotten before all ages,
he has begun to exist in time;

so that, raising up in himself all that was cast down,
he might restore unity to all creation
and call straying humanity back to the heavenly Kingdom.

And so, with all the Angels, we praise you,
as in joyful celebration we acclaim:
Holy, Holy, Holy Lord God of hosts... *(page 35)*

PREFACE 3 OF THE NATIVITY OF THE LORD

It is truly right and just, our duty and our salvation,
always and everywhere to give you thanks,
Lord, holy Father, almighty and eternal God,
through Christ our Lord.

For through him the holy exchange that restores our life
has shone forth today in splendor:
when our frailty is assumed by your Word
not only does human mortality receive unending honor
but by this wondrous union we, too, are made eternal.

And so, in company with the choirs of Angels,
we praise you, and with joy we proclaim:
Holy, Holy, Holy Lord God of hosts... *(page 35)*

PREFACE OF THE EPIPHANY OF THE LORD

It is truly right and just, our duty and our salvation,
always and everywhere to give you thanks,
Lord, holy Father, almighty and eternal God.

For today you have revealed the mystery
of our salvation in Christ
as a light for the nations,

and, when he appeared in our mortal nature,
you made us new by the glory of his immortal nature.

And so, with Angels and Archangels,
with Thrones and Dominions,
and with all the hosts and Powers of heaven,
we sing the hymn of your glory,
as without end we acclaim:
Holy, Holy, Holy Lord God of hosts... *(page 35)*

PREFACE 1 OF LENT

It is truly right and just, our duty and our salvation,
always and everywhere to give you thanks,
Lord, holy Father, almighty and eternal God,
through Christ our Lord.

For by your gracious gift each year
your faithful await the sacred paschal feasts
with the joy of minds made pure,
so that, more eagerly intent on prayer
and on the works of charity,
and participating in the mysteries
by which they have been reborn,
they may be led to the fullness of grace
that you bestow on your sons and daughters.

And so, with Angels and Archangels,
with Thrones and Dominions,
and with all the hosts and Powers of heaven,
we sing the hymn of your glory,
as without end we acclaim:
Holy, Holy, Holy Lord God of hosts... *(page 35)*

PREFACE 2 OF LENT

It is truly right and just, our duty and our salvation,
always and everywhere to give you thanks,
Lord, holy Father, almighty and eternal God.

For you have given your children a sacred time
for the renewing and purifying of their hearts,
that, freed from disordered affections,
they may so deal with the things of this passing world
as to hold rather to the things that eternally endure.

And so, with all the Angels and Saints,
we praise you, as without end we acclaim:
Holy, Holy, Holy Lord God of hosts... *(page 35)*

PREFACE 3 OF LENT

It is truly right and just, our duty and our salvation,
always and everywhere to give you thanks,
Lord, holy Father, almighty and eternal God.

For you will that our self-denial should give you thanks,
humble our sinful pride,
contribute to the feeding of the poor,
and so help us imitate you in your kindness.

And so we glorify you with countless Angels,
as with one voice of praise we acclaim:
Holy, Holy, Holy Lord God of hosts... *(page 35)*

PREFACE 4 OF LENT

It is truly right and just, our duty and our salvation,
always and everywhere to give you thanks,
Lord, holy Father, almighty and eternal God.

For through bodily fasting you restrain our faults,
raise up our minds,
and bestow both virtue and its rewards,
through Christ our Lord.

Through him the Angels praise your majesty,
Dominions adore and Powers tremble before you.
Heaven and the Virtues of heaven and the blessed Seraphim
worship together with exultation.
May our voices, we pray, join with theirs
in humble praise, as we acclaim:
Holy, Holy, Holy Lord God of hosts... *(page 35)*

PREFACE 1 OF THE PASSION OF THE LORD

It is truly right and just, our duty and our salvation,
always and everywhere to give you thanks,
Lord, holy Father, almighty and eternal God.

For through the saving Passion of your Son
the whole world has received a heart
to confess the infinite power of your majesty,
since by the wondrous power of the Cross
your judgment on the world is now revealed
and the authority of Christ crucified.

And so, Lord, with all the Angels and Saints,
we, too, give you thanks, as in exultation we acclaim:
Holy, Holy, Holy Lord God of hosts... *(page 35)*

PREFACE 2 OF THE PASSION OF THE LORD

It is truly right and just, our duty and our salvation,
always and everywhere to give you thanks,

Lord, holy Father, almighty and eternal God,
through Christ our Lord.

For the days of his saving Passion
and glorious Resurrection are approaching,
by which the pride of the ancient foe is vanquished
and the mystery of our redemption in Christ is celebrated.

Through him the host of Angels adores your majesty
and rejoices in your presence for ever.
May our voices, we pray, join with theirs
in one chorus of exultant praise, as we acclaim:
Holy, Holy, Holy Lord God of hosts... *(page 35)*

PREFACE 1 OF EASTER

It is truly right and just, our duty and our salvation,
at all times to acclaim you, O Lord,
but (on this night / on this day / in this time) above all
to laud you yet more gloriously,
when Christ our Passover has been sacrificed.

For he is the true Lamb
who has taken away the sins of the world;
by dying he has destroyed our death,
and by rising, restored our life.

Therefore, overcome with paschal joy,
every land, every people exults in your praise
and even the heavenly Powers, with the angelic hosts,
sing together the unending hymn of your glory,
as they acclaim: ***Holy, Holy, Holy Lord God of hosts...*** *(page 35)*

PREFACE 2 OF EASTER

It is truly right and just, our duty and our salvation,
at all times to acclaim you, O Lord,
but in this time above all to laud you yet more gloriously,
when Christ our Passover has been sacrificed.

Through him the children of light rise to eternal life
and the halls of the heavenly Kingdom
are thrown open to the faithful;
for his Death is our ransom from death,
and in his rising the life of all has risen.

Therefore, overcome with paschal joy,
every land, every people exults in your praise
and even the heavenly Powers, with the angelic hosts,
sing together the unending hymn of your glory,
as they acclaim: ***Holy, Holy, Holy Lord God of hosts...*** *(page 35)*

PREFACE 3 OF EASTER

It is truly right and just, our duty and our salvation,
at all times to acclaim you, O Lord,
but in this time above all to laud you yet more gloriously,
when Christ our Passover has been sacrificed.

He never ceases to offer himself for us
but defends us and ever pleads our cause before you:
he is the sacrificial Victim who dies no more,
the Lamb, once slain, who lives for ever.

Therefore, overcome with paschal joy,
every land, every people exults in your praise
and even the heavenly Powers, with the angelic hosts,

sing together the unending hymn of your glory,
as they acclaim: ***Holy, Holy, Holy Lord God of hosts...*** *(page 35)*

PREFACE 4 OF EASTER

It is truly right and just, our duty and our salvation,
at all times to acclaim you, O Lord,
but in this time above all to laud you yet more gloriously,
when Christ our Passover has been sacrificed.

For, with the old order destroyed,
a universe cast down is renewed,
and integrity of life is restored to us in Christ.

Therefore, overcome with paschal joy,
every land, every people exults in your praise
and even the heavenly Powers, with the angelic hosts,
sing together the unending hymn of your glory,
as they acclaim: ***Holy, Holy, Holy Lord God of hosts...*** *(page 35)*

PREFACE 5 OF EASTER

It is truly right and just, our duty and our salvation,
at all times to acclaim you, O Lord,
but in this time above all to laud you yet more gloriously,
when Christ our Passover has been sacrificed.

By the oblation of his Body,
he brought the sacrifices of old to fulfillment
in the reality of the Cross
and, by commending himself to you for our salvation,
showed himself the Priest, the Altar, and the Lamb of sacrifice.

Therefore, overcome with paschal joy,
every land, every people exults in your praise

and even the heavenly Powers, with the angelic hosts,
sing together the unending hymn of your glory,
as they acclaim: ***Holy, Holy, Holy Lord God of hosts...*** *(page 35)*

PREFACE 1 OF THE ASCENSION OF THE LORD

It is truly right and just, our duty and our salvation,
always and everywhere to give you thanks,
Lord, holy Father, almighty and eternal God.

For the Lord Jesus, the King of glory,
conqueror of sin and death,
ascended (today) to the highest heavens,
as the Angels gazed in wonder.

Mediator between God and man,
judge of the world and Lord of hosts,
he ascended, not to distance himself from our lowly state
but that we, his members, might be confident of following
where he, our Head and Founder, has gone before.

Therefore, overcome with paschal joy,
every land, every people exults in your praise
and even the heavenly Powers, with the angelic hosts,
sing together the unending hymn of your glory,
as they acclaim: ***Holy, Holy, Holy Lord God of hosts...*** *(page 35)*

PREFACE 2 OF THE ASCENSION OF THE LORD

It is truly right and just, our duty and our salvation,
always and everywhere to give you thanks,
Lord, holy Father, almighty and eternal God,
through Christ our Lord.

For after his Resurrection

he plainly appeared to all his disciples
and was taken up to heaven in their sight,
that he might make us sharers in his divinity.

Therefore, overcome with paschal joy,
every land, every people exults in your praise
and even the heavenly Powers, with the angelic hosts,
sing together the unending hymn of your glory,
as they acclaim: ***Holy, Holy, Holy Lord God of hosts...*** *(page 35)*

PREFACE 1 OF THE SUNDAYS IN ORDINARY TIME

It is truly right and just, our duty and our salvation,
always and everywhere to give you thanks,
Lord, holy Father, almighty and eternal God,
through Christ our Lord.

For through his Paschal Mystery,
he accomplished the marvelous deed,
by which he has freed us from the yoke of sin and death,
summoning us to the glory of being now called
a chosen race, a royal priesthood,
a holy nation, a people for your own possession,
to proclaim everywhere your mighty works,
for you have called us out of darkness
into your own wonderful light.

And so, with Angels and Archangels,
with Thrones and Dominions,
and with all the hosts and Powers of heaven,
we sing the hymn of your glory,
as without end we acclaim:
Holy, Holy, Holy Lord God of hosts... *(page 35)*

PREFACE 2 OF THE SUNDAYS IN ORDINARY TIME

It is truly right and just, our duty and our salvation,
always and everywhere to give you thanks,
Lord, holy Father, almighty and eternal God,
through Christ our Lord.

For out of compassion for the waywardness that is ours,
he humbled himself and was born of the Virgin;
by the passion of the Cross he freed us from unending death,
and by rising from the dead he gave us life eternal.

And so, with Angels and Archangels,
with Thrones and Dominions,
and with all the hosts and Powers of heaven,
we sing the hymn of your glory,
as without end we acclaim:
Holy, Holy, Holy Lord God of hosts... *(page 35)*

PREFACE 3 OF THE SUNDAYS IN ORDINARY TIME

It is truly right and just, our duty and our salvation,
always and everywhere to give you thanks,
Lord, holy Father, almighty and eternal God.

For we know it belongs to your boundless glory,
that you came to the aid of mortal beings with your divinity
and even fashioned for us a remedy out of mortality itself,
that the cause of our downfall
might become the means of our salvation,
through Christ our Lord.

Through him the host of Angels adores your majesty
and rejoices in your presence for ever.
May our voices, we pray, join with theirs

in one chorus of exultant praise, as we acclaim:
Holy, Holy, Holy Lord God of hosts... *(page 35)*

PREFACE 4 OF THE SUNDAYS IN ORDINARY TIME

It is truly right and just, our duty and our salvation,
always and everywhere to give you thanks,
Lord, holy Father, almighty and eternal God,
through Christ our Lord.

For by his birth he brought renewal
to humanity's fallen state,
and by his suffering, canceled out our sins;
by his rising from the dead
he has opened the way to eternal life,
and by ascending to you, O Father,
he has unlocked the gates of heaven.

And so, with the company of Angels and Saints,
we sing the hymn of your praise,
as without end we acclaim:
Holy, Holy, Holy Lord God of hosts... *(page 35)*

PREFACE 5 OF THE SUNDAYS IN ORDINARY TIME

It is truly right and just, our duty and our salvation,
always and everywhere to give you thanks,
Lord, holy Father, almighty and eternal God.

For you laid the foundations of the world
and have arranged the changing of times and seasons;
you formed man in your own image
and set humanity over the whole world in all its wonder,

to rule in your name over all you have made
and for ever praise you in your mighty works,
through Christ our Lord.

And so, with all the Angels, we praise you,
as in joyful celebration we acclaim:
Holy, Holy, Holy Lord God of hosts... *(page 35)*

PREFACE 6 OF THE SUNDAYS IN ORDINARY TIME

It is truly right and just, our duty and our salvation,
always and everywhere to give you thanks,
Lord, holy Father, almighty and eternal God.

For in you we live and move and have our being,
and while in this body
we not only experience the daily effects of your care,
but even now possess the pledge of life eternal.

For, having received the first fruits of the Spirit,
through whom you raised up Jesus from the dead,
we hope for an everlasting share in the Paschal Mystery.

And so, with all the Angels, we praise you,
as in joyful celebration we acclaim:
Holy, Holy, Holy Lord God of hosts... *(page 35)*

PREFACE 7 OF THE SUNDAYS IN ORDINARY TIME

It is truly right and just, our duty and our salvation,
always and everywhere to give you thanks,
Lord, holy Father, almighty and eternal God.

For you so loved the world
that in your mercy you sent us the Redeemer,

to live like us in all things but sin,
so that you might love in us what you loved in your Son,
by whose obedience we have been restored to those gifts of yours
that, by sinning, we had lost in disobedience.

And so, Lord, with all the Angels and Saints,
we, too, give you thanks, as in exultation we acclaim:
Holy, Holy, Holy Lord God of hosts... *(page 35)*

PREFACE 8 OF THE SUNDAYS IN ORDINARY TIME

It is truly right and just, our duty and our salvation,
always and everywhere to give you thanks,
Lord, holy Father, almighty and eternal God.

For, when your children were scattered afar by sin,
through the Blood of your Son and the power of the Spirit,
you gathered them again to yourself,
that a people, formed as one by the unity of the Trinity,
made the body of Christ and the temple of the Holy Spirit,
might, to the praise of your manifold wisdom,
be manifest as the Church.

And so, in company with the choirs of Angels,
we praise you, and with joy we proclaim:
Holy, Holy, Holy Lord God of hosts... *(page 35)*

PREFACE 1 OF THE MOST HOLY EUCHARIST

It is truly right and just, our duty and our salvation,
always and everywhere to give you thanks,
Lord, holy Father, almighty and eternal God,
through Christ our Lord.

For he is the true and eternal Priest,
who instituted the pattern of an everlasting sacrifice
and was the first to offer himself as the saving Victim,
commanding us to make this offering as his memorial.
As we eat his flesh that was sacrificed for us,
we are made strong,
and, as we drink his Blood that was poured out for us,
we are washed clean.

And so, with Angels and Archangels,
with Thrones and Dominions,
and with all the hosts and Powers of heaven,
we sing the hymn of your glory,
as without end we acclaim:
Holy, Holy, Holy Lord God of hosts... *(page 35)*

PREFACE 2 OF THE MOST HOLY EUCHARIST

It is truly right and just, our duty and our salvation,
always and everywhere to give you thanks,
Lord, holy Father, almighty and eternal God,
through Christ our Lord.

For at the Last Supper with his Apostles,
establishing for the ages to come the saving memorial of the Cross,
he offered himself to you as the unblemished Lamb,
the acceptable gift of perfect praise.

Nourishing your faithful by this sacred mystery,
you make them holy, so that the human race,
bounded by one world,
may be enlightened by one faith
and united by one bond of charity.

And so, we approach the table of this wondrous Sacrament,
so that, bathed in the sweetness of your grace,
we may pass over to the heavenly realities here foreshadowed.

Therefore, all creatures of heaven and earth
sing a new song in adoration,
and we, with all the host of Angels,
cry out, and without end we acclaim:
Holy, Holy, Holy Lord God of hosts... *(page 35)*

PREFACE 1 OF THE BLESSED VIRGIN MARY

It is truly right and just, our duty and our salvation,
always and everywhere to give you thanks,
Lord, holy Father, almighty and eternal God,
and to praise, bless, and glorify your name
(on the Solemnity of the Motherhood /
on the feast day / on the Nativity / in veneration)
of the Blessed ever-Virgin Mary.

For by the overshadowing of the Holy Spirit
she conceived your Only Begotten Son,
and without losing the glory of virginity,
brought forth into the world the eternal Light,
Jesus Christ our Lord.

Through him the Angels praise your majesty,
Dominions adore and Powers tremble before you.
Heaven and the Virtues of heaven and the blessed Seraphim
worship together with exultation.
May our voices, we pray, join with theirs
in humble praise, as we acclaim:

HOLY, HOLY, HOLY

Holy, Holy, Holy Lord God of hosts.
Heaven and earth are full of your glory.
Hosanna in the highest.
Blessed is he who comes in the name of the Lord.
Hosanna in the highest.

EUCHARISTIC PRAYER 1 *(page 35)*

EUCHARISTIC PRAYER 2 *(page 42)*

EUCHARISTIC PRAYER 3 *(page 45)*

EUCHARISTIC PRAYER 4 *(page 48)*

EUCHARISTIC PRAYER 1

To you, therefore, most merciful Father,
we make humble prayer and petition
through Jesus Christ, your Son, our Lord:
that you accept
and bless these gifts, these offerings,
these holy and unblemished sacrifices,
which we offer you firstly
for your holy catholic Church.
Be pleased to grant her peace,
to guard, unite and govern her
throughout the whole world,
together with your servant N. our Pope
and N. our Bishop,
and all those who, holding to the truth,
hand on the catholic and apostolic faith.

Remember, Lord, your servants N. and N.
and all gathered here,

whose faith and devotion are known to you.
For them, we offer you this sacrifice of praise
or they offer it for themselves
and all who are dear to them:
for the redemption of their souls,
in hope of health and well-being,
and paying their homage to you,
the eternal God, living and true.

On the Nativity of the Lord and throughout the Octave add:
Celebrating the most sacred night (day)
on which blessed Mary the immaculate Virgin
brought forth the Savior for this world,
and

On the Epiphany of the Lord add:
Celebrating the most sacred day
on which your Only Begotten Son,
eternal with you in your glory,
appeared in a human body, truly sharing our flesh,
and

On Holy Thursday add:
Celebrating the most sacred day
on which our Lord Jesus Christ
was handed over for our sake,
and

From the Mass of the Easter Vigil until the Second Sunday of Easter add:
Celebrating the most sacred night (day)

of the Resurrection of our Lord Jesus Christ in the flesh,
and

On the Ascension of the Lord add:

Celebrating the most sacred day
on which your Only Begotten Son, our Lord,
placed at the right hand of your glory
our weak human nature,
which he had united to himself,
and

On Pentecost Sunday add:

Celebrating the most sacred day of Pentecost,
on which the Holy Spirit
appeared to the Apostles in tongues of fire,
and

In communion with those whose memory we venerate,
especially the glorious ever-Virgin Mary,
Mother of our God and Lord, Jesus Christ,
and blessed Joseph, her Spouse,
your blessed Apostles and Martyrs,
Peter and Paul, Andrew,
(James, John,
Thomas, James, Philip,
Bartholomew, Matthew,
Simon and Jude;
Linus, Cletus, Clement, Sixtus,
Cornelius, Cyprian,
Lawrence, Chrysogonus,
John and Paul,
Cosmas and Damian)

and all your Saints;
we ask that through their merits and prayers,
in all things we may be defended
by your protecting help.
(Through Christ our Lord. Amen.)

Therefore, Lord, we pray:
graciously accept this oblation of our service,
that of your whole family;

On Holy Thursday add:

which we make to you
as we observe the day
on which our Lord Jesus Christ
handed on the mysteries of his Body and Blood
for his disciples to celebrate;

From the Mass of the Easter Vigil until the Second Sunday of Easter add:

which we make to you
also for those to whom you have been pleased to give
the new birth of water and the Holy Spirit,
granting them forgiveness of all their sins;

order our days in your peace,
and command that we be delivered from eternal damnation
and counted among the flock of those you have chosen.
(Through Christ our Lord. Amen.)

Be pleased, O God, we pray,
to bless, acknowledge,
and approve this offering in every respect;
make it spiritual and acceptable,

so that it may become for us
the Body and Blood of your most beloved Son,
our Lord Jesus Christ.

On the day before he was to suffer,

On Holy Thursday add:
for our salvation and the salvation of all,
that is today,

he took bread in his holy and venerable hands,
and with eyes raised to heaven
to you, O God, his almighty Father,
giving you thanks, he said the blessing,
broke the bread
and gave it to his disciples, saying:

TAKE THIS, ALL OF YOU, AND EAT OF IT,
FOR THIS IS MY BODY,
WHICH WILL BE GIVEN UP FOR YOU.

In a similar way, when supper was ended,
he took this precious chalice
in his holy and venerable hands,
and once more giving you thanks, he said the blessing
and gave the chalice to his disciples, saying:

TAKE THIS, ALL OF YOU, AND DRINK FROM IT,
FOR THIS IS THE CHALICE OF MY BLOOD,
THE BLOOD OF THE NEW AND ETERNAL COVENANT,
WHICH WILL BE POURED OUT FOR YOU AND FOR MANY
FOR THE FORGIVENESS OF SINS.

DO THIS IN MEMORY OF ME.

The mystery of faith.

1. ***We proclaim your Death, O Lord,***
and profess your Resurrection
until you come again.

2. ***When we eat this Bread and drink this Cup,***
we proclaim your Death, O Lord,
until you come again.

3. ***Save us, Savior of the world,***
for by your Cross and Resurrection
you have set us free.

Therefore, O Lord,
as we celebrate the memorial of the blessed Passion,
the Resurrection from the dead,
and the glorious Ascension into heaven
of Christ, your Son, our Lord,
we, your servants and your holy people,
offer to your glorious majesty
from the gifts that you have given us,
this pure victim,
this holy victim,
this spotless victim,
the holy Bread of eternal life
and the Chalice of everlasting salvation.

Be pleased to look upon these offerings
with a serene and kindly countenance,
and to accept them,
as once you were pleased to accept
the gifts of your servant Abel the just,

the sacrifice of Abraham, our father in faith,
and the offering of your high priest Melchizedek,
a holy sacrifice, a spotless victim.

In humble prayer we ask you, almighty God:
command that these gifts be borne
by the hands of your holy Angel
to your altar on high
in the sight of your divine majesty,
so that all of us, who through this participation at the altar
receive the most holy Body and Blood of your Son,
may be filled with every grace and heavenly blessing.
(Through Christ our Lord. Amen.)

Remember also, Lord, your servants N. and N.,
who have gone before us with the sign of faith
and rest in the sleep of peace.
(Pause)
Grant them, O Lord, we pray,
and all who sleep in Christ,
a place of refreshment, light and peace.
(Through Christ our Lord. Amen.)

To us, also, your servants, who, though sinners,
hope in your abundant mercies,
graciously grant some share
and fellowship with your holy Apostles and Martyrs:
with John the Baptist, Stephen,
Matthias, Barnabas,
(Ignatius, Alexander,
Marcellinus, Peter,
Felicity, Perpetua,

Agatha, Lucy,
Agnes, Cecilia, Anastasia)
and all your Saints;
admit us, we beseech you,
into their company,
not weighing our merits,
but granting us your pardon,
through Christ our Lord.

Through whom
you continue to make all these good things, O Lord;
you sanctify them, fill them with life,
bless them, and bestow them upon us.

Through him, and with him, and in him,
O God, almighty Father,
in the unity of the Holy Spirit,
all glory and honor is yours,
for ever and ever. ***Amen.***

(Turn to the Lord's Prayer, page 53)

EUCHARISTIC PRAYER 2

PREFACE

It is truly right and just, our duty and our salvation,
always and everywhere to give you thanks, Father most holy,
through your beloved Son, Jesus Christ,
your Word through whom you made all things,
whom you sent as our Savior and Redeemer,
incarnate by the Holy Spirit and born of the Virgin.

Fulfilling your will and gaining for you a holy people,
he stretched out his hands as he endured his Passion,
so as to break the bonds of death and manifest the resurrection.

And so, with the Angels and all the Saints
we declare your glory,
as with one voice we acclaim:
Holy, Holy, Holy Lord God of hosts... *(page 35)*

You are indeed Holy, O Lord,
the fount of all holiness.

Make holy, therefore, these gifts, we pray,
by sending down your Spirit upon them like the dewfall,
so that they may become for us
the Body and Blood of our Lord Jesus Christ.

At the time he was betrayed
and entered willingly into his Passion,
he took bread and, giving thanks, broke it,
and gave it to his disciples, saying:

TAKE THIS, ALL OF YOU, AND EAT OF IT,
FOR THIS IS MY BODY,
WHICH WILL BE GIVEN UP FOR YOU.

In a similar way, when supper was ended,
he took the chalice
and, once more giving thanks,
he gave it to his disciples, saying:

TAKE THIS, ALL OF YOU, AND DRINK FROM IT,
FOR THIS IS THE CHALICE OF MY BLOOD,
THE BLOOD OF THE NEW AND ETERNAL COVENANT,

WHICH WILL BE POURED OUT FOR YOU AND FOR MANY
FOR THE FORGIVENESS OF SINS.

DO THIS IN MEMORY OF ME.

The mystery of faith.

We proclaim your Death, O Lord,
and profess your Resurrection
until you come again.

(For other acclamations, see page 40)

Therefore, as we celebrate
the memorial of his Death and Resurrection,
we offer you, Lord,
the Bread of life and the Chalice of salvation,
giving thanks that you have held us worthy
to be in your presence and minister to you.

Humbly we pray
that, partaking of the Body and Blood of Christ,
we may be gathered into one by the Holy Spirit.

Remember, Lord, your Church,
spread throughout the world,
and bring her to the fullness of charity,
together with N. our Pope and N. our Bishop
and all the clergy.

Remember also our brothers and sisters
who have fallen asleep in the hope of the resurrection,
and all who have died in your mercy:
welcome them into the light of your face.

Have mercy on us all, we pray,
that with the Blessed Virgin Mary, Mother of God,
with blessed Joseph, her Spouse,
with the blessed Apostles,
and all the Saints who have pleased you throughout the ages,
we may merit to be coheirs to eternal life,
and may praise and glorify you
through your Son, Jesus Christ.

Through him, and with him, and in him,
O God, almighty Father,
in the unity of the Holy Spirit,
all glory and honor is yours,
for ever and ever. ***Amen.***

(Turn to the Lord's Prayer, page 53)

EUCHARISTIC PRAYER 3

You are indeed Holy, O Lord,
and all you have created
rightly gives you praise,
for through your Son our Lord Jesus Christ,
by the power and working of the Holy Spirit,
you give life to all things and make them holy,
and you never cease to gather a people to yourself,
so that from the rising of the sun to its setting
a pure sacrifice may be offered to your name.

Therefore, O Lord, we humbly implore you:
by the same Spirit graciously make holy
these gifts we have brought to you for consecration,

that they may become the Body and Blood
of your Son our Lord Jesus Christ,
at whose command we celebrate these mysteries.

For on the night he was betrayed
he himself took bread,
and, giving you thanks, he said the blessing,
broke the bread and gave it to his disciples, saying:

TAKE THIS, ALL OF YOU, AND EAT OF IT,
FOR THIS IS MY BODY,
WHICH WILL BE GIVEN UP FOR YOU.

In a similar way, when supper was ended,
he took the chalice,
and, giving you thanks, he said the blessing,
and gave the chalice to his disciples, saying:

TAKE THIS, ALL OF YOU, AND DRINK FROM IT,
FOR THIS IS THE CHALICE OF MY BLOOD,
THE BLOOD OF THE NEW AND ETERNAL COVENANT,
WHICH WILL BE POURED OUT FOR YOU AND FOR MANY
FOR THE FORGIVENESS OF SINS.

DO THIS IN MEMORY OF ME.

The mystery of faith.

When we eat this Bread and drink this Cup,
we proclaim your Death, O Lord,
until you come again.

(For other acclamations, see page 40)

Therefore, O Lord, as we celebrate the memorial
of the saving Passion of your Son,
his wondrous Resurrection
and Ascension into heaven,
and as we look forward to his second coming,
we offer you in thanksgiving
this holy and living sacrifice.

Look, we pray, upon the oblation of your Church
and, recognizing the sacrificial Victim by whose death
you willed to reconcile us to yourself,
grant that we, who are nourished
by the Body and Blood of your Son
and filled with his Holy Spirit,
may become one body, one spirit in Christ.

May he make of us
an eternal offering to you,
so that we may obtain an inheritance with your elect,
especially with the most Blessed Virgin Mary, Mother of God,
with blessed Joseph, her Spouse,
with your blessed Apostles and glorious Martyrs
(with Saint N.)
and with all the Saints,
on whose constant intercession in your presence
we rely for unfailing help.

May this Sacrifice of our reconciliation,
we pray, O Lord,
advance the peace and salvation of all the world.
Be pleased to confirm in faith and charity
your pilgrim Church on earth,

with your servant N. our Pope and N. our Bishop,
the Order of Bishops, all the clergy,
and the entire people you have gained for your own.

Listen graciously to the prayers of this family,
whom you have summoned before you:
in your compassion, O merciful Father,
gather to yourself all your children
scattered throughout the world.

To our departed brothers and sisters
and to all who were pleasing to you
at their passing from this life,
give kind admittance to your kingdom.
There we hope to enjoy for ever the fullness of your glory
through Christ our Lord,
through whom you bestow on the world all that is good.

Through him, and with him, and in him,
O God, almighty Father,
in the unity of the Holy Spirit,
all glory and honor is yours,
for ever and ever. ***Amen.***

(Turn to the Lord's Prayer, page 53)

EUCHARISTIC PRAYER 4

PREFACE

It is truly right to give you thanks,
truly just to give you glory, Father most holy,
for you are the one God living and true,
existing before all ages and abiding for all eternity,

dwelling in unapproachable light;
yet you, who alone are good, the source of life,
have made all that is,
so that you might fill your creatures with blessings
and bring joy to many of them by the glory of your light.

And so, in your presence are countless hosts of Angels,
who serve you day and night
and, gazing upon the glory of your face,
glorify you without ceasing.

With them we, too, confess your name in exultation,
giving voice to every creature under heaven,
as we acclaim:
Holy, Holy, Holy Lord God of hosts... *(page 35)*

We give you praise, Father most holy,
for you are great
and you have fashioned all your works
in wisdom and in love.
You formed man in your own image
and entrusted the whole world to his care,
so that in serving you alone, the Creator,
he might have dominion over all creatures.

And when through disobedience he had lost your friendship,
you did not abandon him to the domain of death.
For you came in mercy to the aid of all,
so that those who seek might find you.
Time and again you offered them covenants
and through the prophets
taught them to look forward to salvation.

And you so loved the world, Father most holy,
that in the fullness of time
you sent your Only Begotten Son to be our Savior.
Made incarnate by the Holy Spirit
and born of the Virgin Mary,
he shared our human nature
in all things but sin.
To the poor he proclaimed the good news of salvation,
to prisoners, freedom,
and to the sorrowful of heart, joy.
To accomplish your plan,
he gave himself up to death,
and, rising from the dead,
he destroyed death and restored life.

And that we might live no longer for ourselves
but for him who died and rose again for us,
he sent the Holy Spirit from you, Father,
as the first fruits for those who believe,
so that, bringing to perfection his work in the world,
he might sanctify creation to the full.

Therefore, O Lord, we pray:
may this same Holy Spirit
graciously sanctify these offerings,
that they may become
the Body and Blood of our Lord Jesus Christ
for the celebration of this great mystery,
which he himself left us
as an eternal covenant.

For when the hour had come
for him to be glorified by you, Father most holy,
having loved his own who were in the world,
he loved them to the end:
and while they were at supper,
he took bread, blessed and broke it,
and gave it to his disciples, saying:

TAKE THIS, ALL OF YOU, AND EAT OF IT,
FOR THIS IS MY BODY,
WHICH WILL BE GIVEN UP FOR YOU.

In a similar way,
taking the chalice filled with the fruit of the vine,
he gave thanks,
and gave the chalice to his disciples, saying:

TAKE THIS, ALL OF YOU, AND DRINK FROM IT,
FOR THIS IS THE CHALICE OF MY BLOOD,
THE BLOOD OF THE NEW AND ETERNAL COVENANT,
WHICH WILL BE POURED OUT FOR YOU AND FOR MANY
FOR THE FORGIVENESS OF SINS.

DO THIS IN MEMORY OF ME.

The mystery of faith.

Save us, Savior of the world,
for by your Cross and Resurrection
you have set us free.

(For other acclamations, see page 40)

Therefore, O Lord,
as we now celebrate the memorial of our redemption,
we remember Christ's Death
and his descent to the realm of the dead,
we proclaim his Resurrection
and his Ascension to your right hand,
and, as we await his coming in glory,
we offer you his Body and Blood,
the sacrifice acceptable to you
which brings salvation to the whole world.

Look, O Lord, upon the Sacrifice
which you yourself have provided for your Church,
and grant in your loving kindness
to all who partake of this one Bread and one Chalice
that, gathered into one body by the Holy Spirit,
they may truly become a living sacrifice in Christ
to the praise of your glory.

Therefore, Lord, remember now
all for whom we offer this sacrifice:
especially your servant N. our Pope,
N. our Bishop, and the whole Order of Bishops,
all the clergy,
those who take part in this offering,
those gathered here before you,
your entire people,
and all who seek you with a sincere heart.

Remember also
those who have died in the peace of your Christ

and all the dead,
whose faith you alone have known.

To all of us, your children,
grant, O merciful Father,
that we may enter into a heavenly inheritance
with the Blessed Virgin Mary, Mother of God,
with blessed Joseph, her Spouse,
and with your Apostles and Saints in your kingdom.
There, with the whole of creation,
freed from the corruption of sin and death,
may we glorify you through Christ our Lord,
through whom you bestow on the world all that is good.

Through him, and with him, and in him,
O God, almighty Father,
in the unity of the Holy Spirit,
all glory and honor is yours,
for ever and ever. ***Amen.***

Communion Rite

LORD'S PRAYER

At the Savior's command
and formed by divine teaching,
we dare to say:

Our Father, who art in heaven,
hallowed be thy name;
thy kingdom come,
thy will be done

on earth as it is in heaven.
Give us this day our daily bread,
and forgive us our trespasses,
as we forgive those who trespass against us;
and lead us not into temptation,
but deliver us from evil.

Deliver us, Lord, we pray, from every evil,
graciously grant peace in our days,
that, by the help of your mercy,
we may be always free from sin
and safe from all distress,
as we await the blessed hope
and the coming of our Savior, Jesus Christ.

For the kingdom,
the power and the glory are yours
now and for ever.

SIGN OF PEACE

Lord Jesus Christ,
who said to your Apostles:
Peace I leave you, my peace I give you,
look not on our sins,
but on the faith of your Church,
and graciously grant her peace and unity
in accordance with your will.
Who live and reign for ever and ever. ***Amen.***

The peace of the Lord be with you always.
And with your spirit.
Let us offer each other the sign of peace.

FRACTION OF THE BREAD

May this mingling of the Body and Blood
of our Lord Jesus Christ
bring eternal life to us who receive it.

Lamb of God, you take away the sins of the world,
have mercy on us.
Lamb of God, you take away the sins of the world,
have mercy on us.
Lamb of God, you take away the sins of the world,
grant us peace.

Lord Jesus Christ, Son of the living God,
who, by the will of the Father
and the work of the Holy Spirit,
through your Death gave life to the world,
free me by this, your most holy Body and Blood,
from all my sins and from every evil;
keep me always faithful to your commandments,
and never let me be parted from you.

Or

May the receiving of your Body and Blood,
Lord Jesus Christ,
not bring me to judgment and condemnation,
but through your loving mercy
be for me protection in mind and body
and a healing remedy.

COMMUNION

Behold the Lamb of God,
behold him who takes away the sins of the world.
Blessed are those called to the supper of the Lamb.

Lord, I am not worthy
that you should enter under my roof,
but only say the word
and my soul shall be healed.

May the Body (Blood) of Christ
keep me safe for eternal life.

COMMUNION ANTIPHON (Turn to the appropriate day)

PRAYER AFTER COMMUNION (Turn to the appropriate day)

Concluding Rites

BLESSING

On certain days or occasions, this blessing is preceded by a solemn formula of blessing (see page 57) or prayer over the people.

The Lord be with you.
And with your spirit.

May almighty God bless you,
the Father, and the Son, and the Holy Spirit.
Amen.

DISMISSAL

1 Go forth, the Mass is ended.
Thanks be to God.

2 Go and announce the Gospel of the Lord.
Thanks be to God.

3 Go in peace, glorifying the Lord by your life.
Thanks be to God.

4 Go in peace.
Thanks be to God.

During the Easter Octave and on Pentecost Sunday, the double alleluia is added:

1 Go forth, the Mass is ended, alleluia, alleluia.
Thanks be to God, alleluia, alleluia.

2 Go in peace, alleluia, alleluia.
Thanks be to God, alleluia, alleluia.

OPTIONAL SOLEMN BLESSINGS

ADVENT

May the almighty and merciful God,
by whose grace you have placed your faith
in the First Coming of his Only Begotten Son
and yearn for his coming again,
sanctify you by the radiance of Christ's Advent
and enrich you with his blessing. ***Amen.***

As you run the race of this present life,
may he make you firm in faith,
joyful in hope and active in charity. ***Amen.***

So that, rejoicing now with devotion
at the Redeemer's coming in the flesh,
you may be endowed with the rich reward of eternal life
when he comes again in majesty. ***Amen.***

And may the blessing of almighty God,
the Father, and the Son, and the Holy Spirit,
come down on you and remain with you for ever. ***Amen.***

THE NATIVITY OF THE LORD

May the God of infinite goodness,
who by the Incarnation of his Son
has driven darkness from the world
and by that glorious Birth has illumined
this most holy night (day),
drive far from you the darkness of vice
and illumine your hearts with the light of virtue. ***Amen.***

May God, who willed that the great joy
of his Son's saving Birth
be announced to shepherds by the Angel,
fill your minds with the gladness he gives
and make you heralds of his Gospel. ***Amen.***

And may God, who by the Incarnation
brought together the earthly and heavenly realm,
fill you with the gift of his peace and favor
and make you sharers with the Church in heaven. ***Amen.***

And may the blessing of almighty God,
the Father, and the Son, and the Holy Spirit,
come down on you and remain with you for ever. ***Amen.***

THE BEGINNING OF THE YEAR

May God, the source and origin of all blessing,
grant you grace,
pour out his blessing in abundance,
and keep you safe from harm throughout the year. ***Amen.***

May he give you integrity in the faith,
endurance in hope,
and perseverance in charity
with holy patience to the end. ***Amen.***

May he order your days and your deeds in his peace,
grant your prayers in this and in every place,
and lead you happily to eternal life. ***Amen.***

And may the blessing of almighty God,
the Father, and the Son, and the Holy Spirit,
come down on you and remain with you for ever. ***Amen.***

THE EPIPHANY OF THE LORD

May God, who has called you
out of darkness into his wonderful light,
pour out in kindness his blessing upon you
and make your hearts firm
in faith, hope and charity. ***Amen.***

And since in all confidence you follow Christ,
who today appeared in the world
as a light shining in darkness,
may God make you, too,
a light for your brothers and sisters. ***Amen.***

And so when your pilgrimage is ended,
may you come to him
whom the Magi sought as they followed the star
and whom they found with great joy, the Light from Light,
who is Christ the Lord. ***Amen.***

And may the blessing of almighty God,
the Father, and the Son, and the Holy Spirit,
come down on you and remain with you for ever. ***Amen.***

THE PASSION OF THE LORD

May God, the Father of mercies,
who has given you an example of love
in the Passion of his Only Begotten Son,
grant that, by serving God and your neighbor,
you may lay hold of the wondrous gift of his blessing. ***Amen.***

So that you may receive the reward of everlasting life from him,
through whose earthly Death
you believe that you escape eternal death. ***Amen.***

And by following the example of his self-abasement,
may you possess a share in his Resurrection. ***Amen.***

And may the blessing of almighty God,
the Father, and the Son, and the Holy Spirit,
come down on you and remain with you for ever. ***Amen.***

EASTER TIME

May God, who by the Resurrection of his Only Begotten Son
was pleased to confer on you
the gift of redemption and of adoption,

give you gladness by his blessing. ***Amen.***

May he, by whose redeeming work
you have received the gift of everlasting freedom,
make you heirs to an eternal inheritance. ***Amen.***

And may you, who have already risen with Christ
in Baptism through faith,
by living in a right manner on this earth,
be united with him in the homeland of heaven. ***Amen.***

And may the blessing of almighty God,
the Father, and the Son, and the Holy Spirit,
come down on you and remain with you for ever. ***Amen.***

THE ASCENSION OF THE LORD

May almighty God bless you,
for on this very day his Only Begotten Son
pierced the heights of heaven
and unlocked for you the way
to ascend to where he is. ***Amen.***

May he grant that,
as Christ after his Resurrection
was seen plainly by his disciples,
so when he comes as Judge
he may show himself merciful to you for all eternity. ***Amen.***

And may you, who believe he is seated
with the Father in his majesty,
know with joy the fulfillment of his promise
to stay with you until the end of time. ***Amen.***

And may the blessing of almighty God,
the Father, and the Son, and the Holy Spirit,
come down on you and remain with you for ever. ***Amen.***

THE HOLY SPIRIT

May God, the Father of lights,
who was pleased to enlighten the disciples' minds
by the outpouring of the Spirit, the Paraclete,
grant you gladness by his blessing
and make you always abound with the gifts
of the same Spirit. ***Amen.***

May the wondrous flame that appeared above the disciples,
powerfully cleanse your hearts from every evil
and pervade them with its purifying light. ***Amen.***

And may God, who has been pleased to unite many tongues
in the profession of one faith,
give you perseverance in that same faith
and, by believing, may you journey from hope
to clear vision. ***Amen.***

And may the blessing of almighty God,
the Father, and the Son, and the Holy Spirit,
come down on you and remain with you for ever. ***Amen.***

THE BLESSED VIRGIN MARY

May God, who through the childbearing
of the Blessed Virgin Mary
willed in his great kindness to redeem the human race,
be pleased to enrich you with his blessing. ***Amen.***

May you know always and everywhere the protection of her,
through whom you have been found worthy
to receive the author of life. ***Amen.***

May you, who have devoutly gathered on this day,
carry away with you the gifts of spiritual joys
and heavenly rewards. ***Amen.***

And may the blessing of almighty God,
the Father, and the Son, and the Holy Spirit,
come down on you and remain with you for ever. ***Amen.***

ALL SAINTS

May God, the glory and joy of the Saints,
who has caused you to be strengthened
by means of their outstanding prayers,
bless you with unending blessings. ***Amen.***

Freed through their intercession from present ills
and formed by the example of their holy way of life,
may you be ever devoted
to serving God and your neighbor. ***Amen.***

So that, together with all,
you may possess the joys of the homeland,
where Holy Church rejoices
that her children are admitted in perpetual peace
to the company of the citizens of heaven. ***Amen.***

And may the blessing of almighty God,
the Father, and the Son, and the Holy Spirit,
come down on you and remain with you for ever. ***Amen.***

Sunday Readings & Prayers

Christ lights our darkness

Advent (literally, "at the coming") prepares for the annual celebration of Jesus' birth at Christmas and his revelation to the nations at Epiphany. The Church year moves in a cycle of promise–fulfillment–proclamation, often using the images of darkness and light to accentuate the movement. With Advent we enter the first part of the cycle—promise—as, in our northern hemisphere, the dark period of the solar year begins. God's goodness gives us light, the light of the Messiah that dawns in the birth of Christ at Bethlehem and that will shine in its fullness at his coming again as King and Judge.

So in this Advent season as we begin a new Church year, we focus our attention on the demands of responding to the light of Jesus' presence. We desire to let his vision and values enlighten us and transform the darkness of our lives so that we may become a light that will lead others to God.

The lectionary focus for this year on Mark's gospel is particularly suited to enhance our experience of enlightenment for following this way of commitment, conversion, and cooperation in the saving work of Jesus for our world today.

As we live through the seasons of the Church year, we will learn that the way of Christian discipleship always leads through the darkness of suffering to the experience of new life in Christ. Preparing the way is the first step to which our Advent experience is directed.

Praying and living the Advent season

An Advent wreath can help you and your household focus on waiting for Christ. Create a wreath from evergreen boughs and four candles (three purple and one rose or white for the joyful third week). Use the following format each week.

INVITATION TO PRAYER *As you light the candles (one for each week of Advent), invite all to share in the response.*

Leader: We look for light, and lo, darkness;
for brightness, but we walk in gloom! *(Isaiah 59:9)*

All: You, Lord, give light to my lamp;
you brighten the darkness about me. *(Psalm 18:28)*

SCRIPTURE READING *When the candles are lit, read aloud one of the Scripture readings from the day or Sunday. Either reflect quietly or invite each household member to respond to these questions:*

- How do I want Jesus to be my light this Advent (tonight)?
- How do the words of this reading help me to wait for Jesus to come?

CLOSING PRAYER *(adapted from Ephesians 5:1-2, 8-14)*

O God of light, help us be imitators of you and live in love.
For we were once darkness, but now we are light in the Lord.
Help us live as children of light,
for light produces every kind of goodness and truth.
Help us learn what is pleasing to the Lord.
We want to take no part in the works of darkness
but rather to expose them.
Christ will give us light! Amen.

November 29

NOV 29

Waiting in faith

Today is the first Sunday of Advent, the season that prepares us for Christmas. However, Mark's Gospel today looks ahead to Christ's betrayal prior to the crucifixion. Jesus tells of a man going on a journey and leaving his slaves in charge. "Be alert!" he says, for no one knows when the master will return. Jesus says to be awake "whether in the evening, or at midnight, or at cockcrow, or in the morning," the four periods of the nighttime watch for the Romans.

For Mark, these are the hours when Jesus is betrayed. Judas abandons Jesus at the Last Supper; Peter denies him at midnight, then consummates his infidelity when the cock crows. Finally, the soldiers arrest Jesus at dawn.

We do not know when we might be called upon, when disaster might strike. Surprises and shocks do not always arrive between nine and five. We cannot anticipate them. What we can do is be ready for the unexpected. We prepare ourselves by rooting our lives in faith, hope, and love. Faith is the conviction of things not seen. When our lives are planted in faith, God gives the grace to withstand what seems humanly impossible. "Be watchful! Be alert! You do not know when the time will come."

■ GLEN ARGAN

ENTRANCE ANTIPHON *(Cf. Psalm 25 [24]:1-3)*
To you, I lift up my soul, O my God. / In you, I have trusted; let me not be put to shame. / Nor let my enemies exult over me; and let none who hope in you be put to shame.

INTRODUCTORY RITES *(page 10)*

COLLECT
Grant your faithful, we pray, almighty God,
the resolve to run forth to meet your Christ
with righteous deeds at his coming,
so that, gathered at his right hand,
they may be worthy to possess the heavenly Kingdom.
Through our Lord Jesus Christ, your Son,
who lives and reigns with you in the unity of the Holy Spirit,
God, for ever and ever. ***Amen.***

FIRST READING *(Isaiah 63:16b-17, 19b; 64:2-7)*
You, **LORD,**+ are our father,
our redeemer you are named forever.
Why do you let us wander, O LORD, from your ways,
and harden our hearts so that we fear you not?
Return for the sake of your servants,
the tribes of your heritage.
Oh, that you would rend the heavens and come down,
with the mountains quaking before you,
while you wrought awesome deeds we could not hope for,
such as they had not heard of from of old.
No ear has ever heard, no eye ever seen, any God but you
doing such deeds for those who wait for him.
Would that you might meet us doing right,
that we were mindful of you in our ways!

Behold, you are angry, and we are sinful;
all of us have become like unclean people,
all our good deeds are like polluted rags;
we have all withered like leaves,
and our guilt carries us away like the wind.
There is none who calls upon your name,
who rouses himself to cling to you;
for you have hidden your face from us
and have delivered us up to our guilt.
Yet, O LORD, you are our father;
we are the clay and you the potter:
we are all the work of your hands.
The word of the Lord. ***Thanks be to God.***

RESPONSORIAL PSALM *(Psalm 80:2-3, 15-16, 18-19)*

℟. Lord, make us turn to you; let us see your face and we shall be saved.

O shepherd of Israel, hearken,
from your throne upon the cherubim,* shine forth.
Rouse your power,
and come to save us. ℟.
Once again, O LORD of hosts,
look down from heaven, and see;
take care of this vine,
and protect what your right hand has planted,
the son of man whom you yourself made strong. ℟.
May your help be with the man of your right hand,
with the son of man whom you yourself made strong.
Then we will no more withdraw from you;
give us new life, and we will call upon your name. ℟.

SECOND READING *(1 Corinthians 1:3-9)*

Brothers and sisters: Grace to you and peace from God our Father and the Lord Jesus Christ.

I give thanks to my God always on your account for the grace of God bestowed on you in Christ Jesus, that in him you were enriched in every way, with all discourse and all knowledge, as the testimony to Christ was confirmed among you, so that you are not lacking in any spiritual gift as you wait for the revelation of our Lord Jesus Christ. He will keep you firm to the end, irreproachable on the day of our Lord Jesus Christ. God is faithful, and by him you were called to fellowship with his Son, Jesus Christ our Lord.

The word of the Lord. ***Thanks be to God.***

ALLELUIA *(Psalm 85:8)*

Alleluia, alleluia. Show us, Lord, your love; / and grant us your salvation. ***Alleluia, alleluia.***

GOSPEL *(Mark 13:33-37)*

A reading from the holy Gospel according to Mark.
Glory to you, O Lord.

Jesus said to his disciples: "Be watchful! Be alert! You do not know when the time will come. It is like a man traveling abroad. He leaves home and places his servants in charge, each with his own work, and orders the gatekeeper to be on the watch. Watch, therefore; you do not know when the lord of the house is coming, whether in the evening, or at midnight, or at cockcrow, or in the morning. May he not come suddenly and find you sleeping. What I say to you, I say to all: 'Watch!'"

The Gospel of the Lord. ***Praise to you, Lord Jesus Christ.***

PROFESSION OF FAITH *(page 13)*

PRAYER OF THE FAITHFUL

PREPARATION OF GIFTS *(page 16)*

PRAYER OVER THE OFFERINGS

Accept, we pray, O Lord, these offerings we make,
gathered from among your gifts to us,
and may what you grant us to celebrate devoutly here below
gain for us the prize of eternal redemption.
Through Christ our Lord. ***Amen.***

PREFACE *(Advent 1, page 17)*

Taking a Closer Look

✝ **Lord** The New American Bible, used for our Sunday Mass readings, uses Lord in small capital letters to indicate the sacred name of God revealed to Moses and the Israelites—*Yahweh*. This choice is appropriate for two reasons. First, Lord has the same number of letters as God's sacred name. Since the Hebrew language wrote only the consonants and not the vowels, God's name was written: YHWH (in English). Since God's name was so sacred, the Jews did not speak it aloud but would instead say *Adonai*, the Hebrew word for Lord. In the Bible, when God is addressed as "Lord Yahweh" (*Adonai YHWH*), God is put in small capital letters. So, when we see Lord or God in small capital letters in the text, we know that the original word is Yahweh, the unique personal name by which God wanted to be known.

COMMUNION ANTIPHON *(Psalm 85 [84]:13)*
The Lord will bestow his bounty, and our earth shall yield its increase.

PRAYER AFTER COMMUNION
May these mysteries, O Lord,
in which we have participated,
profit us, we pray,
for even now, as we walk amid passing things,
you teach us by them to love the things of heaven
and hold fast to what endures.
Through Christ our Lord. ***Amen.***

SOLEMN BLESSING: ADVENT *(Optional, page 57)*

DISMISSAL *(page 57)*

RESPONDING TO THE WORD

Isaiah asks why God lets us wander, and he yearns for God's return.

➡ *Where has my spiritual wandering taken me this past year?*

Paul thanks God, who has given many spiritual gifts.

➡ *Which spiritual gift stands out for me recently?*

Jesus warns us to "watch" and be alert.

➡ *What makes me less attentive to God's presence than I want?*

December 6

DEC 6

Prepare the way!

Isaiah asserted centuries before the birth of Jesus that we should prepare the way of the Lord. John the Baptist repeats this message in the opening verses of Mark's Gospel, apparently with great success, as we are told that people from across Judea and Jerusalem come to be baptized by him in the River Jordan.

I am always struck by the image of John in this passage, clad in camel's hair and eating locusts and wild honey. It is hardly relatable to the modern reader, but the sense of urgency and excitement in his delivery continues to ring clear.

Even if we reside in the heart of the country's biggest cities, we still live in a type of wilderness, for in Scripture the wilderness is a place where people are tested by both physical and spiritual challenges. Do we have a thirst we are unable to quench? Is our faith life as arid as the desert? These tests are an inescapable part of life, but working through them reflectively brings us closer to a more flourishing spiritual landscape.

Thousands of years after John the Baptist, we are still waiting, and the message remains as urgent as ever. *"Prepare the way of the Lord, make straight his paths."* Clearly, there is still work to be done.

CATHERINE MULRONEY

ENTRANCE ANTIPHON *(Cf. Isaiah 30:19, 30)*
O people of Sion, behold, / the Lord will come to save the nations, / and the Lord will make the glory of his voice heard / in the joy of your heart.

INTRODUCTORY RITES *(page 10)*

COLLECT
Almighty and merciful God,
may no earthly undertaking hinder those
who set out in haste to meet your Son,
but may our learning of heavenly wisdom
gain us admittance to his company.
Who lives and reigns with you in the unity of the Holy Spirit,
God, for ever and ever. ***Amen.***

FIRST READING *(Isaiah 40:1–5, 9–11)*
Comfort, give comfort to my people,
says your God.
Speak tenderly to Jerusalem, and proclaim to her
that her service is at an end,
her guilt is expiated;
indeed, she has received from the hand of the LORD
double for all her sins.

A voice cries out:
In the desert prepare the way of the LORD!
Make straight in the wasteland a highway for our God!
Every valley shall be filled in,
every mountain and hill shall be made low;
the rugged land shall be made a plain,
the rough country, a broad valley.

Then the glory of the LORD shall be revealed,
and all people shall see it together;
for the mouth of the LORD has spoken.

Go up on to a high mountain,
Zion,* herald of glad tidings;
cry out at the top of your voice,
Jerusalem, herald of good news!
Fear not to cry out
and say to the cities of Judah:
Here is your God!
Here comes with power
the Lord GOD,
who rules by his strong arm;
here is his reward with him,
his recompense before him.
Like a shepherd he feeds his flock;
in his arms he gathers the lambs,
carrying them in his bosom,
and leading the ewes with care.
The word of the Lord. ***Thanks be to God.***

RESPONSORIAL PSALM *(Psalm 85:9-10, 11-12, 13-14)*

℟. Lord, let us see your kindness, and grant us your salvation.

I will hear what God proclaims;
the LORD—for he proclaims peace to his people.
Near indeed is his salvation to those who fear him,
glory dwelling in our land. ℟.
Kindness and truth shall meet;
justice and peace shall kiss.

Truth shall spring out of the earth,
and justice shall look down from heaven.
℟. **Lord, let us see your kindness, and grant us your salvation.**
The LORD himself will give his benefits;
our land shall yield its increase.
Justice shall walk before him,
and prepare the way of his steps. ℟.

SECOND READING *(2 Peter 3:8–14)*

Do not ignore this one fact, beloved, that with the Lord one day is like a thousand years and a thousand years like one day. The Lord does not delay his promise, as some regard "delay," but he is patient with you, not wishing that any should perish but that all should come to repentance. But the day of the Lord will come like a thief, and then the heavens will pass away with a mighty roar and the elements will be dissolved by fire, and the earth and everything done on it will be found out.

Since everything is to be dissolved in this way, what sort of persons ought you to be, conducting yourselves in holiness and devotion, waiting for and hastening the coming of the day of God, because of which the heavens will be dissolved in flames and the elements melted by fire. But according to his promise we await new heavens and a new earth in which righteousness dwells. Therefore, beloved, since you await these things, be eager to be found without spot or blemish before him, at peace.

The word of the Lord. ***Thanks be to God.***

ALLELUIA *(Luke 3:4, 6)*

Alleluia, alleluia. Prepare the way of the Lord, make straight his paths: / all flesh shall see the salvation of God. ***Alleluia, alleluia.***

GOSPEL *(Mark 1:1-8)*

A reading from the holy Gospel according to Mark.
Glory to you, O Lord.

The beginning of the gospel of Jesus Christ the Son of God.
As it is written in Isaiah the prophet:

Behold, I am sending my messenger ahead of you;
he will prepare your way.
A voice of one crying out in the desert:
"Prepare the way of the Lord,
make straight his paths."

John the Baptist appeared in the desert proclaiming a baptism of **repentance**+ for the forgiveness of sins. People of the whole Judean* countryside and all the inhabitants of Jerusalem were going out to him and were being baptized by him in the Jordan River as they acknowledged their sins. John was clothed in camel's hair, with a leather belt around his waist. He fed on locusts and wild honey. And this is what he proclaimed: "One mightier than I is coming after me. I am not worthy to stoop and loosen the thongs of his sandals. I have baptized you with water; he will baptize you with the Holy Spirit."

The Gospel of the Lord. ***Praise to you, Lord Jesus Christ.***

PROFESSION OF FAITH *(page 13)*

PRAYER OF THE FAITHFUL

PREPARATION OF GIFTS *(page 16)*

PRAYER OVER THE OFFERINGS

Be pleased, O Lord, with our humble prayers and offerings,
and, since we have no merits to plead our cause,
come, we pray, to our rescue
with the protection of your mercy.
Through Christ our Lord. ***Amen.***

PREFACE *(Advent 1, page 17)*

COMMUNION ANTIPHON *(Baruch 5:5; 4:36)*

Jerusalem, arise and stand upon the heights, / and behold the joy which comes to you from God.

TAKING A CLOSER LOOK

+ **Repentance** Because we tend to limit the meaning of repentance to being sorry for something, repentance is a somewhat inadequate translation of the Greek word *metanoia*, which describes a change of mind and heart and attitude demanded by personal conversion. It demands a re-forming of our self and our life by turning toward God and away from the evil forces that pervade our world. It is a lifelong challenge to order ourselves and our world according to the vision and values of Jesus and live out the obligations of belonging to his community of disciples.

PRAYER AFTER COMMUNION

Replenished by the food of spiritual nourishment,
we humbly beseech you, O Lord,
that, through our partaking in this mystery,
you may teach us to judge wisely the things of earth
and hold firm to the things of heaven.
Through Christ our Lord. ***Amen.***

SOLEMN BLESSING: ADVENT *(Optional, page 57)*

DISMISSAL *(page 57)*

RESPONDING TO THE WORD

Isaiah encourages us to prepare the way of the Lord.

What preparations can I make to invite Jesus to be more present in my life this week?

Paul tells us that God's timetable is not like ours.

When has God surprised me with the divine presence?

John the Baptist invites us to repent—to turn from what separates us from God.

What most hinders my relationship with God now?

December 8

Repent and believe

John the Baptist is a perennially challenging and important figure in salvation history. Luke's opening verse situates John's call in a universal context that includes some of the very men—powerful political and religious leaders—who are threatened by, and opposed to, both John and Jesus. In this unique context, the word of God comes to John, a prophet who prepares the way for God's impending intervention in human history.

The renewal that John proclaims has broad-ranging personal and social implications. His baptism of repentance is meant to be an outward sign of *metanoia* or conversion, a radical transformation—grounded in the experience of God's love and forgiveness—that finds expression in commitment to the common good.

As Christians, we naturally associate the new and definitive liberation from sin and suffering that John proclaims with the life, death, and resurrection of Jesus Christ. John's message—his call to repentance in the face of immanent judgment—would have been disturbing back then, but perhaps we need to hear it even more today. His ministry challenges us this Advent season to recall and embrace the radical nature of our baptismal calling to repent and believe in the Good News.

■ Nick Olkovich

ENTRANCE ANTIPHON *(Isaiah 61:10)*
I rejoice heartily in the Lord, / in my God is the joy of my soul; / for he has clothed me with a robe of salvation, / and wrapped me in a mantle of justice, / like a bride adorned with her jewels.

INTRODUCTORY RITES *(page 10)*

COLLECT
O God, who by the Immaculate Conception of the Blessed Virgin
prepared a worthy dwelling for your Son,
grant, we pray,
that, as you preserved her from every stain
by virtue of the Death of your Son, which you foresaw,
so, through her intercession,
we, too, may be cleansed and admitted to your presence.
Through our Lord Jesus Christ, your Son,
who lives and reigns with you in the unity of the Holy Spirit,
God, for ever and ever. ***Amen.***

FIRST READING *(Genesis 3:9–15, 20)*
After the man, Adam, had eaten of the tree, the LORD God called to the man and asked him, "Where are you?" He answered, "I heard you in the garden; but I was afraid, because I was naked, so I hid myself." Then he asked, "Who told you that you were naked? You have eaten, then, from the tree of which I had forbidden you to eat!" The man replied, "The woman whom you put here with me—she gave me fruit from the tree, and so I ate it." The LORD God then asked the woman, "Why did you do such a thing?" The woman answered, "The serpent tricked me into it, so I ate it."

Then the LORD God said to the serpent:
"Because you have done this, you shall be banned
from all the animals
and from all the wild creatures;
on your belly shall you crawl,
and dirt shall you eat
all the days of your life.
I will put enmity between you and the woman,
and between your offspring and hers;
he will strike at your head,
while you strike at his heel."

The man called his wife Eve, because she became the mother of all the living.

The word of the Lord. ***Thanks be to God.***

RESPONSORIAL PSALM *(Psalm 98:1, 2-3ab, 3cd-4)*

℟. Sing to the Lord a new song, for he has done marvelous deeds.

Sing to the LORD a new song,
for he has done wondrous deeds;
His right hand has won victory for him,
his holy arm. ℟.
The LORD has made his salvation known:
in the sight of the nations he has revealed his justice.
He has remembered his kindness and his faithfulness
toward the house of Israel. ℟.
All the ends of the earth have seen
the salvation by our God.
Sing joyfully to the LORD, all you lands;
break into song; sing praise. ℟.

SECOND READING *(Ephesians 1:3-6, 11-12)*

Brothers and sisters: Blessed be the God and Father of our Lord Jesus Christ, who has blessed us in Christ with every spiritual blessing in the heavens, as he chose us in him, before the foundation of the world, to be holy and without blemish before him. In love he destined us for adoption to himself through Jesus Christ, in accord with the favor of his will, for the praise of the glory of his grace that he granted us in the beloved.

In him we were also chosen, destined in accord with the purpose of the One who accomplishes all things according to the intention of his will, so that we might exist for the praise of his glory, we who first hoped in Christ.

The word of the Lord. ***Thanks be to God.***

ALLELUIA *(See Luke 1:28)*

Alleluia, alleluia. Hail, Mary, full of grace, the Lord is with you; / blessed are you among women. ***Alleluia, alleluia.***

GOSPEL *(Luke 1:26-38)*

A reading from the holy Gospel according to Luke.
Glory to you, O Lord.

The angel Gabriel was sent from God to a town of Galilee called Nazareth, to a virgin betrothed to a man named Joseph, of the house of David, and the virgin's name was Mary. And coming to her, he said, "**Hail, full of grace!**✝ The Lord is with you." But she was greatly troubled at what was said and pondered what sort of greeting this might be. Then the angel said to her, "Do not be afraid, Mary, for you have found favor with God. Behold, you will conceive in your womb and bear a son, and you shall name him Jesus. He will be great and will be called Son of the Most High, and the Lord God will give him the throne of David his father, and he will rule over the house of Jacob forever, and of his Kingdom there will be no end." But Mary said to the angel, "How can this be, since I have no relations with a man?" And the angel said to her in reply, "The Holy Spirit will come upon you, and the power of the Most High will overshadow you. Therefore the child to be born will be called holy, the Son of God. And behold, Elizabeth, your relative, has also conceived a son in her old age, and this is the sixth month for her who was called barren; for nothing will be impossible for God." Mary said, "Behold, I am the handmaid of the Lord. May it be done to me according to your word." Then the angel departed from her.

The Gospel of the Lord. ***Praise to you, Lord Jesus Christ.***

PROFESSION OF FAITH *(page 13)*

PRAYER OF THE FAITHFUL

PREPARATION OF GIFTS *(page 16)*

PRAYER OVER THE OFFERINGS

Graciously accept the saving sacrifice
which we offer you, O Lord,
on the Solemnity of the Immaculate Conception
of the Blessed Virgin Mary,
and grant that, as we profess her,
on account of your prevenient grace,
to be untouched by any stain of sin,
so, through her intercession,
we may be delivered from all our faults.
Through Christ our Lord. ***Amen.***

PREFACE: THE MYSTERY OF MARY AND THE CHURCH

It is truly right and just, our duty and our salvation,
always and everywhere to give you thanks,
Lord, holy Father, almighty and eternal God.

For you preserved the most Blessed Virgin Mary
from all stain of original sin,
so that in her, endowed with the rich fullness of your grace,
you might prepare a worthy Mother for your Son
and signify the beginning of the Church,
his beautiful Bride without spot or wrinkle.

She, the most pure Virgin, was to bring forth a Son,
the innocent Lamb who would wipe away our offenses;
you placed her above all others
to be for your people an advocate of grace
and a model of holiness.

Taking a Closer Look

+ **Hail, full of grace!** Although we tend to hear these words as overflowing with theological meaning, note that they are a greeting that Mary finds perplexing. The sense is given by Gabriel, the messenger angel: "You have found favor with God." The basic meaning of the word grace (Greek, *charis*; Latin, *gratia*) describes a free gift that is bestowed not out of merit (then it would be owed rather than a true gift) but because the giver has found some reason to single out or favor the recipient. The choice of one recipient (a favorite) from many possible ones for the gift led to the common connection of grace and honor. As the text indicates, Mary's gift is that God is with her (as God also is with us!), which is indeed both a great favor and an honor.

And so, in company with the choirs of Angels,
we praise you, and with joy we proclaim:
Holy, Holy, Holy Lord God of hosts... *(page 35)*

COMMUNION ANTIPHON

Glorious things are spoken of you, O Mary, / for from you arose the sun of justice, / Christ our God.

PRAYER AFTER COMMUNION

May the Sacrament we have received,
O Lord our God,
heal in us the wounds of that fault
from which in a singular way
you preserved Blessed Mary in her Immaculate Conception.
Through Christ our Lord. ***Amen.***

SOLEMN BLESSING: THE BLESSED VIRGIN MARY *(Optional, page 62)*

DISMISSAL *(page 57)* ❖

RESPONDING TO THE WORD

Adam and Eve shirk their responsibility for sin and blame others.

➔ *Whom have I blamed instead of taking responsibility for my actions?*

Paul reminds us that we have been chosen to participate in God's plan of salvation.

➔ *Where and to whom does it seem that God is directing me to serve today?*

Mary's "yes" to God is unconditional and puts her completely at God's service.

➔ *What conditions do I try to set for what God seems to be asking me to be or do?*

December 13

DEC 13

Jesus, our joy and our light!

Rejoice—Jesus our Messiah is coming soon! Today, we celebrate the Third Sunday of Advent, known as Gaudete Sunday or Rose Sunday. *Gaudete* means rejoice or praise for the Lord who is now close at hand. Pope Francis called this the "Sunday of Joy." It is a time of joyful expectation and hope. Joy in the Christian context is linked to hope.

The readings reflect this rejoicing in the Lord, Christian joy, and the mission of John the Baptist as herald of Jesus' coming birth. In the gospel, John the Baptist comes to testify to the light with honesty and humility. The Baptist is a great antidote to our present times with "fake news" and soaring egos; he is a bearer of "good news" and makes straight the way of the Lord.

An important Advent family tradition is lighting the candles of the Advent wreath for each Sunday of Advent. Churches today light the third candle, which is pink or white. It symbolizes this joyous waiting. Joy brings healing and connection: connection to community, both individually and with others.

May the joy and rejoicing in the readings help us engage in the Mass with gratitude for the coming presence of Jesus. Jesus is our joy and our light as we move closer and prepare for the birth of our Savior. How will we testify to the light?

■ ELIZABETH MEAKES AND TOM O'CONNOR

ENTRANCE ANTIPHON *(Philippians 4:4-5)*
Rejoice in the Lord always; again I say, rejoice. / Indeed, the Lord is near.

INTRODUCTORY RITES *(page 10)*

COLLECT
O God, who see how your people
faithfully await the feast of the Lord's Nativity,
enable us, we pray,
to attain the joys of so great a salvation
and to celebrate them always
with solemn worship and glad rejoicing.
Through our Lord Jesus Christ, your Son,
who lives and reigns with you in the unity of the Holy Spirit,
God, for ever and ever. ***Amen.***

FIRST READING *(Isaiah 61:1-2a, 10-11)*
The spirit of the Lord GOD is upon me,
because the LORD has anointed me;
he has sent me to bring glad tidings to the poor,
to heal the brokenhearted,
to proclaim liberty to the captives
and release to the prisoners,
to announce a year of favor from the LORD
and a day of vindication by our God.

I rejoice heartily in the LORD,
in my God is the joy of my soul;
for he has clothed me with a robe of salvation
and wrapped me in a mantle of justice,
like a bridegroom adorned with a diadem,

like a bride bedecked with her jewels.
As the earth brings forth its plants,
and a garden makes its growth spring up,
so will the Lord GOD make justice and praise
spring up before all the nations.
The word of the Lord. ***Thanks be to God.***

RESPONSORIAL PSALM *(Luke 1:46-48, 49-50, 53-54)*

℟. My soul rejoices in my God.

My soul proclaims the greatness of the Lord;
my spirit rejoices in God my Savior,
for he has looked upon his lowly servant.
From this day all generations will call me blessed. **℟.**
The Almighty has done great things for me,
and holy is his Name.
He has mercy on those who fear him
in every generation. **℟.**
He has filled the hungry with good things,
and the rich he has sent a way empty.
He has come to the help of his servant Israel
for he has remembered his promise of mercy. **℟.**

SECOND READING *(1 Thessalonians 5:16-24)*

Brothers and sisters: Rejoice always. Pray without ceasing. In all circumstances give thanks, for this is the will of God for you in Christ Jesus. Do not quench the Spirit. Do not despise prophetic utterances. Test everything; retain what is good. Refrain from every kind of evil.

May the God of peace make you perfectly holy and may you entirely, **spirit, soul, and body,**† be preserved blameless for the coming of our Lord Jesus Christ. The one who calls you is faithful, and he will also accomplish it.

The word of the Lord: ***Thanks be to God.***

ALLELUIA *(Isaiah 61:1)*

Alleluia, alleluia. The Spirit of the Lord is upon me, / because he has anointed me / to bring glad tidings to the poor. ***Alleluia, alleluia.***

GOSPEL *(John 1:6-8, 19-28)*

A reading from the holy Gospel according to John.

Glory to you, O Lord.

A man named John was sent from God. He came for testimony, to testify to the light, so that all might believe through him. He was not the light, but came to testify to the light.

And this is the testimony of John. When the Jews from Jerusalem sent priests and Levites* to him to ask him, "Who are you?" he admitted and did not deny it, but admitted, "I am not the Christ." So they asked him, "What are you then? Are you Elijah?" And he said, "I am not." "Are you the Prophet?" He answered, "No." So they said to him, "Who are you, so we can give an answer to those who sent us? What do you have to say for yourself?" He said:

"I am *the voice of one crying out in the desert,*
'make straight the way of the Lord,'

as Isaiah the prophet said." Some Pharisees were also sent. They asked him, "Why then do you baptize if you are not the Christ or Elijah or the Prophet?" John answered them, "I baptize with water; but there is one among you whom you do not recognize, the one who is coming after me, whose sandal strap I am not worthy to untie." This happened in Bethany* across the Jordan, where John was baptizing.

The Gospel of the Lord. ***Praise to you, Lord Jesus Christ.***

PROFESSION OF FAITH *(page 13)*

PRAYER OF THE FAITHFUL

PREPARATION OF GIFTS *(page 16)*

PRAYER OVER THE OFFERINGS

May the sacrifice of our worship, Lord, we pray,
be offered to you unceasingly,
to complete what was begun in sacred mystery
and powerfully accomplish for us your saving work.
Through Christ our Lord. ***Amen.***

TAKING A CLOSER LOOK

+ Spirit, soul, and body In our world, we normally describe a human being as composed of body and soul (in which we include all mental and emotional aspects). But Paul follows a slightly different Jewish tradition, identifying the entirety of a person as spirit, soul, and body. These are not three elements blended together, but rather three ways of understanding the entirety of a person in relation to the material or biological realm (Greek, *soma*, "body") and the vital energy for living (*psyche*, "soul"), which are breathed into us through God's Spirit (*pneuma*, "breath or wind," see Genesis 2:7), which then dwells in us and permeates all of these other aspects so that we live in the Spirit (Romans 8:9).

PREFACE *(Advent 1, page 17)*

COMMUNION ANTIPHON *(Cf. Isaiah 35:4)*
Say to the faint of heart: Be strong and do not fear. / Behold, our God will come, and he will save us.

PRAYER AFTER COMMUNION
We implore your mercy, Lord,
that this divine sustenance may cleanse us of our faults
and prepare us for the coming feasts.
Through Christ our Lord. ***Amen.***

SOLEMN BLESSING: ADVENT *(Optional, page 57)*

DISMISSAL *(page 57)* ⁜

Responding to the Word

Isaiah's life is changed because God's Spirit empowers him.

How has God's Spirit empowered me?

Paul advises us not to quench the Holy Spirit.

How have I been hesitant to let God's Spirit work in me this Advent?

John urges us to "make straight the way of the Lord."

What needs to be straightened so God can come more easily to me?

December 20

Nothing is impossible for God

I never truly understood what it meant to trust and wait until my son was overdue. Fittingly, this happened during Advent, when we wait in hope for the birth of Emmanuel, God-with-us. As the days passed with no sign of labor, I had to live in the tension of knowing something remarkable was about to happen and trusting God to lead me into that mystery.

Since then, today's reading of the Annunciation has reconnected me to the intense emotions I experienced all those years ago. Mary knew those same feelings, Luke tells us: wondering, believing, accepting whatever lay ahead.

By saying yes to God's surprising plan for her, Mary becomes the model for us to do likewise in our own lives. But first, we get the same reassurance she received from the Angel Gabriel: "Nothing will be impossible for God." With that never-ending promise given to us, we too can be servants of the Lord, saying, "May it be done to me according to your word."

As we conclude our Advent journey of hope, peace, joy, and love, may Mary's "yes" give us the courage we need to spread the good news of Jesus' presence among us one action, one prayer, one step at a time. Come, Lord Jesus!

■ Anne Louise Mahoney

ENTRANCE ANTIPHON *(Cf. Isaiah 45:8)*
Drop down dew from above, you heavens, / and let the clouds rain down the Just One; / let the earth be opened and bring forth a Savior.

INTRODUCTORY RITES *(page 10)*

COLLECT
Pour forth, we beseech you, O Lord,
your grace into our hearts,
that we, to whom the Incarnation of Christ your Son
was made known by the message of an Angel,
may by his Passion and Cross
be brought to the glory of his Resurrection.
Who lives and reigns with you in the unity of the Holy Spirit,
God, for ever and ever. ***Amen.***

FIRST READING *(2 Samuel 7:1-5, 8b-12, 14a, 16)*
When King David was settled in his palace, and the LORD had given him rest from his enemies on every side, he said to Nathan the prophet, "Here I am living in a house of cedar, while **the ark of God dwells in a tent!**"✝ Nathan answered the king, "Go, do whatever you have in mind, for the LORD is with you." But that night the LORD spoke to Nathan and said: "Go, tell my servant David, 'Thus says the LORD: Should you build me a house to dwell in?

" 'It was I who took you from the pasture and from the care of the flock to be commander of my people Israel. I have been with you wherever you went, and I have destroyed all your enemies before you. And I will make you famous like the great ones of the earth. I will fix a place for my people Israel; I will plant them so that they may dwell in their place without further disturbance.

Neither shall the wicked continue to afflict them as they did of old, since the time I first appointed judges over my people Israel. I will give you rest from all your enemies. The LORD also reveals to you that he will establish a house for you. And when your time comes and you rest with your ancestors, I will raise up your heir after you, sprung from your loins, and I will make his kingdom firm. I will be a father to him, and he shall be a son to me. Your house and your kingdom shall endure forever before me; your throne shall stand firm forever.'"

The word of the Lord. ***Thanks be to God.***

RESPONSORIAL PSALM *(Psalm 24:1-2, 3-4, 5-6)*

℟. For ever I will sing the goodness of the Lord.

The promises of the LORD I will sing forever;
 through all generations my mouth shall proclaim
  your faithfulness.
For you have said, "My kindness is established forever";
 in heaven you have confirmed your faithfulness. **℟.**
"I have made a covenant with my chosen one,
 I have sworn to David my servant:
forever will I confirm your posterity
 and establish your throne for all generations." **℟.**
"He shall say of me, 'You are my father,
 my God, the Rock, my savior.'
Forever I will maintain my kindness toward him,
 and my covenant with him stands firm." **℟.**

SECOND READING *(Romans 16:25-27)*

Brothers and sisters: To him who can strengthen you, according to my gospel and the proclamation of Jesus Christ, according to the revelation of the mystery kept secret for long ages but now manifested through the prophetic writings and, according to the command of the eternal God, made known to all nations to bring about the obedience of faith, to the only wise God, through Jesus Christ be glory forever and ever. Amen.

The word of the Lord. ***Thanks be to God.***

ALLELUIA *(Luke 1:38)*

Alleluia, alleluia. Behold, I am the handmaid of the Lord. / May it be done to me according to your word. ***Alleluia, alleluia.***

GOSPEL *(Luke 1:26–38)*

A reading from the holy Gospel according to Luke.
Glory to you, O Lord.

The angel Gabriel was sent from God to a town of Galilee called Nazareth, to a virgin betrothed to a man named Joseph, of the house of David, and the virgin's name was Mary. And coming to her, he said, "Hail, full of grace! The Lord is with you." But she was greatly troubled at what was said and pondered what sort of greeting this might be. Then the angel said to her, "Do not be afraid, Mary, for you have found favor with God.

"Behold, you will conceive in your womb and bear a son, and you shall name him Jesus. He will be great and will be called Son of the Most High, and the Lord God will give him the throne of David his father, and he will rule over the house of Jacob forever, and of his kingdom there will be no end." But Mary said to the angel, "How can this be, since I have no relations with a man?" And the angel said to her in reply, "The Holy Spirit will come upon you, and the power of the Most High will overshadow you. Therefore the child to be born will be called holy, the Son of God. And behold, Elizabeth, your relative, has also conceived a son in her old age, and this is the sixth month for her who was called barren; for nothing will be impossible for God." Mary said, "Behold, I am the handmaid of the Lord. May it be done to me according to your word." Then the angel departed from her.

The Gospel of the Lord. ***Praise to you, Lord Jesus Christ.***

PROFESSION OF FAITH *(page 13)*

PRAYER OF THE FAITHFUL

PREPARATION OF GIFTS *(page 16)*

PRAYER OVER THE OFFERINGS

May the Holy Spirit, O Lord,
sanctify these gifts laid upon your altar,
just as he filled with his power the womb of the Blessed Virgin Mary.
Through Christ our Lord. ***Amen.***

TAKING A CLOSER LOOK

✝ **The ark of God dwells in a tent** The ark was an ornate portable box containing the tablets of the covenant commandments (Exodus 25). It was also thought of as a throne for God to sit on when Moses and the people met with God in the tent of meeting. This tent was a movable dwelling for God until the people became settled and prosperous. Then it was replaced by the Jerusalem Temple that was God's permanent "house."

PREFACE *(Advent 2, page 18)*

COMMUNION ANTIPHON *(Isaiah 7:14)*
Behold, a Virgin shall conceive and bear a son; / and his name will be called Emmanuel.

PRAYER AFTER COMMUNION
Having received this pledge of eternal redemption,
we pray, almighty God,
that, as the feast day of our salvation draws ever nearer,
so we may press forward all the more eagerly
to the worthy celebration of the mystery of your Son's Nativity.
Who lives and reigns for ever and ever. ***Amen.***

SOLEMN BLESSING: ADVENT *(Optional, page 57)*

DISMISSAL *(page 57)*

Responding to the Word

God desires to dwell within us.

What can I do this week to prepare myself for God's indwelling?

Paul gives praise to God for God's presence among us.

For what would I like to give praise to God?

Mary gives herself completely to God's plans for her.

What is God inviting me to do to share in Christ's work now?

Christ's light shines in the darkness

Christmas celebrates God's becoming incarnate in time and history. The God who promised to be among us has come and continues to be with us, now and always, through Jesus and the Holy Spirit.

As the shortest days of the year end and the light of a new year begins, we celebrate Christ's presence with us to transform our world. The darkness of sin and the reign of evil now must confront the light of the nations and the reign of God. Where Christ's light is allowed to shine, the dark shadows of sin will be illumined, allowing us to live in the light. So each day, as the light intensifies, we proclaim that "Christ's light shines in the darkness, and the darkness has not overcome it" (John 1:5).

Like John the Baptist, we too are called "to testify to the light, so that all might believe through him" (John 1:7). Our testimony to Christ's light will be evident in our words and in our actions. As we are more and more enlightened by Christ, we become beacons of hope for others in a world still steeped in darkness.

Our lives are Christmas in miniature. We are invited to let God enlighten us so that we become "divinized" persons, full of the gift of the divine life and its power to change us completely. In us, God makes an appeal to all humanity to enter into this new life and live in God's light.

Praying and living the Christmas season

The twelve days between Christmas and Epiphany are a special time to celebrate Jesus as God's great gift to us and share gifts with one another. This reminds us that Eucharist (Greek for "thanksgiving") sums up our Christian lives. Let us focus our attention on God's everyday gifts to us and the gifts that we in turn receive and give. As we become more and more attentive to these gifts, we will also grow in our attitude of gratitude and be more aware of how much we have to be thankful for when we celebrate Eucharist.

Whenever your household gathers for a meal or your faith-sharing group meets, take time to thank God for being present in your daily lives. You may wish to do this as part of your grace (another word for "gift"!) before the meal.

INVITATION TO PRAYER

Leader: Jesus said, "I am the light of the world.
Whoever follows me will not walk in darkness,
but will have the light of life." *(John 8:12)*

All: Thanks be to God for this indescribable gift!

AROUND THE TABLE *Invite each member of the household or group to respond to these questions:*

- What gifts did I receive today from others? from God?
- How did I express my gratitude?
- What gifts did I give today to others? to God?

THINGS TO DO *Each day find one way to give a small gift of time, attention, or care for someone in the household, at work, or at school.*

December 25

DEC
25

Christ, our Savior, is born!

As they tended their flocks, the shepherds were the first to hear the angels' message of "good news of great joy that will be for all the people." On that glorious night they were to "find an infant wrapped in swaddling clothes and lying in a manger." No doubt, the shepherds would have wondered at what was being said and how they should respond.

The shepherds chose to trust. They went with haste and found Mary and Joseph, and the child lying in the manger. In awe at finding the Savior, "who is Christ and Lord," they went forth sharing what they had seen and heard, and all were amazed.

We read how Mary treasured the shepherds' words and pondered them in her heart. Will we also choose during the Christmas season, and beyond, to make time to reflect on the good news of our Savior's birth? As we reread the Christmas narratives, ask God to help you grow in your understanding of the mystery of the Incarnation, of Jesus taking on human flesh.

With grateful hearts, let us recommit to bringing the news of Jesus' saving mission to our loved ones, neighbors, and those we encounter each day. God is calling each of us to go forward, like the humble shepherds, as joyful heralds of God's saving message for all.

■ Harry and Jennifer McAvoy

*For the **Mass during the Night,** turn to page 108.*
*For the **Mass at Dawn,** turn to page 114.*
*For the **Mass during the Day,** turn to page 118.*

VIGIL MASS

ENTRANCE ANTIPHON *(Cf. Exodus 16: 6-7)*
Today you will know that the Lord will come, and he will save us, / and in the morning you will see his glory.

INTRODUCTORY RITES *(page 10)*

COLLECT
O God, who gladden us year by year
as we wait in hope for our redemption,
grant that, just as we joyfully welcome
your Only Begotten Son as our Redeemer,
we may also merit to face him confidently
when he comes again as our Judge.
Who lives and reigns with you in the unity of the Holy Spirit,
God, for ever and ever. ***Amen.***

FIRST READING *(Isaiah 62:1-5)*
For Zion's sake I will not be silent,
or Jerusalem's sake I will not be quiet,
until her vindication shines forth like the dawn
and her victory like a burning torch.

Nations shall behold your vindication,
and all the kings your glory;

you shall be called by a new name
pronounced by the mouth of the LORD.
You shall be a glorious crown in the hand of the LORD,
a royal diadem held by your God.
No more shall people call you "Forsaken,"
or your land "Desolate,"
but you shall be called "My Delight,"
and your land "Espoused."
For the LORD delights in you
and makes your land his spouse.
As a young man marries a virgin,
your Builder shall marry you;
and as a bridegroom rejoices in his bride
so shall your God rejoice in you.
The word of the Lord. ***Thanks be to God.***

RESPONSORIAL PSALM *(Psalm 89:4-5, 16-17, 27, 29)*
℟. For ever I will sing the goodness of the Lord.

I have made a covenant with my chosen one,
I have sworn to David my servant:
Forever will I confirm your posterity
and establish your throne for all generations. ℟.
Blessed the people who know the joyful shout;
in the light of your countenance, O LORD, they walk.
At your name they rejoice all the day,
and through your justice they are exalted. ℟.
He shall say of me, "You are my father,
my God, the rock, my savior."
Forever I will maintain my kindness toward him,
and my covenant with him stands firm ℟.

SECOND READING *(Acts 13:16–17, 22–25)*

When Paul reached Antioch in Pisidia and entered the synagogue, he stood up, motioned with his hand, and said, "Fellow Israelites and you others who are God-fearing, listen. The God of this people Israel chose our ancestors and exalted the people during their sojourn in the land of Egypt. With uplifted arm he led them out of it. Then he removed Saul and raised up David as king; of him he testified, 'I have found David, son of Jesse, a man after my own heart; he will carry out my every wish.' From this man's descendants God, according to his promise, has brought to Israel a savior, Jesus. John heralded his coming by proclaiming a baptism of repentance to all the people of Israel; and as John was completing his course, he would say, 'What do you suppose that I am? I am not he. Behold, one is coming after me; I am not worthy to unfasten the sandals of his feet.'"

The word of the Lord. ***Thanks be to God.***

ALLELUIA

Alleluia, alleluia. Tomorrow the wickedness of the earth will be destroyed: / the Savior of the world will reign over us. ***Alleluia, alleluia.***

GOSPEL *(Matthew 1:1–25 or 1:18–25)*

For the shorter version, omit the part in brackets.

A reading from the holy Gospel according to Matthew.
Glory to you, O Lord.

[The book of the genealogy of Jesus Christ, the son of David, the son of Abraham.

Abraham became the father of Isaac, Isaac the father of Jacob, Jacob the father of Judah and his brothers. Judah became the father of Perez and Zerah, whose mother was Tamar. Perez became the father of Hezron, Hezron the father of Ram, Ram the father of Amminadab. Amminadab became the father of Nahshon, Nahshon the father of Salmon, Salmon the father of Boaz, whose mother was Rahab. Boaz became the father of Obed, whose mother was Ruth. Obed became the father of Jesse, Jesse the father of David the king.

David became the father of Solomon, whose mother had been the wife of Uriah. Solomon became the father of Rehoboam, Rehoboam the father of Abijah, Abijah the father of Asaph. Asaph became the father of Jehoshaphat, Jehoshaphat the father of Joram, Joram the father of Uzziah. Uzziah became the father of Jotham, Jotham the father of Ahaz, Ahaz the father of Hezekiah. Hezekiah became the father of Manasseh, Manasseh the father of Amos, Amos the father of Josiah. Josiah became the father of Jechoniah and his brothers at the time of the Babylonian exile.

After the Babylonian exile, Jechoniah became the father of Shealtiel, Shealtiel the father of Zerubbabel, Zerubbabel the father of Abiud, Abiud became the father of Eliakim, Eliakim the father of Azor, Azor the father of Zadok. Zadok became the father of Achim, Achim the father of Eliud, Eliud the father of Eleazar. Eleazar became the father of Matthan, Matthan the father of Jacob, Jacob the father of Joseph, the husband of Mary. Of her was born Jesus who is called the Christ.

Thus the total number of generations from Abraham to David is fourteen generations; from David to the Babylonian exile, fourteen generations; from the Babylonian exile to the Christ, fourteen generations.

Now] this is how the birth of Jesus Christ came about. When his mother Mary was betrothed to Joseph, but before they lived together, she was found with child through the Holy Spirit. Joseph her husband, since he was a righteous man, yet unwilling to expose her to shame, decided to divorce her quietly. Such was his intention when, behold, the angel of the Lord appeared to him in a dream and said, "Joseph, son of David, do not be afraid to take Mary your wife into your home. For it is through the Holy Spirit that this child has been conceived in her. She will bear a son and you are to name him Jesus, because he will save his people from their sins." All this took place to fulfill what the Lord had said through the prophet:

Behold, the virgin shall conceive and bear a son,
and they shall name him Emmanuel,

which means "God is with us." When Joseph awoke, he did as the angel of the Lord had commanded him and took his wife into his home. He had no relations with her until she bore a son, and he named him Jesus.

The Gospel of the Lord. ***Praise to you, Lord Jesus Christ.***

PROFESSION OF FAITH *(page 13)*

PRAYER OF THE FAITHFUL

PREPARATION OF GIFTS *(page 16)*

PRAYER OVER THE OFFERINGS
As we look forward, O Lord,
to the coming festivities,
may we serve you all the more eagerly
for knowing that in them
you make manifest the beginnings of our redemption.
Through Christ our Lord. ***Amen.***

PREFACE *(Nativity 1-3, pages 19-20)*

COMMUNION ANTIPHON *(Cf. Isaiah 40: 5)*
The glory of the Lord will be revealed, / and all flesh will see the salvation of our God.

PRAYER AFTER COMMUNION
Grant, O Lord, we pray,
that we may draw new vigor
from celebrating the Nativity of your Only Begotten Son,
by whose heavenly mystery we receive both food and drink.
Who lives and reigns for ever and ever. ***Amen.***

SOLEMN BLESSING: THE NATIVITY OF THE LORD *(Optional, page 58)*

DISMISSAL *(page 57)*

MASS DURING THE NIGHT

ENTRANCE ANTIPHON *(Psalm 2:7)*
The Lord said to me: You are my Son. / It is I who have begotten you this day.

Or
Let us all rejoice in the Lord, for our Savior has been born in the world. / Today true peace has come down to us from heaven.

INTRODUCTORY RITES *(page 10)*

COLLECT
O God, who have made this most sacred night
radiant with the splendor of the true light,
grant, we pray, that we, who have known the mysteries of his
light on earth,
may also delight in his gladness in heaven.
Who lives and reigns with you in the unity of the Holy Spirit,
God, for ever and ever. ***Amen.***

FIRST READING *(Isaiah 9:1-6)*
The people who walked in darkness
have seen a great light;
upon those who dwelt in the land of gloom
a light has shone.
You have brought them abundant joy
and great rejoicing,
as they rejoice before you as at the harvest,
as people make merry when dividing spoils.
For the yoke that burdened them,
the pole on their shoulder,

and the rod of their taskmaster
  you have smashed, as on the day of Midian.*
For every boot that tramped in battle,
  every cloak rolled in blood,
  will be burned as fuel for flames.
For a child is born to us, a son is given us;
  upon his shoulder dominion rests.
They name him Wonder-Counselor, God-Hero,
  Father-Forever, Prince of Peace.
His dominion is vast
  and forever peaceful,
from David's throne, and over his kingdom,
  which he confirms and sustains
by judgment and justice,
  both now and forever.
The zeal of the LORD of hosts will do this!
The word of the Lord. ***Thanks be to God.***

RESPONSORIAL PSALM *(Psalm 96:1–2, 2–3, 11–12, 13)*

℟. Today is born our Savior, Christ the Lord.

Sing to the LORD a new song;
  sing to the LORD, all you lands.
Sing to the LORD; bless his name. ℟.
Announce his salvation, day after day.
  Tell his **glory**† among the nations;
  among all peoples, his wondrous deeds. ℟.
Let the heavens be glad and the earth rejoice;
  let the sea and what fills it resound;
  let the plains be joyful and all that is in them!
Then shall all the trees of the forest exult. ℟.

They shall exult before the LORD, for he comes;
for he comes to rule the earth.
He shall rule the world with justice
and the peoples with his constancy.
℟. **Today is born our Savior, Christ the Lord.**

SECOND READING *(Titus 2:11–14)*

Beloved: The grace of God has appeared, saving all and training us to reject godless ways and worldly desires and to live temperately, justly, and devoutly in this age, as we await the blessed hope, the appearance of the **glory**✝ of our great God and savior Jesus Christ, who gave himself for us to deliver us from all lawlessness and to cleanse for himself a people as his own, eager to do what is good.

The word of the Lord. ***Thanks be to God.***

ALLELUIA *(Luke 2:10–11)*

Alleluia, alleluia. I proclaim to you good news of great joy: / today a Savior is born for us, / Christ the Lord. ***Alleluia, alleluia.***

GOSPEL *(Luke 2:1–14)*

A reading from the holy Gospel according to Luke.
Glory to you, O Lord.

In those days a decree went out from Caesar* Augustus that the whole world should be enrolled. This was the first enrollment, when Quirinius* was governor of Syria. So all went to be enrolled, each to his own town. And Joseph too went up from Galilee from the town of Nazareth to Judea, to the city of David that is called Bethlehem, because he was of the house and family of David, to be enrolled with Mary, his betrothed, who was with child. While they were there, the time came for her to have her child, and she gave birth to her firstborn son. She wrapped him in swaddling clothes and laid him in a manger, because there was no room for them in the inn.

Now there were shepherds in that region living in the fields and keeping the night watch over their flock. The angel of the Lord appeared to them and the glory of the Lord shone around them, and they were struck with great fear. The angel said to them, "Do not be afraid; for behold, I proclaim to you good news of great joy that will be for all the people. For today in the city of David a savior has been born for you who is Christ and Lord. And this will be a sign for you: you will find an infant wrapped in swaddling clothes and lying in a manger." And suddenly there was a multitude of the heavenly host with the angel, praising God and saying:

"**Glory**+ to God in the highest
and on earth peace to those on whom his favor rests."

The Gospel of the Lord. ***Praise to you, Lord Jesus Christ.***

PROFESSION OF FAITH *(page 13)*

PRAYER OF THE FAITHFUL

PREPARATION OF GIFTS *(page 16)*

PRAYER OVER THE OFFERINGS

May the oblation of this day's feast
be pleasing to you, O Lord, we pray,
that through this most holy exchange
we may be found in the likeness of Christ,
in whom our nature is united to you.
Who lives and reigns for ever and ever. ***Amen.***

PREFACE *(Nativity of the Lord 1-3, pages 19-20)*

COMMUNION ANTIPHON *(John 1:14)*

The Word became flesh, and we have seen his glory.

TAKING A CLOSER LOOK

✝ **Glory** In Hebrew, the word "glory" describes someone's inner worth or importance. When applied to humans, it can be associated with what gives a person dignity and commands respect, such as honor, wealth, or wisdom. When glory is associated with God, the meaning becomes more complex. Glory describes the essence of God's divinity that requires us to respect and honor God. But glory also points to the visible manifestation of God's invisible presence, for example in the cloud and pillar of fire leading the Hebrews during the Exodus. In today's second reading, Paul awaits the glory or reappearance of the risen Christ.

PRAYER AFTER COMMUNION

Grant us, we pray, O Lord our God,
that we, who are gladdened by participation
in the feast of our Redeemer's Nativity,
may through an honorable way of life become worthy of union with him.
Who lives and reigns for ever and ever. ***Amen.***

SOLEMN BLESSING: THE NATIVITY OF THE LORD *(Optional, page 58)*

DISMISSAL *(page 57)* ⁜

RESPONDING TO THE WORD

Isaiah understands how God's presence, like light in darkness, changes the way we see everything.

How has knowing Christ made my life seem clearer?

Paul understands how accepting Christ means rejecting godless ways.

What unhelpful behaviors have I rejected to follow Christ's ways?

God's revelation of Jesus to his family and to the shepherds changed them completely.

How has Jesus' entrance into my life changed me?

MASS AT DAWN

ENTRANCE ANTIPHON *(Cf. Isaiah 9:1, 5; Luke 1:33)*
Today a light will shine upon us, for the Lord is born for us; / and he will be called Wondrous God, / Prince of peace, Father of future ages: / and his reign will be without end.

INTRODUCTORY RITES *(page 10)*

COLLECT
Grant, we pray, almighty God,
that, as we are bathed in the new radiance of your incarnate Word,
the light of faith, which illumines our minds,
may also shine through in our deeds.
Through our Lord Jesus Christ, your Son,
who lives and reigns with you in the unity of the Holy Spirit,
God, for ever and ever. ***Amen.***

FIRST READING *(Isaiah 62:11–12)*
See, the LORD proclaims
to the ends of the earth:
say to daughter Zion,*
your savior comes!
Here is his reward with him,
his recompense before him.
They shall be called the holy people,
the redeemed of the LORD,
and you shall be called "Frequented,"
a city that is not forsaken.
The word of the Lord. ***Thanks be to God.***

RESPONSORIAL PSALM *(Psalm 97:1, 6, 11–12)*

℟. A light will shine on us this day: the Lord is born for us.

The LORD is king; let the earth rejoice;
let the many isles be glad.
The heavens proclaim his justice,
and all peoples see his glory. ℟.
Light dawns for the just;
and gladness, for the upright of heart.
Be glad in the LORD, you just,
and give thanks to his holy name. ℟.

SECOND READING *(Titus 3:4–7)*

Beloved:
When the kindness and generous love
of God our savior appeared,
not because of any righteous deeds we had done
but because of his mercy,
he saved us through the bath of rebirth
and renewal by the Holy Spirit,
whom he richly poured out on us
through Jesus Christ our savior,
so that we might be justified by his grace
and become heirs in hope of eternal life.
The word of the Lord. ***Thanks be to God.***

ALLELUIA *(Luke 2:14)*

Alleluia, alleluia. Glory to God in the highest, / and on earth peace to those / on whom his favor rests. ***Alleluia, alleluia.***

GOSPEL *(Luke 2:15–20)*

A reading from the holy Gospel according to Luke.

Glory to you, O Lord.

When the angels went away from them to heaven, the shepherds said to one another, "Let us go, then, to Bethlehem to see this thing that has taken place, which the Lord has made known to us." So they went in haste and found Mary and Joseph, and the infant lying in the manger. When they saw this, they made known the message that had been told them about this child. All who heard it were amazed by what had been told them by the shepherds. And Mary kept all these things, reflecting on them in her **heart**.+ Then the shepherds returned, glorifying and praising God for all they had heard and seen, just as it had been told to them.

The Gospel of the Lord. ***Praise to you, Lord Jesus Christ.***

PROFESSION OF FAITH *(page 13)*

PRAYER OF THE FAITHFUL

PREPARATION OF GIFTS *(page 16)*

PRAYER OVER THE OFFERINGS

May our offerings be worthy, we pray, O Lord,

TAKING A CLOSER LOOK

+ **Heart** For biblical people, the heart did not just identify the physical organ but rather the psychological activity associated with it. Since the heart was associated with emotional changes (speeding up when we are excited) and physical life (ceasing to beat when we die), "heart" became a general word to identify the location of the distinctively human activities of feeling, thinking, and deciding. Today we might describe this as the "self." So Mary reflects deeply within her "self" about these wondrous experiences arising from her mysterious relationship with Jesus.

of the mysteries of the Nativity this day,
that, just as Christ was born a man and also shone forth as God,
so these earthly gifts may confer on us what is divine.
Through Christ our Lord. ***Amen.***

PREFACE *(Nativity of the Lord 1–3, pages 19–20)*

COMMUNION ANTIPHON *(Cf. Zechariah 9:9)*
Rejoice, O Daughter Sion; lift up praise, Daughter Jerusalem: / Behold, your King will come, the Holy One and Savior of the world.

PRAYER AFTER COMMUNION
Grant us, Lord, as we honor with joyful devotion
the Nativity of your Son,
that we may come to know with fullness of faith
the hidden depths of this mystery
and to love them ever more and more.
Through Christ our Lord. ***Amen.***

SOLEMN BLESSING: THE NATIVITY OF THE LORD *(Optional, page 58)*

DISMISSAL *(page 57)* ✣

Responding to the Word

God's presence brings salvation and makes us a holy people.

➡ *How have I grown in holiness this past year?*

Paul reminds us we are reborn in the Holy Spirit.

➡ *How has the power of God's Holy Spirit made me feel more full of spiritual energy?*

Mary treasured her spiritual experience in her heart.

➡ *How will I make more time to treasure my spiritual experience in prayer this year?*

MASS DURING THE DAY

ENTRANCE ANTIPHON *(Cf. Isaiah 9:5)*
A child is born for us, and a son is given to us; / his scepter of power rests upon his shoulder, / and his name will be called Messenger of great counsel.

INTRODUCTORY RITES *(page 10)*

COLLECT
O God, who wonderfully created the dignity of human nature
and still more wonderfully restored it,
grant, we pray,
that we may share in the divinity of Christ,
who humbled himself to share in our humanity.
Who lives and reigns with you in the unity of the Holy Spirit,
God, for ever and ever. ***Amen.***

FIRST READING *(Isaiah 52:7–10)*
How beautiful upon the mountains
are the feet of him who brings glad tidings,
announcing peace, bearing good news,
announcing salvation, and saying to Zion,*
"Your God is King!"

Hark! Your sentinels raise a cry,
together they shout for joy,
for they see directly, before their eyes,
the LORD restoring Zion.
Break out together in song,
O ruins of Jerusalem!
For the LORD comforts his people,

he redeems Jerusalem.
The LORD has bared his holy arm
in the sight of all the nations;
all the ends of the earth will behold
the salvation of our God.
The word of the Lord. ***Thanks be to God.***

RESPONSORIAL PSALM *(Psalm 98:1, 2-3, 3-4, 5-6)*

℟. All the ends of the earth have seen the saving power of God.

Sing to the LORD a new song,
for he has done wondrous deeds;
his right hand has won victory for him,
his holy arm. ℟.
The LORD has made his salvation known:
in the sight of the nations he has revealed his justice.
He has remembered his kindness and his faithfulness
toward the house of Israel. ℟.
All the ends of the earth have seen
the salvation by our God.
Sing joyfully to the LORD, all you lands;
break into song; sing praise. ℟.
Sing praise to the LORD with the harp,
with the harp and melodious song.
With trumpets and the sound of the horn
sing joyfully before the King, the LORD. ℟.

SECOND READING *(Hebrews 1:1-6)*

Brothers and sisters: In times past, God spoke in partial and various ways to our ancestors through the prophets; in these last days, he has spoken to us through the Son, whom he made heir of all things and through whom he created the universe,

who is the refulgence of his glory, the very imprint of his being,
and who sustains all things by his mighty word.
When he had accomplished purification from sins,
he took his seat at the right hand of the Majesty on high,
as far superior to the angels
as the name he has inherited is more excellent than theirs.

For to which of the angels did God ever say:
You are my son; this day I have begotten you?
Or again:
I will be a father to him, and he shall be a son to me?
And again, when he leads the firstborn into the world, he says:
Let all the angels of God worship him.
The word of the Lord. ***Thanks be to God.***

ALLELUIA

Alleluia, alleluia. A holy day has dawned upon us. / Come, you nations, and adore the Lord. / For today a great light has come upon the earth. ***Alleluia, alleluia.***

GOSPEL *(John 1:1–18 or 1:1–5, 9–14)*

For the shorter version, omit the indented parts in brackets.

A reading from the holy Gospel according to John.
Glory to you, O Lord.

In the beginning was the Word,
and the Word was with God,
and the Word was God.
He was in the beginning with God.
All things came to be through him,
and without him nothing came to be.
What came to be through him was life,

and this life was the light of the human race;
the light shines in the darkness,
and the darkness has not overcome it.
[A man named John was sent from God. He came for testimony, to testify to the light, so that all might believe through him. He was not the light, but came to testify to the light.]
The true light, which enlightens everyone, was coming into the world.
He was in the world,
and the world came to be through him,
but the world did not know him.
He came to what was his own,
but his own people did not accept him.
But to those who did accept him he gave power to become children of God, to those who believe in his name, who were born not by natural generation nor by human choice nor by a man's decision but of God.
And the Word became **flesh**+
and made his dwelling among us,
and we saw his glory,
the glory as of the Father's only Son,
full of grace and truth.
[John testified to him and cried out, saying, "This was he of whom I said, 'The one who is coming after me ranks ahead of me because he existed before me.'" From his fullness we have all received, grace in place of grace, because while the law was given through Moses, grace and truth came through Jesus Christ. No one has ever seen God. The only Son, God, who is at the Father's side, has revealed him.]
The Gospel of the Lord. ***Praise to you, Lord Jesus Christ.***

PROFESSION OF FAITH *(page 13)*

PRAYER OF THE FAITHFUL

PREPARATION OF GIFTS *(page 16)*

PRAYER OVER THE OFFERINGS
Make acceptable, O Lord, our oblation on this solemn day,
when you manifested the reconciliation
that makes us wholly pleasing in your sight
and inaugurated for us the fullness of divine worship.
Through Christ our Lord. ***Amen.***

PREFACE *(Nativity of the Lord 1–3, pages 19–20)*

TAKING A CLOSER LOOK

✝ **Flesh** The word "flesh" does not just refer to the skin but is often used to describe the whole living human body (hence "flesh and blood" to describe a whole living person). But flesh also describes what is corruptible (for we all die) and prone to sin (for we are not perfect). Because "flesh" describes the reality of human existence, it is appropriate to highlight Jesus' becoming human. But because "flesh" points to that which moves us toward sin and alienation from God, it is startling to apply this to Jesus. Normally, God and flesh would not go together, but in the divine-human reality of Jesus they must.

COMMUNION ANTIPHON *(Cf. Psalm 98 [97]:3)*
All the ends of the earth have seen the salvation of our God.

PRAYER AFTER COMMUNION
Grant, O merciful God,
that, just as the Savior of the world, born this day,
is the author of divine generation for us,
so he may be the giver even of immortality.
Who lives and reigns for ever and ever. ***Amen.***

SOLEMN BLESSING: THE NATIVITY OF THE LORD *(Optional, page 58)*

DISMISSAL *(page 57)* ⁜

RESPONDING TO THE WORD

Isaiah foresees a time when God will restore relationships broken by sin.

What might I need to do to restore a broken relationship in my life?

As God's Word, Jesus summarizes in himself all that God wants to tell us about God's hidden self.

How might I listen more attentively to Jesus' words this year?

Jesus is the human image of God.

What particular aspect of God has Jesus revealed to me during this Advent?

December 27

Jesus is God's promise kept to all

The feast of the Holy Family is nominally about Jesus, Mary, and Joseph. And so it is. But today's readings place them in the center of an older and broader relationship: that of God to his people.

In today's gospel, we are reminded of God's covenant by the elders, the keepers of our traditions and stories. Old people remember things that should not be forgotten.

So, when Mary and Joseph present Jesus in the temple, following tradition, the aged Simeon praises God for allowing him to live long enough to see the Redeemer. In the great Canticle of Simeon (aka the *Nunc dimittis*), he says:

"Lord, now let your servant go in peace; your word has been fulfilled: my own eyes have seen the salvation which you have prepared in the sight of every people: a light to reveal you to the nations and the glory of your people Israel" (Luke 2:29-32).

And the old prophet Anna also praises God when she sees Jesus, telling anyone who'll listen of the importance of this tiny child.

Jesus is God's promise kept not just to Anna and Simeon, but to all of us. A great gift for our faithfulness to last the ages. Today, in our eucharistic celebration, we lift our hearts in gratitude as we share with all those before us.

■ Joseph Sinasac

ENTRANCE ANTIPHON *(Luke 2:16)*
The shepherds went in haste, / and found Mary and Joseph and the Infant lying in a manger.

INTRODUCTORY RITES *(page 10)*

COLLECT
O God, who were pleased to give us
the shining example of the Holy Family,
graciously grant that we may imitate them
in practicing the virtues of family life and in the bonds of charity,
and so, in the joy of your house,
delight one day in eternal rewards.
Through our Lord Jesus Christ, your Son,
who lives and reigns with you in the unity of the Holy Spirit,
God, for ever and ever. ***Amen.***

These are the readings for Year B. The first reading, psalm, second reading, and gospel acclamation for Year A (Sirach 3:2-6, 12-14; Psalm 128:1-2, 3, 4-5; Colossians 3:12-21 or 3:12-17; Colossians 3:15a, 16a) may also be used.

FIRST READING *(Genesis 15:1-6; 21:1-3)*
The word of the LORD came to Abram in a vision, saying:
"Fear not, Abram!
I am your shield;
I will make your reward very great."
But Abram said, "O Lord GOD, what good will your gifts be, if I keep on being childless and have as my heir the steward of my house, Eliezer?" Abram continued, "See, you have given me no offspring, and so one of my servants will be my heir." Then the word of the LORD came to him: "No, that one shall not be your

heir; your own issue shall be your heir." The Lord took Abram outside and said, "Look up at the sky and count the stars, if you can. Just so," he added, "shall your descendants be." Abram put his faith in the LORD, who credited it to him as an act of righteousness.

The LORD took note of Sarah as he had said he would; he did for her as he had promised. Sarah became pregnant and bore Abraham a son in his old age, at the set time that God had stated. Abraham gave the name Isaac to this son of his whom Sarah bore him.

The word of the Lord. ***Thanks be to God.***

RESPONSORIAL PSALM *(Psalm 105:1-2, 3-4, 6-7, 8-9)*

℟. The Lord remembers his covenant for ever.

Give thanks to the LORD, invoke his name;
make known among the nations his deeds.
Sing to him, sing his praise,
proclaim all his wondrous deeds. ℟.
Glory in his holy name;
rejoice, O hearts that seek the LORD!
Look to the LORD in his strength;
constantly seek his face. ℟.
You descendants of Abraham, his servants,
sons of Jacob, his chosen ones!
He, the LORD, is our God;
throughout the earth his judgments prevail. ℟.
He remembers forever his covenant
which he made binding for a thousand generations
which he entered into with Abraham
and by his oath to Isaac. ℟.

SECOND READING *(Hebrews 11:8, 11–12, 17–19)*

Brothers and sisters: By faith Abraham obeyed when he was called to go out to a place that he was to receive as an inheritance; he went out, not knowing where he was to go. By faith he received power to generate, even though he was past the normal age—and Sarah herself was sterile—for he thought that the one who had made the promise was trustworthy. So it was that there came forth from one man, himself as good as dead, descendants as numerous as the stars in the sky and as countless as the sands on the seashore.

By faith Abraham, when put to the test, offered up Isaac, and he who had received the promises was ready to offer his only son, of whom it was said, "Through Isaac descendants shall bear your name." He reasoned that God was able to raise even from the dead, and he received Isaac back as a symbol.

The word of the Lord. ***Thanks be to God.***

ALLELUIA *(Hebrews 1:1–2)*

Alleluia, alleluia. In the past God spoke to our ancestors through the prophets; / in these last days, he has spoken to us through the Son. ***Alleluia, alleluia.***

GOSPEL *(Luke 2:22–40 or 2:22, 39–40)*

For the shorter version, omit the indented parts in brackets.

A reading from the holy Gospel according to Luke.
Glory to you, O Lord.

When the days were completed for their **purification**+ according to the law of Moses, they took him up to Jerusalem to present him to the Lord,

[just as it is written in the law of the Lord, *Every male that opens the womb shall be consecrated to the Lord*, and to offer the sacrifice of *a pair of turtledoves or two young pigeons*, in accordance with the dictate in the law of the Lord.

Now there was a man in Jerusalem whose name was Simeon. This man was righteous and devout, awaiting the consolation of Israel, and the Holy Spirit was upon him. It had been revealed to him by the Holy Spirit that he should not see death before he had seen the Christ of the Lord. He came in the Spirit into the temple; and when the parents brought in the child Jesus to perform the custom of the law in regard to him, he took him into his arms and blessed God, saying:

"Now, Master, you may let your servant go
in peace, according to your word,
for my eyes have seen your salvation,
which you prepared in sight of all the peoples,
a light for revelation to the Gentiles,
and glory for your people Israel."

The child's father and mother were amazed at what was said about him; and Simeon blessed them and said to Mary his mother, "Behold, this child is destined for the fall and rise of many in Israel, and to be a sign that will be contradicted—and you yourself a sword will pierce—so that the thoughts of many hearts may be revealed." There was also a prophetess, Anna, the daughter of Phanuel, of the tribe of Asher. She was advanced in years, having lived seven years with her husband after her marriage, and then as a widow until she was eighty-four. She never left the temple, but worshiped night and day with fasting and prayer. And coming forward at that very time, she gave thanks to God and spoke about the child to all who were awaiting the redemption of Jerusalem.]

When they had fulfilled all the prescriptions of the law of the Lord, they returned to Galilee, to their own town of Nazareth.

The child grew and became strong, filled with wisdom; and the favor of God was upon him.

The Gospel of the Lord. ***Praise to you, Lord Jesus Christ.***

PROFESSION OF FAITH *(page 13)*

PRAYER OF THE FAITHFUL

PREPARATION OF GIFTS *(page 16)*

PRAYER OVER THE OFFERINGS

We offer you, Lord, the sacrifice of conciliation,
humbly asking that,
through the intercession of the Virgin Mother of God
and Saint Joseph,
you may establish our families firmly in your grace and your peace.
Through Christ our Lord. ***Amen.***

PREFACE *(Nativity of the Lord 1-3, pages 19-20)*

TAKING A CLOSER LOOK

✝ **Purification** Like many ancient peoples, the Jews had a carefully devised system of meanings that identified and kept order in their lives. When something or someone violated that system, they were "unclean" for a specified time and could not participate in worship until a blessing or a purification rite would reinstate them to the proper relationship with the community. So a mother who gave birth to a boy was ritually "unclean" for forty days (see Leviticus 12:1-8) at which time she brought her purification gift to the priest. Luke reveals that Joseph and Mary fulfill all the ritual obligations of the Jewish law and, from their gift, that they are poor because they could not afford the usual offering of a lamb.

COMMUNION ANTIPHON *(Baruch 3:38)*
Our God has appeared on the earth, and lived among us.

PRAYER AFTER COMMUNION
Bring those you refresh with this heavenly Sacrament,
most merciful Father,
to imitate constantly the example of the Holy Family,
so that, after the trials of this world,
we may share their company for ever.
Through Christ our Lord. ***Amen.***

BLESSING & DISMISSAL *(page 56)*

Responding to the Word

Abraham's faith and trust created the right relationship with God.

How might I express my trust in God today?

Simeon and Anna rejoice because Jesus has come to them.

How can I share with others how Jesus' presence has changed me and my life?

Abraham obeyed God even though he did not know where he was going.

How is God calling me to something new today?

January 1

Begin the year with love and peace

In the very first moments of life, a mother looks upon her child's face in wonder and overwhelming love. Soon enough, that child will open their eyes and look back. The gaze of love then extends to kith and kin. Long before we comprehend their meaning, faces shine upon us in blessing. It is in these mostly silent, intimate encounters that we first know the loving gaze of God. As it is for us, so it would have been in that stable so many years ago. In Mary's eyes, Jesus would have glimpsed the knowledge of his origins in divinity. He would have sensed that his mother's love was a divine collaboration. And Mary would have seen, in her baby, the face of God taken flesh. This kind of love is too big for words. It can only be treasured and pondered in one's heart.

Such attentive looking is fundamental for healthy human development. Only in knowing we are loved can we love and care for others in peace. Our honoring of the Mother of God, who beholds us in love, is not unconnected to our prayers for world peace. Thus, we begin our year: blessed with the gracious countenance of God smiling down upon us and giving us peace—through Mary, through Jesus, and through all those who surround us in love.

CHRISTINE WAY SKINNER

ENTRANCE ANTIPHON

Hail, Holy Mother, who gave birth to the King / who rules heaven and earth for ever.

Or *(Cf. Isaiah 9:1, 5; Luke 1:33)*

Today a light will shine upon us, for the Lord is born for us; / and he will be called Wondrous God, / Prince of peace, Father of future ages: / and his reign will be without end.

INTRODUCTORY RITES *(page 10)*

COLLECT

O God, who through the fruitful virginity of Blessed Mary
bestowed on the human race
the grace of eternal salvation,
grant, we pray,
that we may experience the intercession of her,
through whom we were found worthy
to receive the author of life,
our Lord Jesus Christ, your Son.
Who lives and reigns with you in the unity of the Holy Spirit,
God, for ever and ever. ***Amen.***

FIRST READING *(Numbers 6:22-27)*

The LORD said to Moses: "Speak to Aaron and his sons and tell them: This is how you shall bless the Israelites. Say to them:

The LORD bless you and keep you!
The LORD let his face shine upon you, and be gracious to you!
The LORD look upon you kindly and give you peace!

So shall they invoke my name upon the Israelites, and I will bless them."

The word of the Lord. ***Thanks be to God.***

RESPONSORIAL PSALM *(Psalm 67:2–3, 5, 6, 8)*

℟. May God bless us in his mercy.

May God have pity on us and bless us;
 may he let his face shine upon us.
So may your way be known upon earth;
 among all nations, your salvation. ℟.
May the nations be glad and exult
 because you rule the peoples in equity;
 the nations on the earth you guide. ℟.
May the peoples praise you, O God;
 may all the peoples praise you!
May God bless us,
 and may all the ends of the earth fear him! ℟.

SECOND READING *(Galatians 4:4–7)*

Brothers and sisters: When the fullness of time had come, God sent his Son, born of a woman, born under the law, to ransom those under the law, so that we might receive adoption as sons. As proof that you are sons, God sent the Spirit of his Son into our hearts, crying out, "**Abba,**✝ Father!" So you are no longer a slave but a son, and if a son then also an heir, through God.

The word of the Lord. ***Thanks be to God.***

ALLELUIA *(Hebrews 1:1–2)*

Alleluia, alleluia. In the past God spoke to our ancestors through the prophets; / in these last days, he has spoken to us through the Son. ***Alleluia, alleluia.***

GOSPEL *(Luke 2:16-21)*

A reading from the holy Gospel according to Luke.

Glory to you, O Lord.

The shepherds went in haste to Bethlehem and found Mary and Joseph, and the infant lying in the manger. When they saw this, they made known the message that had been told them about this child. All who heard it were amazed by what had been told them by the shepherds. And Mary kept all these things, reflecting on them in her heart. Then the shepherds returned, glorifying and praising God for all they had heard and seen, just as it had been told to them.

When eight days were completed for his circumcision, he was named Jesus, the name given him by the angel before he was conceived in the womb.

The Gospel of the Lord. ***Praise to you, Lord Jesus Christ.***

PROFESSION OF FAITH *(page 13)*

PRAYER OF THE FAITHFUL

PREPARATION OF GIFTS *(page 16)*

PRAYER OVER THE OFFERINGS

O God, who in your kindness begin all good things

TAKING A CLOSER LOOK

✝ **Abba** This is the Aramaic (the spoken language of Jews in the Holy Land in Jesus' time) word for "father." It is a more familiar form than the common but slightly more formal Greek word for "father," and thus represents the more intimate and close relationship that Jesus has with God. Paul does not expect the Galatians to know its meaning, so he connects the Aramaic term with its Greek translation: "Abba, Father."

and bring them to fulfillment,
grant to us, who find joy in the Solemnity of the holy Mother of God,
that, just as we glory in the beginnings of your grace,
so one day we may rejoice in its completion.
Through Christ our Lord. ***Amen.***

PREFACE *(Blessed Virgin Mary 1, page 34)*

COMMUNION ANTIPHON *(Hebrews 13:8)*
Jesus Christ is the same yesterday, today, and for ever.

PRAYER AFTER COMMUNION
We have received this heavenly Sacrament with joy, O Lord:
grant, we pray,
that it may lead us to eternal life,
for we rejoice to proclaim the blessed ever-Virgin Mary
Mother of your Son and Mother of the Church.
Through Christ our Lord. ***Amen.***

SOLEMN BLESSING: THE BEGINNING OF THE YEAR *(Optional, page 59)*
OR THE BLESSED VIRGIN MARY *(Optional, page 62)*

DISMISSAL *(page 57)*

RESPONDING TO THE WORD

Moses blesses the people, hoping God's face will shine on them.

When have I felt God's loving gaze on me?

Paul reminds us we are all brothers and sisters of Jesus.

Whom do I find hard to think of as a brother or sister in Christ? Why?

Mary reflected in her heart about her experience with Jesus.

How might I find more time for prayer in the coming year?

January 3

Living faithfully in our world

One of the important aspects of today's gospel story is the wisdom displayed by the three kings who arrive from the East, whom we often call "The Wise Men." Herod is clearly threatened by the possibility that the child, whose birth the visitors had foreseen, could one day displace him as monarch. And he is certainly lying when he tells his visitors that he wants to visit and worship the new king of whom they speak. Aided by a dream, the Wise Men recognize Herod's evil intention and, having fulfilled their hearts' desire to see the Holy Child, they make their way home by a different route.

Surely, even though they were foreigners, their decision not to heed King Herod's request to return and tell him the exact location of the kingly baby was not taken lightly. The dream and angelic vision that the Wise Men received concerning Herod's evil intentions, and their courage in ignoring the king's request, can serve as an example for us when we are called to make difficult decisions.

Today's gospel calls us not only to worship the newborn king, the baby Jesus, but also to pay attention to the inner wisdom (here, the message of an angel) that we ourselves may receive from time to time that can help us live faithfully in our world.

■ BETH PORTER

MASS DURING THE DAY

ENTRANCE ANTIPHON *(Cf. Malachi 3:1; 1 Chronicles 29:12)*
Behold, the Lord, the Mighty One, has come; / and kingship is in his grasp, and power and dominion.

INTRODUCTORY RITES *(page 10)*

COLLECT
O God, who on this day
revealed your Only Begotten Son to the nations
by the guidance of a star,
grant in your mercy
that we, who know you already by faith,
may be brought to behold the beauty of your sublime glory.
Through our Lord Jesus Christ, your Son,
who lives and reigns with you in the unity of the Holy Spirit,
God, for ever and ever. ***Amen.***

FIRST READING *(Isaiah 60:1-6)*
Rise up in splendor, Jerusalem! Your light has come,
the glory of the Lord shines upon you.
See, darkness covers the earth,
and thick clouds cover the peoples;
but upon you the LORD shines,
and over you appears his glory.
Nations shall walk by your light,
and kings by your shining radiance.
Raise your eyes and look about;
they all gather and come to you:
your sons come from afar,
and your daughters in the arms of their nurses.

Then you shall be radiant at what you see,
your heart shall throb and overflow,
for the riches of the sea shall be emptied out before you,
the wealth of nations shall be brought to you.
Caravans of camels shall fill you,
dromedaries from Midian* and Ephah;*
all from Sheba* shall come
bearing gold and frankincense,
and proclaiming the praises of the LORD.
The word of the Lord. ***Thanks be to God.***

RESPONSORIAL PSALM *(Psalm 72:1-2, 7-8, 10-11, 12-13)*

℟. Lord, every nation on earth will adore you.

O God, with your judgment endow the king,
and with your justice, the king's son;
he shall govern your people with justice
and your afflicted ones with judgment. **℟.**
Justice shall flower in his days,
and profound peace, till the moon be no more.
May he rule from sea to sea,
and from the River to the ends of the earth. **℟.**
The kings of Tarshish* and the Isles shall offer gifts;
the kings of Arabia and Seba* shall bring tribute.
All kings shall pay him homage,
all nations shall serve him. **℟.**
For he shall rescue the poor when he cries out,
and the afflicted when he has no one to help him.
He shall have pity for the lowly and the poor;
the lives of the poor he shall save. **℟.**

SECOND READING *(Ephesians 3:2–3a, 5–6)*

Brothers and sisters: You have heard of the stewardship of God's grace that was given to me for your benefit, namely, that the **mystery**✝ was made known to me by revelation. It was not made known to people in other generations as it has now been revealed to his holy apostles and prophets by the Spirit: that the Gentiles are coheirs, members of the same body, and copartners in the promise in Christ Jesus through the gospel.

The word of the Lord. ***Thanks be to God.***

ALLELUIA *(Matthew 2:2)*

Alleluia, alleluia. We saw his star at its rising / and have come to do him homage. ***Alleluia, alleluia.***

GOSPEL *(Matthew 2:1–12)*

A reading from the holy Gospel according to Matthew.
Glory to you, O Lord.

When Jesus was born in Bethlehem of Judea, in the days of King Herod, behold, magi from the east arrived in Jerusalem, saying, "Where is the newborn king of the Jews? We saw his star at its rising and have come to do him homage." When King Herod heard this, he was greatly troubled, and all Jerusalem with him. Assembling all the chief priests and the scribes of the people, he inquired of them where the Christ was to be born. They said to him, "In Bethlehem of Judea, for thus it has been written through the prophet:

And you, Bethlehem, land of Judah,
are by no means least among the rulers of Judah;
since from you shall come a ruler,
who is to shepherd my people Israel."

Then Herod called the magi secretly and ascertained from them the time of the star's appearance. He sent them to Bethlehem and said, "Go and search diligently for the child. When you have found him, bring me word, that I too may go and do him homage." After their audience with the king they set out. And behold, the star that they had seen at its rising preceded them, until it came and stopped over the place where the child was. They were overjoyed at seeing the star, and on entering the house they saw the child with Mary his mother. They prostrated themselves and did him homage. Then they opened their treasures and offered him gifts of gold, frankincense, and myrrh.* And having been warned in a dream not to return to Herod, they departed for their country by another way.

The Gospel of the Lord. ***Praise to you, Lord Jesus Christ.***

PROFESSION OF FAITH *(page 13)*

PRAYER OF THE FAITHFUL

PREPARATION OF GIFTS *(page 16)*

PRAYER OVER THE OFFERINGS

Look with favor, Lord, we pray,
on these gifts of your Church,

TAKING A CLOSER LOOK

✝ **Mystery** In the Greek world of early Christianity, "mystery" (singular) referred to what is hidden or secret and cannot be talked about openly. For Christians like Paul, a mystery points to what is hidden unless God reveals it. Paul identifies this revealed mystery as God's desire to unite all humanity—both Jew and Gentile—into one community in Christ. This becomes the core of Paul's Christian message. In later theological terminology, a mystery (such as the Trinity or the Incarnation) is a revealed truth about God that can be affirmed in faith but never completely and adequately expressed in abstract concepts or rational explanations.

in which are offered now not gold or frankincense or myrrh,
but he who by them is proclaimed,
sacrificed and received, Jesus Christ.
Who lives and reigns for ever and ever. ***Amen.***

PREFACE *(Epiphany, page 20)*

COMMUNION ANTIPHON *(Cf. Matthew 2:2)*
We have seen his star in the East, / and have come with gifts to adore the Lord.

PRAYER AFTER COMMUNION
Go before us with heavenly light, O Lord,
always and everywhere,
that we may perceive with clear sight
and revere with true affection
the mystery in which you have willed us to participate.
Through Christ our Lord. ***Amen.***

SOLEMN BLESSING: THE EPIPHANY OF THE LORD *(Optional, page 59)*

DISMISSAL *(page 57)* ⁜

Responding to the Word

Isaiah rejoices that God's light banishes the world's darkness.

When has God's light lifted the shadows of my heart?

The mystery of God's love for us has been made known in Jesus.

How can I share that message with those around me this week?

The magi followed a star to find Jesus.

Like the magi, how willing am I to "go the extra mile" to find Jesus in my daily life?

January 10

Jesus fulfills all righteousness

Actions speak louder than words. So, what do the actions of Jesus tell us? Why does Jesus, who knows no sin, present himself to John for baptism?

Two things are evident here and neither should surprise us. The first is the quality of leadership present in all the actions of Jesus. Jesus never asks us to do something that he himself hasn't done. He leads by accompaniment, sharing with people the experience of their life and calling them to something more, to closer union with God.

The second thing is humility. Given that we believe Jesus to be the Son of God, the Word made flesh, it is astounding to encounter the humble Jesus, born in poverty, a refugee, rejected, mocked, ultimately executed as a criminal. Today's gospel is simply another example of this, accepting a baptism he didn't need because, as he says in Matthew's Gospel, "Allow it now, for thus it is fitting for us to fulfill all righteousness" (Matthew 3:15).

In this moment, Jesus receives the validation of God through the presence of the Holy Trinity. The Father and the Spirit join the Son in affirmation of his mission. For us, this is an invitation to follow the example of Jesus, to accompany others in humility and thereby to lead them to God.

■ Rev. Leonard Altilia, SJ

ENTRANCE ANTIPHON *(Cf. Matthew 3:16-17)*

After the Lord was baptized, the heavens were opened, / and the Spirit descended upon him like a dove, / and the voice of the Father thundered: / This is my beloved Son, with whom I am well pleased.

INTRODUCTORY RITES *(page 10)*

COLLECT

Almighty ever-living God,
who, when Christ had been baptized in the River Jordan
and as the Holy Spirit descended upon him,
solemnly declared him your beloved Son,
grant that your children by adoption,
reborn of water and the Holy Spirit,
may always be well pleasing to you.
Through our Lord Jesus Christ, your Son,
who lives and reigns with you in the unity of the Holy Spirit,
one God, for ever and ever. ***Amen.***

Or

O God, whose Only Begotten Son
has appeared in our very flesh,
grant, we pray, that we may be inwardly transformed
through him whom we recognize as outwardly like ourselves.
Who lives and reigns with you in the unity of the Holy Spirit,
one God, for ever and ever. ***Amen.***

These are the readings for Year B. The first reading, responsorial psalm, second reading, and gospel acclamation from Year A (Isaiah 42:1-4, 6-7; Psalm 29:1-2, 3-4, 3, 9-10; Acts 10:34-38; see Mark 9:7) may also be used.

FIRST READING *(Isaiah 55:1-11)*

Thus says the LORD:
All you who are thirsty,
come to the water!
You who have no money,
come, receive grain and eat;
come, without paying and without cost,
drink wine and milk!
Why spend your money for what is not bread,
your wages for what fails to satisfy?
Heed me, and you shall eat well,
you shall delight in rich fare.
Come to me heedfully,
listen, that you may have life.
I will renew with you the everlasting covenant,
the benefits assured to David.
As I made him a witness to the peoples,
a leader and commander of nations,
so shall you summon a nation you knew not,
and nations that knew you not shall run to you,
because of the LORD, your God,
the Holy One of Israel, who has glorified you.

Seek the LORD while he may be found,
call him while he is near.
Let the scoundrel forsake his way,

and the wicked man his thoughts;
let him turn to the Lord for mercy;
to our God, who is generous in forgiving.
For my thoughts are not your thoughts,
nor are your ways my ways, says the LORD.
As high as the heavens are above the earth
so high are my ways above your ways
and my thoughts above your thoughts.

For just as from the heavens
the rain and snow come down
and do not return there
till they have watered the earth,
making it fertile and fruitful,
giving seed to the one who sows
and bread to the one who eats,
so shall my word be
that goes forth from my mouth;
my word shall not return to me void,
but shall do my will,
achieving the end for which I sent it.
The word of the Lord. ***Thanks be to God.***

RESPONSORIAL PSALM *(Isaiah 12:2–3, 4bcd, 5–6)*

℟. You will draw water joyfully from the springs of salvation.

God indeed is my savior;
I am confident and unafraid.
My strength and my courage is the LORD,
and he has been my savior.
With joy you will draw water

at the fountain of salvation.
℟. You will draw water joyfully from the springs of salvation.
Give thanks to the LORD, acclaim his name;
among the nations make known his deeds,
proclaim how exalted is his name. ℟.
Sing praise to the LORD for his glorious achievement;
let this be known throughout all the earth.
Shout with exultation, O city of Zion,*
for great in your midst
is the Holy One of Israel! ℟.

SECOND READING *(1 John 5:1-9)*

Beloved: Everyone who believes that Jesus is the Christ is begotten by God, and everyone who loves the Father loves also the one begotten by him. In this way we know that we love the children of God when we love God and obey his commandments. For the love of God is this, that we keep his commandments. And his commandments are not burdensome, for whoever is begotten by God conquers the world. And the victory that conquers the world is our faith. Who indeed is the victor over the world but the one who believes that Jesus is the Son of God?

This is the one who came through water and blood, Jesus Christ, not by water alone, but by water and blood. The Spirit is the one who testifies, and the Spirit is truth. So there are three that testify, the Spirit, the water, and the blood, and the three are of one accord. If we accept human testimony, the testimony of God is surely greater. Now the testimony of God is this, that he has testified on behalf of his Son.

The word of the Lord. ***Thanks be to God.***

ALLELUIA *(see John 1:29)*
Alleluia, alleluia. John saw Jesus approaching him, and said: /
Behold the Lamb of God who takes away the sin of the world.
Alleluia, alleluia.

GOSPEL *(Mark 1:7-11)*
A reading from the holy Gospel according to Mark.
Glory to you, O Lord.

This is what John the Baptist proclaimed: "One mightier than I is coming after me. I am not worthy to stoop and loosen the thongs of his sandals. I have baptized you with water; he will **baptize you with the Holy Spirit.**"✝

It happened in those days that Jesus came from Nazareth of Galilee and was baptized in the Jordan by John. On coming up out of the water he saw the heavens being torn open and the Spirit, like a dove, descending upon him. And a voice came from the heavens, "You are my beloved Son; with you I am well pleased."

The Gospel of the Lord. ***Praise to you, Lord Jesus Christ.***

PROFESSION OF FAITH *(page 13)*

PRAYER OF THE FAITHFUL

PREPARATION OF GIFTS *(page 16)*

PRAYER OVER THE OFFERINGS
Accept, O Lord, the offerings
we have brought to honor the revealing of your beloved Son,
so that the oblation of your faithful
may be transformed into the sacrifice of him
who willed in his compassion

to wash away the sins of the world.
Who lives and reigns for ever and ever. ***Amen.***

PREFACE: THE BAPTISM OF THE LORD

It is truly right and just, our duty and our salvation,
always and everywhere to give you thanks,
Lord, holy Father, almighty and eternal God.

For in the waters of the Jordan
you revealed with signs and wonders a new Baptism,
so that through the voice that came down from heaven
we might come to believe in your Word dwelling among us,
and by the Spirit's descending in the likeness of a dove
we might know that Christ your Servant
has been anointed with the oil of gladness
and sent to bring the good news to the poor.

TAKING A CLOSER LOOK

✝ **Baptize you with the Holy Spirit** For the early Christians, there were two great signs of God's saving activity that would bring a new life: the resurrection of Jesus from death to new life and the outpouring of God's Holy Spirit on the community. In this passage, Jesus compares this outpouring of God's Spirit (the power of life associated with breathing) to a baptismal washing that not only purifies the person but signifies one's desire to change one's ways and be more closely united with God's saving activity. Once empowered by the indwelling of God's holy presence, the disciples will be able to carry on the mission and ministry of Jesus in our world.

And so, with the Powers of heaven,
we worship you constantly on earth,
and before your majesty
without end we acclaim:
Holy, Holy, Holy Lord God of hosts... *(page 35)*

COMMUNION ANTIPHON *(John 1:32, 34)*

Behold the One of whom John said: / I have seen and testified that this is the Son of God.

PRAYER AFTER COMMUNION

Nourished with these sacred gifts,
we humbly entreat your mercy, O Lord,
that, faithfully listening to your Only Begotten Son,
we may be your children in name and in truth.
Through Christ our Lord. ***Amen.***

BLESSING & DISMISSAL *(page 56)*

Responding to the Word

Like Jesus at his baptism, we are also identified at our baptism as God's beloved child.

➡ *What does being a child of God mean to me?*

Loving God is expressed by keeping God's commandments.

➡ *Which of God's commandments is most difficult for me to obey?*

Isaiah encourages us to seek and to find God.

➡ *Where do I seek and find God in my everyday life?*

January 17

Growing together in Christ

When I went to church to find comfort and peace, I initially felt lonely and anxious. I was new to Beijing, there for a one-year work stint. However, one parishioner's invitation to join a Singles for Christ group transformed my experience at church. The parishioner and her friends—a mix of Chinese believers and foreigners—welcomed me to their church fellowship meetings and other gatherings. We met regularly for prayer and lunch after Mass. We celebrated Christmas and birthdays. They became my family in China. Together, we supported one another in strengthening our faith and navigating personal challenges.

Today's readings remind us that accepting the invitation to know God can truly transform our lives. How do we respond each day to God's call to be faithful followers? Do we make time to deepen our faith—not just alone, but in community? Do we invite others to encounter Jesus through our words and actions?

As we celebrate Mass today, let us thank God for the opportunity to grow as Christians through fellowship and by living out our faith. May we pray for the courage to be faithful followers of Jesus, leading others to his love by our example.

■ Christl Dabu

ENTRANCE ANTIPHON *(Psalm 66 [65]:4)*
All the earth shall bow down before you, O God, /
and shall sing to you, / shall sing to your name,
O Most High!

INTRODUCTORY RITES *(page 10)*

COLLECT
Almighty ever-living God,
who govern all things,
both in heaven and on earth,
mercifully hear the pleading of your people
and bestow your peace on our times.
Through our Lord Jesus Christ, your Son,
who lives and reigns with you in the unity of the Holy Spirit,
God, for ever and ever. ***Amen.***

FIRST READING *(1 Samuel 3:3b–10, 19)*
Samuel was sleeping in the temple of the LORD where the ark of God was. The LORD called to Samuel, who answered, "Here I am." Samuel ran to Eli and said, "Here I am. You called me." "I did not call you," Eli said. "Go back to sleep." So he went back to sleep. Again the LORD called Samuel, who rose and went to Eli. "Here I am," he said. "You called me." But Eli answered, "I did not call you, my son. Go back to sleep."

At that time Samuel was not familiar with the LORD, because the LORD had not revealed anything to him as yet. The LORD called Samuel again, for the third time. Getting up and going to Eli, he said, "Here I am. You called me." Then Eli understood that the LORD was calling the youth. So he said to Samuel, "Go to sleep, and if you are called, reply, Speak, LORD, for your servant is listening." When Samuel went to sleep in his place, the LORD came and revealed his presence, calling out as before, "Samuel, Samuel!" Samuel answered, "Speak, for your servant is listening."

Samuel grew up, and the LORD was with him, not permitting any word of his to be without effect.

The word of the Lord. ***Thanks be to God.***

RESPONSORIAL PSALM *(Psalm 40:2, 4, 7-8, 8-9, 10)*

℟. Here am I, Lord; I come to do your will.

I have waited, waited for the LORD,
 and he stooped toward me and heard my cry.
And he put a new song into my mouth,
 a hymn to our God. ℟.
Sacrifice or offering you wished not,
 but ears open to obedience you gave me.
Holocausts or sin-offerings+ you sought not;
 then said I, "Behold I come." ℟.
"In the written scroll it is prescribed for me,
to do your will, O my God, is my delight,
 and your law is within my heart!" ℟.
I announced your justice in the vast assembly;
 I did not restrain my lips, as you, O LORD, know. ℟.

SECOND READING *(1 Corinthians 6:13c-15a, 17-20)*

Brothers and sisters: The body is not for immorality, but for the Lord, and the Lord is for the body; God raised the Lord and will also raise us by his power.

Do you not know that your bodies are members of Christ? But whoever is joined to the Lord becomes one Spirit with him. Avoid immorality. Every other sin a person commits is outside the body, but the immoral person sins against his own body. Do you not know that your body is a temple of the Holy Spirit within you, whom you have from God, and that you are not your own? For you have been purchased at a price. Therefore glorify God in your body.

The word of the Lord. ***Thanks be to God.***

ALLELUIA *(John 1:41, 17b)*

Alleluia, alleluia. We have found the Messiah: / Jesus Christ, who brings us truth and grace. ***Alleluia, alleluia.***

GOSPEL *(John 1:35-42)*

A reading from the holy Gospel according to John.

Glory to you, O Lord.

John was standing with two of his disciples, and as he watched Jesus walk by, he said, "Behold, the Lamb of God." The two disciples heard what he said and followed Jesus. Jesus turned and saw them following him and said to them, "What are you looking for?" They said to him, "Rabbi"—which translated means Teacher—, "where are you staying?" He said to them, "Come, and you will see." So they went and saw where Jesus was staying, and they stayed with him that day. It was about four in the afternoon. Andrew, the brother of Simon Peter, was one of the two who heard John and followed Jesus. He first found his own brother Simon and told him, "We have found the Messiah"—which is translated Christ. Then he brought him to Jesus. Jesus looked at him and said, "You are Simon the son of John; you will be called Cephas*"—which is translated Peter.

The Gospel of the Lord. ***Praise to you, Lord Jesus Christ.***

PROFESSION OF FAITH *(page 13)*

PRAYER OF THE FAITHFUL

PREPARATION OF GIFTS *(page 16)*

PRAYER OVER THE OFFERINGS

Grant us, O Lord, we pray,
that we may participate worthily in these mysteries,
for whenever the memorial of this sacrifice is celebrated
the work of our redemption is accomplished.
Through Christ our Lord. ***Amen.***

PREFACE *(Sundays in Ordinary Time, pages 28–32)*

TAKING A CLOSER LOOK

✝ Holocausts or sin-offerings Sacrifice in the biblical world was a way of expressing one's relationship with God by setting apart something for God (thus making it "holy") and offering it as a gift to God. To show the complete character of the gift, it would be burned so that the giver could not take the gift back. This whole burnt offering is a *holocaust* (from the Greek words meaning a complete burning). A sin-offering was a gift offered to God that would help to restore the relationship when it was threatened by unintentional (rather than deliberate) sins.

COMMUNION ANTIPHON *(Cf. Psalm 23 [22]:5)*
You have prepared a table before me, / and how precious is the chalice that quenches my thirst.

Or *(1 John 4:16)*
We have come to know and to believe / in the love that God has for us.

PRAYER AFTER COMMUNION
Pour on us, O Lord, the Spirit of your love,
and in your kindness
make those you have nourished
by this one heavenly Bread
one in mind and heart.
Through Christ our Lord. ***Amen.***

BLESSING & DISMISSAL *(page 56)* ⁜

Responding to the Word

Once he learned how to listen, Samuel responded generously to God's call.

How can I pay closer attention to the surprising ways God might be calling me?

Jesus reminds us that our bodies also belong to God.

What difference might it make in my attitudes or behavior to accept my body as God's gift?

The disciples search out Jesus but are not sure what they want from him.

How would I answer if Jesus asked me, "What are you looking for?"

January 24

A leap of faith

Have you ever taken a leap of faith? If you did, how did that feel? Was it easy? Did you feel alone? Where did it lead you? Where did you land?

In today's gospel, Jesus is inviting Simon, Andrew, James, and John to follow him. They were ordinary men with no specific training, no influence, no power, no wealth. They were not from Jerusalem, the center of power. They were outsiders.

Jesus had no authority, no power, no wealth, and, like them, he was an outsider. So, what inspired them to follow him? What gave them the courage to take the leap of faith to become disciples?

These men took up the call to follow Jesus by the grace of God. The first step in faith begins with God's grace, not with human effort. The disciples' response is based not on their own reason but in trust of God. Was all this going through their minds as they heard the call? Probably not. This is what a leap of faith is all about. There may be no rhyme or reason to it. It just happens.

Today's gospel invites us to take a leap of faith, to examine our lives, to let go of all that hinders our relationship with God so that we can participate in building a world of justice and peace.

■ Anthony Chezzi

ENTRANCE ANTIPHON *(Cf. Psalm 96 [95]:1, 6)*
O sing a new song to the Lord; / sing to the Lord, all the earth. / In his presence are majesty and splendor, / strength and honor in his holy place.

INTRODUCTORY RITES *(page 10)*

COLLECT
Almighty ever-living God,
direct our actions according to your good pleasure,
that in the name of your beloved Son
we may abound in good works.
Through our Lord Jesus Christ, your Son,
who lives and reigns with you in the unity of the Holy Spirit,
God, for ever and ever. ***Amen.***

FIRST READING *(Jonah 3:1–5, 10)*
The word of the LORD came to Jonah, saying: "Set out for the great city of Nineveh, and announce to it the message that I will tell you." So Jonah made ready and went to Nineveh, according to the LORD's bidding. Now Nineveh was an enormously large city; it took three days to go through it. Jonah began his journey through the city, and had gone but a single day's walk announcing, "Forty days more and Nineveh shall be destroyed," when the people of Nineveh believed God; they proclaimed a fast and all of them, great and small, put on sackcloth.

When God saw by their actions how they turned from their evil way, he repented of the evil that he had threatened to do to them; he did not carry it out.

The word of the Lord. ***Thanks be to God.***

RESPONSORIAL PSALM *(Psalm 25:4-5, 6-7, 8-9)*

℟. Teach me your ways, O Lord.

Your ways, O LORD, make known to me;
teach me your paths,
guide me in your truth and teach me,
for you are God my savior. ℟.
Remember that your compassion, O LORD,
and your love are from of old.
In your kindness remember me,
because of your goodness, O LORD. ℟.
Good and upright is the LORD;
thus he shows sinners the way.
He guides the humble to justice
and teaches the humble his way. ℟.

SECOND READING *(1 Corinthians 7:29-31)*

I tell you, brothers and sisters, the time is running out. From now on, let those having wives act as not having them, those weeping as not weeping, those rejoicing as not rejoicing, those buying as not owning, those using the world as not using it fully. For the world in its present form is passing away.

The word of the Lord. ***Thanks be to God.***

ALLELUIA *(Mark 1:15)*

Alleluia, alleluia. The kingdom of God is at hand. / Repent and believe in the Gospel. ***Alleluia, alleluia.***

GOSPEL *(Mark 1:14–20)*

A reading from the holy Gospel according to Mark.
Glory to you, O Lord.

After John had been arrested, Jesus came to Galilee proclaiming the gospel of God: "This is the time of fulfillment. The **kingdom of God**+ is at hand. Repent, and believe in the gospel."

As he passed by the Sea of Galilee, he saw Simon and his brother Andrew casting their nets into the sea; they were fishermen. Jesus said to them, "Come after me, and I will make you fishers of men." Then they abandoned their nets and followed him. He walked along a little farther and saw James, the son of Zebedee, and his brother John. They too were in a boat mending their nets. Then he called them. So they left their father Zebedee in the boat along with the hired men and followed him.

The Gospel of the Lord. ***Praise to you, Lord Jesus Christ.***

PROFESSION OF FAITH *(page 13)*

PRAYER OF THE FAITHFUL

PREPARATION OF GIFTS *(page 16)*

PRAYER OVER THE OFFERINGS

Accept our offerings, O Lord, we pray,
and in sanctifying them
grant that they may profit us for salvation.
Through Christ our Lord. ***Amen.***

PREFACE *(Sundays in Ordinary Time, pages 28–32)*

COMMUNION ANTIPHON *(Cf. Psalm 34 [33]:6)*
Look toward the Lord and be radiant; / let your faces not be abashed.

Or *(John 8:12)*
I am the light of the world, says the Lord; / whoever follows me will not walk in darkness, / but will have the light of life.

TAKING A CLOSER LOOK

✝ **Kingdom of God** In his teaching and preaching, Jesus identifies God's ideal community as the kingdom of God—both the place where God rules and the people who live as God desires. This community is to be characterized by a new way of living together that includes everyone (both Jew and Gentile), who as brothers and sisters will relate to God as their father and as a king whose benevolent rule over them guides every moment of their lives. The kingdom is inaugurated by Jesus and continues today in the Christian community that daily strives to make God's ideal of community a reality.

PRAYER AFTER COMMUNION

Grant, we pray, almighty God,
that, receiving the grace
by which you bring us to new life,
we may always glory in your gift.
Through Christ our Lord. ***Amen.***

BLESSING & DISMISSAL *(page 56)* ⁜

Responding to the Word

Jonah is surprised when he shares God's message with others.

➡ *What has happened when I shared God's good news?*

Paul knows that Jesus makes all things new.

➡ *What is the biggest change going on in my life now because of Christ and his message?*

Jesus calls disciples to use their skills for building God's kingdom community.

➡ *Which gift or skill do I bring to the building of this community?*

January 31

Jesus shows us the way

We don't have to look far to see evidence of evil's impact on our lives, our families, our culture, and our world. As humans, we do a good enough job all on our own of messing things up; but add in the malignant work of demons that seek to divide, deceive, and destroy, and the consequences magnify.

In today's gospel, Jesus amazes the people with his demonstration of authority over the demons. There is to be no doubt by this ordering of events of the importance of the authoritative stance he takes in confronting the demonic: it precedes any healing miracles; it precedes his teaching. There is to be no mistake that there are enemies that seek the ruin of souls and that Jesus has command over them.

We needn't wait to see full-on possession to recognize the influence of Satan and his fallen angels. We can see it where there is deception, where wounds become infected with bitterness, where division inspires hatred.

Jesus shows us the way: first we must follow him, seeking holiness, surrendering to him in all things, obedient to all he has commanded, dying to self. The tradition of the Church is rich with wisdom and prayers to direct us in our battle against evil. St. Michael the Archangel, defend us!

■ Kathleen Giffin

ENTRANCE ANTIPHON *(Psalm 106 (105):47)*
Save us, O Lord our God! / And gather us from the nations, / to give thanks to your holy name, / and make it our glory to praise you.

INTRODUCTORY RITES *(page 10)*

COLLECT
Grant us, Lord our God,
that we may honor you with all our mind,
and love everyone in truth of heart.
Through our Lord Jesus Christ, your Son,
who lives and reigns with you in the unity of the Holy Spirit,
God, for ever and ever. ***Amen.***

FIRST READING *(Deuteronomy 18:15-20)*
Moses spoke to all the people, saying: "A prophet like me will the LORD, your God, raise up for you from among your own kin; to him you shall listen. This is exactly what you requested of the LORD, your God, at Horeb* on the day of the assembly, when you said, 'Let us not again hear the voice of the LORD, our God, nor see this great fire any more, lest we die.' And the LORD said to me, 'This was well said. I will raise up for them a prophet like you from among their kin, and will put my words into his mouth; he shall tell them all that I command him. Whoever will not listen to my words which he speaks in my name, I myself will make him answer for it. But if a prophet presumes to speak in my name an oracle that I have not commanded him to speak, or speaks in the name of other gods, he shall die.'"

The word of the Lord. ***Thanks be to God.***

RESPONSORIAL PSALM *(Psalm 95:1–2, 6–7, 7–9)*

℟ If today you hear his voice, harden not your hearts.

Come, let us sing joyfully to the LORD;
  let us acclaim the rock of our salvation.
Let us come into his presence with thanksgiving;
  let us joyfully sing psalms to him. ℟
Come, let us bow down in worship;
  let us kneel before the LORD who made us.
For he is our God,
  and we are the people he shepherds, the flock he guides. ℟
Oh, that today you would hear his voice:
  "Harden not your hearts as at Meribah,*
  as in the day of Massah* in the desert,
Where your fathers tempted me;
  they tested me though they had seen my works." ℟

SECOND READING *(1 Corinthians 7:32–35)*

Brothers and sisters: I should like you to be free of anxieties. An unmarried man is anxious about the things of the **Lord,**+ how he may please the Lord. But a married man is anxious about the things of the world, how he may please his wife, and he is divided. An unmarried woman or a virgin is anxious about the things of the Lord, so that she may be holy in both body and spirit. A married woman, on the other hand, is anxious about the things of the world, how she may please her husband. I am telling you this for your own benefit, not to impose a restraint upon you, but for the sake of propriety and adherence to the Lord without distraction.

The word of the Lord. ***Thanks be to God.***

ALLELUIA *(Matthew 4:16)*
Alleluia, alleluia. The people who sit in darkness have seen a great light; / on those dwelling in a land overshadowed by death, / light has arisen. ***Alleluia, alleluia.***

GOSPEL *(Mark 1:21–28)*
A reading from the holy Gospel according to Mark.
Glory to you, O Lord.

Then they came to Capernaum,* and on the sabbath Jesus entered the synagogue and taught. The people were astonished at his teaching, for he taught them as one having authority and not as the scribes. In their synagogue was a man with an unclean spirit; he cried out, "What have you to do with us, Jesus of Nazareth? Have you come to destroy us? I know who you are—the Holy One of God!" Jesus rebuked him and said, "Quiet! Come out of him!" The unclean spirit convulsed him and with a loud cry came out of him. All were amazed and asked one another, "What is this? A new teaching with authority. He commands even the unclean spirits and they obey him." His fame spread everywhere throughout the whole region of Galilee.

The Gospel of the Lord. ***Praise to you, Lord Jesus Christ.***

PROFESSION OF FAITH *(page 13)*

PRAYER OF THE FAITHFUL

PREPARATION OF GIFTS *(page 16)*

PRAYER OVER THE OFFERINGS

O Lord, we bring to your altar
these offerings of our service:
be pleased to receive them, we pray,
and transform them
into the Sacrament of our redemption.
Through Christ our Lord. ***Amen.***

PREFACE *(Sundays in Ordinary Time, pages 28–32)*

COMMUNION ANTIPHON *(Cf. Psalm 31 (30):17–18)*

Let your face shine on your servant. / Save me in your merciful love. / O Lord, let me never be put to shame, for I call on you.

Or *(Matthew 5:3–4)*

Blessed are the poor in spirit, / for theirs is the Kingdom of Heaven. / Blessed are the meek, for they shall possess the land.

TAKING A CLOSER LOOK

✚ **Lord** Since God's personal name, *Yahweh* (Lord printed in small capital letters as LORD in our Bible), which was revealed to Moses and the Israelites (Exodus 3:14) was so sacred, the Jews did not speak it aloud but would instead often say Adonai, the Hebrew word for "Lord." Thus "Lord" (Greek, *Kyrios*; Latin, *Dominus*) describes the exalted status of God—higher in power, honor, and glory than any creature. When Christians began to recognize that Jesus did most of the things that God did (except to create, which God the Father alone did), they reasoned that since Jesus did what God did, Jesus must also be divine and hence worthy of the name "Lord." As St. Paul realized, although God the Father remains Lord, the name "Lord" is now also honorably bestowed on Jesus (see Philippians 2:6-11, Palm Sunday), who thus becomes Our Lord Jesus Christ.

PRAYER AFTER COMMUNION

Nourished by these redeeming gifts,
we pray, O Lord,
that through this help to eternal salvation
true faith may ever increase.
Through Christ our Lord. ***Amen.***

BLESSING & DISMISSAL *(page 56)* ✣

Responding to the Word

God promises to send prophets who will reveal God's presence among us.

➔ *Who has shown me where God is hidden in our midst?*

Paul encourages us to be free of anxieties in our relationships.

➔ *How has my anxiety about a relationship influenced my behavior toward God or others?*

Jesus' mastery of unclean spirits shows he is reordering the world for God.

➔ *How has my life been reordered because of my faith in Christ?*

February 7

Jesus knows our struggles

Caring is exhausting. As a mother, I truly understand this sentiment. Taking care of other people's emotions, needs, and health is draining. As mothers, we experience pressure to do this vocation perfectly, easily, and without complaint. We are forever holding two truths in our hands: I will give myself completely to this beautiful human, and yet I long for a moment of peace where I am relieved of this mental load.

Being fully human, Jesus experiences this duality. After two days of casting out demons, this element of Jesus' ministry starts to take a physical and mental toll. People are in awe of his ability to cast out demons, and his disciples want him to perform even more miracles for the crowds. While meaningful, it pulls him away from preaching the message of finding salvation in the love of God. Ultimately, Jesus feels stretched thin.

Today we see Jesus take a step back. He wakes early to spend time with God the Father in solitude and regain clarity. As we prepare to begin Lent later this week, may we take time to rest in the humanity of our Savior. Let us share with him our vulnerabilities and the struggles we experience, allowing him to grant us peace. With our burden lessened, let us continue to live our vocations to the fullest.

■ Elizabeth Chesley-Jewell

ENTRANCE ANTIPHON *(Psalm 95 [94]:6-7)*
O come, let us worship God / and bow low before the God who made us, / for he is the Lord our God.

INTRODUCTORY RITES *(page 10)*

COLLECT
Keep your family safe, O Lord, with unfailing care,
that, relying solely on the hope of heavenly grace,
they may be defended always by your protection.
Through our Lord Jesus Christ, your Son,
who lives and reigns with you in the unity of the Holy Spirit,
God, for ever and ever. ***Amen.***

FIRST READING *(Job 7:1-4, 6-7)*
Job spoke, saying:
Is not man's life on earth a drudgery?
  Are not his days those of hirelings?
He is a slave who longs for the shade,
  a hireling who waits for his wages.
So I have been assigned months of misery,
  and troubled nights have been allotted to me.
If in bed I say, "When shall I arise?"
  then the night drags on;
  I am filled with restlessness until the dawn.
My days are swifter than a weaver's shuttle;
  they come to an end without hope.
Remember that my life is like the wind;
  I shall not see happiness again.
The word of the Lord. ***Thanks be to God.***

RESPONSORIAL PSALM *(Psalm 147:1-2, 3-4, 5-6)*

℟. Praise the Lord, who heals the brokenhearted. *Or* **Alleluia.**

Praise the LORD, for he is good;
sing praise to our God, for he is gracious;
it is fitting to praise him.
The LORD rebuilds Jerusalem;
the dispersed of Israel he gathers. **℟.**
He heals the brokenhearted
and binds up their wounds.
He tells the number of the stars;
he calls each by name. **℟.**
Great is our Lord and mighty in power;
to his wisdom there is no limit.
The LORD sustains the lowly;
the wicked he casts to the ground. **℟.**

SECOND READING *(1 Corinthians 9:16-19, 22-23)*

Brothers and sisters: If I preach the gospel, this is no reason for me to boast, for an obligation has been imposed on me, and woe to me if I do not preach it! If I do so willingly, I have a recompense, but if unwillingly, then I have been entrusted with a stewardship. What then is my recompense? That, when I preach, I offer the gospel free of charge so as not to make full use of my right in the gospel.

Although I am free in regard to all, I have made myself a slave to all so as to win over as many as possible. To the weak I became weak, to win over the weak. I have become all things to all, to save at least some. All this I do for the sake of the gospel, so that I too may have a share in it.

The word of the Lord. ***Thanks be to God.***

ALLELUIA *(Matthew 8:17)*
Alleluia, alleluia. Christ took away our infirmities / and bore our diseases. ***Alleluia, alleluia.***

GOSPEL *(Mark 1:29–39)*
A reading from the holy Gospel according to Mark.
Glory to you, O Lord.

On leaving the **synagogue**+ Jesus entered the house of Simon and Andrew with James and John. Simon's mother-in-law lay sick with a fever. They immediately told him about her. He approached, grasped her hand, and helped her up. Then the fever left her and she waited on them.

When it was evening, after sunset, they brought to him all who were ill or possessed by demons. The whole town was gathered at the door. He cured many who were sick with various diseases, and he drove out many demons, not permitting them to speak because they knew him.

Rising very early before dawn, he left and went off to a deserted place, where he prayed. Simon and those who were with him pursued him and on finding him said, "Everyone is looking for you." He told them, "Let us go on to the nearby villages that I may preach there also. For this purpose have I come." So he went into their synagogues, preaching and driving out demons throughout the whole of Galilee.

The Gospel of the Lord. ***Praise to you, Lord Jesus Christ.***

PROFESSION OF FAITH *(page 13)*

PRAYER OF THE FAITHFUL

PREPARATION OF GIFTS *(page 16)*

PRAYER OVER THE OFFERINGS

O Lord our God,
who once established these created things
to sustain us in our frailty,
grant, we pray,
that they may become for us now
the Sacrament of eternal life.
Through Christ our Lord. ***Amen.***

PREFACE *(Sundays in Ordinary Time, pages 28–32)*

COMMUNION ANTIPHON *(Cf. Psalm 107 [106]:8–9)*

Let them thank the Lord for his mercy, / his wonders for the children of men, / for he satisfies the thirsty soul, / and the hungry he fills with good things.

Or *(Matthew 5:5–6)*

Blessed are those who mourn, for they shall be consoled. / Blessed are those who hunger and thirst for righteousness, / for they shall have their fill.

TAKING A CLOSER LOOK

✝ **Synagogue** The synagogue was not, like the Temple in Jerusalem, a place where God dwelt and where Jews worshipped and offered sacrifices. It was primarily a meeting place for community prayer and for the study and discussion of the Scriptures. Hence, it was not organized and run by priests but by lay people, in particular the elders of the community. Synagogues became even more important after the Jerusalem Temple was destroyed in 70 AD by the Romans and sacrifices ceased to be offered. Synagogues also helped affirm Jewish identity and community belonging when Jews emigrated to other nations.

PRAYER AFTER COMMUNION

O God, who have willed that we be partakers
in the one Bread and the one Chalice,
grant us, we pray, so to live
that, made one in Christ,
we may joyfully bear fruit
for the salvation of the world.
Through Christ our Lord. ***Amen.***

BLESSING & DISMISSAL *(page 56)*

Responding to the Word

Job recognizes the difficulties of life and how they push us to give up hope.

How does Christ's presence in my life offer hope?

Paul feels compelled to share the gospel message.

What makes Jesus' good news so good that I want to share it?

Despite his busy ministry, Jesus prayed alone in the morning.

When can I find time each day to pray and be alone with God?

Christ lights our darkness

We may be surprised to hear that the Church's liturgy reminds us that Lent is meant to be a joyful season.

> For by your gracious gift each year
> your faithful await the sacred paschal feasts
> with the joy of minds made pure...
> PREFACE I OF LENT

The season of Lent finds its meaning and origin in Easter, the annual celebration of our Lord's resurrection and our salvation. As the Church's time to prepare for the high point of the Christian year, it is the most appropriate time for persons to enter into Christ's new life through baptism. How can it not be a time of joy?

Over the centuries, Lent has become a special time for fasting, abstinence, communal and private prayer, self-discipline, serving others, study, reflection, and penance. With the whole Church we re-examine our priorities, leaving sin and self behind and intensifying our love and service of God and our neighbors.

The joy of this time of preparation is all about the surprise of new life coming from what may have appeared dead—just as fresh buds break through each spring on trees that seemed dead during the long winter.

If we use these forty days of Lent for honest examination and careful "pruning" of our lives, we will be ready to celebrate the great feast of Easter with our risen Lord and to be joyful witnesses of the power of his resurrection in our world so broken by sin.

Praying and living the Lenten season

It's a common practice to "give things up" for Lent. But when we give something up, we create an empty space into which we must then put some new form of loving behavior.

Give yourself and each household member an index card. Either divide the card into five weeks or, better, use a new card each week. Invite everyone to write on one side what they want to give up to create space for something new, and on the other side what they want to fill the space with.

For example, giving up calories by fasting creates a space for feeling a little of the hunger that haunts millions of the world's poor. The money we save from fasting can also be donated to groups that help feed the hungry. Giving up some television time as a household creates space for spending time together in conversation, prayer, or even playing games. Giving up an attitude of complaining makes space for a more cooperative approach to fixing dinners or doing chores.

When everyone is finished, take the cards and place them in the center of the dinner table or in your household Lenten prayer space. Light a candle and pray together:

God, giver of all gifts,
you have given us so much.
Now we want to give up something
so that we might experience
the emptiness that reminds us
how much we want to be filled
by your loving presence.
May our sacrifice show our willingness
to change our lives this Lent. Amen.

February 10

Listen to the Spirit

On Ash Wednesday, we mark the beginning of our Lenten journey by literally marking our foreheads with ashes. These ashes symbolize our ongoing need to grow in humility and gratitude. Lent is a time to slow down: a time to reflect, to take stock of our prayer life, to determine what we need to change in our lives.

The gospel for today provides guidance on how to go about fasting and almsgiving through this liturgical season. We may feel distracted in the busy-ness of life: family and work can overwhelm us. We may feel as though we are juggling too many things. If our children have grown, we may feel tired and lost, with time on our hands. But there is always something we can change.

As children, many of us were encouraged to "give something up" during Lent, like dessert. As adults, we could "give up" complaining, or work harder at making family time, or be more patient with others. Perhaps if we pray and listen to the Spirit more, we may find a way to be more generous in our community.

Lent gives us an opportunity, a chance to grow and be changed by the Spirit. Let us pray as we begin this journey that our sacrifices will declare our praises to God even (especially) if we do not make a show of them.

■ Jeanne Lambert

If the blessing and distribution of ashes take place outside Mass, it is appropriate that the complete Liturgy of the Word precede it, using texts assigned to the Mass of Ash Wednesday.

ENTRANCE ANTIPHON *(Wisdom 11:24, 25, 27)*
You are merciful to all, O Lord, / and despise nothing that you have made. / You overlook people's sins, to bring them to repentance, / and you spare them, for you are the Lord our God.

INTRODUCTORY RITES *(page 10)*

COLLECT
Grant, O Lord, that we may begin with holy fasting
this campaign of Christian service,
so that, as we take up battle against spiritual evils,
we may be armed with weapons of self-restraint.
Through our Lord Jesus Christ, your Son,
who lives and reigns with you in the unity of the Holy Spirit,
God, for ever and ever. ***Amen.***

FIRST READING *(Joel 2:12–18)*
Even now, says the LORD,
return to me with your whole heart,
with fasting, and weeping, and mourning;
Rend your hearts, not your garments,
and return to the LORD, your God.
For gracious and merciful is he,
slow to anger, rich in kindness,
and relenting in punishment.
Perhaps he will again relent
and leave behind him a blessing,

Offerings and libations
  for the LORD, your God.

Blow the trumpet in Zion!*
  proclaim a fast,
  call an assembly;
Gather the people,
  notify the congregation;
Assemble the elders,
  gather the children
  and the infants at the breast;
Let the bridegroom quit his room
  and the bride her chamber.
Between the porch and the altar
  let the priests, the ministers of the LORD, weep,
And say, "Spare, O LORD, your people,
  and make not your heritage a reproach,
  with the nations ruling over them!
Why should they say among the peoples,
  'Where is their God?' "

Then the LORD was stirred to concern for his land
  and took pity on his people.
  The word of the Lord. ***Thanks be to God.***

RESPONSORIAL PSALM *(Psalm 51:3-4, 5-6ab, 12-13, 14, 17)*
℟. Be merciful, O Lord, for we have sinned.

Have mercy on me, O God, in your goodness;
  in the greatness of your compassion wipe out my offense.
Thoroughly wash me from my guilt

and of my sin cleanse me. **℟.**
For I acknowledge my offense,
and my sin is before me always:
"Against you only have I sinned,
and done what is evil in your sight." **℟.**
A clean heart create for me, O God,
and a steadfast spirit renew within me.
Cast me not out from your presence,
and your Holy Spirit take not from me. **℟.**
Give me back the joy of your salvation,
and a willing spirit sustain in me.
O Lord, open my lips,
and my mouth shall proclaim your praise. **℟.**

SECOND READING *(2 Corinthians 5:20–6:2)*

Brothers and sisters: We are ambassadors for Christ, as if God were appealing through us. We implore you on behalf of Christ, be reconciled to God. For our sake he made him to be sin who did not know sin, so that we might become the righteousness of God in him.

Working together, then, we appeal to you not to receive the grace of God in vain. For he says:

In an acceptable time I heard you,
and on the day of salvation I helped you.

Behold, now is a very acceptable time; behold, now is the day of salvation.

The word of the Lord. ***Thanks be to God.***

VERSE BEFORE THE GOSPEL *(See Psalm 95:8)*
Glory and praise to you, Lord Jesus Christ! If today you hear his voice, / harden not your hearts. ***Glory and praise to you, Lord Jesus Christ!***

GOSPEL *(Matthew 6:1–6, 16–18)*
A reading from the holy Gospel according to Matthew.
Glory to you, O Lord.

Jesus said to his disciples: "Take care not to perform righteous deeds in order that people may see them; otherwise, you will have no recompense from your heavenly Father. When you give alms, do not blow a trumpet before you, as the **hypocrites**+ do in the synagogues and in the streets to win the praise of others. Amen, I say to you, they have received their reward. But when you give alms, do not let your left hand know what your right is doing, so that your almsgiving may be secret. And your Father who sees in secret will repay you.

"When you pray, do not be like the hypocrites, who love to stand and pray in the synagogues and on street corners so that others may see them. Amen, I say to you, they have received their reward. But when you pray, go to your inner room, close the door, and pray to your Father in secret. And your Father who sees in secret will repay you.

"When you fast, do not look gloomy like the hypocrites. They neglect their appearance, so that they may appear to others to be fasting. Amen, I say to you, they have received their reward. But when you fast, anoint your head and wash your face, so that you may not appear to be fasting, except to your Father who is hidden. And your Father who sees what is hidden will repay you."

The Gospel of the Lord. ***Praise to you, Lord Jesus Christ.***

BLESSING AND DISTRIBUTION OF ASHES

After the homily, the priest, standing with hands joined, says:

Dear brethren (brothers and sisters), let us humbly ask God
our Father
that he be pleased to bless with the abundance of his grace
these ashes, which we will put on our heads in penitence.

After a brief prayer in silence he continues:

O God, who are moved by acts of humility
and respond with forgiveness to works of penance,
lend your merciful ear to our prayers
and in your kindness pour out the grace of your blessing
on your servants who are marked with these ashes,
that, as they follow the Lenten observances,
they may be worthy to come with minds made pure
to celebrate the Paschal Mystery of your Son.
Who lives and reigns for ever and ever. ***Amen.***

Or

O God, who desire not the death of sinners,
but their conversion,
mercifully hear our prayers
and in your kindness be pleased to bless these ashes,
which we intend to receive upon our heads,
that we, who acknowledge we are but ashes
and shall return to dust,
may, through a steadfast observance of Lent,
gain pardon for sins and newness of life
after the likeness of your Risen Son.
Who lives and reigns for ever and ever. ***Amen.***

The priest sprinkles the ashes with holy water, places ashes on the heads of all those present who come to him, and says to each one:

Repent, and believe in the Gospel.

Or

Remember that you are dust, and to dust you shall return.

PRAYER OF THE FAITHFUL

PREPARATION OF GIFTS *(page 16)*

PRAYER OVER THE OFFERINGS

As we solemnly offer
the annual sacrifice for the beginning of Lent,
we entreat you, O Lord,
that, through works of penance and charity,
we may turn away from harmful pleasures
and, cleansed from our sins, may become worthy
to celebrate devoutly the Passion of your Son.
Who lives and reigns for ever and ever. ***Amen.***

TAKING A CLOSER LOOK

Hypocrites *Hypokrites* is a Greek word for an actor in the theater. Since Greek plays were performed outdoors and the audience was at a distance, actors wore large stereotyped masks to identify their characters. So in popular usage, a hypocrite was someone who pretended to be something that he or she was not, and hypocrisy described the general mismatch between one's external appearance and one's internal attitudes or intentions. Just as the actor hid behind a mask and performed a role, so the hypocrite hides something behind a pleasing external appearance.

PREFACE *(Lent 3-4, page 22)*

COMMUNION ANTIPHON *(Cf. Psalm 1:2-3)*
He who ponders the law of the Lord day and night / will yield fruit in due season.

PRAYER AFTER COMMUNION
May the Sacrament we have received sustain us, O Lord,
that our Lenten fast may be pleasing to you
and be for us a healing remedy.
Through Christ our Lord. ***Amen.***

PRAYER OVER THE PEOPLE
Pour out a spirit of compunction, O God,
on those who bow before your majesty,
and by your mercy may they merit the rewards you promise
to those who do penance.
Through Christ our Lord. ***Amen.***

DISMISSAL *(page 57)* ⁜

Responding to the Word

Joel wants us to change on the inside and not just externally.

➡ *What change of attitude do I most want to make this Lent?*

Paul says that now is the acceptable time to be an ambassador of Christ.

➡ *With whom will I share the good news of salvation today?*

Jesus warns against hypocritical behavior.

➡ *What do I need to do to match my words with my actions?*

February 14

We never face our perils alone

The events described in today's gospel take place immediately after Jesus was baptized by John the Baptist and he heard those wonderful words: "You are my beloved Son; with you I am well pleased."

Those words of God's changed everything for Jesus. And the gospel account of Jesus in the wilderness changes our perspective, too. We are conditioned to think of the wilderness as a place of threat, of danger. The gospel passage today opens a new way of looking at the wilderness. Although there is danger in the wilderness, there is also great possibility.

It's a matter of seeing things through God's eyes. The gospel reminds us that Jesus did not decide on his own to go out into the wilderness. Jesus was led into the wilderness by the Holy Spirit, encountered God in the wilderness, and was ministered to in the wilderness by angels. Through it all, he was sustained and strengthened by God's words: "You are my beloved Son; with you I am well pleased."

Whatever our personal wilderness might be, we who have been baptized have received God's assurance that we are beloved and God is well pleased. The Holy Spirit leads us, and Jesus walks with us, assuring us that we will never face our perils alone.

■ Anne Walsh

Parishes engaged in the Order of Christian Initiation of Adults (OCIA) may celebrate the Rite of Election today.

ENTRANCE ANTIPHON *(Cf. Psalm 91 [90]:15-16)*
When he calls on me, I will answer him; / I will deliver him and give him glory, / I will grant him length of days.

INTRODUCTORY RITES *(page 10)*

COLLECT
Grant, almighty God,
through the yearly observances of holy Lent,
that we may grow in understanding
of the riches hidden in Christ
and by worthy conduct pursue their effects.
Through our Lord Jesus Christ, your Son,
who lives and reigns with you in the unity of the Holy Spirit,
God, for ever and ever. ***Amen.***

FIRST READING *(Genesis 9:8-15)*
God said to Noah and to his sons with him: "See, I am now establishing my **covenant**✝ with you and your descendants after you and with every living creature that was with you: all the birds, and the various tame and wild animals that were with you and came out of the ark. I will establish my covenant with you, that never again shall all bodily creatures be destroyed by the waters of a flood; there shall not be another flood to devastate the earth." God added: "This is the sign that I am giving for all ages to come, of the covenant between me and you and every living creature with you: I set my bow in the clouds to serve as a sign of the covenant

between me and the earth. When I bring clouds over the earth, and the bow appears in the clouds, I will recall the covenant I have made between me and you and all living beings, so that the waters shall never again become a flood to destroy all mortal beings."

The word of the Lord. ***Thanks be to God.***

RESPONSORIAL PSALM *(Psalm 25:4-5, 6-7, 8-9)*

℟ Your ways, O Lord, are love and truth to those who keep your covenant.

Your ways, O LORD, make known to me;
teach me your paths.
Guide me in your truth and teach me,
for you are God my savior. ℟
Remember that your compassion, O LORD,
and your love are from of old.
In your kindness remember me,
because of your goodness, O LORD. ℟
Good and upright is the LORD,
thus he shows sinners the way.
He guides the humble to justice,
and he teaches the humble his way. ℟

SECOND READING *(1 Peter 3:18-22)*

Beloved: Christ suffered for sins once, the righteous for the sake of the unrighteous, that he might lead you to God. Put to death in the flesh, he was brought to life in the Spirit. In it he also went to preach to the spirits in prison, who had once been disobedient while God patiently waited in the days of Noah during the building of the ark, in which a few persons, eight in all, were saved through water. This prefigured baptism, which saves you now. It is not a removal of dirt from the body but an appeal to God for a clear conscience, through the resurrection of Jesus Christ, who has gone into heaven and is at the right hand of God, with angels, authorities, and powers subject to him.

The word of the Lord. ***Thanks be to God.***

VERSE BEFORE THE GOSPEL *(Matthew 4:4b)*

Glory and praise to you, Lord Jesus Christ! One does not live on bread alone, / but on every word that comes forth from the mouth of God. ***Glory and praise to you, Lord Jesus Christ!***

GOSPEL *(Mark 1:12–15)*

A reading from the holy Gospel according to Mark.
Glory to you, O Lord.

The Spirit drove Jesus out into the desert, and he remained in the desert for forty days, tempted by Satan. He was among wild beasts, and the angels ministered to him.

After John had been arrested, Jesus came to Galilee proclaiming the gospel of God: "This is the time of fulfillment. The kingdom of God is at hand. Repent, and believe in the gospel."

The Gospel of the Lord. ***Praise to you, Lord Jesus Christ.***

RITE OF ELECTION

PROFESSION OF FAITH *(page 13)*

PRAYER OF THE FAITHFUL

PREPARATION OF GIFTS *(page 16)*

PRAYER OVER THE OFFERINGS

Give us the right dispositions, O Lord, we pray,
to make these offerings,
for with them we celebrate the beginning
of this venerable and sacred time.
Through Christ our Lord. ***Amen.***

PREFACE: THE TEMPTATION OF THE LORD

It is truly right and just, our duty and our salvation,
always and everywhere to give you thanks,
Lord, holy Father, almighty and eternal God,
through Christ our Lord.

By abstaining forty long days from earthly food,
he consecrated through his fast
the pattern of our Lenten observance
and, by overturning all the snares of the ancient serpent,
taught us to cast out the leaven of malice,
so that, celebrating worthily the Paschal Mystery,
we might pass over at last to the eternal paschal feast.

And so, with the company of Angels and Saints,
we sing the hymn of your praise,
as without end we acclaim:
Holy, Holy, Holy Lord God of hosts... *(page 35)*

COMMUNION ANTIPHON *(Matthew 4:4)*
One does not live by bread alone, / but by every word that comes forth from the mouth of God.

Or *(Cf. Psalm 91 [90]:4)*
The Lord will conceal you with his pinions, / and under his wings you will trust.

PRAYER AFTER COMMUNION
Renewed now with heavenly bread,
by which faith is nourished, hope increased,
and charity strengthened,
we pray, O Lord,
that we may learn to hunger for Christ,
the true and living Bread,
and strive to live by every word
which proceeds from your mouth.
Through Christ our Lord. ***Amen.***

TAKING A CLOSER LOOK

✢ **Covenant** A covenant is a formal agreement between two persons or parties that spells out the obligations of their relationship. In the biblical world, the general expectations were modeled on the customs that guided relationships between persons of unequal honor, status, and wealth. These relationships were voluntary and freely entered into and were not required by law. The covenant bound the parties in mutual and reciprocal obligations. The "patron" or more powerful person (like God) promised to provide for and protect the less powerful "clients" (from the Latin word for dependents). In return, to enhance the honor and reputation of the patron, the clients offered respect, praise, and gratitude, and other favors when requested.

PRAYER OVER THE PEOPLE

May bountiful blessing, O Lord, we pray,
come down upon your people,
that hope may grow in tribulation,
virtue be strengthened in temptation,
and eternal redemption be assured.
Through Christ our Lord. ***Amen.***

DISMISSAL *(page 57)* ⁜

Responding to the Word

The rainbow was Noah's reminder of God's covenant with all creation.

➡ *What, like the rainbow, reminds me of God's loving care for creation?*

Peter reminds us it is not outer dirt but the inner spirit that needs cleansing.

➡ *What inner renewal do I most desire this Lent?*

Jesus' desert experience led to a new ministry for others.

➡ *How might my Lenten changes make me a better announcer for God's good news?*

February 21

Jesus doesn't demand perfection

Jesus is perfect, and we are not. How should we respond to that? Is it something to be ashamed of? Is it an excuse to stop trying? In today's gospel, both Jesus' behavior and Peter's response can inspire us.

Peter, James, and John didn't ask to go up the mountain with Jesus, and they didn't ask for anything while they were there. Jesus freely showed them his divine nature, his absolute perfection. He was completely honest with them. Understandably, the sight was so monumental that Peter didn't know how to respond. He didn't hide or run away and even had the presence of mind to say, "Rabbi, it is good that we are here!" However, the rest of his words come across as nervous rambling.

At times, when I have something on my mind, I hesitate to pray about it because I doubt that I will understand Jesus' response. Today's gospel shows us that Jesus can present us with amazing insights even when we can't fully process them or know what to do with them right away. He doesn't demand a perfect response: he just gives.

Jesus' perfection offers us the security to be honest in prayer. He won't reject us. Our imperfections shouldn't keep us from Jesus but rather drive us to him. It is good for us to be here.

■ Kate Larson

ENTRANCE ANTIPHON *(Cf. Psalm 27 [26]:8-9)*
Of you my heart has spoken: Seek his face. / It is your face, O Lord, that I seek; / hide not your face from me.

Or *(Cf. Psalm 25 [24]:6, 2, 22)*
Remember your compassion, O Lord, / and your merciful love, for they are from of old. / Let not our enemies exult over us. / Redeem us, O God of Israel, from all our distress.

INTRODUCTORY RITES *(page 10)*

COLLECT
O God, who have commanded us
to listen to your beloved Son,
be pleased, we pray,
to nourish us inwardly by your word,
that, with spiritual sight made pure,
we may rejoice to behold your glory.
Through our Lord Jesus Christ, your Son,
who lives and reigns with you in the unity of the Holy Spirit,
God, for ever and ever. ***Amen.***

FIRST READING *(Genesis 22:1-2, 9a, 10-13, 15-18)*
God put Abraham to the test. He called to him, "Abraham!" "Here I am!" he replied. Then God said: "Take your son Isaac, your only one, whom you love, and go to the land of Moriah.* There you shall offer him up as a holocaust on a height that I will point out to you."

When they came to the place of which God had told him, Abraham built an altar there and arranged the wood on it. Then he reached out and took the knife to slaughter his son. But the LORD's messenger called to him from heaven, "Abraham,

Abraham!" "Here I am!" he answered. "Do not lay your hand on the boy," said the messenger. "Do not do the least thing to him. I know now how devoted you are to God, since you did not withhold from me your own beloved son." As Abraham looked about, he spied a ram caught by its horns in the thicket. So he went and took the ram and offered it up as a holocaust in place of his son.

Again the LORD's messenger called to Abraham from heaven and said: "I swear by myself, declares the LORD, that because you acted as you did in not withholding from me your beloved son, I will bless you abundantly and make your descendants as countless as the stars of the sky and the sands of the seashore; your descendants shall take possession of the gates of their enemies, and in your descendants all the nations of the earth shall find blessing—all this because you obeyed my command."

The word of the Lord. ***Thanks be to God.***

RESPONSORIAL PSALM *(Psalm 116:10, 15, 16–17, 18–19)*

℟. I will walk before the Lord, in the land of the living.

I believed, even when I said,
  "I am greatly afflicted."
Precious in the eyes of the LORD
  is the death of his faithful ones. ℟.
O LORD, I am your servant;
  I am your servant, the son of your handmaid;
  you have loosed my bonds.
To you will I offer sacrifice of thanksgiving,
  and I will call upon the name of the LORD. ℟.
My vows to the LORD I will pay
  in the presence of all his people,

in the courts of the house of the LORD,
  in your midst, O Jerusalem.
℟. I will walk before the Lord, in the land of the living.

SECOND READING *(Romans 8:31b–34)*

Brothers and sisters: If God is for us, who can be against us? He who did not spare his own Son but handed him over for us all, how will he not also give us everything else along with him?

Who will bring a charge against God's chosen ones? It is God who acquits us. Who will condemn? Christ Jesus it is who died—or, rather, was raised—who also is at the right hand of God, who indeed intercedes for us.

The word of the Lord. ***Thanks be to God.***

VERSE BEFORE THE GOSPEL *(See Matthew 17:5)*

Glory and praise to you, Lord Jesus Christ! From the shining cloud the Father's voice is heard: / This is my beloved Son, listen to him. ***Glory and praise to you, Lord Jesus Christ!***

GOSPEL *(Mark 9:2–10)*

A reading from the holy Gospel according to Mark.
Glory to you, O Lord.

Jesus took Peter, James, and John and led them up a high mountain apart by themselves. And he was **transfigured**+ before them, and his clothes became dazzling white, such as no fuller on earth could bleach them. Then Elijah appeared to them along with Moses, and they were conversing with Jesus. Then Peter said to Jesus in reply, "Rabbi, it is good that we are here! Let us make three tents: one for you, one for Moses, and one for Elijah." He hardly knew what to say, they were so terrified. Then a cloud came, casting a shadow over them; from the cloud came a voice, "This is my beloved Son. Listen to him." Suddenly, looking around, they no longer saw anyone but Jesus alone with them.

As they were coming down from the mountain, he charged them not to relate what they had seen to anyone, except when the Son of Man had risen from the dead. So they kept the matter to themselves, questioning what rising from the dead meant.

The Gospel of the Lord. ***Praise to you, Lord Jesus Christ.***

PROFESSION OF FAITH *(page 13)*

PRAYER OF THE FAITHFUL

PREPARATION OF GIFTS *(page 16)*

PRAYER OVER THE OFFERINGS

May this sacrifice, O Lord, we pray,
cleanse us of our faults
and sanctify your faithful in body and mind
for the celebration of the paschal festivities.
Through Christ our Lord. ***Amen.***

PREFACE: THE TRANSFIGURATION OF THE LORD

It is truly right and just, our duty and our salvation,
always and everywhere to give you thanks,
Lord, holy Father, almighty and eternal God,
through Christ our Lord.

For after he had told the disciples of his coming Death,
on the holy mountain he manifested to them his glory,
to show, even by the testimony of the law and the prophets,
that the Passion leads to the glory of the Resurrection.

And so, with the Powers of heaven,
we worship you constantly on earth,
and before your majesty
without end we acclaim:
Holy, Holy, Holy Lord God of hosts... *(page 35)*

COMMUNION ANTIPHON *(Matthew 17:5)*
This is my beloved Son, with whom I am well pleased; /
listen to him.

PRAYER AFTER COMMUNION
As we receive these glorious mysteries,
we make thanksgiving to you, O Lord,
for allowing us while still on earth
to be partakers even now of the things of heaven.
Through Christ our Lord. ***Amen.***

TAKING A CLOSER LOOK

+ **Transfigured** Although the Greek word here (*metamorphosis*) commonly described a change in form or appearance that a god might make to appear to humans, the gospel writers suggest a completely new meaning. The transfiguration is a glimpse of God's glory breaking forth from Jesus' human form. After revealing to the disciples that, as Messiah, he would have to suffer, Jesus' changed appearance previews the change that he will undergo at his resurrection. The dazzling light, the divine voice of approval, and the support of the whole Jewish tradition represented by Moses (the Jewish Law) and Elijah (the prophets) signal that Jesus' messianic suffering is the fulfillment of God's plan for salvation.

PRAYER OVER THE PEOPLE

Bless your faithful, we pray, O Lord,
with a blessing that endures for ever,
and keep them faithful
to the Gospel of your Only Begotten Son,
so that they may always desire and at last attain
that glory whose beauty he showed in his own Body,
to the amazement of his Apostles.
Through Christ our Lord. ***Amen.***

DISMISSAL *(page 57)* ⁜

Responding to the Word

Abraham was asked to sacrifice what was most dear to him—his beloved son.

What might I need to give up to live more closely with God?

Paul feels that God is for us, bringing new life through Christ.

What sign gives me confidence that God is for me?

Jesus' baptism affirms that he is God's beloved son.

What evidence from my life shows that I am God's beloved child?

February 28

God endures forever

Everyone has their tipping point, their "up to here and no further." When we reach it, our emotions can run high with our actions louder and larger than usual. So too with Jesus. Take today's gospel with the money changers in the temple. Drama and dismay aside, there is something refreshing about this exercise of humanity. We can relate to Jesus' feelings of anger, disrespect, and frustration, and can likely name those moments when we have also taken up a whip of cords in speech or action.

The shock of that moment in the temple must have been great, and the impact greater still over time, with the meaning behind an outburst often understood only later. The clearing of the market is more than an impassioned response to a personal affront. It is only after Jesus is raised from the dead on the third day that the depth of his actions and meaning of his words are fully known.

Today's gospel speaks to a coherence and breadth of vision that has its origin in God alone: God before whom there shall be no other gods and who brought his people out of the land of slavery; God who is not a commodity to be bought, sold, or traded; God who is sweeter than honey and who endures forever.

■ Sr. Kimberly King, RSCJ

Parishes engaged in the Order of Christian Initiation of Adults (OCIA) may celebrate the First Scrutiny today (see page 205).

ENTRANCE ANTIPHON *(Cf. Psalm 25 [24]:15–16)*
My eyes are always on the Lord, / for he rescues my feet from the snare. / Turn to me and have mercy on me, / for I am alone and poor.

Or *(Cf. Ezekiel 36:23–26)*
When I prove my holiness among you, / I will gather you from all the foreign lands; / and I will pour clean water upon you / and cleanse you from all your impurities, / and I will give you a new spirit, says the Lord.

INTRODUCTORY RITES *(page 10)*

COLLECT
O God, author of every mercy and of all goodness,
who in fasting, prayer and almsgiving
have shown us a remedy for sin,
look graciously on this confession of our lowliness,
that we, who are bowed down by our conscience,
may always be lifted up by your mercy.
Through our Lord Jesus Christ, your Son,
who lives and reigns with you in the unity of the Holy Spirit,
God, for ever and ever. ***Amen.***

These are the readings for Year B. The readings for Year A may also be used *(see page 205).*

FIRST READING *(Exodus 20:1–17 or 20:1–3, 7–8, 12–17)*

For the shorter version, omit the indented parts in brackets.

In those days, God delivered all these commandments: "I, the LORD, am your God, who brought you out of the land of Egypt, that place of slavery. You shall not have other gods besides me.

[You shall not carve idols for yourselves in the shape of anything in the sky above or on the earth below or in the waters beneath the earth; you shall not bow down before them or worship them. For I, the LORD, your God, am a jealous God, inflicting punishment for their fathers' wickedness on the children of those who hate me, down to the third and fourth generation; but bestowing mercy down to the thousandth generation on the children of those who love me and keep my commandments.]

"You shall not take the name of the LORD, your God, in vain. For the LORD will not leave unpunished the one who takes his name in vain.

"Remember to keep holy the sabbath day.

[Six days you may labor and do all your work, but the seventh day is the sabbath of the LORD, your God. No work may be done then either by you, or your son or daughter, or your male or female slave, or your beast, or by the alien who lives with you. In six days the LORD made the heavens and the earth, the sea and all that is in them; but on the seventh day he rested. That is why the LORD has blessed the sabbath day and made it holy.]

"Honor your father and your mother, that you may have a long life in the land which the LORD, your God, is giving you.

You shall not kill. You shall not commit adultery. You shall not steal. You shall not bear false witness against your neighbor. You shall not covet your neighbor's house. You shall not covet your neighbor's wife, nor his male or female slave, nor his ox or ass, nor anything else that belongs to him."

The word of the Lord. ***Thanks be to God.***

RESPONSORIAL PSALM *(Psalm 19:8, 9, 10, 11)*

℟. Lord, you have the words of everlasting life.

The law of the LORD is perfect,
refreshing the soul;
the decree of the LORD is trustworthy,
giving wisdom to the simple. ℟.
The precepts of the LORD are right,
rejoicing the heart;
the command of the LORD is clear,
enlightening the eye. ℟.
The fear of the LORD is pure,
enduring forever;
the ordinances of the LORD are true,
all of them just. ℟.
They are more precious than gold,
than a heap of purest gold;
sweeter also than syrup
or honey from the comb. ℟.

SECOND READING *(1 Corinthians 1:22–25)*

Brothers and sisters: Jews demand signs and Greeks look for wisdom, but we proclaim Christ crucified, a stumbling block to Jews and foolishness to Gentiles, but to those who are called, Jews and Greeks alike, Christ the power of God and the wisdom of God. For the foolishness of God is wiser than human wisdom, and the weakness of God is stronger than human strength.

The word of the Lord. ***Thanks be to God.***

VERSE BEFORE THE GOSPEL *(John 3:16)*

Glory and praise to you, Lord Jesus Christ! God so loved the world that he gave his only Son, / so that everyone who believes in him might have eternal life. ***Glory and praise to you, Lord Jesus Christ!***

GOSPEL *(John 2:13–25)*

A reading from the holy Gospel according to John.

Glory to you, O Lord.

Since the Passover of the Jews was near, Jesus went up to Jerusalem. He found in the temple area those who sold oxen, sheep, and doves, as well as the **money changers**+ seated there. He made a whip out of cords and drove them all out of the temple area, with the sheep and oxen, and spilled the coins of the money changers and overturned their tables, and to those who sold doves he said, "Take these out of here, and stop making my Father's house a marketplace." His disciples recalled the words of Scripture, *Zeal for your house will consume me.* At this the Jews answered and said to him, "What sign can you show us for doing this?" Jesus answered and said to them, "Destroy this temple and in three days I will raise it up." The Jews said, "This temple has been under construction for forty-six years, and you will raise it up in three days?" But he was speaking about the temple of his body. Therefore, when he was raised from the dead, his disciples remembered that he had said this, and they came to believe the Scripture and the word Jesus had spoken.

While he was in Jerusalem for the feast of Passover, many began to believe in his name when they saw the signs he was doing. But Jesus would not trust himself to them because he knew them all, and did not need anyone to testify about human nature. He himself understood it well.

The Gospel of the Lord. ***Praise to you, Lord Jesus Christ.***

PROFESSION OF FAITH *(page 13)*

PRAYER OF THE FAITHFUL

PREPARATION OF GIFTS *(page 16)*

PRAYER OVER THE OFFERINGS

Be pleased, O Lord, with these sacrificial offerings,
and grant that we who beseech pardon for our own sins,
may take care to forgive our neighbor.
Through Christ our Lord. ***Amen.***

PREFACE *(Lent 1–2, page 21)*

Taking a Closer Look

✝ **Money changers** The Jerusalem temple was not merely a place of worship but also a market where sacrificial animals were sold and a bank where the state treasury was kept (recall the widow who is contributing to the treasury in Mark 12:41-44). Jews throughout the world were obligated to pay a special tax each year to provide for the upkeep of the temple. But since Roman and Greek coins were stamped with images of their gods and emperors, these coins could not be used to pay the temple tax. Thus money changers congregated in the outer court of the temple and exchanged these pagan coins for Jewish coins that could be used for temple business.

COMMUNION ANTIPHON *(Cf. Psalm 84 [83]:4-5)*
The sparrow finds a home, / and the swallow a nest for her young: / by your altars, O Lord of hosts, my King and my God. / Blessed are they who dwell in your house, / for ever singing your praise.

PRAYER AFTER COMMUNION
As we receive the pledge
of things yet hidden in heaven
and are nourished while still on earth
with the Bread that comes from on high,
we humbly entreat you, O Lord,
that what is being brought about in us in mystery
may come to true completion.
Through Christ our Lord. ***Amen.***

PRAYER OVER THE PEOPLE
Direct, O Lord, we pray, the hearts of your faithful,
and in your kindness grant your servants this grace:
that, abiding in the love of you and their neighbor,
they may fulfill the whole of your commands.
Through Christ our Lord. ***Amen.***

DISMISSAL *(page 57)*

RESPONDING TO THE WORD

God's commandments reveal the way for us to have a good community.

Which commandment is hardest for me to observe?

Jesus' crucifixion as a criminal was a stumbling block for many.

What makes it hard for me to accept Jesus today?

Jesus disrupts the non-religious activities in the temple.

What might I need to disrupt to restore a more religious attitude when I go to Mass?

CHRISTIAN INITIATION: FIRST SCRUTINY

The Mass prayers and readings below are for use in parishes celebrating the First Scrutiny.

ENTRANCE ANTIPHON *(Ezekiel 36:23-26)*
When I prove my holiness among you, / I will gather you from all the foreign lands / and I will pour clean water upon you / and cleanse you from all your impurities, / and I will give you a new spirit, says the Lord.

Or *(Cf. Isaiah 55:1)*
Come to the waters, you who are thirsty, says the Lord; / you who have no money, come and drink joyfully.

COLLECT
Grant, we pray, O Lord,
that these chosen ones may come worthily and wisely
to the confession of your praise,
so that in accordance with that first dignity
which they lost by original sin
they may be fashioned anew through your glory.
Through our Lord Jesus Christ, your Son,
who lives and reigns with you in the unity of the Holy Spirit,
God, for ever and ever. ***Amen.***

FIRST READING *(Exodus 17:3-7)*
In those days, in their thirst for water, the people grumbled against Moses, saying, "Why did you ever make us leave Egypt? Was it just to have us die here of thirst with our children and our livestock?" So Moses cried out to the LORD, "What shall I do with this

people? A little more and they will stone me!" The LORD answered Moses, "Go over there in front of the people, along with some of the elders of Israel, holding in your hand, as you go, the staff with which you struck the river. I will be standing there in front of you on the rock in Horeb.* Strike the rock, and the water will flow from it for the people to drink." This Moses did, in the presence of the elders of Israel. The place was called Massah* and Meribah,* because the Israelites quarreled there and tested the LORD, saying, "Is the LORD in our midst or not?"

The word of the Lord. ***Thanks be to God.***

RESPONSORIAL PSALM *(Psalm 95:1-2, 6-7, 8-9)*

℟. If today you hear his voice, harden not your hearts.

Come, let us sing joyfully to the LORD;
  let us acclaim the Rock of our salvation.
Let us come into his presence with thanksgiving;
  let us joyfully sing psalms to him. ℟.
Come, let us bow down in worship;
  let us kneel before the LORD who made us.
For he is our God,
  and we are the people he shepherds, the flock he guides. ℟.
Oh, that today you would hear his voice:
  "Harden not your hearts as at Meribah,*
  as in the day of Massah* in the desert,
where your fathers tempted me;
  they tested me though they had seen my works." ℟.

SECOND READING *(Romans 5:1-2, 5-8)*

Brothers and sisters: Since we have been justified by faith, we have peace with God through our Lord Jesus Christ, through whom we have gained access by faith to this grace in which we stand, and we boast in hope of the glory of God.

And hope does not disappoint, because the love of God has been poured out into our hearts through the Holy Spirit who has been given to us. For Christ, while we were still helpless, died at the appointed time for the ungodly. Indeed, only with difficulty does one die for a just person, though perhaps for a good person one might even find courage to die. But God proves his love for us in that while we were still sinners Christ died for us.

The word of the Lord. ***Thanks be to God.***

VERSE BEFORE THE GOSPEL *(See John 4:42, 15)*
Glory and praise to you, Lord Jesus Christ! Lord, you are truly the Savior of the world; / give me living water, that I may never thirst again. ***Glory and praise to you, Lord Jesus Christ!***

GOSPEL *(John 4:5–42 or 4:5–15, 19b–26, 39a, 40–42)*
For the shorter version, omit the indented parts in brackets.

A reading from the holy Gospel according to John.
Glory to you, O Lord.

Jesus came to a town of Samaria* called Sychar,* near the plot of land that Jacob had given to his son Joseph. Jacob's well was there. Jesus, tired from his journey, sat down there at the well. It was about noon.

A woman of Samaria came to draw water. Jesus said to her, "Give me a drink." His disciples had gone into the town to buy food. The Samaritan woman said to him, "How can you, a Jew, ask me, a Samaritan woman, for a drink?"—For Jews use nothing in common with Samaritans.—Jesus answered and said to her, "If you knew the gift of God and who is saying to you, 'Give me a drink,' you would have asked him and he would have given you living water." The woman said to him, "Sir, you do not even have a bucket and the cistern is deep; where then can you get this living water? Are you greater than our father Jacob, who gave us this cistern and drank from it himself with his children and his flocks?" Jesus answered and said to her, "Everyone who drinks this water will be thirsty again; but whoever drinks the water I shall give will never thirst; the water I shall give will become in him a spring of water welling up to eternal life." The woman said to him, "Sir, give me this water, so that I may not be thirsty or have to keep coming here to draw water."

[Jesus said to her, "Go call your husband and come back." The woman answered and said to him, "I do not have a husband." Jesus answered her, "You are right in saying, 'I do not have a husband.' For you have had five husbands, and the one you have now is not your husband. What you have said is true." The woman said to him, "Sir,]

"I can see that you are a prophet. Our ancestors worshiped on this mountain; but you people say that the place to worship is in Jerusalem." Jesus said to her, "Believe me, woman, the hour is coming when you will worship the Father neither on this mountain nor in Jerusalem. You people worship what you do not understand; we worship what we understand, because salvation is from the Jews. But the hour is coming, and is now here, when true worshipers will worship the Father in Spirit and truth; and indeed the Father seeks such people to worship him. God is Spirit, and those who worship him must worship in Spirit and truth." The woman said to him, "I know that the Messiah is coming, the one called the Christ; when he comes, he will tell us everything." Jesus said to her, "I am he, the one (who is) speaking with you."

[At that moment his disciples returned, and were amazed that he was talking with a woman, but still no one said, "What are you looking for?" or "Why are you talking with her?" The woman left her water jar and went into the town and said to the people, "Come see a man who told me everything I have done. Could he possibly be the Christ?" They went out of the town and came to him. Meanwhile, the disciples urged him, "Rabbi, eat." But he said to them, "I have food to eat of which you do not know." So the disciples said to one another, "Could someone have brought him something to eat?" Jesus said to them, "My food is to do the will of the one who sent me and to finish his work. Do you not say, 'In four months the harvest will be here'? I tell you, look up and see the fields ripe for the harvest. The reaper is already receiving payment and gathering crops for eternal life, so that the sower and reaper can rejoice together. For here the saying is verified that 'One sows and another reaps.' I sent you to reap what you have not worked for; others have done the work, and you are sharing the fruits of their work."]

Many of the Samaritans of that town began to believe in him [because of the word of the woman who testified, "He told me everything I have done."]

When the Samaritans came to him, they invited him to stay with them; and he stayed there two days. Many more began to believe in him because of his word, and they said to the woman, "We no longer believe because of your word; for we have heard for ourselves, and we know that this is truly the savior of the world."

The Gospel of the Lord. ***Praise to you, Lord Jesus Christ.***

PRAYER OVER THE OFFERINGS

May your merciful grace prepare your servants, O Lord,
for the worthy celebration of these mysteries
and lead them to it by a devout way of life.
Through Christ our Lord. ***Amen.***

PREFACE : THE SAMARITAN WOMAN

It is truly right and just, our duty and our salvation,
always and everywhere to give you thanks,
Lord, holy Father, almighty and eternal God,
through Christ our Lord.

For when he asked the Samaritan woman for water to drink,
he had already created the gift of faith within her
and so ardently did he thirst for her faith,
that he kindled in her the fire of divine love.

And so we, too, give you thanks
and with the Angels
praise your mighty deeds, as we acclaim:
Holy, Holy, Holy Lord God of hosts... *(page 35)*

COMMUNION ANTIPHON *(Cf. John 4:13-14)*

For anyone who drinks it, says the Lord, / the water I shall give will become in him a spring / welling up to eternal life.

PRAYER AFTER COMMUNION

Give help, O Lord, we pray,
by the grace of your redemption
and be pleased to protect and prepare
those you are to initiate
through the Sacraments of eternal life.
Through Christ our Lord. ***Amen.*** ⁂

March 7

Have courage, come into the light!

In today's gospel, Jesus is teaching Nicodemus, a pharisee who has come to him by night. Nicodemus wishes to be a disciple of Jesus, but he is afraid of judgment. Jesus is not speaking to a criminal, to murderers or thieves, but to a man of God. It is a man of faith whom Jesus warns about preferring darkness over light, preferring sin to God.

How often do we prefer our sin to God? How often do we refuse to trust in the Lord and patiently accept the suffering that God permits in our lives? How often do we hold on to some little corner of our heart that we wish to be just our own, that we wish to rule in our own way, when the Lord asks us to give ourselves to him entirely?

To be good is difficult. It is demanding. And we would much prefer our own passing comfort, our little delights, to our relationship with God.

It is easy to prefer the darkness. The darkness is comfortable and familiar. In the darkness, we don't need to feel the weight of our sin. In the light, we see the cross. It takes courage to come into the light, to be lifted up with Christ crucified. But it is only by dying with Jesus that we may rise with him to eternal life.

■ Gabrielle Tonelli

Parishes engaged in the Order of Christian Initiation of Adults (OCIA) may celebrate the Second Scrutiny today *(see page 218).*

ENTRANCE ANTIPHON *(Cf. Isaiah 66:10–11)*
Rejoice, Jerusalem, and all who love her. / Be joyful, all who were in mourning; / exult and be satisfied at her consoling breast.

INTRODUCTORY RITES *(page 10)*

COLLECT
O God, who through your Word
reconcile the human race to yourself in a wonderful way,
grant, we pray,
that with prompt devotion and eager faith
the Christian people may hasten
toward the solemn celebrations to come.
Through our Lord Jesus Christ, your Son,
who lives and reigns with you in the unity of the Holy Spirit,
God, for ever and ever. ***Amen.***

These are the readings for Year B. The readings for Year A may also be used *(see page 218).*

FIRST READING *(2 Chronicles 36:14–16, 19–23)*
In those days, all the princes of Judah, the priests, and the people added infidelity to infidelity, practicing all the abominations of the nations and polluting the LORD's temple which he had consecrated in Jerusalem.

Early and often did the LORD, the God of their fathers, send his messengers to them, for he had compassion on his people and his dwelling place. But they mocked the messengers of God, despised his warnings, and scoffed at his prophets, until the anger of the LORD against his people was so inflamed that there was no remedy. Their enemies burnt the house of God, tore down the walls of Jerusalem, set all its palaces afire, and destroyed all its precious objects. Those who escaped the sword were carried captive to Babylon,* where they became servants of the king of the Chaldeans* and his sons until the kingdom of the Persians came to power. All this was to fulfill the word of the LORD spoken by Jeremiah: "Until the land has retrieved its lost sabbaths, during all the time it lies waste it shall have rest while seventy years are fulfilled."

In the first year of Cyrus, king of Persia, in order to fulfill the word of the LORD spoken by Jeremiah, the LORD inspired King Cyrus of Persia to issue this proclamation throughout his kingdom, both by word of mouth and in writing: "Thus says Cyrus, king of Persia: All the kingdoms of the earth the LORD, the God of heaven, has given to me, and he has also charged me to build him a house in Jerusalem, which is in Judah. Whoever, therefore, among you belongs to any part of his people, let him go up, and may his God be with him!"

The word of the Lord. ***Thanks be to God.***

RESPONSORIAL PSALM *(Psalm 137:1-2, 3, 4-5, 6)*

℟. Let my tongue be silenced, if I ever forget you!

By the streams of Babylon*
we sat and wept
when we remembered Zion.*
On the aspens of that land
we hung up our harps. ℟.
For there our captors asked of us
the lyrics of our songs,

and our despoilers urged us to be joyous:
"Sing for us the songs of Zion!"
℟. **Let my tongue be silenced, if I ever forget you!**
How could we sing a song of the LORD
in a foreign land?
If I forget you, Jerusalem,
may my right hand be forgotten! ℟.
May my tongue cleave to my palate
if I remember you not,
if I place not Jerusalem
ahead of my joy. ℟.

SECOND READING *(Ephesians 2:4-10)*

Brothers and sisters: God, who is rich in **mercy,**✝ because of the great love he had for us, even when we were dead in our transgressions, brought us to life with Christ—by grace you have been saved—, raised us up with him, and seated us with him in the heavens in Christ Jesus, that in the ages to come he might show the immeasurable riches of his grace in his kindness to us in Christ Jesus. For by grace you have been saved through faith, and this is not from you; it is the gift of God; it is not from works, so no one may boast. For we are his handiwork, created in Christ Jesus for the good works that God has prepared in advance, that we should live in them.

The word of the Lord. ***Thanks be to God.***

VERSE BEFORE THE GOSPEL *(John 3:16)*
Glory and praise to you, Lord Jesus Christ! God so loved the world that he gave his only Son, / so everyone who believes in him might have eternal life. ***Glory and praise to you, Lord Jesus Christ!***

GOSPEL *(John 3:14–21)*
A reading from the holy Gospel according to John.
Glory to you, O Lord.
Jesus said to Nicodemus: "Just as Moses lifted up the serpent in the desert, so must the Son of Man be lifted up, so that everyone who believes in him may have eternal life."

For God so loved the world that he gave his only Son, so that everyone who believes in him might not perish but might have eternal life. For God did not send his Son into the world to condemn the world, but that the world might be saved through him. Whoever believes in him will not be condemned, but whoever does not believe has already been condemned, because he has not believed in the name of the only Son of God. And this is the verdict, that the light came into the world, but people preferred darkness to light, because their works were evil. For everyone who does wicked things hates the light and does not come toward the light, so that his works might not be exposed. But whoever lives the truth comes to the light, so that his works may be clearly seen as done in God.

The Gospel of the Lord. ***Praise to you, Lord Jesus Christ.***

PROFESSION OF FAITH *(page 13)*

PRAYER OF THE FAITHFUL

PREPARATION OF GIFTS *(page 16)*

PRAYER OVER THE OFFERINGS
We place before you with joy these offerings,
which bring eternal remedy, O Lord,
praying that we may both faithfully revere them
and present them to you, as is fitting,
for the salvation of all the world.
Through Christ our Lord. ***Amen.***

PREFACE *(Lent 1-2, page 21)*

COMMUNION ANTIPHON *(Cf. Psalm 122 [121]:3-4)*
Jerusalem is built as a city bonded as one together. / It is there that the tribes go up, the tribes of the Lord, / to praise the name of the Lord.

TAKING A CLOSER LOOK

✝ **Mercy** In the Old Testament, mercy usually identifies a complex Hebrew idea that describes God's special covenant love. God's attitude of love or attachment to the covenant partners includes aspects of loyalty, dependability, trustworthiness, and an eagerness to help when situations turn bad. Paul echoes this fierce fidelity by describing God's eagerness to rescue or save us when we were alienated by sin. God's desire to be in relationship with us keeps God alert to our cries for help and eager to deliver us from what separates us from God.

PRAYER AFTER COMMUNION

O God, who enlighten everyone who comes into this world,
illuminate our hearts, we pray,
with the splendor of your grace,
that we may always ponder
what is worthy and pleasing to your majesty
and love you in all sincerity.
Through Christ our Lord. ***Amen.***

PRAYER OVER THE PEOPLE

Look upon those who call to you, O Lord,
and sustain the weak;
give life by your unfailing light
to those who walk in the shadow of death,
and bring those rescued by your mercy from every evil
to reach the highest good.
Through Christ our Lord. ***Amen.***

DISMISSAL *(page 57)*

Responding to the Word

God sends messengers to invite the people to change their ways.

Who is God sending me to help me make my Lenten changes?

Our salvation or right relationship with God is God's gift to us.

How might I express my gratitude for this divine gift?

Jesus is the light that drives away the shadows in our hearts.

What shadowy areas in me has Christ's light been shining into this Lent?

CHRISTIAN INITIATION: SECOND SCRUTINY

The Mass prayers and readings below are for use in parishes celebrating the Second Scrutiny.

ENTRANCE ANTIPHON *(Cf. Psalm 25 [24]:15-16)*
My eyes are always on the Lord, for he rescues my feet from the snare. / Turn to me and have mercy on me, for I am alone and poor.

COLLECT
Almighty ever-living God,
give to your Church an increase in spiritual joy,
so that those once born of earth
may be reborn as citizens of heaven.
Through our Lord Jesus Christ, your Son,
who lives and reigns with you in the unity of the Holy Spirit,
God, for ever and ever. ***Amen.***

FIRST READING *(1 Samuel 16:1b, 6-7, 10-13a)*
The LORD said to Samuel: "Fill your horn with oil, and be on your way. I am sending you to Jesse of Bethlehem, for I have chosen my king from among his sons."

As Jesse and his sons came to the sacrifice, Samuel looked at Eliab and thought, "Surely the LORD's anointed is here before him." But the LORD said to Samuel: "Do not judge from his appearance or from his lofty stature, because I have rejected him. Not as man sees does God see, because man sees the appearance but the LORD looks into the heart." In the same way Jesse presented seven sons before Samuel, but Samuel said to Jesse,

"The LORD has not chosen any one of these." Then Samuel asked Jesse, "Are these all the sons you have?" Jesse replied, "There is still the youngest, who is tending the sheep." Samuel said to Jesse, "Send for him; we will not begin the sacrificial banquet until he arrives here." Jesse sent and had the young man brought to them. He was ruddy, a youth handsome to behold and making a splendid appearance. The LORD said, "There—anoint him, for this is the one!" Then Samuel, with the horn of oil in hand, anointed David in the presence of his brothers; and from that day on, the spirit of the LORD rushed upon David.

The word of the Lord. ***Thanks be to God.***

RESPONSORIAL PSALM *(Psalm 23:1-3a, 3b-4, 5, 6)*

℟. The Lord is my shepherd; there is nothing I shall want.

The LORD is my shepherd; I shall not want.
  In verdant pastures he gives me repose;
beside restful waters he leads me;
  he refreshes my soul. ℟.
He guides me in right paths
  for his name's sake.
Even though I walk in the dark valley
  I fear no evil; for you are at my side
with your rod and your staff
  that give me courage. ℟.
You spread the table before me
  in the sight of my foes;
you anoint my head with oil;
  my cup overflows. ℟.
Only goodness and kindness follow me
  all the days of my life;

and I shall dwell in the house of the LORD
for years to come.
℟. **The Lord is my shepherd; there is nothing I shall want.**

SECOND READING *(Ephesians 5:8-14)*

Brothers and sisters: You were once darkness, but now you are light in the Lord. Live as children of light, for light produces every kind of goodness and righteousness and truth. Try to learn what is pleasing to the Lord. Take no part in the fruitless works of darkness; rather expose them, for it is shameful even to mention the things done by them in secret; but everything exposed by the light becomes visible, for everything that becomes visible is light. Therefore, it says:

"Awake, O sleeper,
and arise from the dead,
and Christ will give you light."

The word of the Lord. ***Thanks be to God.***

VERSE BEFORE THE GOSPEL *(John 8:12)*

Glory and praise to you, Lord Jesus Christ! I am the light of the world, says the Lord; / whoever follows me will have the light of life. ***Glory and praise to you, Lord Jesus Christ!***

GOSPEL *(John 9:1-41 or 9:1, 6-9, 13-17, 34-38)*

For the shorter version, omit the indented parts in brackets.

A reading from the holy Gospel according to John.
Glory to you, O Lord.

As Jesus passed by he saw a man blind from birth.

[His disciples asked him, "Rabbi, who sinned, this man or his parents, that he was born blind?" Jesus answered, "Neither he nor his parents sinned; it is so that the works of God might be made visible through him. We have to do the works of the one who sent me while it is day. Night is coming when no one can work. While I am in the world, I am the light of the world." When he had said this,]

he spat on the ground and made clay with the saliva, and smeared the clay on his eyes, and said to him, "Go wash in the Pool of Siloam*"—which means Sent—. So he went and washed, and came back able to see.

His neighbors and those who had seen him earlier as a beggar said, "Isn't this the one who used to sit and beg?" Some said, "It is," but others said, "No, he just looks like him." He said, "I am."

[So they said to him, "How were your eyes opened?" He replied, "The man called Jesus made clay and anointed my eyes and told me, 'Go to Siloam and wash.' So I went there and washed and was able to see." And they said to him, "Where is he?" He said, "I don't know."]

They brought the one who was once blind to the Pharisees. Now Jesus had made clay and opened his eyes on a sabbath. So then the Pharisees also asked him how he was able to see. He said to them, "He put clay on my eyes, and I washed, and now I can see." So some of the Pharisees said, "This man is not from God, because he does not keep the sabbath." But others said, "How can a sinful man do such signs?" And there was a division among them. So they said to the blind man again, "What do you have to say about him, since he opened your eyes?" He said, "He is a prophet."

[Now the Jews did not believe that he had been blind and gained his sight until they summoned the parents of the one who had gained his sight. They asked them, "Is this your son, who you say was born blind? How does he now see?" His parents answered and said, "We know that this is our son and that he was born blind. We do not know how he sees now, nor do we know who opened his eyes. Ask him, he is of age; he can speak for himself." His parents said this because they were afraid of the Jews, for the Jews had already agreed that if anyone acknowledged him as the Christ, he would be expelled from the synagogue. For this reason his parents said, "He is of age; question him."

So a second time they called the man who had been blind and said to him, "Give God the praise! We know that this man is a sinner." He replied, "If he is a sinner, I do not know. One thing I do know is that I was blind and now I see." So they said to him, "What did he do to you? How did he open your eyes?" He answered them, "I told you already and you did not listen. Why do you want to hear it again? Do you want to become his disciples, too?" They ridiculed him and said, "You are that man's disciple; we are disciples of Moses! We know that God spoke to Moses, but we do not know where this one is from." The man answered and said to them, "This is what is so amazing, that you do not know where he is from, yet he opened my eyes. We know that God does not listen to sinners, but if one is devout and does his will, he listens to him. It is unheard of that anyone ever opened the eyes of a person born blind. If this man were not from God, he would not be able to do anything."]

They answered and said to him, "You were born totally in sin, and are you trying to teach us?" Then they threw him out.

When Jesus heard that they had thrown him out, he found him and said, "Do you believe in the Son of Man?" He answered and said, "Who is he, sir, that I may believe in him?" Jesus said to him, "You have seen him, the one speaking with you is he." He said, "I do believe, Lord," and he worshiped him.

[Then Jesus said, "I came into this world for judgment, so that those who do not see might see, and those who do see might become blind."

Some of the Pharisees who were with him heard this and said to him, "Surely we are not also blind, are we?" Jesus said to them, "If you were blind, you would have no sin; but now you are saying, 'We see,' so your sin remains."]

The Gospel of the Lord. ***Praise to you, Lord Jesus Christ.***

PRAYER OVER THE OFFERINGS

We place before you with joy these offerings,
which bring eternal remedy, O Lord,
praying that we may both faithfully revere them
and present them to you, as is fitting,
for those who seek salvation.
Through Christ our Lord. ***Amen.***

PREFACE: THE MAN BORN BLIND

It is truly right and just, our duty and our salvation,
always and everywhere to give you thanks,
Lord, holy Father, almighty and eternal God,
through Christ our Lord.

By the mystery of the Incarnation,
he has led the human race that walked in darkness
into the radiance of the faith
and has brought those born in slavery to ancient sin
through the waters of regeneration
to make them your adopted children.

Therefore, all creatures of heaven and earth
sing a new song in adoration,
and we, with all the host of Angels,
cry out, and without end acclaim:
Holy, Holy, Holy Lord God of hosts... *(page 35)*

COMMUNION ANTIPHON *(Cf. John 9:11, 38)*
The Lord anointed my eyes; I went, I washed, / I saw and I believed in God.

PRAYER AFTER COMMUNION
Sustain your family always in your kindness,
O Lord, we pray,
correct them, set them in order,
graciously protect them under your rule,
and in your unfailing goodness
direct them along the way of salvation.
Through Christ our Lord. ***Amen.*** ⁂

March 14

MAR 14

Allow God to begin something new

One of my neighbors was in her nineties when we met. Anne told me she only counted her blessings and trips around the sun. Her childlike exuberance and sunny attitude were contagious! As we age, we too can choose to be positive and share our optimism in the face of life's challenges.

In today's gospel, Jesus addresses his own painful future using the familiar image of a grain of wheat. In this way, he foretells his death and resurrection so his followers can be better prepared. It is a prophetic, powerful, and profound teaching: beyond our human sight there is also spiritual activity we may not yet see or understand. Jesus tries to explain what is unfolding because of his love for others and unshakable belief in the divine love of his Father.

As in the natural world, so new life within us germinates and flourishes only when something changes or ends. If we resist, this unseen transformation may be disrupted, delayed, or even derailed. Over time, we all face pain, loss, decay, and death. However, Jesus invites us to look beyond to the good, green, and God within us, each other, and each spiritual season of our life. This Easter, let us look within and allow God to begin something new in the next season of our souls.

KAREN LAHAISE

Parishes engaged in the Order of Christian Initiation of Adults (OCIA) may celebrate the Third Scrutiny today *(see page 231).*

ENTRANCE ANTIPHON *(Cf. Psalm 43 [42]:1-2)*

Give me justice, O God, / and plead my cause against a nation that is faithless. / From the deceitful and cunning rescue me, / for you, O God, are my strength.

INTRODUCTORY RITES *(page 10)*

COLLECT

By your help, we beseech you, Lord our God,
may we walk eagerly in that same charity
with which, out of love for the world,
your Son handed himself over to death.
Through our Lord Jesus Christ, your Son,
who lives and reigns with you in the unity of the Holy Spirit,
God, for ever and ever. ***Amen.***

These are the readings for Year B. The readings for Year A may also be used *(see page 231).*

FIRST READING *(Jeremiah 31:31-34)*

The days are coming, says the LORD, when I will make a new covenant with the house of Israel and the house of Judah. It will not be like the covenant I made with their fathers the day I took them by the hand to lead them forth from the land of Egypt; for they broke my covenant, and I had to show myself their master, says the LORD. But this is the covenant that I will make with the house of Israel after those days, says the LORD. I will place my law within them and write it upon their hearts; I will be their God, and they shall be my people. No longer will they have need to teach their friends and relatives how to know the LORD. All, from least to greatest, shall know me, says the LORD, for I will forgive their evildoing and remember their sin no more.

The word of the Lord. ***Thanks be to God.***

RESPONSORIAL PSALM *(Psalm 51:3-4, 12-13, 14-15)*

℟. Create a clean heart in me, O God.

Have mercy on me, O God, in your goodness;
  in the greatness of your compassion wipe out my offense.
Thoroughly wash me from my guilt
  and of my sin cleanse me. **℟.**
A clean heart create for me, O God,
  and a steadfast spirit renew within me.
Cast me not out from your presence,
  and your Holy Spirit take not from me. **℟.**
Give me back the joy of your salvation,
  and a willing spirit sustain in me.
I will teach transgressors your ways,
  and sinners shall return to you. **℟.**

SECOND READING *(Hebrews 5:7-9)*

In the days when Christ Jesus was in the flesh, he offered prayers and supplications with loud cries and tears to the one who was able to save him from death, and he was heard because of his reverence. Son though he was, he learned obedience from what he suffered; and when he was made perfect, he became the source of eternal salvation for all who obey him.

The word of the Lord. ***Thanks be to God.***

VERSE BEFORE THE GOSPEL *(John 12:26)*

Glory and praise to you, Lord Jesus Christ! Whoever serves me must follow me, says the Lord; / and where I am, there also will my servant be. ***Glory and praise to you, Lord Jesus Christ!***

GOSPEL *(John 12:20–33)*

A reading from the holy Gospel according to John.
Glory to you, O Lord.

Some Greeks who had come to worship at the Passover Feast came to Philip, who was from Bethsaida* in Galilee, and asked him, "Sir, we would like to see Jesus." Philip went and told Andrew; then Andrew and Philip went and told Jesus. Jesus answered them, "The hour has come for the Son of Man to be glorified. **Amen,**+ amen, I say to you, unless a grain of wheat falls to the ground and dies, it remains just a grain of wheat; but if it dies, it produces much fruit. Whoever loves his life loses it, and whoever hates his life in this world will preserve it for eternal life. Whoever serves me must follow me, and where I am, there also will my servant be. The Father will honor whoever serves me.

"I am troubled now. Yet what should I say? 'Father, save me from this hour'? But it was for this purpose that I came to this hour. Father, glorify your name." Then a voice came from heaven, "I have glorified it and will glorify it again." The crowd there heard it and said it was thunder; but others said, "An angel has spoken to him." Jesus answered and said, "This voice did not come for my sake but for yours. Now is the time of judgment on this world; now the ruler of this world will be driven out. And when I am lifted up from the earth, I will draw everyone to myself." He said this indicating the kind of death he would die.

The Gospel of the Lord. ***Praise to you, Lord Jesus Christ.***

PROFESSION OF FAITH *(page 13)*

PRAYER OF THE FAITHFUL

PREPARATION OF GIFTS *(page 16)*

PRAYER OVER THE OFFERINGS
Hear us, almighty God,
and, having instilled in your servants
the teachings of the Christian faith,
graciously purify them
by the working of this sacrifice.
Through Christ our Lord. ***Amen.***

PREFACE *(Lent 1-2, page 21)*

COMMUNION ANTIPHON *(John 12:24)*
Amen, amen I say to you: Unless a grain of wheat / falls to the ground and dies, it remains a single grain. / But if it dies, it bears much fruit.

TAKING A CLOSER LOOK

+ **Amen** "Amen" is a Hebrew word that affirms what has been said—"It is true!" It appears often throughout the Bible both in normal speech and in prayer whenever people want to signal their acceptance and affirmation. So it is used at Mass as the people's affirmation of what the priest has prayed in their name. In the gospels, Jesus often begins his teaching with the phrase "Amen, I say to you" to emphasize the importance of what follows. And in John's gospel, when Jesus wants to really stress the importance of what he is about to say, he uses the curious double "Amen, amen" to invite his audience to pay close attention to his message.

PRAYER AFTER COMMUNION

We pray, almighty God,
that we may always be counted among the members of Christ,
in whose Body and Blood we have communion.
Who lives and reigns for ever and ever. ***Amen.***

PRAYER OVER THE PEOPLE

Bless, O Lord, your people,
who long for the gift of your mercy,
and grant that what, at your prompting, they desire
they may receive by your generous gift.
Through Christ our Lord. ***Amen.***

DISMISSAL *(page 57)*

RESPONDING TO THE WORD

Jeremiah foresees a time when God's law will be written on our hearts.

What new experience of God's loving guidance have I felt this Lent?

Jesus' suffering led to a deeper relationship with God.

How has my suffering helped me to discover new dimensions of God's love?

Jesus connects death and service because for us to live, some other animals and plants must die.

What little deaths of service have I experienced during this Lenten season?

CHRISTIAN INITIATION: THIRD SCRUTINY

The Mass prayers and readings below are for use in parishes celebrating the Third Scrutiny.

ENTRANCE ANTIPHON *(Cf. Psalm 18 [17]:5-7)*
The waves of death rose about me; / the pains of the netherworld surrounded me. / In my anguish I called to the Lord; / and from his holy temple he heard my voice.

COLLECT
Grant, O Lord, to these chosen ones
that, instructed in the holy mysteries,
they may receive new life at the font of Baptism
and be numbered among the members of your Church.
Through our Lord Jesus Christ, your Son,
who lives and reigns with you in the unity of the Holy Spirit,
God, for ever and ever. ***Amen.***

FIRST READING *(Ezekiel 37:12-14)*
Thus says the Lord GOD: O my people, I will open your graves and have you rise from them, and bring you back to the land of Israel. Then you shall know that I am the LORD, when I open your graves and have you rise from them, O my people! I will put my spirit in you that you may live, and I will settle you upon your land; thus you shall know that I am the LORD. I have promised, and I will do it, says the LORD.

The word of the Lord. ***Thanks be to God.***

RESPONSORIAL PSALM *(Psalm 130:1-2, 3-4, 5-6, 7-8)*

℟. With the Lord there is mercy and fullness of redemption.

Out of the depths I cry to you, O LORD;
  LORD, hear my voice!
Let your ears be attentive
  to my voice in supplication. ℟.
If you, O LORD, mark iniquities,
  LORD, who can stand?
But with you is forgiveness,
  that you may be revered. ℟.
I trust in the LORD;
  my soul trusts in his word.
More than sentinels wait for the dawn,
  let Israel wait for the LORD. ℟.
For with the LORD is kindness
  and with him is plenteous redemption;
and he will redeem Israel
  from all their iniquities. ℟.

SECOND READING *(Romans 8:8-11)*

Brothers and sisters: Those who are in the flesh cannot please God. But you are not in the flesh; on the contrary, you are in the spirit, if only the Spirit of God dwells in you. Whoever does not have the Spirit of Christ does not belong to him. But if Christ is in you, although the body is dead because of sin, the spirit is alive because of righteousness. If the Spirit of the one who raised Jesus from the dead dwells in you, the one who raised Christ from the dead will give life to your mortal bodies also, through his Spirit dwelling in you.

The word of the Lord. ***Thanks be to God.***

VERSE BEFORE THE GOSPEL *(John 11:25a, 26)*
Glory and praise to you, Lord Jesus Christ! I am the resurrection and the life, says the Lord; / whoever believes in me, even if he dies, will never die. ***Glory and praise to you, Lord Jesus Christ!***

GOSPEL *(John 11:1–45 or 11:3–7, 17, 20–27, 33b–45)*
For the shorter version, omit the indented text in brackets and add words in parentheses.

A reading from the holy Gospel according to John.
Glory to you, O Lord.

[Now a man was ill, Lazarus from Bethany,* the village of Mary and her sister Martha. Mary was the one who had anointed the Lord with perfumed oil and dried his feet with her hair; it was her brother Lazarus who was ill. So]

The sisters (of Lazarus) sent word to Jesus saying, "Master, the one you love is ill." When Jesus heard this he said, "This illness is not to end in death, but is for the glory of God, that the Son of God may be glorified through it." Now Jesus loved Martha and her sister and Lazarus. So when he heard that he was ill, he remained for two days in the place where he was. Then after this he said to his disciples, "Let us go back to Judea."

[The disciples said to him, "Rabbi, the Jews were just trying to stone you, and you want to go back there?" Jesus answered, "Are there not twelve hours in a day? If one walks during the day, he does not stumble, because he sees the light of this world. But if one walks at night, he stumbles, because the light is not in him." He said this, and then told them, "Our friend Lazarus is asleep, but I am going to awaken him." So the disciples said to him, "Master, if he is asleep, he will be saved." But Jesus was talking about his death, while they thought that he meant ordinary sleep. So then Jesus said to them clearly, "Lazarus has died. And I am glad for you that I was not there, that you may believe. Let us go to him." So Thomas, called Didymus,* said to his fellow disciples, "Let us also go to die with him."]

When Jesus arrived, he found that Lazarus had already been in the tomb for four days.

[Now Bethany was near Jerusalem, only about two miles away. And many of the Jews had come to Martha and Mary to comfort them about their brother.]

When Martha heard that Jesus was coming, she went to meet him; but Mary sat at home. Martha said to Jesus, "Lord, if you had been here, my brother would not have died. But even now I know that whatever you ask of God, God will give you." Jesus said to her, "Your brother will rise." Martha said to him, "I know he will rise, in the resurrection on the last day." Jesus told her, "I am the resurrection and the life; whoever believes in me, even if he dies, will live, and everyone who lives and believes in me will never die. Do you believe this?" She said to him, "Yes, Lord. I have come to believe that you are the Christ, the Son of God, the one who is coming into the world."

[When she had said this, she went and called her sister Mary secretly, saying, "The teacher is here and is asking for you." As soon as she heard this, she rose quickly and went to him. For Jesus had not yet come into the village, but was still where Martha had met him. So when the Jews who were with her in the house comforting her saw Mary get up quickly and go out, they followed her, presuming that she was going to the tomb to weep there. When Mary came to where Jesus was and saw him, she fell at his feet and said to him, "Lord, if you had been here, my brother would not have died." When Jesus saw her weeping and the Jews who had come with her weeping,] He became perturbed and deeply troubled, and said, "Where have you laid him?" They said to him, "Sir, come and see." And Jesus wept. So the Jews said, "See how he loved him." But some of them said, "Could not the one who opened the eyes of the blind man have done something so that this man would not have died?"

So Jesus, perturbed again, came to the tomb. It was a cave, and a stone lay across it. Jesus said, "Take away the stone." Martha, the dead man's sister, said to him, "Lord, by now there will be a stench; he has been dead for four days." Jesus said to her, "Did I not tell you that if you believe you will see the glory of God?" So they took away the stone. And Jesus raised his eyes and said, "Father, I thank you for hearing me. I know that you always hear me; but because of the crowd here I have said this, that they may believe that you sent me." And when he had said this, He cried out in a loud voice, "Lazarus, come out!" The dead man came out, tied hand and foot with burial bands, and his face was wrapped in a cloth. So Jesus said to them, "Untie him and let him go."

Now many of the Jews who had come to Mary and seen what he had done began to believe in him.

The Gospel of the Lord. ***Praise to you, Lord Jesus Christ.***

PRAYER OVER THE OFFERINGS

Hear us, almighty God,
and, having instilled in your servants
the first fruits of the Christian faith,
graciously purify them by the working of this sacrifice.
Through Christ our Lord. ***Amen.***

PREFACE: LAZARUS

It is truly right and just, our duty and our salvation,
always and everywhere to give you thanks,
Lord, holy Father, almighty and eternal God,
through Christ our Lord.

For as true man he wept for Lazarus his friend
and as eternal God raised him from the tomb,
just as, taking pity on the human race,
he leads us by sacred mysteries to new life.

Through him the host of Angels adores your majesty
and rejoices in your presence for ever.
May our voices, we pray, join with theirs
in one chorus of exultant praise, as we acclaim:
Holy, Holy, Holy Lord God of hosts... *(page 35)*

COMMUNION ANTIPHON *(Cf. John 11:26)*

Everyone who lives and believes in me / will not die for ever, says the Lord.

PRAYER AFTER COMMUNION

May your people be at one, O Lord, we pray,
and in wholehearted submission to you
may they obtain this grace:
that, safe from all distress,
they may readily live out their joy at being saved
and remember in loving prayer those to be reborn.
Through Christ our Lord. ***Amen.*** ⁜

March 21

God will not abandon us

When I first heard the word "passion" in reference to the brutal events of Christ's crucifixion, my young mind was confused. Why did those around me cherish these horrifying events? Learning that this was but a middle episode in the love story of God's passion for our wholeness was transformative.

In the beginning, God who so loved the world sent his beloved Son, Jesus: episode one. Jesus, in response, emptied himself, loving us to the end, one human being to another. He wasn't appeasing a vengeful Father, but embodying God's mercy: healing the sick, befriending impure outcasts, raising the dead, cleansing the temple. Episode two.

There were mortal consequences for such fidelity. Thus unfolds today's episode: the authorities, Roman and Jewish, were outraged. Jesus did not save himself with shows of divine strength. The self-emptying was total: he accepted death by crucifixion, reserved for criminals, with Jewish law confident that those crucified are also damned by God.

Today we remember, knowing that a new beginning for all humanity, for all creation, rises from this episode: God's love does not abandon Jesus in death. Therefore, we walk this week together, to rediscover the depths, the height, and the richness of God's faithfulness to Jesus and to us.

■ BERNADETTE GASSLEIN

THE COMMEMORATION OF THE LORD'S ENTRANCE INTO JERUSALEM

FIRST FORM: THE PROCESSION

INTRODUCTION

The assembly, carrying palm branches, gather in a place distinct from the church to which the procession will move. They may sing Hosanna! or another hymn.

Dear brethren (brothers and sisters),
since the beginning of Lent until now
we have prepared our hearts by penance and charitable works.
Today we gather together to herald with the whole Church
the beginning of the celebration
of our Lord's Paschal Mystery,
that is to say, of his Passion and Resurrection.
For it was to accomplish this mystery
that he entered his own city of Jerusalem.
Therefore, with all faith and devotion,
let us commemorate
the Lord's entry into the city for our salvation,
following in his footsteps,
so that, being made by his grace partakers of the Cross,
we may have a share also in his Resurrection and in his life.

Let us pray:

Almighty ever-living God,
sanctify these branches with your blessing,
that we, who follow Christ the King in exultation,

may reach the eternal Jerusalem through him.
Who lives and reigns for ever and ever. ***Amen.***

Or

Increase the faith of those who place their hope in you, O God,
and graciously hear the prayers of those who call on you,
that we, who today hold high these branches
to hail Christ in his triumph,
may bear fruit for you by good works accomplished in him.
Who lives and reigns for ever and ever. ***Amen.***

An alternate reading follows.

GOSPEL *(Mark 11:1–10)*

A reading from the holy Gospel according to Mark.
Glory to you, O Lord.

When Jesus and his disciples drew near to Jerusalem, to Bethphage* and Bethany* at the Mount of Olives, he sent two of his disciples and said to them, "Go into the village opposite you, and immediately on entering it, you will find a colt tethered on which no one has ever sat. Untie it and bring it here. If anyone should say to you, 'Why are you doing this?' reply, 'The Master has need of it and will send it back here at once.'" So they went off and found a colt tethered at a gate outside on the street, and they untied it. Some of the bystanders said to them, "What are you doing, untying the colt?" They answered them just as Jesus had told them to, and they permitted them to do it. So they brought the colt to Jesus and put their cloaks over it. And he sat on it. Many people spread their cloaks on the road, and others spread leafy branches that they had cut from the fields. Those preceding him as well as those following kept crying out:

"Hosanna!
Blessed is he who comes in the name of the Lord!
Blessed is the kingdom of our father David that is to come!
Hosanna in the highest!"
The Gospel of the Lord. ***Praise to you, Lord Jesus Christ.***

Or

GOSPEL *(John 12:12–16)*
A reading from the holy Gospel according to John.
Glory to you, O Lord.
When the great crowd that had come to the feast heard that Jesus was coming to Jerusalem, they took palm branches and went out to meet him, and cried out:
"Hosanna!
"Blessed is he who comes in the name of the Lord,
the king of Israel."
Jesus found an ass and sat upon it, as is written:
*Fear no more, O daughter Zion;**
see, your king comes, seated upon an ass's colt.
His disciples did not understand this at first, but when Jesus had been glorified they remembered that these things were written about him and that they had done this for him.
The Gospel of the Lord. ***Praise to you, Lord Jesus Christ.***

PROCESSION
Dear brethren (brothers and sisters),
like the crowds who acclaimed Jesus in Jerusalem,
let us go forth in peace.

All process to the church singing a hymn in honor of Christ the King. Mass continues with the Collect.

SECOND FORM: THE SOLEMN ENTRANCE

The blessing of branches and proclamation of the gospel take place, as above, but in the church. After the gospel, the celebrant moves solemnly through the church to the sanctuary, while all sing. Mass continues with the Collect.

THIRD FORM: THE SIMPLE ENTRANCE

The people gather in the church as usual. While the celebrant goes to the altar, the following entrance antiphon or a suitable hymn is sung.

ENTRANCE ANTIPHON *(Cf. John 12:1, 12–13; Psalm 24 [23]:9–10)*
Six days before the Passover, / when the Lord came into the city of Jerusalem, / the children ran to meet him; / in their hands they carried palm branches / and with a loud voice cried out: / Hosanna in the highest! / Blessed are you, who have come in your abundant mercy! / O gates, lift high your heads; / grow higher, ancient doors. / Let him enter, the king of glory! / Who is this king of glory? / He, the Lord of hosts, he is the king of glory. / Hosanna in the highest! / Blessed are you, who have come in your abundant mercy!

INTRODUCTORY RITES *(page 10)*

COLLECT
Almighty ever-living God,
who as an example of humility for the human race to follow
caused our Savior to take flesh and submit to the Cross,
graciously grant that we may heed his lesson of patient suffering
and so merit a share in his Resurrection.
Who lives and reigns with you in the unity of the Holy Spirit,
God, for ever and ever. ***Amen.***

FIRST READING *(Isaiah 50:4–7)*

The Lord GOD has given me
a well-trained tongue,
that I might know how to speak to the weary
a word that will rouse them.
Morning after morning
he opens my ear that I may hear;
and I have not rebelled,
have not turned back.
I gave my back to those who beat me,
my cheeks to those who plucked my beard;
my face I did not shield
from buffets and spitting.

The Lord GOD is my help,
therefore I am not disgraced;
I have set my face like flint,
knowing that I shall not be put to shame.
The word of the Lord. ***Thanks be to God.***

RESPONSORIAL PSALM *(Psalm 22:8–9, 17–18, 19–20, 23–24)*

℟. My God, my God, why have you abandoned me?

All who see me scoff at me;
they mock me with parted lips, they wag their heads:
"He relied on the LORD; let him deliver him,
let him rescue him, if he loves him." ℟.
Indeed, many dogs surround me,
a pack of evildoers closes in upon me;
they have pierced my hands and my feet;
I can count all my bones. ℟.
They divide my garments among them,

and for my vesture they cast lots.
But you, O LORD, be not far from me;
O my help, hasten to aid me. ℟.
I will proclaim your name to my brethren;
in the midst of the assembly I will praise you:
"You who fear the LORD, praise him;
all you descendants of Jacob, give glory to him;
revere him, all you descendants of Israel!" ℟.

SECOND READING *(Philippians 2:6-11)*

Christ Jesus, though he was in the form of God,
did not regard equality with God
something to be grasped.
Rather, he emptied himself,
taking the form of a slave,
coming in human likeness;
and found human in appearance,
he humbled himself,
becoming obedient to the point of death,
even death on a cross.
Because of this, God greatly exalted him
and bestowed on him the name
which is above every name,
that at the name of Jesus
every knee should bend,
of those in heaven and on earth and under the earth,
and every tongue confess that
Jesus Christ is Lord,
to the glory of God the Father.
The word of the Lord. ***Thanks be to God.***

VERSE BEFORE THE GOSPEL *(Philippians 2:8-9)*

Glory and praise to you, Lord Jesus Christ! Christ became obedient to the point of death, / even death on a cross. / Because of this, God greatly exalted him / and bestowed on him the name which is above every name. ***Glory and praise to you, Lord Jesus Christ!***

GOSPEL *(Mark 14:1–15:47 or 15:1-39)*

Several readers may proclaim the passion narrative today. **(N)** *indicates the narrator,* (†) *the words of Jesus,* **(V)** *a voice, and* **(C)** *the crowd. The shorter version begins (page 250) and ends (page 254) at the asterisks.*

N The Passion of our Lord Jesus Christ according to Mark.

The **Passover**+ and the **Feast of Unleavened Bread**+ were to take place in two days' time. So the chief priests and the scribes were seeking a way to arrest him by treachery and put him to death. They said,

C **"Not during the festival, for fear that there may be a riot among the people."**

N When he was in Bethany* reclining at table in the house of Simon the leper, a woman came with an alabaster jar of perfumed oil, costly genuine spikenard. She broke the alabaster jar and poured it on his head. There were some who were indignant.

C **"Why has there been this waste of perfumed oil? It could have been sold for more than three hundred days' wages and the money given to the poor."**

N They were infuriated with her. Jesus said,

† "Let her alone. Why do you make trouble for her? She has

done a good thing for me. The poor you will always have with you, and whenever you wish you can do good to them, but you will not always have me. She has done what she could. She has anticipated anointing my body for burial. Amen, I say to you, wherever the gospel is proclaimed to the whole world, what she has done will be told in memory of her."

N Then Judas Iscariot, one of the Twelve, went off to the chief priests to hand him over to them. When they heard him they were pleased and promised to pay him money. Then he looked for an opportunity to hand him over.

On the first day of the Feast of Unleavened Bread, when they sacrificed the Passover lamb, his disciples said to him,

C "Where do you want us to go and prepare for you to eat the Passover?"

N He sent two of his disciples and said to them,

† "Go into the city and a man will meet you, carrying a jar of water. Follow him. Wherever he enters, say to the master of the house, 'The Teacher says, "Where is my guest room where I may eat the Passover with my disciples?" ' Then he will show you a large upper room furnished and ready. Make the preparations for us there."

N The disciples then went off, entered the city, and found it just as he had told them; and they prepared the Passover.

When it was evening, he came with the Twelve. And as they reclined at table and were eating, Jesus said,

† "Amen, I say to you, one of you will betray me, one who is eating with me."

N They began to be distressed and to say to him, one by one,

V "Surely it is not I?"

N He said to them,

† "One of the Twelve, the one who dips with me into the dish. For the Son of Man indeed goes, as it is written of him, but woe to that man by whom the Son of Man is betrayed. It would be better for that man if he had never been born."

N While they were eating, he took bread, said the blessing, broke it, and gave it to them, and said,

† "Take it; this is my body."

N Then he took a cup, gave thanks, and gave it to them, and they all drank from it. He said to them,

† "This is my blood of the covenant, which will be shed for many. Amen, I say to you, I shall not drink again the fruit of the vine until the day when I drink it new in the kingdom of God."

N Then, after singing a hymn, they went out to the Mount of Olives.
Then Jesus said to them,

† "All of you will have your faith shaken, for it is written:

I will strike the shepherd,
and the sheep will be dispersed.

But after I have been raised up, I shall go before you to Galilee."

N Peter said to him,

V "Even though all should have their faith shaken, mine will not be."

N Then Jesus said to him,

† "Amen, I say to you, this very night before the cock crows twice you will deny me three times."

N But he vehemently replied,

V "Even though I should have to die with you, I will not deny you."

N And they all spoke similarly.

Then they came to a place named Gethsemane,* and he said to his disciples,

† "Sit here while I pray."

N He took with him Peter, James, and John, and began to be troubled and distressed. Then he said to them,

† "My soul is sorrowful even to death. Remain here and keep watch."

N He advanced a little and fell to the ground and prayed that if it were possible the hour might pass by him; he said,

† "Abba, Father, all things are possible to you. Take this cup away from me, but not what I will but what you will."

N When he returned he found them asleep. He said to Peter,

† "Simon, are you asleep? Could you not keep watch for one hour? Watch and pray that you may not undergo the test. The spirit is willing but the flesh is weak."

N Withdrawing again, he prayed, saying the same thing. Then he returned once more and found them asleep, for they could not keep their eyes open and did not know what to answer him. He returned a third time and said to them,

† "Are you still sleeping and taking your rest? It is enough. The hour has come. Behold, the Son of Man is to be handed over to sinners. Get up, let us go. See, my betrayer is at hand."

N Then, while he was still speaking, Judas, one of the Twelve, arrived, accompanied by a crowd with swords and clubs who had come from the chief priests, the scribes, and the elders. His betrayer had arranged a signal with them, saying,

V "The man I shall kiss is the one; arrest him and lead him away securely."

N He came and immediately went over to him and said,

V "Rabbi."

N And he kissed him. At this they laid hands on him and arrested him. One of the bystanders drew his sword, struck the high priest's servant, and cut off his ear. Jesus said to them in reply,

† "Have you come out as against a robber, with swords and clubs, to seize me? Day after day I was with you teaching in the temple area, yet you did not arrest me; but that the Scriptures may be fulfilled."

N And they all left him and fled. Now a young man followed him wearing nothing but a linen cloth about his body. They seized him, but he left the cloth behind and ran off naked.

They led Jesus away to the high priest, and all the chief priests and the elders and the scribes came together. Peter followed him at a distance into the high priest's courtyard and was seated with the guards, warming himself at the fire. The chief priests and the entire Sanhedrin* kept trying to obtain testimony against Jesus in order to put him to death, but they found none. Many gave false witness against him, but their testimony did not agree. Some took the stand and testified falsely against him, alleging,

C **"We heard him say, 'I will destroy this temple made with hands and within three days I will build another not made with hands.'"**

N Even so their testimony did not agree. The high priest rose before the assembly and questioned Jesus, saying,

V "Have you no answer? What are these men testifying against you?"

N But he was silent and answered nothing. Again the high priest asked him and said to him,

V "Are you the Christ, the son of the Blessed One?"

N Then Jesus answered,

† "I am;
and 'you will see the Son of Man
seated at the right hand of the Power
and coming with the clouds of heaven.'"

N At that the high priest tore his garments and said,

V "What further need have we of witnesses? You have heard the blasphemy. What do you think?"

N They all condemned him as deserving to die. Some began to spit on him. They blindfolded him and struck him and said to him,

C "Prophesy!"

N And the guards greeted him with blows.

While Peter was below in the courtyard, one of the high priest's maids came along. Seeing Peter warming himself, she looked intently at him and said,

C "You too were with the Nazarene, Jesus."

N But he denied it saying,

V "I neither know nor understand what you are talking about."

N So he went out into the outer court. Then the cock crowed. The maid saw him and began again to say to the bystanders,

C "This man is one of them."

N Once again he denied it. A little later the bystanders said to Peter once more,

C "Surely you are one of them; for you too are a Galilean."

N He began to curse and to swear,

V "I do not know this man about whom you are talking."

N And immediately a cock crowed a second time. Then Peter remembered the word that Jesus had said to him, "Before the cock crows twice you will deny me three times." He broke down and wept.

* * *

N As soon as morning came, the chief priests with the elders and the scribes, that is, the whole Sanhedrin, held a council. They bound Jesus, led him away, and handed him over to Pilate. Pilate questioned him,

V "Are you the king of the Jews?"

N He said to him in reply,

† "You say so."

N The chief priests accused him of many things. Again Pilate questioned him,

V "Have you no answer? See how many things they accuse you of."

N Jesus gave him no further answer, so that Pilate was amazed.

Now on the occasion of the feast he used to release to them one prisoner whom they requested. A man called Barabbas* was then in prison along with the rebels who had committed murder in a rebellion. The crowd came forward and began to ask him to do for them as he was accustomed. Pilate answered,

V "Do you want me to release to you the king of the Jews?"

N For he knew that it was out of envy that the chief priests had handed him over. But the chief priests stirred up the crowd to have him release Barabbas for them instead. Pilate again said to them in reply,

V "Then what do you want me to do with the man you call the king of the Jews?"

N They shouted again,

C "Crucify him."

N Pilate said to them,

V "Why? What evil has he done?"

N They only shouted the louder,

C **"Crucify him."**

N So Pilate, wishing to satisfy the crowd, released Barabbas to them and, after he had Jesus scourged, handed him over to be crucified.

The soldiers led him away inside the palace, that is, the praetorium,* and assembled the whole cohort. They clothed him in purple and, weaving a crown of thorns, placed it on him. They began to salute him with,

C **"Hail, King of the Jews!"**

N and kept striking his head with a reed and spitting upon him. They knelt before him in homage. And when they had mocked him, they stripped him of the purple cloak, dressed him in his own clothes, and led him out to crucify him.

They pressed into service a passer-by, Simon, a Cyrenian,* who was coming in from the country, the father of Alexander and Rufus, to carry his cross.

They brought him to the place of Golgotha*—which is translated Place of the Skull—. They gave him wine drugged with myrrh,* but he did not take it. Then they crucified him and divided his garments by casting lots for them to see what each should take. It was nine o'clock in the morning when they crucified him. The inscription of the charge against him read, "The King of the Jews." With him they crucified two revolutionaries, one on his right and one on his left. Those passing by reviled him, shaking their heads and saying,

C "Aha! You who would destroy the temple and rebuild it in three days, save yourself by coming down from the cross."

N Likewise the chief priests, with the scribes, mocked him among themselves and said,

C "He saved others; he cannot save himself. Let the Christ, the King of Israel, come down now from the cross that we may see and believe."

N Those who were crucified with him also kept abusing him.
At noon darkness came over the whole land until three in the afternoon. And at three o'clock Jesus cried out in a loud voice,

† "*Eloi, Eloi, lema sabachthani?*"*

N which is translated,

† "My God, my God, why have you forsaken me?"

N Some of the bystanders who heard it said,

C "Look, he is calling Elijah."

N One of them ran, soaked a sponge with wine, put it on a reed and gave it to him to drink saying,

V "Wait, let us see if Elijah comes to take him down."

N Jesus gave a loud cry and breathed his last.

(Here all kneel and pause for a short time.)

N The veil of the sanctuary was torn in two from top to bottom. When the centurion who stood facing him saw how he breathed his last he said,

V "Truly this man was the Son of God!"

* * *

N There were also women looking on from a distance. Among them were Mary Magdalene, Mary the mother of the younger James and of Joses, and Salome.* These women had followed him when he was in Galilee and ministered to him. There were also many other women who had come up with him to Jerusalem.

When it was already evening, since it was the day of preparation, the day before the sabbath, Joseph of Arimathea,* a distinguished member of the council, who was himself awaiting the kingdom of God, came and courageously went to Pilate and asked for the body of Jesus. Pilate was amazed that he was already dead. He summoned the centurion and asked him if Jesus had already died. And when he learned of it from the centurion, he gave the body to Joseph. Having bought a linen cloth, he took him down, wrapped him in the linen cloth, and laid him in a tomb that had been hewn out of the rock. Then he rolled a stone against the entrance to the tomb. Mary Magdalene and Mary the mother of Joses watched where he was laid.

The Gospel of the Lord. ***Praise to you, Lord Jesus Christ.***

PROFESSION OF FAITH *(page 13)*

PRAYER OF THE FAITHFUL

PREPARATION OF GIFTS *(page 16)*

PRAYER OVER THE OFFERINGS

Through the Passion of your Only Begotten Son, O Lord,
may our reconciliation with you be near at hand,
so that, though we do not merit it by our own deeds,
yet by this sacrifice made once for all,
we may feel already the effects of your mercy.
Through Christ our Lord. ***Amen.***

PREFACE: THE PASSION OF THE LORD

It is truly right and just, our duty and our salvation,
always and everywhere to give you thanks,
Lord, holy Father, almighty and eternal God,
through Christ our Lord.

For, though innocent, he suffered willingly for sinners
and accepted unjust condemnation to save the guilty.
His Death has washed away our sins,
and his Resurrection has purchased our justification.

And so, with all the Angels,
we praise you, as in joyful celebration we acclaim:
Holy, Holy, Holy Lord God of hosts... *(page 35)*

COMMUNION ANTIPHON *(Matthew 26:42)*
Father, if this chalice cannot pass without my drinking it, / your will be done.

PRAYER AFTER COMMUNION
Nourished with these sacred gifts,
we humbly beseech you, O Lord,
that, just as through the death of your Son
you have brought us to hope for what we believe,
so by his Resurrection
you may lead us to where you call.
Through Christ our Lord. ***Amen.***

TAKING A CLOSER LOOK

+ Passover / Feast of Unleavened Bread

Passover (Greek, *ta pascha*) was the annual Jewish family celebration remembering God's deliverance of Israel from Egypt. In particular, the term recalls God's striking down of every Egyptian firstborn, both children and animals, and "passing over" the Hebrews whose houses were marked with lamb's blood (see Exodus 12). To this feast was joined an eight-day period when only unleavened bread could be eaten. Their leaven was not like our powdered yeast, but rather a fermentation agent as is used in making sourdough bread today. Thus leavened bread contained a corrupting agent that would render it "unclean" for ritual use on this most sacred feast.

PRAYER OVER THE PEOPLE

Look, we pray, O Lord, on this your family,
for whom our Lord Jesus Christ
did not hesitate to be delivered into the hands of the wicked
and submit to the agony of the Cross.
Who lives and reigns for ever and ever. ***Amen.***

DISMISSAL *(page 57)* ⁜

Responding to the Word

Isaiah describes God's faithful servant, who suffers but is later rewarded.

What has been the hardest aspect of my Lenten time?

Paul's hymn characterizes Jesus' earthly career as self-emptying service.

What self-emptying service have I experienced this Lent?

In Mark's gospel, Jesus is abandoned by everybody to die alone.

How have I felt abandoned and alone when I had to suffer?

The Triduum (Latin for "three days") comes at the end of Holy Week and comprises the three-day period of prayer that culminates in the Easter feast, the fulfillment of the whole liturgical year.

Holy Thursday

On Holy Thursday (also called Maundy Thursday), the Church celebrates the Lord's Supper and the institution of the Eucharist. The word "Maundy" stems from the Latin word *mandatum*, meaning "commandment," and refers to the new commandment of love that Jesus gave his disciples that night.

Most parishes now observe the custom of foot-washing, recalling how Jesus washed his disciples' feet at the Last Supper (John 13:1-20). After the liturgy, the consecrated bread is transferred to a side altar and kept in the tabernacle of repose. Then the altar is stripped.

Good Friday

Good Friday is the only day of the year on which Mass is not celebrated. The altar is bare, and the liturgy consists of proclaiming John's passion account, intercessions, veneration of the cross, and Holy Communion.

Many churches, in addition to the liturgy of Good Friday, have a meditation on the Way of the Cross commemorating the events of Jesus' passion. Some parishes have also introduced Good Friday meditations on the seven last words of Christ on the cross, taken from all four gospels.

The Great Vigil of Easter

Only the Eucharist itself is older than the liturgy of the Easter Vigil. This service commemorates the passage from death into life. On this night, we celebrate our deliverance by Christ and look forward to the day when we shall see him face to face. As the Roman Missal explains, "the Church, keeping watch, awaits the Resurrection of Christ and celebrates it in the Sacraments."

The liturgy begins at the fire. The paschal candle is lighted as the "Light of Christ" is proclaimed and praised. In many churches, after the paschal candle is put in place, small candles are lit from it and held by the worshippers. Next, several readings from the Old Testament summarize the story of salvation, telling of God's work of creation, the calling of the Hebrews to be God's people, their deliverance in the Exodus, and God's constant care until Christ came. An air of expectancy surrounds the prayers and singing of psalms and canticles that follow each reading.

Then, the altar candles are lighted from the paschal candle, and, in a blaze of light and triumphant music, the first Easter Eucharist begins. The Gloria is joyfully sung, echoing the angels' hymn of praise. This moment of triumph leads into the solemn proclamation of the Gospel, announcing the Resurrection of Christ. Our risen Lord comes, in word and sacrament, into the darkness of our lives with the light of his risen life.

Baptisms follow the Scripture readings. If there are no candidates for baptism, the congregation may join in the renewal of baptismal promises. The Easter Vigil continues with the sprinkling of the congregation, the Liturgy of the Eucharist—where the newly baptized receive communion for the first time—and concludes with a joyful dismissal, sending forth the faithful to celebrate the risen Christ.

Praying and living Holy Week

When a Jewish household gathers for its Passover meal, the youngest child begins the reminiscing by asking: "Why is this night different from all other nights?" So likewise, we Christians might ask, "Why are these three days different from all other days?" The answer, of course, is that they encapsulate the deepest meaning of the story of our salvation. Through his death and resurrection, Jesus brings us all into the right relationships with God and with others.

During Holy Week and the Triduum, in order to recall the story of our salvation, individuals and family members might read the Scriptures appointed for each day or, if there are young children, read the events of Holy Week from a Bible storybook.

But knowing the story is only half the challenge. We need to connect its life-giving possibilities with our own lives. Use the following questions (based on Exodus 14:15–15:1) as a way for household members to discover the "exodus" character of their own lives.

- Tell a story of your experience of freedom and deliverance. What part did God play in this experience?
- When did you escape your own form of slavery and head for the promised land of freedom?
- When did you pass through the waters of your Red Sea and dance like Miriam on the other side?
- Tell a story of your passing over from some form of death to new life.

March 25

We are all worthy

Jesus washing the feet of his disciples teaches us a lesson in worthiness and service. Too often, we walk through life evaluating the worthiness of ourselves and others. Jesus, in this simple action, turns the notion of worthiness upside down.

Jesus shows us that servant leadership breaks down any notion of privilege or entitlement. We cling to the idea that power, privilege, and social standing are important and determine our value. Jesus shows that we are all worthy. Even Judas, whom Jesus knew would betray him, received this act of cleansing service from the Lord.

Correspondingly, Jesus rejects any sense of unworthiness from Peter. We are all worthy, and none of us are unworthy. Likewise, not one of us is too important to reject the call to serve others. All people deserve our service. Their perceived goodness or importance, or their perceived malevolence or offensiveness, do not have any role in determining how we live out our call to serve each person we encounter. We are called to put aside any notions of worthiness and unworthiness. We simply serve.

MICHAEL WAY SKINNER

ENTRANCE ANTIPHON *(Cf. Galatians 6:14)*
We should glory in the Cross of our Lord Jesus Christ, / in whom is our salvation, life and resurrection, / through whom we are saved and delivered.

INTRODUCTORY RITES *(page 10)*

COLLECT
O God, who have called us to participate
in this most sacred Supper,
in which your Only Begotten Son,
when about to hand himself over to death,
entrusted to the Church a sacrifice new for all eternity,
the banquet of his love,
grant, we pray,
that we may draw from so great a mystery,
the fullness of charity and of life.
Through our Lord Jesus Christ, your Son,
who lives and reigns with you in the unity of the Holy Spirit,
God, for ever and ever. ***Amen.***

FIRST READING *(Exodus 12:1-8, 11-14)*
The LORD said to Moses and Aaron in the land of Egypt, "This month shall stand at the head of your calendar; you shall reckon it the first month of the year. Tell the whole community of Israel: On the tenth of this month every one of your families must procure for itself a lamb, one apiece for each household. If a family is too small for a whole lamb, it shall join the nearest household in procuring one and shall share in the lamb in proportion to the number of persons who partake of it. The lamb must be a year-old male and without blemish. You may take it from either the sheep or the goats. You shall keep it

until the fourteenth day of this month, and then, with the whole assembly of Israel present, it shall be slaughtered during the evening twilight. They shall take some of its blood and apply it to the two doorposts and the lintel of every house in which they partake of the lamb. That same night they shall eat its roasted flesh with unleavened bread and bitter herbs.

"This is how you are to eat it: with your loins girt, sandals on your feet and your staff in hand, you shall eat like those who are in flight. It is the Passover of the LORD. For on this same night I will go through Egypt, striking down every firstborn of the land, both man and beast, and executing judgment on all the gods of Egypt—I, the LORD! But the blood will mark the houses where you are. Seeing the blood, I will pass over you; thus, when I strike the land of Egypt, no destructive blow will come upon you.

"This day shall be a memorial feast for you, which all your generations shall celebrate with pilgrimage to the LORD, as a perpetual institution."

The word of the Lord. ***Thanks be to God.***

RESPONSORIAL PSALM *(Psalm 116:12-13, 15-16bc, 17-18)*

℟. Our blessing-cup is a communion with the Blood of Christ.

How shall I make a return to the LORD
for all the good he has done for me?
The cup of salvation I will take up,
and I will call upon the name of the LORD. ℟.
Precious in the eyes of the LORD
is the death of his faithful ones.
I am your servant, the son of your handmaid;
you have loosed my bonds. ℟.
To you will I offer sacrifice of thanksgiving,

and I will call upon the name of the LORD.
My vows to the LORD I will pay
in the presence of all his people.
℟. **Our blessing-cup is a communion with the Blood of Christ.**

SECOND READING *(1 Corinthians 11:23-26)*

Brothers and sisters: I received from the Lord what I also handed on to you, that the Lord Jesus, on the night he was handed over, took bread, and, after he had given thanks, broke it and said, "This is my body that is for you. Do this in remembrance of me." In the same way also the cup, after supper, saying, "This cup is the new covenant in my blood. Do this, as often as you drink it, in remembrance of me." For as often as you eat this bread and drink the cup, you proclaim the death of the Lord until he comes.

The word of the Lord. ***Thanks be to God.***

VERSE BEFORE THE GOSPEL *(John 13:34)*

Glory and praise to you, Lord Jesus Christ! I give you a new commandment, says the Lord: / love one another as I have loved you. ***Glory and praise to you, Lord Jesus Christ!***

GOSPEL *(John 13:1-15)*

A reading from the holy Gospel according to John.
Glory to you, O Lord.

Before the feast of Passover, Jesus knew that his hour had come to pass from this world to the Father. He loved his own in the world and he loved them to the end. The devil had already induced Judas, son of Simon the Iscariot, to hand him over. So, during supper, fully aware that the Father had put everything into his power and that he had come from God and was returning to God, he rose from supper and took off his outer garments. He took a towel and tied it around his waist. Then he poured water into a basin and began to **wash the disciples' feet**+ and dry them with the towel around his waist. He came to Simon Peter, who said to him, "Master, are you going to wash my feet?" Jesus answered and said to him, "What I am doing, you do not understand now, but you will understand later." Peter said to him, "You will never wash my feet." Jesus answered him, "Unless I wash you, you will have no inheritance with me." Simon Peter said to him, "Master, then not only my feet, but my hands and head as well." Jesus said to him, "Whoever has bathed has no need except to have his feet washed, for he is clean all over; so you are clean, but not all." For he knew who would betray him; for this reason, he said, "Not all of you are clean."

So when he had washed their feet and put his garments back on and reclined at table again, he said to them, "Do you realize what I have done for you? You call me 'teacher' and 'master,' and rightly so, for indeed I am. If I, therefore, the master and teacher, have washed your feet, you ought to wash one another's feet. I have given you a model to follow, so that as I have done for you, you should also do."

The Gospel of the Lord. ***Praise to you, Lord Jesus Christ.***

THE WASHING OF FEET

During the washing of feet, the assembly may sing an appropriate song.

PRAYER OF THE FAITHFUL

PREPARATION OF GIFTS *(page 16)*

PRAYER OVER THE OFFERINGS

Grant us, O Lord, we pray,
that we may participate worthily in these mysteries,
for whenever the memorial of this sacrifice is celebrated
the work of our redemption is accomplished.
Through Christ our Lord. ***Amen.***

PREFACE *(Most Holy Eucharist 1, page 32)*

COMMUNION ANTIPHON *(1 Corinthians 11:24–25)*

This is the Body that will be given up for you; / this is the Chalice of the new covenant in my Blood, says the Lord; / do this, whenever you receive it, in memory of me.

PRAYER AFTER COMMUNION

Grant, almighty God,
that, just as we are renewed
by the Supper of your Son in this present age,
so we may enjoy his banquet for all eternity.
Who lives and reigns for ever and ever. ***Amen.***

TAKING A CLOSER LOOK

+ **The washing of feet** Footwashing was not part of the Passover ritual, but for John it is clearly an acting out of the deepest meaning of the Eucharist—giving oneself in loving service for others. In the biblical world, sandals that protected the bottom of the foot did not keep the dirt away, so a customary sign of hospitality upon entering a house was to provide water for a guest to wash their feet. This was usually the task of a servant. So, when Jesus assumes the role of the servant instead of the master that he is, what would normally be considered undignified and humiliating becomes a sign of love for his disciples.

The Blessing and Dismissal are omitted tonight.

TRANSFER OF THE MOST BLESSED SACRAMENT

The consecrated eucharistic bread is carried through the church in procession to the place of repose. During the procession, the hymn "Pange lingua" or another eucharistic song is sung.

When the procession reaches the place of repose, the celebrant incenses the eucharistic bread, while the "Tantum ergo" (stanzas 5-6 of the "Pange lingua") is sung. The tabernacle of repose is then closed.

After a few moments of silent adoration, the priests and ministers of the altar leave. The faithful are encouraged to continue adoration before the Blessed Sacrament for a suitable period of time through the evening and night, but there should be no solemn adoration after midnight. ⁜

RESPONDING TO THE WORD

At the Passover, the Jews remembered God's powerful presence that transformed their oppression into freedom.

➔ *How has God freed me from some oppression this Lent?*

At the Eucharist, we remember Christ's powerful presence that is always transforming us.

➔ *How might I express my gratitude to Christ for what he has done for me?*

In John's gospel, Jesus' footwashing is the model of eucharistic service.

➔ *What service for others might I undertake to show my thanks to Christ for his gift of life to me?*

March 26

"The passion narratives are proclaimed in full so that all see vividly the love of Christ for each person. In light of this, the crimes during the Passion of Christ cannot be attributed, in either preaching or catechesis, indiscriminately to all Jews of that time, nor to Jews today. The Jewish people should not be referred to as though rejected or cursed, as if this view followed from Scripture. The Church ever keeps in mind that Jesus, his mother Mary, and the apostles all were Jewish. As the Church has always held, Christ freely suffered his passion and death because of the sins of all, that all might be saved."

The United States Conference of Catholic Bishops Committee on Divine Worship and the Committee on Ecumenical and Interreligious Affairs

Nothing can extinguish God's love

No words can do justice to the sheer intensity of violence that Jesus undergoes in today's gospel. He is tormented physically, psychologically, and emotionally. Even at the moment of his betrayal, his concern is not for himself but for his cherished friends.

Despite the appalling cruelty inflicted upon him, Jesus never stops loving. In his passion we are shown that Jesus—God incarnate—is love in its fullness. Nothing in the universe—no evil, no violence, no human malice—can extinguish the love of God.

If Christ's love did not cease on Good Friday, then we can trust that when we face our own struggles, Christ does not cease loving us.

■ Andrew Hume

No Mass is celebrated today. The celebration of the Lord's Passion consists of three parts: the Liturgy of the Word, the Adoration of the Holy Cross, and Holy Communion.

PRAYER

Remember your mercies, O Lord,
and with your eternal protection sanctify your servants,
for whom Christ your Son,
by the shedding of his Blood,
established the Paschal Mystery.
Who lives and reigns for ever and ever. ***Amen.***

Or

O God, who by the Passion of Christ your Son, our Lord,
abolished the death inherited from ancient sin
by every succeeding generation,
grant that just as, being conformed to him,
we have borne by the law of nature
the image of the man of earth,
so by the sanctification of grace
we may bear the image of the Man of heaven.
Through Christ our Lord. ***Amen.***

LITURGY OF THE WORD

FIRST READING *(Isaiah 52:13–53:12)*

See, my servant shall prosper,
he shall be raised high and greatly exalted.

Even as many were amazed at him—
  so marred was his look beyond human semblance
  and his appearance beyond that of the sons of man—
so shall he startle many nations,
  because of him kings shall stand speechless;
for those who have not been told shall see,
  those who have not heard shall ponder it.

Who would believe what we have heard?
  To whom has the arm of the LORD been revealed?
He grew up like a sapling before him,
  like a shoot from the parched earth;
there was in him no stately bearing to make us look at him,
  nor appearance that would attract us to him.
He was spurned and avoided by people,
  a man of suffering, accustomed to infirmity,
one of those from whom people hide their faces,
  spurned, and we held him in no esteem.

Yet it was our infirmities that he bore,
  our sufferings that he endured,
while we thought of him as stricken,
  as one smitten by God and afflicted.
But he was pierced for our offenses,
  crushed for our sins;
upon him was the chastisement that makes us whole,
  by his stripes we were healed.
We had all gone astray like sheep,
  each following his own way;
but the LORD laid upon him
  the guilt of us all.

Though he was harshly treated, he submitted
and opened not his mouth;
like a lamb led to the slaughter
or a sheep before the shearers,
he was silent and opened not his mouth.
Oppressed and condemned, he was taken away,
and who would have thought any more of his destiny?
When he was cut off from the land of the living,
and smitten for the sin of his people,
a grave was assigned him among the wicked
and a burial place with evildoers,
though he had done no wrong
nor spoken any falsehood.
But the LORD was pleased
to crush him in infirmity.

If he gives his life as an offering for sin,
he shall see his descendants in a long life,
and the will of the LORD shall be accomplished through him.

Because of his affliction
he shall see the light in fullness of days;
through his suffering, my servant shall justify many,
and their guilt he shall bear.
Therefore I will give him his portion among the great,
and he shall divide the spoils with the mighty,
because he surrendered himself to death
and was counted among the wicked;
and he shall take away the sins of many,
and win pardon for their offenses.
The word of the Lord. ***Thanks be to God.***

RESPONSORIAL PSALM *(Psalm 31:2, 6, 12-13, 15-16, 17, 25)*

℟. Father, into your hands I commend my spirit.

In you, O LORD, I take refuge;
  let me never be put to shame.
In your justice rescue me.
Into your hands I commend my spirit;
  you will redeem me, O LORD, O faithful God. ℟.
For all my foes I am an object of reproach,
  a laughingstock to my neighbors, and a dread to my friends;
  they who see me abroad flee from me.
I am forgotten like the unremembered dead;
  I am like a dish that is broken. ℟.
But my trust is in you, O LORD;
  I say, "You are my God.
In your hands is my destiny; rescue me
  from the clutches of my enemies and my persecutors." ℟.
Let your face shine upon your servant;
  save me in your kindness.
Take courage and be stouthearted,
  all you who hope in the LORD. ℟.

SECOND READING *(Hebrews 4:14-16; 5:7-9)*

Brothers and sisters: Since we have a great high priest who has passed through the heavens, Jesus, the Son of God, let us hold fast to our confession. For we do not have a high priest who is unable to sympathize with our weaknesses, but one who has similarly been tested in every way, yet without sin. So let us confidently approach the throne of grace to receive mercy and to find grace for timely help.

In the days when Christ was in the flesh, he offered prayers and supplications with loud cries and tears to the one who was able to save him from death, and he was heard because of his reverence. Son though he was, he learned obedience from what he suffered; and when he was made perfect, he became the source of eternal salvation for all who obey him.

The word of the Lord. ***Thanks be to God.***

VERSE BEFORE THE GOSPEL *(Philippians 2:8–9)*

Glory and praise to you, Lord Jesus Christ! Christ became obedient to the point of death, / even death on a cross. / Because of this, God greatly exalted him / and bestowed on him the name which is above every other name. ***Glory and praise to you, Lord Jesus Christ!***

GOSPEL *(John 18:1–19:42)*

*Several readers may proclaim the passion narrative today. (**N**) indicates the narrator, (†) the words of Jesus, (**V**) a voice, and (**C**) the crowd.*

N The Passion of our Lord Jesus Christ according to John.

Jesus went out with his disciples across the Kidron* valley to where there was a garden, into which he and his disciples entered. Judas his betrayer also knew the place, because Jesus had often met there with his disciples. So Judas got a band of soldiers and guards from the chief priests and the Pharisees and went there with lanterns, torches, and weapons. Jesus, knowing everything that was going to happen to him, went out and said to them,

† "Whom are you looking for?"

N They answered him,

C "Jesus the Nazorean.*"

N He said to them,

† **"I AM."**+

N Judas his betrayer was also with them. When he said to them, "I AM," they turned away and fell to the ground. So he again asked them,

† "Whom are you looking for?"

N They said,

C "Jesus the Nazorean."

N Jesus answered,

† "I told you that I AM. So if you are looking for me, let these men go."

N This was to fulfill what he had said, "I have not lost any of those you gave me." Then Simon Peter, who had a sword, drew it, struck the high priest's slave, and cut off his right ear. The slave's name was Malchus.* Jesus said to Peter,

† "Put your sword into its scabbard. Shall I not drink the cup that the Father gave me?"

N So the band of soldiers, the tribune, and the Jewish guards seized Jesus, bound him, and brought him to Annas first. He was the father-in-law of Caiaphas,* who was high priest that year. It was Caiaphas who had counseled the Jews that it was better that one man should die rather than the people.

Simon Peter and another disciple followed Jesus. Now the other disciple was known to the high priest, and he entered the courtyard of the high priest with Jesus. But Peter stood at the gate outside. So the other disciple, the acquaintance of the high priest, went out and spoke to the gatekeeper and brought Peter in. Then the maid who was the gatekeeper said to Peter,

C **"You are not one of this man's disciples, are you?"**

N He said,

V "I am not."

N Now the slaves and the guards were standing around a charcoal fire that they had made, because it was cold, and were warming themselves. Peter was also standing there keeping warm.

The high priest questioned Jesus about his disciples and about his doctrine. Jesus answered him,

† "I have spoken publicly to the world. I have always taught in a synagogue or in the temple area where all the Jews gather, and in secret I have said nothing. Why ask me? Ask those who heard me what I said to them. They know what I said."

N When he had said this, one of the temple guards standing there struck Jesus and said,

V "Is this the way you answer the high priest?"

N Jesus answered him,

† "If I have spoken wrongly, testify to the wrong; but if I have spoken rightly, why do you strike me?"

N Then Annas sent him bound to Caiaphas the high priest.

Now Simon Peter was standing there keeping warm. And they said to him,

C **"You are not one of his disciples, are you?"**

N He denied it and said,

V "I am not."

N One of the slaves of the high priest, a relative of the one whose ear Peter had cut off, said,

C "Didn't I see you in the garden with him?"

N Again Peter denied it. And immediately the cock crowed.

Then they brought Jesus from Caiaphas to the praetorium.* It was morning. And they themselves did not enter the praetorium, in order not to be defiled so that they could eat the Passover. So Pilate came out to them and said,

V "What charge do you bring against this man?"

N They answered and said to him,

C "If he were not a criminal, we would not have handed him over to you."

N At this, Pilate said to them,

V "Take him yourselves, and judge him according to your law."

N The Jews answered him,

C "We do not have the right to execute anyone,"

N in order that the word of Jesus might be fulfilled that he said indicating the kind of death he would die. So Pilate went back into the praetorium and summoned Jesus and said to him,

V "Are you the King of the Jews?"

N Jesus answered,

† "Do you say this on your own or have others told you about me?"

N Pilate answered,

V "I am not a Jew, am I? Your own nation and the chief priests handed you over to me. What have you done?"

N Jesus answered,

† "My kingdom does not belong to this world. If my kingdom did belong to this world, my attendants would be fighting to keep me from being handed over to the Jews. But as it is, my kingdom is not here."

N So Pilate said to him,

V "Then you are a king?"

N Jesus answered,

† "You say I am a king. For this I was born and for this I came into the world, to testify to the truth. Everyone who belongs to the truth listens to my voice."

N Pilate said to him,

V "What is truth?"

N When he had said this, he again went out to the Jews and said to them,

V "I find no guilt in him. But you have a custom that I release one prisoner to you at Passover. Do you want me to release to you the King of the Jews?"

N They cried out again,

C **"Not this one but Barabbas!*"**

N Now Barabbas was a revolutionary.

Then Pilate took Jesus and had him scourged. And the soldiers wove a crown out of thorns and placed it on his head, and clothed him in a purple cloak, and they came to him and said,

C **"Hail, King of the Jews!"**

N And they struck him repeatedly. Once more Pilate went out and said to them,

V "Look, I am bringing him out to you, so that you may know that I find no guilt in him."

N So Jesus came out, wearing the crown of thorns and the purple cloak. And he said to them,

V "Behold, the man!"

N When the chief priests and the guards saw him they cried out,

C **"Crucify him, crucify him!"**

N Pilate said to them,

V "Take him yourselves and crucify him. I find no guilt in him."

N The Jews answered,

C **"We have a law, and according to that law he ought to die, because he made himself the Son of God."**

N Now when Pilate heard this statement, he became even more afraid, and went back into the praetorium and said to Jesus,

V "Where are you from?"

N Jesus did not answer him. So Pilate said to him,

V "Do you not speak to me? Do you not know that I have power to release you and I have power to crucify you?"

N Jesus answered him,

† "You would have no power over me if it had not been given to you from above. For this reason the one who handed me over to you has the greater sin."

N Consequently, Pilate tried to release him; but the Jews cried out,

C **"If you release him, you are not a Friend of Caesar.* Everyone who makes himself a king opposes Caesar."**

N When Pilate heard these words he brought Jesus out and seated him on the judge's bench in the place called Stone Pavement, in Hebrew, Gabbatha.* It was preparation day for Passover, and it was about noon. And he said to the Jews,

V "Behold, your king!"

N They cried out,

C **"Take him away, take him away! Crucify him!"**

N Pilate said to them,

V "Shall I crucify your king?"

N The chief priests answered,

C **"We have no king but Caesar."**

N Then he handed him over to them to be crucified.

So they took Jesus, and, carrying the cross himself, he went out to what is called the Place of the Skull, in Hebrew, Golgotha.* There they crucified him, and with him two others, one on either side, with Jesus in the middle. Pilate also had an inscription written and put on the cross. It read, "Jesus the Nazorean, the King of the Jews." Now many of the Jews read this inscription, because the place where Jesus was crucified was near the city; and it was written in Hebrew, Latin, and Greek. So the chief priests of the Jews said to Pilate,

C "Do not write 'The King of the Jews,' but that he said, 'I am the King of the Jews.'"

N Pilate answered,

V "What I have written, I have written."

N When the soldiers had crucified Jesus, they took his clothes and divided them into four shares, a share for each soldier. They also took his tunic, but the tunic was seamless, woven in one piece from the top down. So they said to one another,

C "Let's not tear it, but cast lots for it to see whose it will be,"

N in order that the passage of Scripture might be fulfilled that says:

They divided my garments among them,
and for my vesture they cast lots.

This is what the soldiers did. Standing by the cross of Jesus were his mother and his mother's sister, Mary the wife of Clopas, and Mary of Magdala. When Jesus saw his mother and the disciple there whom he loved he said to his mother,

† "Woman, behold, your son."

N Then he said to the disciple,

† "Behold, your mother."

N And from that hour the disciple took her into his home.
After this, aware that everything was now finished, in order that the Scripture might be fulfilled, Jesus said,

† "I thirst."

N There was a vessel filled with common wine. So they put a sponge soaked in wine on a sprig of hyssop* and put it up to his mouth. When Jesus had taken the wine, he said,

† "It is finished."

N And bowing his head, he handed over the spirit.

(Here all kneel and pause for a short time.)

N Now since it was preparation day, in order that the bodies might not remain on the cross on the sabbath, for the sabbath day of that week was a solemn one, the Jews asked Pilate that their legs be broken and that they be taken down. So the soldiers came and broke the legs of the first and then of the other one who was crucified with Jesus. But when they came to Jesus and saw that he was already dead, they did not break his legs, but one soldier thrust his lance into his side, and immediately blood and water flowed out. An eyewitness has testified, and his testimony is true; he knows that he is speaking the truth, so that you also may come to believe. For this happened so that the Scripture passage might be fulfilled:
Not a bone of it will be broken.

And again another passage says:

They will look upon him whom they have pierced.

After this, Joseph of Arimathea,* secretly a disciple of Jesus for fear of the Jews, asked Pilate if he could remove the body of Jesus. And Pilate permitted it. So he came and took his body. Nicodemus, the one who had first come to him at night, also came bringing a mixture of myrrh and aloes weighing about one hundred pounds. They took the body of Jesus and bound it with burial cloths along with the spices, according to the Jewish burial custom. Now in the place where he had been crucified there was a garden, and in the garden a new tomb, in which no one had yet been buried. So they laid Jesus there because of the Jewish preparation day; for the tomb was close by.

The Gospel of the Lord. ***Praise to you, Lord Jesus Christ.***

THE SOLEMN INTERCESSIONS

For Holy Church

Let us pray, dearly beloved, for the holy Church of God,
that our God and Lord be pleased to give her peace,
to guard her and to unite her throughout the whole world
and grant that, leading our life in tranquility and quiet,
we may glorify God the Father almighty.

(Prayer in silence.)

Almighty ever-living God,
who in Christ revealed your glory to all the nations,
watch over the works of your mercy,
that your Church, spread throughout all the world,
may persevere with steadfast faith in confessing your name.
Through Christ our Lord. ***Amen.***

For the Pope

Let us pray also for our most Holy Father Pope N.,
that our God and Lord,
who chose him for the Order of Bishops,
may keep him safe and unharmed for the Lord's holy Church,
to govern the holy People of God.
(Prayer in silence.)
Almighty ever-living God,
by whose decree all things are founded,
look with favor on our prayers
and in your kindness protect the Pope chosen for us,
that, under him, the Christian people,
governed by you their maker,
may grow in merit by reason of their faith.
Through Christ our Lord. ***Amen.***

For all orders and degrees of the faithful

Let us pray also for our Bishop N.,
for all Bishops, Priests, and Deacons of the Church
and for the whole of the faithful people.
(Prayer in silence.)
Almighty ever-living God,
by whose Spirit the whole body of the Church
is sanctified and governed,
hear our humble prayer for your ministers,
that, by the gift of your grace,
all may serve you faithfully.
Through Christ our Lord. ***Amen.***

For catechumens

Let us pray also for (our) catechumens,
that our God and Lord
may open wide the ears of their inmost hearts
and unlock the gates of his mercy,
that, having received forgiveness of all their sins
through the waters of rebirth,
they, too, may be one with Christ Jesus our Lord.
(Prayer in silence.)
Almighty ever-living God,
who make your Church ever fruitful with new offspring,
increase the faith and understanding of (our) catechumens,
that, reborn in the font of Baptism,
they may be added to the number of your adopted children.
Through Christ our Lord. ***Amen.***

For the unity of Christians

Let us pray also for all our brothers and sisters who believe in Christ,
that our God and Lord may be pleased,
as they live the truth,
to gather them together and keep them in his one Church.
(Prayer in silence.)
Almighty ever-living God,
who gather what is scattered
and keep together what you have gathered,
look kindly on the flock of your Son,
that those whom one Baptism has consecrated
may be joined together by integrity of faith
and united in the bond of charity.
Through Christ our Lord. ***Amen.***

For the Jewish people
Let us pray also for the Jewish people,
to whom the Lord our God spoke first,
that he may grant them to advance in love of his name
and in faithfulness to his covenant.
(Prayer in silence.)
Almighty ever-living God,
who bestowed your promises on Abraham and his descendants,
graciously hear the prayers of your Church,
that the people you first made your own
may attain the fullness of redemption.
Through Christ our Lord. ***Amen.***

For those who do not believe in Christ
Let us pray also for those who do not believe in Christ,
that, enlightened by the Holy Spirit,
they, too, may enter on the way of salvation.
(Prayer in silence.)
Almighty ever-living God,
grant to those who do not confess Christ
that, by walking before you with a sincere heart,
they may find the truth
and that we ourselves, being constant in mutual love
and striving to understand more fully the mystery of your life,
may be made more perfect witnesses to your love in the world.
Through Christ our Lord. ***Amen.***

For those who do not believe in God
Let us pray also for those who do not acknowledge God,
that, following what is right in sincerity of heart,

they may find the way to God himself.
(Prayer in silence.)
Almighty ever-living God,
who created all people
to seek you always by desiring you
and, by finding you, come to rest,
grant, we pray,
that, despite every harmful obstacle,
all may recognize the signs of your fatherly love
and the witness of the good works
done by those who believe in you,
and so in gladness confess you,
the one true God and Father of our human race.
Through Christ our Lord. ***Amen.***

For those in public office
Let us pray also for those in public office,
that our God and Lord
may direct their minds and hearts according to his will
for the true peace and freedom of all.
(Prayer in silence.)
Almighty ever-living God,
in whose hand lies every human heart
and the rights of peoples,
look with favor, we pray,
on those who govern with authority over us,
that throughout the whole world,
the prosperity of peoples,
the assurance of peace,
and freedom of religion

may through your gift be made secure.
Through Christ our Lord. ***Amen.***

For those in tribulation
Let us pray, dearly beloved,
to God the Father almighty,
that he may cleanse the world of all errors,
banish disease, drive out hunger,
unlock prisons, loosen fetters,
granting to travelers safety, to pilgrims return,
health to the sick, and salvation to the dying.
(Prayer in silence.)
Almighty ever-living God,
comfort of mourners, strength of all who toil,
may the prayers of those who cry out in any tribulation
come before you,
that all may rejoice,
because in their hour of need
your mercy was at hand.
Through Christ our Lord. ***Amen.***

ADORATION OF THE HOLY CROSS

Three times the celebrant invites the assembly to proclaim its faith:

Behold the wood of the Cross,
on which hung the salvation of the world.
Come, let us adore.
After each response all venerate the cross briefly in silence. After the third response, the people approach to venerate the cross. They make a simple

genuflection or perform some other appropriate sign of reverence according to local custom.

During the veneration, appropriate songs may be sung. All who have venerated the cross return to their places and sit. Where large numbers of people make individual veneration difficult, the celebrant may raise the cross briefly for all to venerate in silence.

HOLY COMMUNION

THE LORD'S PRAYER *(page 53)*

PRAYER AFTER COMMUNION

Almighty ever-living God,
who have restored us to life
by the blessed Death and Resurrection of your Christ,
preserve in us the work of your mercy,

TAKING A CLOSER LOOK

✝ **I AM** These words have multiple levels of meaning. In everyday conversation, Jesus' statement "I am he" (John 4:26) would simply identify him as the one sought. The "I AM" of Exodus 3:14 (in capital letters) is God's personal name, *Yahweh*, which was closely related to the verb "I am." When Jesus says these words, his adversaries understand their deeper meaning, that Jesus shares God's power and, as Jesus says later to Pilate (John 19:11), they have no power over him unless he willingly permits it. It also accounts for the response of the soldiers and guards who fall to the ground, indicating that something more was being understood (John 18:3-6).

that, by partaking of this mystery,
we may have a life unceasingly devoted to you.
Through Christ our Lord. ***Amen.***

PRAYER OVER THE PEOPLE

May abundant blessing, O Lord, we pray,
descend upon your people,
who have honored the Death of your Son
in the hope of their resurrection:
may pardon come,
comfort be given,
holy faith increase,
and everlasting redemption be made secure.
Through Christ our Lord. ***Amen.***

All depart in silence.

Responding to the Word

The suffering of God's servant is hard for Isaiah to understand.

How does suffering make me more aware of who I am and of who God is for me?

Jesus shares our human weakness but never lets that create a separation from God.

What weakness or suffering has tempted me to question God's love for me?

John's narrative contrasts Jesus and the other characters—including Peter, the Jewish leaders, Pilate, and the crowds.

Which of these other characters do I feel most like today?

March 27

Proclaim Christ's triumph

On this "night of nights," we celebrate the resurrection of Jesus Christ, the climax in an epic narrative of salvation history with a curiously open-ended conclusion. That story—running from Creation through the Exodus and the messianic expectation of the later prophets—culminates in the paschal mystery of Jesus Christ, the suffering servant, crucified and now risen.

The angel's proclamation is brief and no doubt startling. He tells the women—the same women who had been present at the crucifixion—that Jesus is risen, that he goes before them, and that they will meet him again. They are told to proclaim this Good News to the disciples and Peter: but instead, they leave bewildered, even frightened.

The story seems to end here—but we know this episode is not the last word. All of us who gather here tonight—those about to be baptized into Christ's death and resurrection as well as those who will renew their baptismal promises—are invited to continue this story, to make it our own. As disciples of Jesus Christ, we are called to proclaim his triumph over sin and death, to shine the light of love and compassion in a world too often marked by darkness and division. How will you respond this Easter season?

Nick Olkovich

There is no Mass celebrated during the day on Holy Saturday. But during the night, we anticipate Jesus' resurrection with one of the most ancient rites—a solemn vigil, which leads into the celebration of the 50 days of the Easter Season.

The Easter Vigil is arranged in four parts: the Service of Light (Lucernarium), the Liturgy of the Word, the Liturgy of Baptism, and the Liturgy of the Eucharist.

LUCERNARIUM

BLESSING OF THE FIRE

Dear brethren (brothers and sisters),
on this most sacred night,
in which our Lord Jesus Christ
passed over from death to life,
the Church calls upon her sons and daughters,
scattered throughout the world,
to come together to watch and pray.
If we keep the memorial
of the Lord's paschal solemnity in this way,
listening to his word and celebrating his mysteries,
then we shall have the sure hope
of sharing his triumph over death
and living with him in God.

Let us pray.

O God, who through your Son
bestowed upon the faithful the fire of your glory,

sanctify this new fire, we pray,
and grant that,
by these paschal celebrations,
we may be so inflamed with heavenly desires,
that with minds made pure
we may attain festivities of unending splendor.
Through Christ our Lord. ***Amen.***

PREPARATION OF THE CANDLE

The celebrant cuts a cross in the Easter candle and traces the Greek letters alpha (Α) and omega (Ω) and the numerals 2027, saying:

Christ yesterday and today;
the Beginning and the End;
the Alpha; and the Omega.
All time belongs to him;
and all the ages.
To him be glory and power;
through every age and for ever. Amen.

When the marks have been made, the celebrant may insert five grains of incense in the candle, saying:

By his holy and glorious wounds,
may Christ the Lord guard us and protect us. Amen.

LIGHTING OF THE CANDLE

The celebrant lights the Easter candle from the new fire, saying:

May the light of Christ rising in glory
dispel the darkness of our hearts and minds.

PROCESSION WITH THE EASTER CANDLE

The priest or deacon takes the Easter candle and, three times during the procession to the altar, lifts it high and sings alone. Then the people respond.

The Light of Christ.
Thanks be to God.

EASTER PROCLAMATION *(Exsultet)*

For the shorter version, omit the indented parts in brackets.

Exult, let them exult, the hosts of heaven,
exult, let Angel ministers of God exult,
let the trumpet of salvation
sound aloud our mighty King's triumph!
Be glad, let earth be glad, as glory floods her,
ablaze with light from her eternal King,
let all corners of the earth be glad,
knowing an end to gloom and darkness.
Rejoice, let Mother Church also rejoice,
arrayed with the lightning of his glory,
let this holy building shake with joy,
filled with the mighty voices of the peoples.

> [(Therefore, dearest friends,
> standing in the awesome glory of this holy light,
> invoke with me, I ask you,
> the mercy of God almighty,
> that he, who has been pleased to number me,
> though unworthy, among the Levites,
> may pour into me his light unshadowed,
> that I may sing this candle's perfect praises).]

(The Lord be with you.
And with your spirit.)
Lift up your hearts.
We lift them up to the Lord.
Let us give thanks to the Lord our God.
It is right and just.

It is truly right and just,
with ardent love of mind and heart
and with devoted service of our voice,
to acclaim our God invisible, the almighty Father,
and Jesus Christ, our Lord, his Son, his Only Begotten.

Who for our sake paid Adam's debt to the eternal Father,
and, pouring out his own dear Blood,
wiped clean the record of our ancient sinfulness.

These then are the feasts of Passover,
in which is slain the Lamb, the one true Lamb,
whose Blood anoints the doorposts of believers.

This is the night,
when once you led our forebears, Israel's children,
from slavery in Egypt
and made them pass dry-shod through the Red Sea.

This is the night
that with a pillar of fire
banished the darkness of sin.

This is the night
that even now, throughout the world,
sets Christian believers apart from worldly vices

and from the gloom of sin,
leading them to grace
and joining them to his holy ones.

This is the night,
when Christ broke the prison-bars of death
and rose victorious from the underworld.

[Our birth would have been no gain,
had we not been redeemed.]
O wonder of your humble care for us!
O love, O charity beyond all telling,
to ransom a slave you gave away your Son!

O truly necessary sin of Adam,
destroyed completely by the Death of Christ!

O happy fault
that earned so great, so glorious a Redeemer!

[O truly blessed night,
worthy alone to know the time and hour
when Christ rose from the underworld!

This is the night
of which it is written:
The night shall be as bright as day,
dazzling is the night for me,
and full of gladness.]

The sanctifying power of this night
dispels wickedness, washes faults away,
restores innocence to the fallen, and joy to mourners,
[drives out hatred, fosters concord, and brings down the mighty.]

The longer version ending:

On this, your night of grace, O holy Father,
accept this candle, a solemn offering,
the work of bees and of your servants' hands,
an evening sacrifice of praise,
this gift from your most holy Church.

But now we know the praises of this pillar,
which glowing fire ignites for God's honor,
a fire into many flames divided,
yet never dimmed by sharing of its light,
for it is fed by melting wax,
drawn out by mother bees
to build a torch so precious.

O truly blessed night,
when things of heaven are wed to those of earth,
and divine to the human.

Therefore, O Lord,
we pray you that this candle,
hallowed to the honor of your name,
may persevere undimmed,
to overcome the darkness of this night.
Receive it as a pleasing fragrance,
and let it mingle with the lights of heaven.
May this flame be found still burning
by the Morning Star:
the one Morning Star who never sets,
Christ your Son,
who, coming back from death's domain,

has shed his peaceful light on humanity,
and lives and reigns for ever and ever. ***Amen.***

The shorter version ending:

O truly blessed night,
when things of heaven are wed to those of earth
and divine to the human.

On this, your night of grace, O holy Father,
accept this candle, a solemn offering,
the work of bees and of your servants' hands,
an evening sacrifice of praise,
this gift from your most holy Church.

Therefore, O Lord,
we pray you that this candle,
hallowed to the honor of your name,
may persevere undimmed,
to overcome the darkness of this night.
Receive it as a pleasing fragrance,
and let it mingle with the lights of heaven.
May this flame be found still burning
by the Morning Star:
the one Morning Star who never sets,
Christ your Son,
who, coming back from death's domain,
has shed his peaceful light on humanity,
and lives and reigns for ever and ever. ***Amen.***

LITURGY OF THE WORD

Dear brethren (brothers and sisters),
now that we have begun our solemn Vigil,
let us listen with quiet hearts to the Word of God.
Let us meditate on how God in times past saved his people
and in these, the last days, has sent us his Son as our Redeemer.
Let us pray that our God may complete this paschal work
of salvation
by the fullness of redemption.

FIRST READING *(Genesis 1:1–2:2 or 1:1, 26–31a)*
For the shorter version, omit the indented parts in brackets.

In the beginning, when God created the heavens and the earth, [the earth was a formless wasteland, and darkness covered the abyss, while a mighty wind swept over the waters.

Then God said, "Let there be light," and there was light. God saw how good the light was. God then separated the light from the darkness. God called the light "day," and the darkness he called "night." Thus evening came, and morning followed—the first day.

Then God said, "Let there be a dome in the middle of the waters, to separate one body of water from the other." And so it happened: God made the dome, and it separated the water above the dome from the water below it. God called the dome "the sky." Evening came, and morning followed—the second day.

Then God said, "Let the water under the sky be gathered into a single basin, so that the dry land may appear." And so it happened: the water under the sky was gathered into its basin, and the dry land appeared. God called the dry land "the earth," and the basin of the water he called "the sea." God saw how good it was. Then God said, "Let the earth bring forth vegetation: every kind of plant that bears seed and every kind of fruit tree on earth that bears fruit with its seed in it." And so it happened: the earth brought forth every kind of plant that bears seed and every kind of fruit tree on earth that bears fruit with its seed in it. God saw how good it was. Evening came, and morning followed—the third day.

Then God said: "Let there be lights in the dome of the sky, to separate day from night. Let them mark the fixed times, the days and the years, and serve as luminaries in the dome of the sky, to shed light upon the earth." And so it happened: God made the two great lights, the greater one to govern the day, and the lesser one to govern the night; and he made the stars. God set them in the dome of the sky, to shed light upon the earth, to govern the day and the night, and to separate the light from the darkness. God saw how good it was. Evening came, and morning followed—the fourth day.

Then God said, "Let the water teem with an abundance of living creatures, and on the earth let birds fly beneath the dome of the sky." And so it happened: God created the great sea monsters and all kinds of swimming creatures with which the water teems, and all kinds of winged birds. God saw how good it was, and God blessed them, saying, "Be fertile, multiply, and fill the water of the seas; and let the birds multiply on the earth." Evening came, and morning followed—the fifth day.

Then God said, "Let the earth bring forth all kinds of living creatures: cattle, creeping things, and wild animals of all kinds." And so it happened: God made all kinds of wild animals, all kinds of cattle, and all kinds of creeping things of

the earth. God saw how good it was. Then]
God said: "Let us make man in our image, after our likeness. Let them have dominion over the fish of the sea, the birds of the air, and the cattle, and over all the wild animals and all the creatures that crawl on the ground."

God created man in his image;
in the image of God he created him;
male and female he created them.

God blessed them, saying: "Be fertile and multiply; fill the earth and subdue it. Have dominion over the fish of the sea, the birds of the air, and all the living things that move on the earth." God also said: "See, I give you every seed-bearing plant all over the earth and every tree that has seed-bearing fruit on it to be your food; and to all the animals of the land, all the birds of the air, and all the living creatures that crawl on the ground, I give all the green plants for food." And so it happened. God looked at everything he had made, and he found it very good.

[Evening came, and morning followed—the sixth day.

Thus the heavens and the earth and all their array were completed. Since on the seventh day God was finished with the work he had been doing, he rested on the seventh day from all the work he had undertaken.]

The word of the Lord. ***Thanks be to God.***

An alternate psalm follows.

RESPONSORIAL PSALM *(Psalm 104:1-2, 5-6, 10, 12, 13-14, 24, 35)*

℟. Lord, send out your Spirit, and renew the face of the earth.

Bless the LORD, O my soul!
O LORD, my God, you are great indeed!
You are clothed with majesty and glory,

robed in light as with a cloak. ℟
You fixed the earth upon its foundation,
not to be moved forever;
with the ocean, as with a garment, you covered it;
above the mountains the waters stood. ℟
You send forth springs into the watercourses
that wind among the mountains.
Beside them the birds of heaven dwell;
from among the branches they send forth their song. ℟
You water the mountains from your palace;
the earth is replete with the fruit of your works.
You raise grass for the cattle,
and vegetation for man's use,
producing bread from the earth. ℟
How manifold are your works, O LORD!
In wisdom you have wrought them all—
the earth is full of your creatures.
Bless the LORD, O my soul! ℟

OR

RESPONSORIAL PSALM *(Psalm 33:4-5, 6-7, 12-13, 20 and 22)*
℟ The earth is full of the goodness of the Lord.

Upright is the word of the LORD,
and all his works are trustworthy.
He loves justice and right;
of the kindness of the LORD the earth is full. ℟
By the word of the LORD the heavens were made;
by the breath of his mouth all their host.
He gathers the waters of the sea as in a flask;
in cellars he confines the deep. ℟

Blessed the nation whose God is the LORD,
 the people he has chosen for his own inheritance.
From heaven the LORD looks down;
 he sees all mankind.
℟. The earth is full of the goodness of the Lord.
Our soul waits for the LORD,
 who is our help and our shield.
May your kindness, O LORD, be upon us
 who have put our hope in you. ℟.

PRAYER

Almighty ever-living God,
who are wonderful in the ordering of all your works,
may those you have redeemed understand
that there exists nothing more marvelous
than the world's creation in the beginning
except that, at the end of the ages,
Christ our Passover has been sacrificed.
Who lives and reigns for ever and ever. ***Amen.***

Or

O God, who wonderfully created human nature
and still more wonderfully redeemed it,
grant us, we pray,
to set our minds against the enticements of sin,
that we may merit to attain eternal joys.
Through Christ our Lord. ***Amen.***

SECOND READING *(Genesis 22:1–18 or 22:1–2, 9a, 10–13, 15–18)*
For the shorter version, omit the indented parts in brackets.

God put Abraham to the test. He called to him, "Abraham!" "Here I am," he replied. Then God said: "Take your son Isaac, your only one, whom you love, and go to the land of Moriah.* There you shall offer him up as a holocaust on a height that I will point out to you."

> [Early the next morning Abraham saddled his donkey, took with him his son Isaac and two of his servants as well, and with the wood that he had cut for the holocaust, set out for the place of which God had told him.
>
> On the third day Abraham got sight of the place from afar. Then he said to his servants: "Both of you stay here with the donkey, while the boy and I go on over yonder. We will worship and then come back to you." Thereupon Abraham took the wood for the holocaust and laid it on his son Isaac's shoulders, while he himself carried the fire and the knife. As the two walked on together, Isaac spoke to his father Abraham: "Father!" Isaac said. "Yes, son," he replied. Isaac continued, "Here are the fire and the wood, but where is the sheep for the holocaust?" "Son," Abraham answered, "God himself will provide the sheep for the holocaust." Then the two continued going forward.]

When they came to the place of which God had told him, Abraham built an altar there and arranged the wood on it.

> [Next he tied up his son Isaac, and put him on top of the wood on the altar.]

Then he reached out and took the knife to slaughter his son. But the LORD's messenger called to him from heaven, "Abraham, Abraham!" "Here I am," he answered. "Do not lay your hand on the boy," said the messenger. "Do not do the least thing to him.

I know now how devoted you are to God, since you did not withhold from me your own beloved son." As Abraham looked about, he spied a ram caught by its horns in the thicket. So he went and took the ram and offered it up as a holocaust in place of his son.

[Abraham named the site Yahweh-yireh;* hence people now say, "On the mountain the LORD will see."]

Again the LORD's messenger called to Abraham from heaven and said: "I swear by myself, declares the LORD, that because you acted as you did in not withholding from me your beloved son, I will bless you abundantly and make your descendants as countless as the stars of the sky and the sands of the seashore; your descendants shall take possession of the gates of their enemies, and in your descendants all the nations of the earth shall find blessing—all this because you obeyed my command."

The word of the Lord. ***Thanks be to God.***

RESPONSORIAL PSALM *(Psalm 16:5, 8, 9-10, 11)*

℟. You are my inheritance, O Lord.

O LORD, my allotted portion and my cup,
you it is who hold fast my lot.
I set the LORD ever before me;
with him at my right hand I shall not be disturbed. ℟.
Therefore my heart is glad and my soul rejoices,
my body, too, abides in confidence;
because you will not abandon my soul to the netherworld,
nor will you suffer your faithful one to undergo corruption. ℟.
You will show me the path to life,
fullness of joys in your presence,
the delights at your right hand forever. ℟.

PRAYER

O God, supreme Father of the faithful,
who increase the children of your promise
by pouring out the grace of adoption
throughout the whole world
and who through the Paschal Mystery
make your servant Abraham father of nations,
as once you swore,
grant, we pray,
that your peoples may enter worthily
into the grace to which you call them.
Through Christ our Lord. ***Amen.***

THIRD READING *(Exodus 14:15–15:1)*

The LORD said to Moses, "Why are you crying out to me? Tell the Israelites to go forward. And you, lift up your staff and, with hand outstretched over the sea, split the sea in two, that the Israelites may pass through it on dry land. But I will make the Egyptians so obstinate that they will go in after them. Then I will receive glory through Pharaoh and all his army, his chariots and charioteers. The Egyptians shall know that I am the LORD, when I receive glory through Pharaoh and his chariots and charioteers."

The angel of God, who had been leading Israel's camp, now moved and went around behind them. The column of cloud also, leaving the front, took up its place behind them, so that it came between the camp of the Egyptians and that of Israel. But the cloud now became dark, and thus the night passed without the rival camps coming any closer together all night long. Then Moses stretched out his hand over the sea, and the LORD swept the sea with a strong east wind throughout the night and so turned it into dry land. When the water was thus divided, the

Israelites marched into the midst of the sea on dry land, with the water like a wall to their right and to their left.

The Egyptians followed in pursuit; all Pharaoh's horses and chariots and charioteers went after them right into the midst of the sea. In the night watch just before dawn the LORD cast through the column of the fiery cloud upon the Egyptian force a glance that threw it into a panic; and he so clogged their chariot wheels that they could hardly drive. With that the Egyptians sounded the retreat before Israel, because the LORD was fighting for them against the Egyptians.

Then the LORD told Moses, "Stretch out your hand over the sea, that the water may flow back upon the Egyptians, upon their chariots and their charioteers." So Moses stretched out his hand over the sea, and at dawn the sea flowed back to its normal depth. The Egyptians were fleeing head on toward the sea, when the LORD hurled them into its midst. As the water flowed back, it covered the chariots and the charioteers of Pharaoh's whole army which had followed the Israelites into the sea. Not a single one of them escaped. But the Israelites had marched on dry land through the midst of the sea, with the water like a wall to their right and to their left. Thus the LORD saved Israel on that day from the power of the Egyptians. When Israel saw the Egyptians lying dead on the seashore and beheld the great power that the LORD had shown against the Egyptians, they feared the LORD and believed in him and in his servant Moses.

Then Moses and the Israelites sang this song to the LORD:
I will sing to the LORD, for he is gloriously triumphant;
horse and chariot he has cast into the sea.
The word of the Lord. ***Thanks be to God.***

RESPONSORIAL CANTICLE *(Exodus 15:1-2, 3-4, 5-6, 17-18)*

℟ Let us sing to the Lord; he has covered himself in glory.

I will sing to the LORD, for he is gloriously triumphant;
horse and chariot he has cast into the sea.
My strength and my courage is the LORD,
and he has been my savior.
He is my God, I praise him;
the God of my father, I extol him. ℟
The LORD is a warrior,
LORD is his name!
Pharaoh's chariots and army he hurled into the sea;
the elite of his officers were submerged in the Red Sea. ℟
The flood waters covered them,
they sank into the depths like a stone.
Your right hand, O LORD, magnificent in power,
your right hand, O LORD, has shattered the enemy. ℟
You brought in the people you redeemed
and planted them on the mountain of your inheritance—
the place where you made your seat, O LORD,
the sanctuary, LORD, which your hands established.
The LORD shall reign forever and ever. ℟

PRAYER

O God, whose ancient wonders
remain undimmed in splendor even in our day,
for what you once bestowed on a single people,
freeing them from Pharaoh's persecution
by the power of your right hand,
now you bring about as the salvation of the nations
through the waters of rebirth,

grant, we pray, that the whole world
may become children of Abraham
and inherit the dignity of Israel's birthright.
Through Christ our Lord. ***Amen.***

Or

O God, who by the light of the New Testament
have unlocked the meaning
of wonders worked in former times,
so that the Red Sea prefigures the sacred font
and the nation delivered from slavery
foreshadows the Christian people,
grant, we pray, that all nations,
obtaining the privilege of Israel by merit of faith,
may be reborn by partaking of your Spirit.
Through Christ our Lord. ***Amen.***

FOURTH READING *(Isaiah 54:5–14)*

The One who has become your husband is your Maker;
his name is the LORD of hosts;
your redeemer is the Holy One of Israel,
called God of all the earth.
The LORD calls you back,
like a wife forsaken and grieved in spirit,
a wife married in youth and then cast off,
says your God.
For a brief moment I abandoned you,
but with great tenderness I will take you back.
In an outburst of wrath, for a moment
I hid my face from you;
but with enduring love I take pity on you,

says the LORD, your redeemer.
This is for me like the days of Noah,
when I swore that the waters of Noah
should never again deluge the earth;
so I have sworn not to be angry with you,
or to rebuke you.
Though the mountains leave their place
and the hills be shaken,
my love shall never leave you
nor my covenant of peace be shaken,
says the LORD, who has mercy on you.
O afflicted one, storm-battered and unconsoled,
I lay your pavements in carnelians,
and your foundations in sapphires;
I will make your battlements of rubies,
your gates of carbuncles,
and all your walls of precious stones.
All your children shall be taught by the LORD,
and great shall be the peace of your children.
In justice shall you be established,
far from the fear of oppression,
where destruction cannot come near you.
The word of the Lord. ***Thanks be to God.***

RESPONSORIAL PSALM *(Psalm 30:2, 4, 5-6, 11-12, 13)*
℟. I will praise you, Lord, for you have rescued me.

I will extol you, O LORD, for you drew me clear
and did not let my enemies rejoice over me.
O LORD, you brought me up from the netherworld;
you preserved me from among those going down into the pit. ℟.

Sing praise to the LORD, you his faithful ones,
  and give thanks to his holy name.
For his anger lasts but a moment;
  a lifetime, his good will.
At nightfall, weeping enters in,
  but with the dawn, rejoicing.
℟. I will praise you, Lord, for you have rescued me.
Hear, O LORD, and have pity on me;
  O LORD, be my helper.
You changed my mourning into dancing;
  O LORD, my God, forever will I give you thanks. ℟.

PRAYER

Almighty ever-living God,
surpass, for the honor of your name,
what you pledged to the Patriarchs by reason of their faith,
and through sacred adoption increase the children of your promise,
so that what the Saints of old never doubted would come to pass
your Church may now see in great part fulfilled.
Through Christ our Lord. *Amen.*

FIFTH READING *(Isaiah 55:1-11)*

Thus says the LORD:
  All you who are thirsty,
    come to the water!
  You who have no money,
    come, receive grain and eat;
  come, without paying and without cost,
    drink wine and milk!
  Why spend your money for what is not bread,
    your wages for what fails to satisfy?

Heed me, and you shall eat well,
 you shall delight in rich fare.
Come to me heedfully,
 listen, that you may have life.
I will renew with you the everlasting covenant,
 the benefits assured to David.
As I made him a witness to the peoples,
 a leader and commander of nations,
so shall you summon a nation you knew not,
 and nations that knew you not shall run to you,
because of the LORD, your God,
 the Holy One of Israel, who has glorified you.

Seek the LORD while he may be found,
 call him while he is near.
Let the scoundrel forsake his way,
 and the wicked man his thoughts;
let him turn to the LORD for mercy;
 to our God, who is generous in forgiving.
For my thoughts are not your thoughts,
 nor are your ways my ways, says the LORD.
As high as the heavens are above the earth,
 so high are my ways above your ways
 and my thoughts above your thoughts.

For just as from the heavens
 the rain and snow come down
and do not return there
 till they have watered the earth,
 making it fertile and fruitful,
giving seed to the one who sows

and bread to the one who eats,
so shall my word be
that goes forth from my mouth;
my word shall not return to me void,
but shall do my will,
achieving the end for which I sent it.
The word of the Lord. ***Thanks be to God.***

RESPONSORIAL CANTICLE *(Isaiah 12:2–3, 4, 5–6)*

℟ You will draw water joyfully from the springs of salvation.

God indeed is my savior;
I am confident and unafraid.
My strength and my courage is the LORD,
and he has been my savior.
With joy you will draw water
at the fountain of salvation. ℟
Give thanks to the LORD, acclaim his name;
among the nations make known his deeds,
proclaim how exalted is his name. ℟
Sing praise to the LORD for his glorious achievement;
let this be known throughout all the earth.
Shout with exultation, O city of Zion,*
for great in your midst
is the Holy One of Israel! ℟

PRAYER

Almighty ever-living God,
sole hope of the world,
who by the preaching of your Prophets
unveiled the mysteries of this present age,
graciously increase the longing of your people,

for only at the prompting of your grace
do the faithful progress in any kind of virtue.
Through Christ our Lord. ***Amen.***

SIXTH READING *(Baruch 3:9–15, 32–4:4)*

Hear, O Israel, the commandments of life:
listen, and know prudence!
How is it, Israel,
that you are in the land of your foes,
grown old in a foreign land,
defiled with the dead,
accounted with those destined for the netherworld?
You have forsaken the fountain of wisdom!
Had you walked in the way of God,
you would have dwelt in enduring peace.
Learn where prudence is,
where strength, where understanding;
that you may know also
where are length of days, and life,
where light of the eyes, and peace.
Who has found the place of wisdom,
who has entered into her treasuries?

The One who knows all things knows her;
he has probed her by his knowledge—
the One who established the earth for all time,
and filled it with four-footed beasts;
he who dismisses the light, and it departs,
calls it, and it obeys him trembling;
before whom the stars at their posts
shine and rejoice;

when he calls them, they answer, "Here we are!"
shining with joy for their Maker.
Such is our God;
no other is to be compared to him:
he has traced out the whole way of understanding,
and has given her to Jacob, his servant,
to Israel, his beloved son.

Since then she has appeared on earth,
and moved among people.
She is the book of the precepts of God,
the law that endures forever;
all who cling to her will live,
but those will die who forsake her.
Turn, O Jacob, and receive her:
walk by her light toward splendor.
Give not your glory to another,
your privileges to an alien race.
Blessed are we, O Israel;
for what pleases God is known to us!
The word of the Lord. ***Thanks be to God.***

RESPONSORIAL PSALM *(Psalm 19:8, 9, 10, 11)*

℟. Lord, you have the words of everlasting life.

The law of the LORD is perfect,
refreshing the soul;
the decree of the LORD is trustworthy,
giving wisdom to the simple. ℟.
The precepts of the LORD are right,
rejoicing the heart;
the command of the LORD is clear,

enlightening the eye. ℟.
The fear of the LORD is pure,
enduring forever;
the ordinances of the LORD are true,
all of them just. ℟.
They are more precious than gold,
than a heap of purest gold;
sweeter also than syrup
or honey from the comb. ℟.

PRAYER

O God, who constantly increase your Church
by your call to the nations,
graciously grant
to those you wash clean in the waters of Baptism
the assurance of your unfailing protection.
Through Christ our Lord. ***Amen.***

SEVENTH READING *(Ezekiel 36:16-17a, 18-28)*

The word of the LORD came to me, saying: Son of man, when the house of Israel lived in their land, they defiled it by their conduct and deeds. Therefore I poured out my fury upon them because of the blood that they poured out on the ground, and because they defiled it with idols. I scattered them among the nations, dispersing them over foreign lands; according to their conduct and deeds I judged them. But when they came among the nations wherever they came, they served to profane my holy name, because it was said of them: "These are the people of the LORD, yet they had to leave their land." So I have relented because of my holy name which the house of Israel profaned among the nations where they came. Therefore say to the house of Israel: Thus says the Lord GOD: Not for your sakes do I act, house of Israel, but for the sake of my holy name, which you profaned among the nations to which you came. I will prove the holiness of my great name, profaned among the nations, in whose midst you have profaned it. Thus the nations shall know that I am the LORD, says the Lord GOD, when in their sight I prove my holiness through you. For I will take you away from among the nations, gather you from all the foreign lands, and bring you back to your own land. I will sprinkle clean water upon you to cleanse you from all your impurities, and from all your idols I will cleanse you. I will give you a new heart and place a new spirit within you, taking from your bodies your stony hearts and giving you natural hearts. I will put my spirit within you and make you live by my statutes, careful to observe my decrees. You shall live in the land I gave your fathers; you shall be my people, and I will be your God.

The word of the Lord. ***Thanks be to God.***

When baptism is celebrated, sing Psalm 42/43 (below); when baptism is not celebrated, sing Isaiah 12 (from after the Fifth Reading, page 312) or Psalm 51 (page 317).

RESPONSORIAL PSALM *(Psalm 42:3, 5; 43:3, 4)*

℟ **Like a deer that longs for running streams,**
my soul longs for you, my God.

Athirst is my soul for God, the living God.
When shall I go and behold the face of God? ℟
I went with the throng
and led them in procession to the house of God,
amid loud cries of joy and thanksgiving,

with the multitude keeping festival. ℟.
Send forth your light and your fidelity;
they shall lead me on
and bring me to your holy mountain,
to your dwelling-place. ℟.
Then will I go in to the altar of God,
the God of my gladness and joy;
then will I give you thanks upon the harp,
O God, my God! ℟.

OR

RESPONSORIAL PSALM *(Psalm 51:12-13, 14-15, 18-19)*
℟. Create a clean heart in me, O God.

A clean heart create for me, O God,
and a steadfast spirit renew within me.
Cast me not out from your presence,
and your Holy Spirit take not from me. ℟.
Give me back the joy of your salvation,
and a willing spirit sustain in me.
I will teach transgressors your ways,
and sinners shall return to you. ℟.
For you are not pleased with sacrifices;
should I offer a holocaust, you would not accept it.
My sacrifice, O God, is a contrite spirit;
a heart contrite and humbled, O God, you will not spurn. ℟.

PRAYER
O God of unchanging power and eternal light,
look with favor on the wondrous mystery of the whole Church
and serenely accomplish the work of human salvation,

which you planned from all eternity;
may the whole world know and see
that what was cast down is raised up,
what had become old is made new,
and all things are restored to integrity through Christ,
just as by him they came into being.
Who lives and reigns for ever and ever. ***Amen.***

Or

O God, who by the pages of both Testaments
instruct and prepare us to celebrate the Paschal Mystery,
grant that we may comprehend your mercy,
so that the gifts we receive from you this night
may confirm our hope of the gifts to come.
Through Christ our Lord. ***Amen.***

GLORY TO GOD *(page 12)*

COLLECT

O God, who make this most sacred night radiant
with the glory of the Lord's Resurrection,
stir up in your Church a spirit of adoption,
so that, renewed in body and mind,
we may render you undivided service.
Through our Lord Jesus Christ, your Son,
who lives and reigns with you in the unity of the Holy Spirit,
God, for ever and ever. ***Amen.***

EPISTLE *(Romans 6:3–11)*

Brothers and sisters: Are you unaware that we who were baptized into Christ Jesus were baptized into his death? We were indeed buried with him through baptism into death, so that, just as Christ was raised from the dead by the glory of the Father, we too might live in newness of life.

For if we have grown into union with him through a death like his, we shall also be united with him in the **resurrection.**✝ We know that our old self was crucified with him, so that our sinful body might be done away with, that we might no longer be in slavery to sin. For a dead person has been absolved from sin. If, then, we have died with Christ, we believe that we shall also live with him. We know that Christ, raised from the dead, dies no more; death no longer has power over him. As to his death, he died to sin once and for all; as to his life, he lives for God. Consequently, you too must think of yourselves as being dead to sin and living for God in Christ Jesus.

The word of the Lord. ***Thanks be to God.***

RESPONSORIAL PSALM *(Psalm 118:1-2, 16-17, 22-23)*

℟. Alleluia, alleluia, alleluia.

Give thanks to the LORD, for he is good,
 for his mercy endures forever.
Let the house of Israel say,
 "His mercy endures forever." **℟.**
The right hand of the LORD has struck with power;
 the right hand of the LORD is exalted.
I shall not die, but live,
 and declare the works of the LORD. **℟.**
The stone which the builders rejected
 has become the cornerstone.
By the LORD has this been done;
 it is wonderful in our eyes. **℟.**

GOSPEL *(Mark 16:1-7)*
A reading from the holy Gospel according to Mark.
Glory to you, O Lord.

When the sabbath was over, Mary Magdalene, Mary, the mother of James, and Salome* bought spices so that they might go and anoint him. Very early when the sun had risen, on the first day of the week, they came to the tomb. They were saying to one another, "Who will roll back the stone for us from the entrance to the tomb?" When they looked up, they saw that the stone had been rolled back; it was very large. On entering the tomb they saw a young man sitting on the right side, clothed in a white robe, and they were utterly amazed. He said to them, "Do not be amazed! You seek Jesus of Nazareth, the crucified. He has been raised; he is not here. Behold the place where they laid him. But go and tell his disciples and Peter, 'He is going before you to Galilee; there you will see him, as he told you.' "

The Gospel of the Lord. ***Praise to you, Lord Jesus Christ.***

LITURGY OF BAPTISM

INVITATION

When baptism is celebrated:

Dearly beloved,
with one heart and one soul, let us by our prayers
come to the aid of these our brothers and sisters
in their blessed hope,
so that, as they approach the font of rebirth,
the almighty Father may bestow on them
all his merciful help.

When baptism is not celebrated, but the font is blessed:

Dearly beloved,
let us humbly invoke upon this font
the grace of God the almighty Father,
that those who from it are born anew
may be numbered among the children of adoption in Christ.

If baptism is not celebrated and the font is not blessed, proceed to the blessing of the water outside of baptism *(page 325).*

LITANY OF SAINTS

Lord, have mercy. ***Lord, have mercy.***
Christ, have mercy. ***Christ, have mercy.***
Lord, have mercy. ***Lord, have mercy.***

Holy Mary, Mother of God, ***pray for us.***

Saint Michael, ***pray for us.***
Holy Angels of God,
Saint John the Baptist,
Saint Joseph,
Saint Peter and Saint Paul,
Saint Andrew,
Saint John,
Saint Mary Magdalene,
Saint Stephen,
Saint Ignatius of Antioch,
Saint Lawrence,
Saint Perpetua
  and Saint Felicity,
Saint Agnes,
Saint Gregory,
Saint Augustine,
Saint Athanasius,
Saint Basil,
Saint Martin,
Saint Benedict,
Saint Francis
  and Saint Dominic,
Saint Francis Xavier,
Saint John Vianney,
Saint Catherine of Siena,
Saint Teresa of Jesus,
All holy men and women,
  Saints of God,

Lord, be merciful.
Lord, deliver us, we pray.
From all evil,
From every sin,
From everlasting death,
By your Incarnation,
By your Death and Resurrection,
By the outpouring of the Holy Spirit,

Be merciful to us sinners,
Lord, we ask you, hear our prayer.

When baptism is celebrated add:

Bring these chosen ones to new birth through the grace of Baptism,
Lord, we ask you, hear our prayer.

Or, when baptism is not celebrated:

Make this font holy by your grace for the new birth of your children,
Lord, we ask you, hear our prayer.

Jesus, Son of the living God,
Lord, we ask you, hear our prayer.
Christ, hear us.
Christ, hear us.
Christ, graciously hear us.
Christ, graciously hear us.

When baptism is celebrated, the priest prays:

Almighty ever-living God,
be present by the mysteries of your great love
and send forth the spirit of adoption
to create the new peoples
brought to birth for you in the font of Baptism,
so that what is to be carried out by our humble service
may be brought to fulfillment by your mighty power.
Through Christ our Lord. ***Amen.***

BLESSING OF BAPTISMAL WATER

O God, who by invisible power
accomplish a wondrous effect
through sacramental signs
and who in many ways have prepared water, your creation,
to show forth the grace of Baptism;

O God, whose Spirit
in the first moments of the world's creation
hovered over the waters,

so that the very substance of water
would even then take to itself the power to sanctify;

O God, who by the outpouring of the flood
foreshadowed regeneration,
so that from the mystery of one and the same element of water
would come an end to vice and a beginning of virtue;

O God, who caused the children of Abraham
to pass dry-shod through the Red Sea,
so that the chosen people,
set free from slavery to Pharaoh,
would prefigure the people of the baptized;

O God, whose Son,
baptized by John in the waters of the Jordan,
was anointed with the Holy Spirit,
and, as he hung upon the Cross,
gave forth water from his side along with blood,
and after his Resurrection, commanded his disciples:
"Go forth, teach all nations, baptizing them
in the name of the Father and of the Son and of the Holy Spirit,"
look now, we pray, upon the face of your Church
and graciously unseal for her the fountain of Baptism.

May this water receive by the Holy Spirit
the grace of your Only Begotten Son,
so that human nature, created in your image
and washed clean through the Sacrament of Baptism
from all the squalor of the life of old,
may be found worthy to rise to the life of newborn children
through water and the Holy Spirit.

May the power of the Holy Spirit,
O Lord, we pray,
come down through your Son
into the fullness of this font,
so that all who have been buried with Christ
by Baptism into death
may rise again to life with him.
Who lives and reigns with you in the unity of the Holy Spirit,
one God, for ever and ever. ***Amen.***

Springs of water, bless the Lord;
praise and exalt him above all for ever.

Baptism is now conferred, and for adults, Confirmation follows immediately after. Those already baptized in another Christian tradition are formally received into full communion with the Catholic Church before being confirmed.

If there is no baptism and the font is not blessed, the priest blesses the water and invites the assembly to renew their baptismal commitment:

THE BLESSING OF WATER *(OUTSIDE OF BAPTISM)*

Dear brothers and sisters,
let us humbly beseech the Lord our God
to bless this water he has created,
which will be sprinkled upon us
as a memorial of our Baptism.
May he graciously renew us,
that we may remain faithful to the Spirit
whom we have received.

Lord our God,
in your mercy be present to your people

who keep vigil on this most sacred night,
and, for us who recall the wondrous work of our creation
and the still greater work of our redemption,
graciously bless this water.
For you created water to make the fields fruitful
and to refresh and cleanse our bodies.
You also made water the instrument of your mercy:
for through water you freed your people from slavery
and quenched their thirst in the desert;
through water the Prophets proclaimed the new covenant
you were to enter upon with the human race;
and last of all,
through water, which Christ made holy in the Jordan,
you have renewed our corrupted nature
in the bath of regeneration.
Therefore, may this water be for us
a memorial of the Baptism we have received,
and grant that we may share
in the gladness of our brothers and sisters,
who at Easter have received their Baptism.
Through Christ our Lord. ***Amen.***

When the Rite of Baptism (and Confirmation) has been completed or, if this has not taken place, after the blessing of water, all stand, holding lighted candles in their hands, and renew the promise of baptismal faith, unless this has already been done together with those to be baptized.

RENEWAL OF BAPTISMAL PROMISES

Dear brethren (brothers and sisters), through the Paschal Mystery
we have been buried with Christ in Baptism,
so that we may walk with him in newness of life.

And so, now that our Lenten observance is concluded,
let us renew the promises of Holy Baptism,
by which we once renounced Satan and his works
and promised to serve God in the holy Catholic Church.
And so I ask you:

1 Do you renounce Satan? ***I do.***
And all his works? ***I do.***
And all his empty show? ***I do.***

2 Do you renounce sin,
so as to live in the freedom of the children of God? ***I do.***
Do you renounce the lure of evil,
so that sin may have no mastery over you? ***I do.***
Do you renounce Satan,
the author and prince of sin? ***I do.***

PROFESSION OF FAITH

Do you believe in God, the Father almighty,
Creator of heaven and earth? ***I do.***

Do you believe in Jesus Christ, his only Son, our Lord,
who was born of the Virgin Mary,
suffered death and was buried,
rose again from the dead
and is seated at the right hand of the Father? ***I do.***

Do you believe in the Holy Spirit,
the holy catholic Church,
the communion of saints,
the forgiveness of sins,
the resurrection of the body,
and life everlasting? ***I do.***

And may almighty God, the Father of our Lord Jesus Christ,
who has given us new birth by water and the Holy Spirit
and bestowed on us forgiveness of our sins,
keep us by his grace,
in Christ Jesus our Lord,
for eternal life. ***Amen.***

SPRINKLING WITH BAPTISMAL WATER

The priest sprinkles all the people with the blessed baptismal water, while an appropriate song may be sung.

PRAYER OF THE FAITHFUL

LITURGY OF THE EUCHARIST

PREPARATION OF GIFTS *(page 16)*

PRAYER OVER THE OFFERINGS

Accept, we ask, O Lord,
the prayers of your people
with the sacrificial offerings,
that what has begun in the paschal mysteries
may, by the working of your power,
bring us to the healing of eternity.
Through Christ our Lord. ***Amen.***

PREFACE *(Easter 1, page 24)*

COMMUNION ANTIPHON *(1 Corinthians 5:7–8)*
Christ our Passover has been sacrificed; / therefore let us keep the feast / with the unleavened bread of purity and truth, alleluia.

PRAYER AFTER COMMUNION
Pour out on us, O Lord, the Spirit of your love,
and in your kindness make those you have nourished
by this paschal Sacrament
one in mind and heart.
Through Christ our Lord. ***Amen.***

SOLEMN BLESSING: MASS OF THE EASTER VIGIL
May almighty God bless you
through today's Easter Solemnity
and, in his compassion,
defend you from every assault of sin. ***Amen.***

• TAKING A CLOSER LOOK •

+ **Resurrection** What happened on Easter was a complete surprise to the disciples. The Jesus that they had known and who had died was suddenly experienced as alive again. This new life, described as resurrection, was not just a restoration of one's former life—a resuscitation from the dead. The prophets Elijah and Elisha had brought people back to this life, as had Jesus for the daughter of Jairus, the son of the widow of Nain, and Jesus' beloved friend Lazarus. Although their return from the dead left them temporarily alive, they would die again. Jesus' resurrection was a new life that would not be subject to death again. It was eternal life, permanent and undying existence in the presence of God forever.

And may he, who restores you to eternal life
in the Resurrection of his Only Begotten,
endow you with the prize of immortality. ***Amen.***

Now that the days of the Lord's Passion have drawn to a close,
may you who celebrate the gladness of the Paschal Feast
come with Christ's help, and exulting in spirit,
to those feasts that are celebrated in eternal joy. ***Amen.***

And may the blessing of almighty God,
the Father, and the Son, and the Holy Spirit,
come down on you and remain with you for ever. ***Amen.***

DISMISSAL *(page 57)*

Responding to the Word

The Old Testament readings recall the whole story of God's desire to create a covenant community that would follow God's guidelines.

➔ *What word, phrase, or idea in these readings most interested me tonight?*

Paul reminds us that, through our relationship with Jesus, we are drawn into the mystery of life and death and new life.

➔ *What hint of new life is beginning in me at this Easter time?*

The three women do not find Jesus' body, but they are told he is risen and where to meet him.

➔ *Where have I met or experienced the risen Jesus most clearly in my life?*

March 28

Let us rejoice and be glad!

Less than half a mile along the Via Dolorosa from the Antonia Fortress where Pilate judged Jesus to Calvary, and another half mile to the garden tomb: this short distance marked the final earthly journey of Jesus. Or so his followers thought. Another passage took place between Good Friday and Easter morning: a redemptive one.

The Sabbath was over when Mary Magdalene made her way to the garden tomb early that first Easter morning. The horror of the last days had brought doubt and fear. Her hope crushed, would the forces of repression and violence that claimed Jesus now come for her and the disciples? Still, she went. Grief-bound, she needed to be close to him. She found the tomb empty. Profound loss now turned to desperation. Where had they taken him?

Are we also bound by doubt and fear, unable to see? Today's growing crises afflicting our world—climate change, violence, rampant injustices—can make it difficult for us to recognize the presence of Jesus and his promise. Has fear overwhelmed us, too?

Peter and the other discipe returned to the tomb and found the burial cloths. And they believed, their hope restored.

Let us rejoice and be glad!

■ Michael Dougherty

ENTRANCE ANTIPHON *(Cf. Psalm 139 (138):18, 5-6)*
I have risen, and I am with you still, alleluia. / You have laid your hand upon me, alleluia. / Too wonderful for me, this knowledge, alleluia, alleluia.

Or *(Luke 24:34; cf. Revelation 1:6)*
The Lord is truly risen, alleluia. / To him be glory and power / for all the ages of eternity, alleluia, alleluia.

INTRODUCTORY RITES *(page 10)*

COLLECT
O God, who on this day,
through your Only Begotten Son,
have conquered death
and unlocked for us the path to eternity,
grant, we pray, that we who keep
the solemnity of the Lord's Resurrection
may, through the renewal brought by your Spirit,
rise up in the light of life.
Through our Lord Jesus Christ, your Son,
who lives and reigns with you in the unity of the Holy Spirit,
God, for ever and ever. ***Amen.***

FIRST READING *(Acts 10:34a, 37-43)*
Peter proceeded to speak and said: "You know what has happened all over Judea, beginning in Galilee after the baptism that John preached, how God anointed Jesus of Nazareth with the Holy Spirit and power. He went about doing good and healing all those oppressed by the devil, for God was with him. We are witnesses of all that he did both in the country of the Jews and in Jerusalem. They put him to death by hanging him on a

tree. This man God raised on the third day and granted that he be visible, not to all the people, but to us, the witnesses chosen by God in advance, who ate and drank with him after he rose from the dead. He commissioned us to preach to the people and testify that he is the one appointed by God as judge of the living and the dead. To him all the prophets bear witness, that everyone who believes in him will receive forgiveness of sins through his name."

The word of the Lord. ***Thanks be to God.***

RESPONSORIAL PSALM *(Psalm 118:1-2, 16-17, 22-23)*

℟. This is the day the Lord has made; let us rejoice and be glad.
Or **Alleluia.**

Give thanks to the LORD, for he is good,
for his mercy endures forever.
Let the house of Israel say,
"His mercy endures forever." **℟.**
"The right hand of the LORD has struck with power;
the right hand of the LORD is exalted.
I shall not die, but live,
and declare the works of the LORD." **℟.**
The stone which the builders rejected
has become the cornerstone.
By the LORD has this been done;
it is wonderful in our eyes. **℟.**

An alternate reading follows.

SECOND READING *(Colossians 3:1–4)*

Brothers and sisters: If then you were raised with Christ, seek what is above, where Christ is seated at the right hand of God. Think of what is above, not of what is on earth. For you have died, and your life is hidden with Christ in God. When Christ your life appears, then you too will appear with him in glory.

The word of the Lord. ***Thanks be to God.***

OR

SECOND READING *(1 Corinthians 5:6b–8)*

Brothers and sisters: Do you not know that a little yeast leavens all the dough? Clear out the old yeast, so that you may become a fresh batch of dough, inasmuch as you are unleavened. For our paschal lamb, Christ, has been sacrificed. Therefore, let us celebrate the feast, not with the old yeast, the yeast of malice and wickedness, but with the unleavened bread of sincerity and truth.

The word of the Lord. ***Thanks be to God.***

SEQUENCE

Christians, to the Paschal Victim
Offer your thankful praises!
A Lamb the sheep redeems;
Christ, who only is sinless,
Reconciles sinners to the Father.
Death and life have contended in that combat stupendous:
The Prince of life, who died, reigns immortal.
Speak, Mary, declaring
What you saw, wayfaring.
"The tomb of Christ, who is living,
The glory of Jesus' resurrection;

Bright angels attesting,
  The shroud and napkin resting.
Yes, Christ my hope is arisen;
  To Galilee he goes before you."
Christ indeed from death is risen, our new life obtaining.
  Have mercy, victor King, ever reigning!
  Amen. Alleluia.

ALLELUIA *(See 1 Corinthians 5:7b–8a)*
Alleluia, alleluia. Christ, our paschal lamb, has been sacrificed; / let us then feast with joy in the Lord. ***Alleluia, alleluia.***

The gospel from the Easter Vigil (Mark 16:1-7, page 320) may be read instead. For an afternoon or evening Mass, Luke 24:13-35 (page 336) may be used.

GOSPEL *(John 20:1–9)*
A reading from the holy Gospel according to John.
Glory to you, O Lord.

On the first day of the week, Mary of Magdala came to **the tomb**✝ early in the morning, while it was still dark, and saw the stone removed from the tomb. So she ran and went to Simon Peter and to the other disciple whom Jesus loved, and told them, "They have taken the Lord from the tomb, and we don't know where they put him." So Peter and the other disciple went out and came to the tomb. They both ran, but the other disciple ran faster than Peter and arrived at the tomb first; he bent down and saw the burial cloths there, but did not go in. When Simon Peter arrived after him, he went into the tomb and saw the burial cloths there, and the cloth that had covered his head, not with the burial cloths but rolled up in a separate place.

Then the other disciple also went in, the one who had arrived at the tomb first, and he saw and believed. For they did not yet understand the Scripture that he had to rise from the dead.

The Gospel of the Lord. ***Praise to you, Lord Jesus Christ.***

Alternate reading for an afternoon or evening Mass:

GOSPEL *(Luke 24:13–35)*
A reading from the holy Gospel according to Luke.
Glory to you, Lord.

That very day, the first day of the week, two of Jesus' disciples were going to a village seven miles from Jerusalem called Emmaus, and they were conversing about all the things that had occurred. And it happened that while they were conversing and debating, Jesus himself drew near and walked with them, but their eyes were prevented from recognizing him. He asked them, "What are you discussing as you walk along?" They stopped, looking downcast. One of them, named Cleopas, said to him in reply, "Are you the only visitor to Jerusalem who does not know of the things that have taken place there in these days?" And he replied to them, "What sort of things?" They said to him, "The things that happened to Jesus the Nazarene, who was a prophet mighty in deed and word before God and all the people, how our chief priests and rulers both handed him over to a sentence of death and crucified him. But we were hoping that he would be the one to redeem Israel; and besides all this, it is now the third day since this took place. Some women from our group, however, have astounded us: they were at the tomb early in the morning and did not find his body; they came back and reported that they had indeed seen a vision of angels who announced that he was alive.

Then some of those with us went to the tomb and found things just as the women had described, but him they did not see." And he said to them, "Oh, how foolish you are! How slow of heart to believe all that the prophets spoke! Was it not necessary that the Christ should suffer these things and enter into his glory?" Then beginning with Moses and all the prophets, he interpreted to them what referred to him in all the Scriptures. As they approached the village to which they were going, he gave the impression that he was going on farther. But they urged him, "Stay with us, for it is nearly evening and the day is almost over." So he went in to stay with them. And it happened that, while he was with them at table, he took bread, said the blessing, broke it, and gave it to them. With that their eyes were opened and they recognized him, but he vanished from their sight. Then they said to each other, "Were not our hearts burning within us while he spoke to us on the way and opened the Scriptures to us?" So they set out at once and returned to Jerusalem where they found gathered together the eleven and those with them who were saying, "The Lord has truly been raised and has appeared to Simon!" Then the two recounted what had taken place on the way and how he was made known to them in the breaking of bread.

The Gospel of the Lord. ***Praise to you, Lord Jesus Christ.***

RENEWAL OF BAPTISMAL PROMISES AND PROFESSION OF FAITH

(See page 326)

In Easter Sunday Masses, the rite of the renewal of baptismal promises may take place after the homily, according to the text used at the Easter Vigil.

PRAYER OF THE FAITHFUL

PREPARATION OF GIFTS *(page 16)*

PRAYER OVER THE OFFERINGS

Exultant with paschal gladness, O Lord,
we offer the sacrifice
by which your Church
is wondrously reborn and nourished.
Through Christ our Lord. ***Amen.***

PREFACE *(Easter 1, page 24)*

TAKING A CLOSER LOOK

✝ **The tomb** What is most apparent from the resurrection accounts in the gospels is that the meaning of the event was not immediately intelligible. The empty tomb was not proof of the resurrection but a fact whose meaning needed to be discovered. Finding the empty tomb made Jesus' followers bewildered and confused, grasping for various possible answers to account for it. Only when the disciples experienced the risen Lord did the meaning of the empty tomb become clear. The stone was rolled back not so Jesus could get out, but so we could get in and be assured that his tomb of death will remain empty forever. He is risen!

COMMUNION ANTIPHON *(1 Corinthians 5:7-8)*
Christ our Passover has been sacrificed, alleluia; / therefore let us keep the feast with the unleavened bread / of purity and truth, alleluia, alleluia.

PRAYER AFTER COMMUNION
Look upon your Church, O God,
with unfailing love and favor,
so that, renewed by the paschal mysteries,
she may come to the glory of the resurrection.
Through Christ our Lord. ***Amen.***

SOLEMN BLESSING: MASS OF THE EASTER VIGIL *(Optional, page 329)*

DISMISSAL *(page 57)* ⁜

Responding to the Word

Peter summarizes the Christian motive for mission: when we experience the risen Christ, we proclaim this message to others.

➔ *How might I share my belief in Jesus' resurrection with others today?*

Our connection to the risen Christ influences all our behavior.

➔ *What is the biggest change that Christ's presence to me this Lent has made in my life?*

The risen Christ is always present with us but not always noticed.

➔ *How can I be more attentive to Christ's presence now?*

These fifty days are like one great Sunday

The season of Easter is actually a celebration of fifty days, from Easter until Pentecost. The word "Pentecost" means "fiftieth" and is the Greek translation of the Hebrew word *Shavuot*. *Shavuot*, the Jewish Feast of Weeks, began as a harvest festival in Canaan, coming approximately seven weeks after the first day of Passover.

What Sunday is to our Christian week, the Easter season is to the whole liturgical year. The fifty days of Easter have been observed longer than any other season of the Christian year. In the early Church, it was celebrated as an "unbroken Sunday," a week of weeks (7 times 7, or 49 days) plus the eighth day of the new creation. During these fifty days of joy, we are called upon in our life and worship to proclaim the lordship of Jesus revealed through his resurrection and ascension, and the outpouring of the Holy Spirit.

This season is a time to grow in our understanding of the paschal mystery and to make it part of our lives through our renewed attentiveness to God's word that we hear each Sunday and talk about in our households, through our fuller participation in the Eucharist, and through our renewed dedication to acts of charity and justice.

As we celebrate this season, we become more deeply aware of Christ's abiding but hidden presence with us that is daily transforming us into the image of Jesus.

Praying and living the Easter season

Since the Easter season is fifty days long, it will take some effort on our part to extend its celebration for the full seven weeks until Pentecost.

As Christians we each share in the Easter experience because we have in one way or another met the risen Christ and so become connected to the community that witnesses to the good news of his resurrection.

One way to make Easter into a season of celebrations and keep its spirit alive is to adopt the daily practice of using the Collect for Sunday as the gathering prayer for a household meal.

Another practice is to connect ourselves to the long chain of Christian witnesses that have preceded us. Gather your household or faith-sharing group and explain that when Paul locates himself in the Christian tradition, he creates a chain of witnesses connecting those who experienced Christ's first Easter appearance to himself.

Invite the household to bring this chain of witnesses from Paul's time down to our present time by naming those who have been most important in handing on the living tradition (e.g., family, relatives, friends, mentors, spiritual persons you have admired, patron saints, etc.).

Write down the names to create your household's or group's unique connection to the Easter tradition. To express your solidarity, share a sign of peace with one another. Then conclude by praying the Lord's Prayer together.

April 4

Jesus offers his incarnate mercy

When Pope John Paul II declared today Divine Mercy Sunday in 2000, he invited the world to recognize Christ as love and mercy personified. We are invited to remember that the generosity of God's love flows out through his tender mercy, which lifts the burden of our needs and has an immense capacity for forgiveness.

We hope that in our best moments, our marriage and family are akin to what the early Christians described in the first reading: a community dedicated to the common good, selflessly supporting each other in anticipation of Christ's return. In times of struggle, though, our marriage can feel like being locked in doubt like Thomas. When we feel stuck, we find consolation in remembering how Jesus helped Thomas move through fear by offering his incarnate mercy. Jesus' invocation of peace opens our hearts to forgive each other, our children, and ourselves.

It is not easy to love with a deep love that lies in the authentic gift of self. Today's gospel reminds all of us that this love flows to us freely through God's mercy. Christ's grace invites us into living mercy in our own relationships with an attitude of generosity, solidarity, and forgiveness. God's mercy overcomes fear and invites us, like Thomas, to joyfully believe and have life in Christ's name.

■ VANESSA & MICHAEL NICHOLAS-SCHMIDT

ENTRANCE ANTIPHON *(1 Peter 2:2)*
Like newborn infants, you must long for the pure, spiritual milk, / that in him you may grow to salvation, alleluia.

Or *(4 Esdras 2:36–37)*
Receive the joy of your glory, giving thanks to God, / who has called you into the heavenly kingdom, alleluia.

INTRODUCTORY RITES *(page 10)*

COLLECT
God of everlasting mercy,
who in the very recurrence of the paschal feast
kindle the faith of the people you have made your own,
increase, we pray, the grace you have bestowed,
that all may grasp and rightly understand
in what font they have been washed,
by whose Spirit they have been reborn,
by whose Blood they have been redeemed.
Through our Lord Jesus Christ, your Son,
who lives and reigns with you in the unity of the Holy Spirit,
God, for ever and ever. ***Amen.***

FIRST READING *(Acts 4:32–35)*
The community of believers was of one heart and mind, and no one claimed that any of his possessions was his own, but they had everything in common. With great power the apostles bore witness to the resurrection of the Lord Jesus, and great favor was accorded them all. There was no needy person among them, for those who owned property or houses would sell them, bring the proceeds of the sale, and put them at the feet of the

apostles, and they were distributed to each according to need.
The word of the Lord. ***Thanks be to God.***

RESPONSORIAL PSALM *(Psalm 118:2-4, 13-15, 22-24)*

℟. Give thanks to the Lord for he is good, his love is everlasting. *Or* **Alleluia.**

Let the house of Israel say,
"His **mercy endures forever.**" ✠
Let the house of Aaron say,
"His mercy endures forever."
Let those who fear the LORD say,
"His mercy endures forever." ℟.
I was hard pressed and was falling,
but the LORD helped me.
My strength and my courage is the LORD,
and he has been my savior.
The joyful shout of victory
in the tents of the just. ℟.
The stone which the builders rejected
has become the cornerstone.
By the LORD has this been done;
it is wonderful in our eyes.
This is the day the LORD has made;
let us be glad and rejoice in it. ℟.

SECOND READING *(1 John 5:1-6)*

Beloved: Everyone who believes that Jesus is the Christ is begotten by God, and everyone who loves the Father loves also the one begotten by him. In this way we know that we love the children of God when we love God and obey his commandments. For the love of God is this, that we keep his commandments. And his commandments are not burdensome, for whoever is begotten by God conquers the world. And the victory that conquers the world is our faith. Who indeed is the victor over the world but the one who believes that Jesus is the Son of God?

This is the one who came through water and blood, Jesus Christ, not by water alone, but by water and blood. The Spirit is the one that testifies, and the Spirit is truth.

The word of the Lord. ***Thanks be to God.***

ALLELUIA *(John 20:29)*

Alleluia, alleluia. You believe in me, Thomas, because you have seen me, says the Lord; / blessed are they who have not seen me, but still believe! ***Alleluia, alleluia.***

GOSPEL *(John 20:19-31)*

A reading from the holy Gospel according to John.

Glory to you, O Lord.

On the evening of that first day of the week, when the doors were locked, where the disciples were, for fear of the Jews, Jesus came and stood in their midst and said to them, "Peace be with you." When he had said this, he showed them his hands and his side. The disciples rejoiced when they saw the Lord. Jesus said to them again, "Peace be with you. As the Father has sent me, so I send you." And when he had said this, he breathed on them and said to them, "Receive the Holy Spirit. Whose sins you forgive are forgiven them, and whose sins you retain are retained."

Thomas, called Didymus, one of the Twelve, was not with them when Jesus came. So the other disciples said to him, "We have seen the Lord." But he said to them, "Unless I see the mark of the nails in his hands and put my finger into the nailmarks and put my hand into his side, I will not believe."

Now a week later his disciples were again inside and Thomas was with them. Jesus came, although the doors were locked, and stood in their midst and said, "Peace be with you." Then he said to Thomas, "Put your finger here and see my hands, and bring your hand and put it into my side, and do not be unbelieving, but believe." Thomas answered and said to him, "My Lord and my God!" Jesus said to him, "Have you come to believe because you have seen me? Blessed are those who have not seen and have believed."

Now Jesus did many other signs in the presence of his disciples that are not written in this book. But these are written that you may come to believe that Jesus is the Christ, the Son of God, and that through this belief you may have life in his name.

The Gospel of the Lord. ***Praise to you, Lord Jesus Christ.***

PROFESSION OF FAITH *(page 13)*

PRAYER OF THE FAITHFUL

PREPARATION OF GIFTS *(page 16)*

PRAYER OVER THE OFFERINGS

Accept, O Lord, we pray,
the oblations of your people
(and of those you have brought to new birth),
that, renewed by confession of your name and by Baptism,
they may attain unending happiness.
Through Christ our Lord. ***Amen.***

PREFACE *(Easter 1, page 24)*

TAKING A CLOSER LOOK

✝ **Mercy endures forever** In the Old Testament, mercy (Hebrew, *hesed*) usually identifies a complex Hebrew idea that describes God's special covenant love. God's desire to be in communion with us as covenant partners reveals an attitude of divine love and faithfulness that includes loyalty, compassion, dependability, trustworthiness, and an eagerness to help when situations turn bad. And once God commits to the people in covenant fidelity, there is no question of God ever retracting that commitment. So God's covenant love will never end—hence it can aptly be described as enduring forever, as in the words of today's psalm.

COMMUNION ANTIPHON *(Cf. John 20:27)*
Bring your hand and feel the place of the nails, / and do not be unbelieving but believing, alleluia.

PRAYER AFTER COMMUNION
Grant, we pray, almighty God,
that our reception of this paschal Sacrament
may have a continuing effect
in our minds and hearts.
Through Christ our Lord. ***Amen.***

SOLEMN BLESSING: EASTER TIME *(Optional, page 60)*

DISMISSAL *(page 57)* ⁜

Responding to the Word

The earliest Christian community was distinguished by its sharing of goods.

➡ *What sharing of my goods might I undertake this week?*

John knows that love can make obedience much easier.

➡ *How has love made keeping God's commandments easier at times for me?*

Thomas wanted proof rather than relying on the word of the other disciples.

➡ *When has it been difficult for me to trust the word of others about Jesus?*

April 11

APR 11

"Peace be with you"

In today's gospel, Jesus models a way forward for the disciples, past their fears and doubts. He knows their humanity and struggles. Why else would he appear so many times, guiding them in their understanding? "Peace be with you." His message reminds them that all will be okay. They are in his presence.

When we long for someone or we are grieving a loss, touch becomes a healing gesture. Jesus invites the disciples to touch him and see him. He shows them his wounds. In flesh and blood, he reminds them to believe in the hope that resurrection brings.

As people of faith, we are like the disciples in this moment. What about our fear of death and loss? How can we deal with the doubts we face? What meaning does God's forgiveness hold in our lives? God is always present, helping us again and again to return to the Scriptures, to come together in community, and to share a meal in his presence.

Like a family, we gather and break bread. We remember and we celebrate. This is where love is revealed and community is strengthened. Still struggling with our doubts and fears, Jesus comes to us, wounded with arms outstretched. We are gifted with Christ's presence in this Eucharist today.

JAN BENTHAM

ENTRANCE ANTIPHON *(Cf. Psalm 66 [65]:1-2)*
Cry out with joy to God, all the earth; / O sing to the glory of his name. / O render him glorious praise, alleluia.

INTRODUCTORY RITES *(page 10)*

COLLECT
May your people exult for ever, O God,
in renewed youthfulness of spirit,
so that, rejoicing now in the restored glory of our adoption,
we may look forward in confident hope
to the rejoicing of the day of resurrection.
Through our Lord Jesus Christ, your Son,
who lives and reigns with you in the unity of the Holy Spirit,
God, for ever and ever. ***Amen.***

FIRST READING *(Acts 3:13-15, 17-19)*
Peter said to the people: "The God of Abraham, the God of Isaac, and the God of Jacob, the God of our fathers, has glorified his servant Jesus, whom you handed over and denied in Pilate's presence when he had decided to release him. You denied the Holy and Righteous One and asked that a murderer be released to you. The author of life you put to death, but God raised him from the dead; of this we are witnesses. Now I know, brothers, that you acted out of ignorance, just as your leaders did; but God has thus brought to fulfillment what he had announced beforehand through the mouth of all the prophets, that his Christ would suffer. Repent, therefore, and be converted, that your sins may be wiped away."

The word of the Lord. ***Thanks be to God.***

RESPONSONIAL PSALM *(Psalm 4:2, 4, 7–8, 9)*

℟. Lord, let your face shine on us. *Or* **Alleluia.**

When I call, answer me, O my just God,
you who relieve me when I am in distress;
have pity on me, and hear my prayer! **℟.**
Know that the LORD does wonders for his faithful one;
the LORD will hear me when I call upon him. **℟.**
O LORD, let the light of your countenance shine upon us!
You put gladness into my heart. **℟.**
As soon as I lie down, I fall peacefully asleep,
for you alone, O LORD,
bring security to my dwelling. **℟.**

SECOND READING *(1 John 2:1–5a)*

My children, I am writing this to you so that you may not commit sin. But if anyone does sin, we have an Advocate with the Father, Jesus Christ the righteous one. He is expiation for our sins, and not for our sins only but for those of the whole world. The way we may be sure that we know him is to keep his commandments. Those who say, "I know him," but do not keep his commandments are liars, and the truth is not in them. But whoever keeps his word, the love of God is truly perfected in him.

The word of the Lord. ***Thanks be to God.***

ALLELUIA *(Luke 24:32)*

Alleluia, alleluia. Lord Jesus, open the Scriptures to us; / make our hearts burn while you speak to us. ***Alleluia, alleluia.***

GOSPEL *(Luke 24:35–48)*

A reading from the holy Gospel according to Luke.

Glory to you, O Lord.

The two disciples recounted what had taken place on the way, and how Jesus was made known to them in the breaking of bread.

While they were still speaking about this, he stood in their midst and said to them, "Peace be with you." But they were startled and terrified and thought that they were seeing a ghost. Then he said to them, "Why are you troubled? And why do questions arise in your hearts? Look at my hands and my feet, that it is I myself. Touch me and see, because a ghost does not have flesh and bones as you can see I have." And as he said this, he showed them his hands and his feet. While they were still incredulous for joy and were amazed, he asked them, "Have you anything here to eat?" They gave him a piece of baked fish; he took it and ate it in front of them.

He said to them, "These are my words that I spoke to you while I was still with you, that everything written about me **in the law of Moses and in the prophets and psalms**✝ must be fulfilled." Then he opened their minds to understand the Scriptures. And he said to them, "Thus it is written that the Christ would suffer and rise from the dead on the third day and that repentance, for the forgiveness of sins, would be preached in his name to all the nations, beginning from Jerusalem. You are witnesses of these things."

The Gospel of the Lord. ***Praise to you, Lord Jesus Christ.***

PROFESSION OF FAITH *(page 13)*

PRAYER OF THE FAITHFUL

PREPARATION OF GIFTS *(page 16)*

PRAYER OVER THE OFFERINGS

Receive, O Lord, we pray,
these offerings of your exultant Church,
and, as you have given her cause for such great gladness,
grant also that the gifts we bring
may bear fruit in perpetual happiness.
Through Christ our Lord. ***Amen.***

PREFACE *(Easter 1–5, pages 24–26)*

TAKING A CLOSER LOOK

+ In the law of Moses and in the prophets and psalms

This phrase summarizes the three general categories of Jewish sacred texts. The Law (Hebrew *Torah*, "instruction") consisted of the first five books of the Old Testament that tell of God's search for an appropriate covenant partner. The Prophets (*Nevi'im*) collected the prophetic stories and God's messages to the community. The Writings (*Ketuvim*) was a catch-all for everything else. It included the song book of the Psalms and wisdom writings for living a happy life. The first letter of each of these categories in Hebrew, T-N-K, forms the acronym that identifies the Jewish Scriptures as TaNaKh.

COMMUNION ANTIPHON *(Luke 24:35)*
The disciples recognized the Lord Jesus / in the breaking of the bread, alleluia.

Or Optional for Year B: *(Luke 24:46–47)*
The Christ had to suffer and on the third day rise from the dead; / in his name repentance and remission of sins / must be preached to all the nations, alleluia.

PRAYER AFTER COMMUNION
Look with kindness upon your people, O Lord,
and grant, we pray,
that those you were pleased to renew by eternal mysteries
may attain in their flesh
the incorruptible glory of the resurrection.
Through Christ our Lord. ***Amen.***

SOLEMN BLESSING: EASTER TIME *(Optional, page 60)*

DISMISSAL *(page 57)* ⁘

Responding to the Word

Peter encourages repentance—changing our lives to relate in a new way to God.

How can I continue the changes I began during Lent and grow in my relationships to God and others?

John joins together knowing Jesus and keeping his commandments.

How has my attempt to keep Jesus' commands helped me understand him better?

Jesus invites us to be witnesses of what we have experienced with him.

How might I share my love for Jesus with others today?

APR 18

April 18

Reflecting Jesus' love in the world

Here in the Gospel of John, Jesus describes his relationship with God's people using the metaphor of a shepherd. The description is of a personal relationship. It is one of deep care, commitment, and of great and free sacrifice. He sacrifices for his people and "will lay down his life." He knows them and they know him, "just as the Father knows me and I know the Father." The shepherding relationship described here reflects the dynamic within the love of the Trinity.

We are his people! We are truly known. We are cared for—sacrificed for completely, without reservation. We are loved with the unconditional, unending love-in-action of the Trinity. And we are called to reflect this love in the world, to know and care deeply for God's people. If we are like the hired hand, we might care for the sheep—but it's just a job and they are someone else's sheep. We would still look out for ourselves most of all.

We must become more like the Good Shepherd. If we are to respond to Jesus' call, we must learn from our relationship with him how to lay our own lives down. It is only by being in a deepening relationship with the Trinity that we begin to reflect Jesus' love-in-action for God's people.

KELLY BOURKE

ENTRANCE ANTIPHON *(Cf. Psalm 33 [32]:5-6)*
The merciful love of the Lord fills the earth; / by the word of the Lord the heavens were made, alleluia.

INTRODUCTORY RITES *(page 10)*

COLLECT
Almighty ever-living God,
lead us to a share in the joys of heaven,
so that the humble flock may reach
where the brave Shepherd has gone before.
Who lives and reigns with you in the unity of the Holy Spirit,
God, for ever and ever. ***Amen.***

FIRST READING *(Acts 4:8-12)*
Peter, filled with the Holy Spirit, said: "Leaders of the people and elders: If we are being examined today about a good deed done to a cripple, namely, by what means he was saved, then all of you and all the people of Israel should know that it was in the name of Jesus Christ the Nazorean whom you crucified, whom God raised from the dead; in his name this man stands before you healed. He is *the stone rejected by you, the builders, which has become the cornerstone.* There is no salvation through anyone else, nor is there any other name under heaven given to the human race by which we are to be saved."

The word of the Lord. ***Thanks be to God.***

RESPONSORIAL PSALM *(Psalm 118:1, 8-9, 21-23, 26, 28, 29)*

℟. The stone rejected by the builders has become the cornerstone. *Or* **Alleluia.**

Give thanks to the LORD, for he is good,
for his mercy endures forever.
It is better to take refuge in the LORD
than to trust in man.
It is better to take refuge in the LORD
than to trust in princes. ℟.

I will give thanks to you, for you have answered me
and have been my savior.
The stone which the builders rejected
has become the cornerstone.
By the LORD has this been done;
it is wonderful in our eyes. ℟.

Blessed is he who comes in the name of the LORD;
we bless you from the house of the LORD.
I will give thanks to you, for you have answered me
and have been my savior.
Give thanks to the LORD, for he is good;
for his kindness endures forever. ℟.

SECOND READING *(1 John 3:1-2)*

Beloved: See what love the Father has bestowed on us that we may be called the children of God. Yet so we are. The reason **the world**✢ does not know us is that it did not know him. Beloved, we are God's children now; what we shall be has not yet been revealed. We do know that when it is revealed we shall be like him, for we shall see him as he is.

The word of the Lord. ***Thanks be to God.***

ALLELUIA *(John 10:14)*
Alleluia, alleluia. I am the good shepherd, says the Lord; /
I know my sheep, and mine know me. ***Alleluia, alleluia.***

GOSPEL *(John 10:11–18)*
A reading from the holy Gospel according to John.
Glory to you, O Lord.

Jesus said: "I am the good shepherd. A good shepherd lays down his life for the sheep. A hired man, who is not a shepherd and whose sheep are not his own, sees a wolf coming and leaves the sheep and runs away, and the wolf catches and scatters them. This is because he works for pay and has no concern for the sheep. I am the good shepherd, and I know mine and mine know me, just as the Father knows me and I know the Father; and I will lay down my life for the sheep. I have other sheep that do not belong to this fold. These also I must lead, and they will hear my voice, and there will be one flock, one shepherd. This is why the Father loves me, because I lay down my life in order to take it up again. No one takes it from me, but I lay it down on my own. I have power to lay it down, and power to take it up again. This command I have received from my Father."

The Gospel of the Lord. ***Praise to you, Lord Jesus Christ.***

PROFESSION OF FAITH *(page 13)*

PRAYER OF THE FAITHFUL

PREPARATION OF GIFTS *(page 16)*

PRAYER OVER THE OFFERINGS

Grant, we pray, O Lord,
that we may always find delight in these paschal mysteries,
so that the renewal constantly at work within us
may be the cause of our unending joy.
Through Christ our Lord. ***Amen.***

PREFACE *(Easter 1-5, pages 24–26)*

COMMUNION ANTIPHON

The Good Shepherd has risen, / who laid down his life for his sheep / and willingly died for his flock, alleluia.

TAKING A CLOSER LOOK

✝ **The world** As so often in John's gospel and letters, many terms have two levels of meaning. Usually "the world" (Greek, *cosmos*) would describe the ordered quality of God's creation. But since John also sees a spiritual dimension to all of our existence, he uses "the world" as a shorthand way to refer to the forces that we often experience that resist the ordering power of God and so stand in opposition to Jesus and the Christian community. Though the world is hostile to God, God is not hostile to the world but sends Jesus "into the world" for its salvation.

PRAYER AFTER COMMUNION

Look upon your flock, kind Shepherd,
and be pleased to settle in eternal pastures
the sheep you have redeemed
by the Precious Blood of your Son.
Who lives and reigns for ever and ever. ***Amen.***

SOLEMN BLESSING: EASTER TIME *(Optional, page 60)*

DISMISSAL *(page 57)*

Responding to the Word

Peter knows that Jesus has the power to heal us.

What thanks can I give to Jesus for my healing (whether spiritual, physical, or emotional)?

John recognizes that we are all God's children.

How might this awareness change the way I deal with a difficult person at work or at school this week?

Jesus knows our uniqueness just like a shepherd knows his sheep.

How does it change me to know that Jesus loves me the way I am, and that he can help me be the person God wants me to be?

APR
25

April 25

Jesus is way, the truth, and the life

Today's gospel from John is a simple eight verses, repeating the word "remain" eight times. When I pray with this text, I breathe in deeply on the word "remain," and it feels as though I am resting in the palms of God's hands. *Remain in my love; remain in my peace; remain in my joy; remain in my hope.* As a prayer, close your eyes and repeat these four short phrases, adding your own name at the beginning or ending of each phrase.

We are so blessed to have an incarnate God who wants us to be content, deeply content. Living in the 50 days of Easter offers us a steadfast awareness that we are resurrection people, and Alleluia is our song!

Follow the truth of who Jesus is: Jesus is the way, the truth, and the life. He loves us as though we are the only one! "Ask for whatever you want and it will be done for you." Do we really believe this invitation? Do we believe that Jesus' love is completely given to us? What more does Jesus have to do, to convince us that his love is enough? As we move toward Pentecost, may the Holy Spirit ground us in the conviction of God's love for us personally. Amen.

Sr. Pat Carter, CSJ

ENTRANCE ANTIPHON *(Cf. Psalm 98 [97]:1-2)*
O sing a new song to the Lord, / for he has worked wonders; / in the sight of the nations / he has shown his deliverance, alleluia.

INTRODUCTORY RITES *(page 10)*

COLLECT
Almighty ever-living God,
constantly accomplish the Paschal Mystery within us,
that those you were pleased to make new in Holy Baptism
may, under your protective care, bear much fruit
and come to the joys of life eternal.
Through our Lord Jesus Christ, your Son,
who lives and reigns with you in the unity of the Holy Spirit,
God, for ever and ever. ***Amen.***

FIRST READING *(Acts 9:26-31)*
When Saul arrived in Jerusalem he tried to join the disciples, but they were all afraid of him, not believing that he was a disciple. Then Barnabas took charge of him and brought him to the apostles, and he reported to them how he had seen the Lord, and that he had spoken to him, and how in Damascus he had spoken out boldly in the name of Jesus. He moved about freely with them in Jerusalem, and spoke out boldly in the name of the Lord. He also spoke and debated with the **Hellenists,**✢ but they tried to kill him. And when the brothers learned of this, they took him down to Caesarea and sent him on his way to Tarsus.

The church throughout all Judea, Galilee, and Samaria was at peace. It was being built up and walked in the fear of the Lord, and with the consolation of the Holy Spirit it grew in numbers.

The word of the Lord. ***Thanks be to God.***

RESPONSORIAL PSALM *(Psalm 22:26-27, 28, 30, 31-32)*

℟. I will praise you, Lord, in the assembly of your people.
Or **Alleluia.**

I will fulfill my vows before those who fear the LORD.
The lowly shall eat their fill;
they who seek the LORD shall praise him:
"May your hearts live forever!" ℟.
All the ends of the earth
shall remember and turn to the LORD;
all the families of the nations
shall bow down before him. ℟.
To him alone shall bow down
all who sleep in the earth;
before him shall bend
all who go down into the dust. ℟.
And to him my soul shall live;
my descendants shall serve him.
Let the coming generation be told of the LORD
that they may proclaim to a people yet to be born
the justice he has shown. ℟.

SECOND READING *(1 John 3:18-24)*

Children, let us love not in word or speech but in deed and truth.

Now this is how we shall know that we belong to the truth and reassure our hearts before him in whatever our hearts condemn, for God is greater than our hearts and knows everything. Beloved, if our hearts do not condemn us, we have confidence in God and receive from him whatever we ask, because we keep his commandments and do what pleases him. And his commandment is this: we should believe in the name of his Son, Jesus Christ, and love one another just as he commanded us. Those who keep his commandments remain in him, and he in them, and the way we know that he remains in us is from the Spirit he gave us.

The word of the Lord. ***Thanks be to God.***

ALLELUIA *(John 15:4a, 5b)*

Alleluia, alleluia. Remain in me as I remain in you, says the Lord. / Whoever remains in me will bear much fruit. ***Alleluia, alleluia.***

GOSPEL *(John 15:1-8)*

A reading from the holy Gospel according to John.
Glory to you, O Lord.

Jesus said to his disciples: "I am the true vine, and my Father is the vine grower. He takes away every branch in me that does not bear fruit, and every one that does he prunes so that it bears more fruit. You are already pruned because of the word that I spoke to you. Remain in me, as I remain in you. Just as a branch cannot bear fruit on its own unless it remains on the vine, so neither can you unless you remain in me. I am the vine, you are the branches. Whoever remains in me and I in him will bear much fruit, because without me you can do nothing. Anyone who does not remain in me will be thrown out like a branch and wither; people will gather them and throw them into a fire and they will be burned. If you remain in me and my words remain in you, ask for whatever you want and it will be done for you. By this is my Father glorified, that you bear much fruit and become my disciples."

The Gospel of the Lord. ***Praise to you, Lord Jesus Christ.***

PROFESSION OF FAITH *(page 13)*

PRAYER OF THE FAITHFUL

PREPARATION OF GIFTS *(page 16)*

PRAYER OVER THE OFFERINGS
O God, who by the wonderful exchange effected in this sacrifice
have made us partakers of the one supreme Godhead,
grant, we pray,
that, as we have come to know your truth,
we may make it ours by a worthy way of life.
Through Christ our Lord. ***Amen.***

PREFACE *(Easter 1–5, pages 24–26)*

Taking a Closer Look

+ **Hellenists** "Hellenists" (from *Hellas*, Greek for Greece) were those from other nations who spoke Greek and were more receptive to the influence of Greek culture. Though the Romans ruled the Mediterranean nations, Greek literature and ideas formed the basis for education, and the Greek language was used for international communication and business. To be educated often meant to be able to speak and read Greek (like St. Paul and the other New Testament authors who all wrote in Greek). For Jews, Hellenism posed a threat because its education was rooted in religious beliefs and social values that were not compatible with the Jewish monotheistic belief that Yahweh was the one and only God.

COMMUNION ANTIPHON *(Cf. John 15:1, 5)*
I am the true vine and you are the branches, says the Lord. / Whoever remains in me, and I in him, bears fruit in plenty, alleluia.

PRAYER AFTER COMMUNION
Graciously be present to your people, we pray, O Lord,
and lead those you have imbued with heavenly mysteries
to pass from former ways to newness of life.
Through Christ our Lord. ***Amen.***

SOLEMN BLESSING: EASTER TIME *(Optional, page 60)*

DISMISSAL *(page 57)* ⁜

RESPONDING TO THE WORD

The disciples were afraid of Saul the persecutor and did not trust his "conversion."

What evidence do I trust to accept someone's religious sincerity?

John tells us that genuine love is shown not just in words but in everyday deeds.

When have my Christian words not been matched by my Christian deeds?

Jesus tells us that we can only survive if we join ourselves to his life.

What can I do this week to invite Jesus to "remain in me"?

Order By July 31 To Take Advantage Of Special Prepublication Pricing

- **GREAT GIFT** FOR YOUR LOVED ONES!
- **DISCOUNTS TO PARISHES** FOR MULTIPLE COPIES!

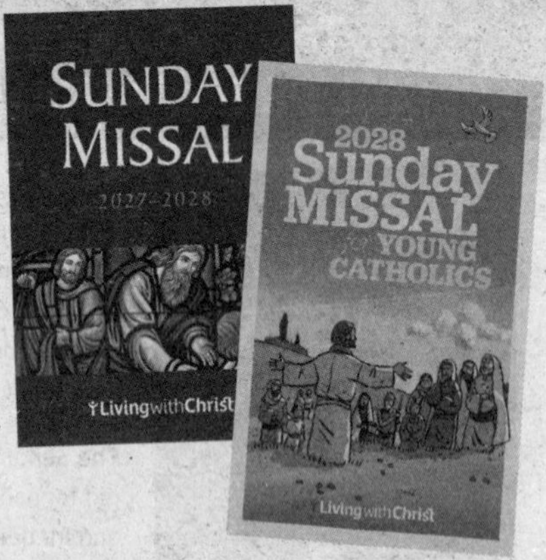

HOW TO ORDER

Call us at **1-800-321-0411**
(Please refer to LSM27P1-PVB when placing your order)

Online at
www.livingwithchrist.us/1missal

Sunday Readings are from the U.S. Lectionary. Missals will ship in October—in time for the first Sunday of Advent. All missals must ship to the same address for discounted pricing.

bayard *Living with Christ* is published by Bayard USA

May 2

Numbered among the beloved

The Easter season, for newly initiated Christians, is meant for reflection on what has happened to them (at the Easter Vigil, of course, but in their life of faith in general), and the entire Church stands in solidarity with them through the period of *mystagogy*, also pondering what it means to be numbered among the beloved of God.

That term, "beloved," by which we are addressed in today's second reading, is at the heart of what Jesus means by "friends." The idea of servanthood has not been lost, but to it has been added a new bond with Jesus that reflects his intimate union with the Father. Jesus is the beloved of the Father; we are the beloved of Jesus.

That these relationships are real is demonstrated every time we love others as Jesus loved us. Peter expanded his vision in response to the Spirit. The elder's community strove to allow the love of God to form and inform them in their every action and attitude.

Let us then also recall and take to heart that God sought us out and loved us first, that Jesus came to reveal and demonstrate that love, even to death on a cross, and that he remains faithful in his abiding presence: in the Eucharist, the gift of the Spirit, and every encounter of selfless love we experience.

CHRISTINE MADER

ENTRANCE ANTIPHON *(Cf. Isaiah 48:20)*
Proclaim a joyful sound and let it be heard; / proclaim to the ends of the earth: / The Lord has freed his people, alleluia.

INTRODUCTORY RITES *(page 10)*

COLLECT
Grant, almighty God,
that we may celebrate with heartfelt devotion these days of joy,
which we keep in honor of the risen Lord,
and that what we relive in remembrance
we may always hold to in what we do.
Through our Lord Jesus Christ, your Son,
who lives and reigns with you in the unity of the Holy Spirit,
God, for ever and ever. ***Amen.***

FIRST READING *(Acts 10:25-26, 34-35, 44-48)*
When Peter entered, Cornelius met him and, falling at his feet, paid him homage. Peter, however, raised him up, saying, "Get up. I myself am also a human being."

Then Peter proceeded to speak and said, "In truth, I see that God shows **no partiality.**✝ Rather, in every nation whoever fears him and acts uprightly is acceptable to him."

While Peter was still speaking these things, the Holy Spirit fell upon all who were listening to the word. The circumcised believers who had accompanied Peter were astounded that the gift of the Holy Spirit should have been poured out on the Gentiles also, for they could hear them speaking in tongues and glorifying God. Then Peter responded, "Can anyone withhold the water for baptizing these people, who have received the Holy Spirit even as we have?" He ordered them to be baptized in the name of Jesus Christ.

The word of the Lord. ***Thanks be to God.***

RESPONSORIAL PSALM *(Psalm 98:1, 2-3, 3-4)*

℟. The Lord has revealed to the nations his saving power.
Or **Alleluia.**

Sing to the LORD a new song,
for he has done wondrous deeds;
his right hand has won victory for him,
his holy arm. **℟.**
The LORD has made his salvation known:
in the sight of the nations he has revealed his justice.
He has remembered his kindness and his faithfulness
toward the house of Israel. **℟.**
All the ends of the earth have seen
the salvation by our God.
Sing joyfully to the LORD, all you lands;
break into song; sing praise. **℟.**

SECOND READING *(1 John 4:7-10)*

Beloved, let us love one another, because love is of God; everyone who loves is begotten by God and knows God. Whoever is without love does not know God, for God is love. In this way the love of God was revealed to us: God sent his only Son into the world so that we might have life through him. In this is love: not that we have loved God, but that he loved us and sent his Son as expiation for our sins.

The word of the Lord. ***Thanks be to God.***

ALLELUIA *(John 14:23)*
Alleluia, alleluia. Whoever loves me will keep my word, says the Lord, / and my Father will love him and we will come to him.
Alleluia, alleluia.

GOSPEL *(John 15:9–17)*
A reading from the holy Gospel according to John.
Glory to you, O Lord.

Jesus said to his disciples: "As the Father loves me, so I also love you. Remain in my love. If you keep my commandments, you will remain in my love, just as I have kept my Father's commandments and remain in his love.

"I have told you this so that my joy may be in you and your joy might be complete. This is my commandment: love one another as I love you. No one has greater love than this, to lay down one's life for one's friends. You are my friends if you do what I command you. I no longer call you slaves, because a slave does not know what his master is doing. I have called you friends, because I have told you everything I have heard from my Father. It was not you who chose me, but I who chose you and appointed you to go and bear fruit that will remain, so that whatever you ask the Father in my name he may give you. This I command you: love one another."

The Gospel of the Lord. ***Praise to you, Lord Jesus Christ.***

PROFESSION OF FAITH *(page 13)*

PRAYER OF THE FAITHFUL

PREPARATION OF GIFTS *(page 16)*

PRAYER OVER THE OFFERINGS
May our prayers rise up to you, O Lord,
together with the sacrificial offerings,
so that, purified by your graciousness,
we may be conformed to the mysteries of your mighty love.
Through Christ our Lord. ***Amen.***

PREFACE *(Easter 1-5, pages 24-26)*

TAKING A CLOSER LOOK

✝ **No partiality** In the first century, personal relationships were most often strictly voluntary and so were based on the benefactor's favoritism or partiality. A wealthy or powerful person (the benefactor) could freely choose who among many potential candidates would receive his or her favor or gift. In religious terms, God's partiality was revealed in the free choice of Israel from among all the nations to be God's covenant partner. Peter realized that he had misunderstood God's partiality as limiting the covenant relationship only to Jews. God actually shows no partiality but invites all humanity—both Jews and Gentiles—into the new covenant.

COMMUNION ANTIPHON *(John 14:15-16)*
If you love me, keep my commandments, says the Lord, / and I will ask the Father and he will send you another Paraclete, / to abide with you for ever, alleluia.

PRAYER AFTER COMMUNION
Almighty ever-living God,
who restore us to eternal life in the Resurrection of Christ,
increase in us, we pray, the fruits of this paschal Sacrament
and pour into our hearts the strength of this saving food.
Through Christ our Lord. ***Amen.***

SOLEMN BLESSING: EASTER TIME *(Optional, page 60)*

DISMISSAL *(page 57)*

RESPONDING TO THE WORD

Peter's life is changed when he realizes that God shows no partiality.

➡ *What might I do this week to notice and affirm God's love for those outside the Church?*

John summarizes God's whole existence as love—the power uniting us into a new community.

➡ *How might I imitate God's love in some small way by relating more deeply to others?*

Jesus challenges us to love others as we love him.

➡ *How might I respond to this challenge by my love for others at home, at work, or at school this week?*

May 6

All dioceses in the United States, except those within the ecclesiastical provinces of Boston, Hartford, New York, Philadelphia, and Omaha, transfer the celebration of the Ascension of the Lord from Thursday to this coming Sunday.

If the Ascension is celebrated on Thursday in your diocese, see the Mass for the Ascension on page 377. Then on Sunday use the Mass for the Seventh Sunday of Easter on page 383.

May 9

Embrace Christ's mission

We know the sorrow of saying goodbye to someone we love. The apostles were deeply saddened with Jesus' departure. Yet Jesus' leaving was not an act of abandonment but of trust. Jesus entrusted them, and us, with a greater mission: go out into the world and proclaim the Good News.

By ascending, Jesus became even more present in our hearts through the Holy Spirit. Like a relay, the baton of gospel values has been placed in our hands to pass on to others. Nobody is left behind. We are Christ's Body—the Church—commissioned to build God's kingdom here and now.

Carrying the baton of faith in our time requires courage, humility, and perseverance. Gathering for our eucharistic celebration gives us hope, strength, and sustenance. God's word nourishes our souls and receiving the Eucharist fuels us with Christ's love. With heartfelt thanks, we go forth renewed and reminded to be Christ's presence of love, mercy, and compassion bringing justice and healing to our suffering world.

Our Redeemer lives in our everyday lives and firmly within us. Let us embrace Christ's mission with resilience, leaving our legacy of faith and love as an enduring path for future generations.

■ Julie Cachia

THE ASCENSION OF THE LORD (MASS DURING THE DAY)

ENTRANCE ANTIPHON *(Acts 1:11)*
Men of Galilee, why gaze in wonder at the heavens? / This Jesus whom you saw ascending into heaven /will return as you saw him go, alleluia.

INTRODUCTORY RITES *(page 10)*

COLLECT
Gladden us with holy joys, almighty God,
and make us rejoice with devout thanksgiving,
for the Ascension of Christ your Son
is our exaltation,
and, where the Head has gone before in glory,
the Body is called to follow in hope.
Through our Lord Jesus Christ, your Son,
who lives and reigns with you in the unity of the Holy Spirit,
God, for ever and ever. ***Amen.***

Or
Grant, we pray, almighty God,
that we, who believe that your Only Begotten Son, our Redeemer,
ascended this day to the heavens,
may in spirit dwell already in heavenly realms.
Who lives and reigns with you in the unity of the Holy Spirit,
one God, for ever and ever. ***Amen.***

FIRST READING *(Acts 1:1-11)*
In the first book, Theophilus, I dealt with all that Jesus did and taught until the day he was taken up, after giving instructions

through the Holy Spirit to the apostles whom he had chosen. He presented himself alive to them by many proofs after he had suffered, appearing to them during forty days and speaking about the kingdom of God. While meeting with them, he enjoined them not to depart from Jerusalem, but to wait for "the promise of the Father about which you have heard me speak; for John baptized with water, but in a few days you will be baptized with the Holy Spirit."

When they had gathered together they asked him, "Lord, are you at this time going to restore the kingdom to Israel?" He answered them, "It is not for you to know the times or seasons that the Father has established by his own authority. But you will receive power when the Holy Spirit comes upon you, and you will be my witnesses in Jerusalem, throughout Judea and Samaria, and to the ends of the earth." When he had said this, as they were looking on, he was lifted up, and a cloud took him from their sight. While they were looking intently at the sky as he was going, suddenly two men dressed in white garments stood beside them. They said, "Men of Galilee, why are you standing there looking at the sky? This Jesus who has been taken up from you into heaven will return in the same way you have seen him going into heaven."

The word of the Lord. ***Thanks be to God.***

RESPONSORIAL PSALM *(Psalm 47:2-3, 6-7, 8-9)*

℟. God mounts his throne to shouts of joy: a blare of trumpets for the Lord. *Or* **Alleluia.**

All you peoples, clap your hands,
shout to God with cries of gladness.
For the LORD, the Most High, the awesome,
is the great king over all the earth. **℟.**
God mounts his throne amid shouts of joy;

the LORD, amid trumpet blasts.
Sing praise to God, sing praise;
sing praise to our king, sing praise. ℟.
For king of all the earth is God;
sing hymns of praise.
God reigns over the nations,
God sits upon his holy throne. ℟.

An alternate reading follows.

SECOND READING *(Ephesians 1:17–23)*

Brothers and sisters: May the God of our Lord Jesus Christ, the Father of glory, give you a Spirit of wisdom and revelation resulting in knowledge of him. May the eyes of your hearts be enlightened, that you may know what is the hope that belongs to his call, what are the riches of glory in his inheritance among the holy ones, and what is the surpassing greatness of his power for us who believe, in accord with the exercise of his great might: which he worked in Christ, raising him from the dead and seating him at his right hand in the heavens, far above every principality, authority, power, and dominion, and every name that is named not only in this age but also in the one to come. And he put all things beneath his feet and gave him as head over all things to the church, which is his body, the fullness of the one who fills all things in every way.

The word of the Lord. ***Thanks be to God.***

Or

SECOND READING *(Ephesians 4:1–13 or 4:1–7, 11–13)*

For the shorter version, omit the indented parts in brackets.

Brothers and sisters, I, a prisoner for the Lord, urge you to live in a manner worthy of the call you have received, with all humility and gentleness, with patience, bearing with one another through love, striving to preserve the unity of the Spirit through the bond of peace: one body and one Spirit, as you were also called to the one hope of your call; one Lord, one faith, one baptism; one God and Father of all, who is over all and through all and in all.

But grace was given to each of us according to the measure of Christ's gift.

[Therefore, it says:

He ascended on high and took prisoners captive;
he gave gifts to men.

What does "he ascended" mean except that he also descended into the lower regions of the earth? The one who descended is also the one who ascended far above all the heavens, that he might fill all things.]

And he gave some as apostles, others as prophets, others as evangelists, others as pastors and teachers, to equip the holy ones for the work of ministry, for building up the body of Christ, until we all attain to the unity of faith and knowledge of the Son of God, to mature manhood, to the extent of the full stature of Christ.

The word of the Lord. ***Thanks be to God.***

ALLELUIA *(Matthew 28:19a, 20b)*

Alleluia, alleluia. Go and teach all nations, says the Lord; / I am with you always, until the end of the world. ***Alleluia, alleluia.***

GOSPEL *(Mark 16:15–20)*

A reading from the holy Gospel according to Mark.

Glory to you, O Lord.

Jesus said to his disciples: "Go into the whole world and proclaim **the gospel**✝ to every creature. Whoever believes and is baptized will be saved; whoever does not believe will be condemned. These signs will accompany those who believe: in my name they will drive out demons, they will speak new languages. They will pick up serpents with their hands, and if they drink any deadly thing, it will not harm them. They will lay hands on the sick, and they will recover."

So then the Lord Jesus, after he spoke to them, was taken up into heaven and took his seat at the right hand of God. But they went forth and preached everywhere, while the Lord worked with them and confirmed the word through accompanying signs.

The Gospel of the Lord. ***Praise to you, Lord Jesus Christ.***

PROFESSION OF FAITH *(page 13)*

PRAYER OF THE FAITHFUL

PREPARATION OF GIFTS *(page 16)*

PRAYER OVER THE OFFERINGS

We offer sacrifice now in supplication, O Lord,
to honor the wondrous Ascension of your Son:
grant, we pray,

TAKING A CLOSER LOOK

✝ **The gospel** In everyday usage the word "gospel" (Greek, *evangelion*; Anglo-Saxon, *godspell*), meant "good news," often about an important event, such as the birthday of the emperor or a national victory in war. The Christian good news of Jesus Christ includes both his message about a new kind of community for all and his victory over the forces of evil, sin, and death by his resurrection. In the hands of the gospel writers, "gospel" became a unique Christian format for proclaiming the good news through the retelling of Jesus' life story.

that through this most holy exchange
we, too, may rise up to the heavenly realms.
Through Christ our Lord. ***Amen.***

PREFACE *(Ascension of the Lord 1-2, page 27)*

COMMUNION ANTIPHON *(Matthew 28:20)*
Behold, I am with you always, / even to the end of the age, alleluia.

PRAYER AFTER COMMUNION
Almighty ever-living God,
who allow those on earth to celebrate divine mysteries,
grant, we pray,
that Christian hope may draw us onward
to where our nature is united with you.
Through Christ our Lord. ***Amen.***

SOLEMN BLESSING: THE ASCENSION OF THE LORD *(Optional, page 61)*

DISMISSAL *(page 57)*

Responding to the Word

Jesus' ascension ends his time on earth but not his presence for salvation.

➡ *How might I witness to the good news of Jesus' abiding presence with us still?*

Paul asks that we grow in the knowledge of Christ and the new relationship he made possible with God.

➡ *What new insight about Christ has been most meaningful for me this Easter season?*

After his ascension, Jesus continued to work through the disciples.

➡ *When have I most felt that God was working though me?*

SEVENTH SUNDAY OF EASTER

ENTRANCE ANTIPHON *(Cf. Psalm 27 [26]:7-9)*
O Lord, hear my voice, for I have called to you; / of you my heart has spoken: Seek his face; / hide not your face from me, alleluia.

INTRODUCTORY RITES *(page 10)*

COLLECT
Graciously hear our supplications, O Lord,
so that we, who believe that the Savior of the human race
is with you in your glory,
may experience, as he promised,
until the end of the world,
his abiding presence among us.
Who lives and reigns with you in the unity of the Holy Spirit,
God, for ever and ever. ***Amen.***

FIRST READING *(Acts 1:15-17, 20a, 20c-26)*
Peter stood up in the midst of the brothers—there was a group of about one hundred and twenty persons in the one place—. He said, "My brothers, the Scripture had to be fulfilled which the Holy Spirit spoke beforehand through the mouth of David, concerning Judas, who was the guide for those who arrested Jesus. He was numbered among us and was allotted a share in this ministry.

"For it is written in the Book of Psalms:

May another take his office.

"Therefore, it is necessary that one of the men who accompanied us the whole time the Lord Jesus came and went among us, beginning from the baptism of John until the day on which he was taken up from us, become with us a witness to his resurrection." So they proposed two, Judas called Barsabbas, who was also known as Justus, and Matthias. Then they prayed, "You, Lord, who know the hearts of all, show which one of these two you have chosen to take the place in this apostolic ministry from which Judas turned away to go to his own place." Then they gave lots to them, and the lot fell upon Matthias, and he was counted with the eleven apostles.

The word of the Lord. ***Thanks be to God.***

RESPONSORIAL PSALM *(Psalm 103:1–2, 11–12, 19–20)*

℟ The Lord has set his throne in heaven. *Or* **Alleluia.**

Bless the LORD, O my soul;
and all my being, bless his holy name.
Bless the LORD, O my soul,
and forget not all his benefits. **℟**
For as the heavens are high above the earth,
so surpassing is his kindness toward those who fear him.
As far as the east is from the west,
so far has he put our transgressions from us. **℟**
The LORD has established his throne in heaven,
and his kingdom rules over all.
Bless the LORD, all you his angels,
you mighty in strength, who do his bidding. **℟**

SECOND READING *(1 John 4:11–16)*

Beloved, if God so loved us, we also must love one another. No one has ever seen God. Yet, if we love one another, God remains in us, and his love is brought to perfection in us.

This is how we know that we remain in him and he in us, that he has given us of his Spirit. Moreover, we have seen and testify that the Father sent his Son as **savior of the world.** ✝ Whoever acknowledges that Jesus is the Son of God, God remains in him and he in God. We have come to know and to believe in the love God has for us.

God is love, and whoever remains in love remains in God and God in him.

The word of the Lord. ***Thanks be to God.***

ALLELUIA *(See John 14:18)*
Alleluia, alleluia. I will not leave you orphans, says the Lord. / I will come back to you, and your hearts will rejoice. ***Alleluia, alleluia.***

GOSPEL *(John 17:11b–19)*
A reading from the holy Gospel according to John.
Glory to you, O Lord.

Lifting up his eyes to heaven, Jesus prayed, saying: "Holy Father, keep them in your name that you have given me, so that they may be one just as we are one. When I was with them I protected them in your name that you gave me, and I guarded them, and none of them was lost except the son of destruction, in order that the Scripture might be fulfilled. But now I am coming to you. I speak this in the world so that they may share my joy completely. I gave them your word, and the world hated them, because they do not belong to the world any more than I belong to the world. I do not ask that you take them out of the world but that you keep them from the evil one. They do not belong to the world any more than I belong to the world. Consecrate them in the truth. Your word is truth. As you sent me into the world, so I sent them into the world. And I consecrate myself for them, so that they also may be consecrated in truth."

The Gospel of the Lord. ***Praise to you, Lord Jesus Christ.***

PROFESSION OF FAITH *(page 13)*

PRAYER OF THE FAITHFUL

PREPARATION OF GIFTS *(page 16)*

PRAYER OVER THE OFFERINGS

Accept, O Lord, the prayers of your faithful
with the sacrificial offerings,
that through these acts of devotedness
we may pass over to the glory of heaven.
Through Christ our Lord. ***Amen.***

PREFACE *(Easter 1-5, pages 24–26, or Ascension 1-2, page 27)*

TAKING A CLOSER LOOK

+ **Savior of the world** Before it became a theological term, "savior" meant one who rescued someone from a difficult situation. Thus it was commonly attributed to the king, emperor, or general who saved the nation by winning a war. For the Jews, God was their primary savior because God rescued them from their oppression in Egypt. For Christians, Jesus is the savior because he rescued us from our broken relationship with God and offered us a new relationship under God's rule. In John's gospel, Jesus also overcomes the hostile forces resisting God's reordering of creation and community (which John calls "the world").

COMMUNION ANTIPHON *(John 17: 22)*
Father, I pray that they may be one / as we also are one, alleluia.

PRAYER AFTER COMMUNION
Hear us, O God our Savior,
and grant us confidence,
that through these sacred mysteries
there will be accomplished in the body of the whole Church
what has already come to pass in Christ her Head.
Who lives and reigns for ever and ever. ***Amen.***

SOLEMN BLESSING: EASTER TIME *(Optional, page 60)*

DISMISSAL *(page 57)*

Responding to the Word

The eleven disciples chose to replace Judas so the group would be complete again.

How would I have felt if the choice had been me?

God's love for us is the reason that God desires to be close to us.

What might I do to encourage God to remain with me today and throughout this week?

Jesus prays that we continue his work and stay free of evil.

What can I do to be more attentive to the way that evil wants to change my relation to God and others?

Witnesses of the good news

As the gospels show, every time the disciples experience the risen and ascended Christ, they are told to share this with others. Being a Christian can never be just a "me and Jesus" experience. We must continue the ministry and mission of Jesus in our world. Pentecost reminds us of this task and invites us to take the Easter message of Christ's resurrection and spread this good news to our world.

The remainder of the Church's year is called "ordinary time." This does not mean that this time is not important, but rather that it is "ordered" by our ever-deepening appreciation of how the mystery of our faith must be lived in our everyday lives.

During this time, Sunday by Sunday, we listen and respond to the Scripture readings and thus deepen our awareness of Jesus' life and teaching. As we better understand who he was, we also better understand who we are as his followers today.

Jesus' message was a new way to relate to God and to others, and this is what we share with our family, our friends, our fellow parishioners, and all those with whom we work and play. As individuals and communities, we begin to live right now as the kingdom community that Christ envisioned. We must dare to create communities based on justice and right relationships with one another, built on love and respect for each person as a beloved child of God.

Praying and living Pentecost all year

Find a time to pray quietly or gather the household. (You may wish to do this several times between Pentecost and the end of the liturgical year.) Pray this prayer to the Holy Spirit:

Come, Holy Spirit, fill the hearts of your faithful
and enkindle in them the fire of your love.
Send forth your Spirit and they shall be created,
and you shall renew the face of the earth.

The Holy Spirit has given each of us personal gifts to use for building the Christian community. Consider the following questions (if you are with others, reflect and share together):

- What are the Holy Spirit's gifts to me?
- What situation or event illustrates how that gift helps others?
- In what other ways might I use my gifts?

If you are with others, invite each person to proceed around the circle, laying a hand on each person's head, while saying:

May you use your gifts in the service of God and others.

When all have had a chance to bless and be blessed, pray:

O God, help us to use your gifts
to make the world a better place—
more filled with your presence,
more in keeping with your desires,
and more aligned with your will.
Send your Holy Spirit upon us now
so that we can recognize the gifts you have given,
more eagerly make them our own,
and more willingly share them with others.
Amen.

May 16

Proclaim the Good News!

It is Holy! What began as sorrow-full despair became holy peace and enlightening joy. What began as eleven disciples cowering in fear behind closed doors after the resurrection became a growing band proclaiming the Good News of the Son of God to the world. What began as the visit of a crucified—but now living—Shepherd to his followers became the manifestation of the wounded Lamb of God, the Messiah, to the world. But how did these transformations take place?

It is the Spirit! What began as a single breath of Jesus in an upper room on Easter evening became a magnificent, fire-infused, polyglot, out-pouring of the Holy Spirit publicly in Jerusalem a mere 50 days later. This is the power of Pentecost! None of our sorrows, our despair, our fearful unknowing, or our own wounds can separate us from the love and the mercy of God proclaimed for all time in the incarnation, death, and resurrection of Christ Jesus. And like the disciples of old, each one of us who has received even a breath of the Holy Spirit is sent by Jesus, just like he was, into the world to proclaim redemption from sin.

This year, let us live into the goal of "Mass" (*Missa*, Latin for "sent") and go where God sends us to proclaim the Good News.

■ Beverly Illauq

*For the **Mass during the Day,***
turn to page 405.

VIGIL MASS

The Vigil Mass of Pentecost can be celebrated in an Extended Form, which is similar to the Easter Vigil, or in a Simple Form, which is like a standard Vigil Mass.

First Form: Extended Vigil

(For the Simple Form, see page 401.)

Two options are given for the manner of celebrating the Extended form of the Pentecost Vigil Mass. The first option allows for First Vespers to precede Mass, in which case the proper rubrics are observed, as found in the Roman Missal. For the second option, Mass begins in the usual way.

ENTRANCE ANTIPHON *(Romans 5: 5; cf. 8: 11)*
The love of God has been poured into our hearts / through the Spirit of God dwelling within us, alleluia.

INTRODUCTORY RITES *(page 10)*
After the Kyrie (Lord, have mercy), the priest says the following prayer:

Grant, we pray, almighty God,
that your Church may always remain that holy people,
formed as one by the unity of Father, Son and Holy Spirit,
which manifests to the world
the Sacrament of your holiness and unity
and leads it to the perfection of your charity.
Through Christ our Lord. ***Amen.***

Then the Priest may address the people in these or similar words:

Dear brethren (brothers and sisters),
we have now begun our Pentecost Vigil,
after the example of the Apostles and disciples,
who with Mary, the Mother of Jesus, persevered in prayer,
awaiting the Spirit promised by the Lord;
like them, let us, too, listen with quiet hearts to the Word of God.
Let us meditate on how many great deeds
God in times past did for his people
and let us pray that the Holy Spirit,
whom the Father sent as the first fruits for those who believe,
may bring to perfection his work in the world.

FIRST READING *(Genesis 11:1–9)*

The whole world spoke the same language, using the same words. While the people were migrating in the east, they came upon a valley in the land of Shinar and settled there. They said to one another, "Come, let us mold bricks and harden them with fire." They used bricks for stone, and bitumen for mortar. Then they said, "Come, let us build ourselves a city and a tower with its top in the sky, and so make a name for ourselves; otherwise we shall be scattered all over the earth."

The LORD came down to see the city and the tower that the people had built. Then the LORD said: "If now, while they are one people, all speaking the same language, they have started to do this, nothing will later stop them from doing whatever they presume to do. Let us then go down there and confuse their language, so that one will not understand what another says." Thus the LORD scattered them from there all over the earth, and they stopped building the city. That is why it was called Babel, because there the LORD confused the speech of all the world. It was from that place that he scattered them all over the earth.

The word of the Lord. ***Thanks be to God.***

RESPONSORIAL PSALM *(Psalm 33:10-11, 12-13, 14-15)*

℟. Blessed the people the Lord has chosen to be his own.

The LORD brings to nought the plans of nations;
he foils the designs of peoples.
But the plan of the LORD stands forever;
the design of his heart, through all generations. **℟.**
Blessed the nation whose God is the LORD,
the people he has chosen for his own inheritance.
From heaven the LORD looks down;
he sees all mankind. **℟.**
From his fixed throne he beholds
all who dwell on the earth,
He who fashioned the heart of each,
he who knows all their works. **℟.**

PRAYER

Grant, we pray, almighty God,
that your Church may always remain that holy people,
formed as one by the unity of Father, Son and Holy Spirit,
which manifests to the world
the Sacrament of your holiness and unity
and leads it to the perfection of your charity.
Through Christ our Lord. ***Amen.***

SECOND READING *(Exodus 19:3-8a, 16-20b)*

Moses went up the mountain to God. Then the LORD called to him and said, "Thus shall you say to the house of Jacob; tell the Israelites: You have seen for yourselves how I treated the Egyptians and how I bore you up on eagle wings and brought you here to myself. Therefore, if you hearken to my voice and keep my covenant, you shall be my special possession, dearer to me than all other people, though all the earth is mine. You shall be to me a kingdom of priests, a holy nation. That is what you must tell the Israelites." So Moses went and summoned the elders of the people. When he set before them all that the LORD had ordered him to tell them, the people all answered together, "Everything the LORD has said, we will do."

On the morning of the third day there were peals of thunder and lightning, and a heavy cloud over the mountain, and a very loud trumpet blast, so that all the people in the camp trembled. But Moses led the people out of the camp to meet God, and they stationed themselves at the foot of the mountain. Mount Sinai was all wrapped in smoke, for the LORD came down upon it in fire. The smoke rose from it as though from a furnace, and the whole mountain trembled violently. The trumpet blast grew louder and louder, while Moses was speaking, and God answering him with thunder.

When the LORD came down to the top of Mount Sinai, he summoned Moses to the top of the mountain.

The word of the Lord. ***Thanks be to God.***

An alternate Responsorial Psalm follows.

RESPONSORIAL PSALM *(Daniel 3:52, 53, 54, 55, 56)*
℟. Glory and praise forever!

"Blessed are you, O Lord, the God of our fathers,
praiseworthy and exalted above all forever;
And blessed is your holy and glorious name,
praiseworthy and exalted above all for all ages." ℟.
"Blessed are you in the temple of your holy glory,
praiseworthy and glorious above all forever." ℟.
"Blessed are you on the throne of your Kingdom,
praiseworthy and exalted above all forever." ℟.
"Blessed are you who look into the depths
from your throne upon the cherubim,
praiseworthy and exalted above all forever." ℟.
"Blessed are you in the firmament of heaven,
praiseworthy and glorious forever." ℟.

Or

RESPONSORIAL PSALM *(Psalm 19:8, 9, 10, 11)*
℟. Lord, you have the words of everlasting life.

The law of the LORD is perfect,
refreshing the soul;
The decree of the LORD is trustworthy,
giving wisdom to the simple. ℟.
The precepts of the LORD are right,
rejoicing the heart;
The command of the LORD is clear,
enlightening the eye. ℟.

The fear of the LORD is pure,
enduring forever;
The ordinances of the LORD are true,
all of them just.
℟. **Lord, you have the words of everlasting life.**
They are more precious than gold,
than a heap of purest gold;
Sweeter also than syrup
or honey from the comb. ℟.

PRAYER

O God, who in fire and lightning
gave the ancient Law to Moses on Mount Sinai
and on this day manifested the new covenant
in the fire of the Spirit,
grant, we pray,
that we may always be aflame with that same Spirit
whom you wondrously poured out on your Apostles,
and that the new Israel,
gathered from every people,
may receive with rejoicing
the eternal commandment of your love.
Through Christ our Lord. ***Amen.***

THIRD READING *(Ezekiel 37:1–14)*

The hand of the LORD came upon me, and he led me out in the spirit of the LORD and set me in the center of the plain, which was now filled with bones. He made me walk among the bones in every direction so that I saw how many they were on the surface of the plain. How dry they were! He asked me: Son of man, can these bones come to life? I answered, "Lord GOD, you alone know that." Then he said to me: Prophesy over these bones, and say to them: Dry bones, hear the word of the LORD! Thus says the Lord GOD to these bones: See! I will bring spirit into you, that you may come to life. I will put sinews upon you, make flesh grow over you, cover you with skin, and put spirit in you so that you may come to life and know that I am the LORD. I, Ezekiel, prophesied as I had been told, and even as I was prophesying I heard a noise; it was a rattling as the bones came together, bone joining bone. I saw the sinews and the flesh come upon them, and the skin cover them, but there was no spirit in them. Then the LORD said to me: Prophesy to the spirit, prophesy, son of man, and say to the spirit: Thus says the Lord GOD: From the four winds come, O spirit, and breathe into these slain that they may come to life. I prophesied as he told me, and the spirit came into them; they came alive and stood upright, a vast army. Then he said to me: Son of man, these bones are the whole house of Israel. They have been saying, "Our bones are dried up, our hope is lost, and we are cut off." Therefore, prophesy and say to them: Thus says the Lord GOD: O my people, I will open your graves and have you rise from them, and bring you back to the land of Israel. Then you shall know that I am the LORD, when I open your graves and have you rise from them, O my people! I will put my spirit in you that you may live, and I will settle you upon your land; thus you shall know that I am the LORD. I have promised, and I will do it, says the LORD.

The word of the Lord. ***Thanks be to God.***

RESPONSORIAL PSALM *(Psalm 107:2-3, 4-5, 6-7, 8-9)*

℟. Give thanks to the Lord; his love is everlasting. *Or* **Alleluia.**

Let the redeemed of the LORD say,
those whom he has redeemed from the hand of the foe

And gathered from the lands,
  from the east and the west, from the north and the south.
℟. Give thanks to the Lord; his love is everlasting. *Or* **Alleluia.**
They went astray in the desert wilderness;
  the way to an inhabited city they did not find.
Hungry and thirsty,
  their life was wasting away within them. ℟.
They cried to the LORD in their distress;
  from their straits he rescued them.
And he led them by a direct way
  to reach an inhabited city. ℟.
Let them give thanks to the LORD for his mercy
  and his wondrous deeds to the children of men,
Because he satisfied the longing soul
  and filled the hungry soul with good things. ℟.

PRAYER

Lord, God of power,
who restore what has fallen
and preserve what you have restored,
increase, we pray, the peoples
to be renewed by the sanctification of your name,
that all who are washed clean by holy Baptism
may always be directed by your prompting.
Through Christ our Lord. ***Amen.***

Or

O God, who have brought us to rebirth by the word of life,
pour out upon us your Holy Spirit,
that walking in oneness of faith,
may attain in our flesh

the incorruptible glory of the resurrection.
Through Christ our Lord. ***Amen.***

Or

May your people exult for ever, O God,
in renewed youthfulness of spirit,
so that, rejoicing now in the restored glory of our adoption,
we may look forward in confident hope
to the rejoicing of the day of resurrection.
Through Christ Our Lord. ***Amen.***

FOURTH READING *(Joel 3:1-5)*

Thus says the LORD:
I will pour out my spirit upon all flesh.
Your sons and daughters shall prophesy,
your old men shall dream dreams,
your young men shall see visions;
even upon the servants and the handmaids,
in those days, I will pour out my spirit.
And I will work wonders in the heavens and on the earth,
blood, fire, and columns of smoke;
the sun will be turned to darkness,
and the moon to blood,
at the coming of the day of the LORD,
the great and terrible day.
Then everyone shall be rescued
who calls on the name of the LORD;
for on Mount Zion there shall be a remnant,
as the LORD has said,
and in Jerusalem survivors
whom the LORD shall call.
The word of the Lord. ***Thanks be to God.***

RESPONSORIAL PSALM *(Psalm 104:1-2, 24, 35, 27-28, 29, 30)*

℟. Lord, send out your Spirit, and renew the face of the earth. *Or* **Alleluia.**

Bless the LORD, O my soul!
O LORD, my God, you are great indeed!
You are clothed with majesty and glory,
robed in light as with a cloak. ℟.
How manifold are your works, O LORD!
In wisdom you have wrought them all —
the earth is full of your creatures;
bless the LORD, O my soul! Alleluia. ℟.
Creatures all look to you
to give them food in due time.
When you give it to them, they gather it;
when you open your hand, they are filled with good things. ℟.
If you take away their breath, they perish
and return to their dust.
When you send forth your spirit, they are created,
and you renew the face of the earth. ℟.

PRAYER

Fulfill for us your gracious promise,
O Lord, we pray, so that by his coming
the Holy Spirit may make us witnesses before the world
to the Gospel of our Lord Jesus Christ.
Who lives and reigns for ever and ever. ***Amen.***

GLORIA

When the hymn is concluded, the priest says the Collect in the usual way:

COLLECT

Almighty ever-living God,
who willed the Paschal Mystery
to be encompassed as a sign in fifty days,
grant that from out of the scattered nations
the confusion of many tongues
may be gathered by heavenly grace
into one great confession of your name.
Through our Lord Jesus Christ, your Son,
who lives and reigns with you in the unity of the Holy Spirit,
one God, for ever and ever. ***Amen.***

The reader proclaims the Epistle, found on page 402, and Mass continues in the usual way.

SIMPLE FORM

ENTRANCE ANTIPHON *(Romans 5: 5; cf. 8: 11)*

The love of God has been poured into our hearts / through the Spirit of God dwelling within us, alleluia.

INTRODUCTORY RITES

COLLECT

Almighty ever-living God,
who willed the Paschal Mystery
to be encompassed as a sign in fifty days,
grant that from out of the scattered nations

the confusion of many tongues
may be gathered by heavenly grace
into one great confession of your name.
Through our Lord Jesus Christ, your Son,
who lives and reigns with you in the unity of the Holy Spirit,
one God, for ever and ever. ***Amen.***

Or

Grant, we pray, almighty God,
that the splendor of your glory
may shine forth upon us
and that, by the bright rays of the Holy Spirit,
the light of your light may confirm the hearts
of those born again by your grace.
Through our Lord Jesus Christ, your Son,
who lives and reigns with you in the unity of the Holy Spirit,
one God, for ever and ever.

FIRST READING

A First Reading is chosen from among the Old Testament readings prescribed for the Extended Vigil on pages 392-399 (Genesis 11:1-9; Exodus 19:3-8a, 16-20b; Ezekiel 37:1-14; or Joel 3:1-5).

RESPONSORIAL PSALM

Psalm 104, page 400.

EPISTLE *(Romans 8:22-27)*

Brothers and sisters: We know that all creation is groaning in labor pains even until now; and not only that, but we ourselves, who have the firstfruits of the Spirit, we also groan within ourselves as we wait for adoption, the redemption of our bodies.

For in hope we were saved. Now hope that sees is not hope. For who hopes for what one sees? But if we hope for what we do not see, we wait with endurance.

In the same way, the Spirit too comes to the aid of our weakness; for we do not know how to pray as we ought, but the Spirit himself intercedes with inexpressible groanings. And the one who searches hearts knows what is the intention of the Spirit, because he intercedes for the holy ones according to God's will.

The word of the Lord. ***Thanks be to God.***

ALLELUIA

Alleluia, alleluia. Come, Holy Spirit, fill the hearts of your faithful / and kindle in them the fire of your love. ***Alleluia, alleluia.***

GOSPEL *(John 7:37-39)*

A reading from the holy Gospel according to John.

Glory to you, O Lord.

On the last and greatest day of the feast, Jesus stood up and exclaimed, "Let anyone who thirsts come to me and drink. As Scripture says:

Rivers of living water will flow from within him
who believes in me."

He said this in reference to the Spirit that those who came to believe in him were to receive. There was, of course, no Spirit yet, because Jesus had not yet been glorified.

The Gospel of the Lord. ***Praise to you, Lord Jesus Christ.***

PROFESSION OF FAITH *(page 13)*

PRAYER OF THE FAITHFUL

PREPARATION OF GIFTS *(page 16)*

PRAYER OVER THE OFFERINGS

Pour out upon these gifts the blessing of your Spirit,
we pray, O Lord,
so that through them your Church may be imbued with such love
that the truth of your saving mystery
may shine forth for the whole world.
Through Christ our Lord. ***Amen.***

PREFACE: THE MYSTERY OF PENTECOST

It is truly right and just, our duty and our salvation,
always and everywhere to give you thanks,
Lord, holy Father, almighty and eternal God.

For, bringing your Paschal Mystery to completion,
you bestowed the Holy Spirit today
on those you made your adopted children
by uniting them to your Only Begotten Son.
This same Spirit, as the Church came to birth,
opened to all peoples the knowledge of God
and brought together the many languages of the earth
in profession of the one faith.

Therefore, overcome with paschal joy,
every land, every people exults in your praise
and even the heavenly Powers, with the angelic hosts,
sing together the unending hymn of your glory,
as they acclaim:
Holy, Holy, Holy Lord God of hosts... *(page 35)*

COMMUNION ANTIPHON *(John 7:37)*
On the last day of the festival, Jesus stood and cried out:/ If anyone is thirsty, let him come to me and drink, alleluia.

PRAYER AFTER COMMUNION
May these gifts we have consumed
benefit us, O Lord,
that we may always be aflame with the same Spirit,
whom you wondrously poured out on your Apostles.
Through Christ our Lord. ***Amen.***

SOLEMN BLESSING: THE HOLY SPIRIT *(Optional, page 62)*

DISMISSAL *(page 57)* ✠

MASS DURING THE DAY

ENTRANCE ANTIPHON *(Wisdom 1:7)*
The Spirit of the Lord has filled the whole world / and that which contains all things / understands what is said, alleluia.

Or *(Romans 5:5; cf. 8:11)*
The love of God has been poured into our hearts / through the Spirit of God dwelling within us, alleluia.

INTRODUCTORY RITES *(page 10)*

COLLECT
O God, who by the mystery of today's great feast
sanctify your whole Church in every people and nation,
pour out, we pray, the gifts of the Holy Spirit

across the face of the earth
and, with the divine grace that was at work
when the Gospel was first proclaimed,
fill now once more the hearts of believers.
Through our Lord Jesus Christ, your Son,
who lives and reigns with you in the unity of the Holy Spirit,
God, for ever and ever. ***Amen.***

FIRST READING *(Acts 2:1-11)*

When the time for **Pentecost**✝ was fulfilled, they were all in one place together. And suddenly there came from the sky a noise like a strong driving wind, and it filled the entire house in which they were. Then there appeared to them tongues as of fire, which parted and came to rest on each one of them. And they were all filled with the Holy Spirit and began to speak in different tongues, as the Spirit enabled them to proclaim.

Now there were devout Jews from every nation under heaven staying in Jerusalem. At this sound, they gathered in a large crowd, but they were confused because each one heard them speaking in his own language. They were astounded, and in amazement they asked, "Are not all these people who are speaking Galileans? Then how does each of us hear them in his native language? We are Parthians, Medes, and Elamites, inhabitants of Mesopotamia, Judea and Cappadocia, Pontus and Asia, Phrygia and Pamphylia, Egypt and the districts of Libya near Cyrene, as well as travelers from Rome, both Jews and converts to Judaism, Cretans and Arabs, yet we hear them speaking in our own tongues of the mighty acts of God."

The word of the Lord. ***Thanks be to God.***

RESPONSORIAL PSALM *(Psalm 104:1, 24, 29-30, 31, 34)*

℟. Lord, send out your Spirit, and renew the face of the earth.
Or **Alleluia.**

Bless the LORD, O my soul!
O LORD, my God, you are great indeed!
How manifold are your works, O LORD!
The earth is full of your creatures. ℟.
If you take away their breath, they perish
and return to their dust.
When you send forth your spirit, they are created,
and you renew the face of the earth. ℟.
May the glory of the LORD endure forever;
may the LORD be glad in his works!
Pleasing to him be my theme;
I will be glad in the LORD. ℟.

An alternate reading follows.

SECOND READING *(1 Corinthians 12:3b-7, 12-13)*

Brothers and sisters: No one can say, "Jesus is Lord," except by the Holy Spirit.

There are different kinds of spiritual gifts but the same Spirit; there are different forms of service but the same Lord; there are different workings but the same God who produces all of them in everyone. To each individual the manifestation of the Spirit is given for some benefit.

As a body is one though it has many parts, and all the parts of the body, though many, are one body, so also Christ. For in one Spirit we were all baptized into one body, whether Jews or

Greeks, slaves or free persons, and we were all given to drink of one Spirit.

The word of the Lord. ***Thanks be to God.***

Or

SECOND READING *(Galatians 5:16-25)*

Brothers and sisters, live by the Spirit and you will certainly not gratify the desire of the flesh. For the flesh has desires against the Spirit, and the Spirit against the flesh; these are opposed to each other, so that you may not do what you want. But if you are guided by the Spirit, you are not under the law. Now the works of the flesh are obvious: immorality, impurity, lust, idolatry, sorcery, hatreds, rivalry, jealousy, outbursts of fury, acts of selfishness, dissensions, factions, occasions of envy, drinking bouts, orgies, and the like. I warn you, as I warned you before, that those who do such things will not inherit the kingdom of God. In contrast, the fruit of the Spirit is love, joy, peace, patience, kindness, generosity, faithfulness, gentleness, self-control. Against such there is no law. Now those who belong to Christ Jesus have crucified their flesh with its passions and desires. If we live in the Spirit, let us also follow the Spirit.

The word of the Lord. ***Thanks be to God.***

SEQUENCE *(Veni, Sancte Spiritus)*

Come, Holy Spirit, come!
And from your celestial home
   Shed a ray of light divine!
Come, Father of the poor!
Come, source of all our store!
   Come, within our bosoms shine.
You, of comforters the best;

You, the soul's most welcome guest;
Sweet refreshment here below.
In our labor, rest most sweet;
Grateful coolness in the heat;
Solace in the midst of woe.
O most blessed Light divine,
Shine within these hearts of yours,
And our inmost being fill!
Where you are not, we have naught,
Nothing good in deed or thought,
Nothing free from taint of ill.
Heal our wounds, our strength renew;
On our dryness pour your dew;
Wash the stains of guilt away.
Bend the stubborn heart and will;
Melt the frozen, warm the chill;
Guide the steps that go astray.
On the faithful, who adore
And confess you, evermore
In your sevenfold gift descend.
Give them virtue's sure reward;
Give them your salvation, Lord;
Give them joys that never end. Amen.
Alleluia.

ALLELUIA

Alleluia, alleluia. Come, Holy Spirit, fill the hearts of your faithful / and kindle in them the fire of your love. ***Alleluia, alleluia.***

An alternate reading follows.

GOSPEL *(John 20:19–23)*
A reading from the holy Gospel according to John.
Glory to you, O Lord.

On the evening of that first day of the week, when the doors were locked, where the disciples were, for fear of the Jews, Jesus came and stood in their midst and said to them, "Peace be with you." When he had said this, he showed them his hands and his side. The disciples rejoiced when they saw the Lord. Jesus said to them again, "Peace be with you. As the Father has sent me, so I send you." And when he had said this, he breathed on them and said to them, "Receive the Holy Spirit. Whose sins you forgive are forgiven them, and whose sins you retain are retained."

The Gospel of the Lord. ***Praise to you, Lord Jesus Christ.***

Or

GOSPEL *(John 15:26–27; 16:12–15)*
A reading from the holy Gospel according to John.
Glory to you, O Lord.

Jesus said to his disciples: "When the Advocate comes whom I will send you from the Father, the Spirit of truth that proceeds from the Father, he will testify to me. And you also testify, because you have been with me from the beginning.

"I have much more to tell you, but you cannot bear it now. But when he comes, the Spirit of truth, he will guide you to all truth. He will not speak on his own, but he will speak what he hears, and will declare to you the things that are coming. He will glorify me, because he will take from what is mine and declare it to you. Everything that the Father has is mine; for this reason I told you that he will take from what is mine and declare it to you.'"

The Gospel of the Lord. ***Praise to you, Lord Jesus Christ.***

PROFESSION OF FAITH *(page 13)*

PRAYER OF THE FAITHFUL

PREPARATION OF GIFTS *(page 16)*

PRAYER OVER THE OFFERINGS

Grant, we pray, O Lord,
that, as promised by your Son,
the Holy Spirit may reveal to us more abundantly
the hidden mystery of this sacrifice
and graciously lead us into all truth.
Through Christ our Lord. ***Amen.***

PREFACE: THE MYSTERY OF PENTECOST *(page 404)*

TAKING A CLOSER LOOK

✝ **Pentecost** *Pentecost* (Greek, the "fiftieth day") was the Jewish feast that came fifty days after Passover. It celebrated the spring grain harvest and the offering to God of the firstfruits of the crop (Exodus 23:14-17). One of the three major Jewish feast days, over the centuries it became associated with the giving of the Law (or *Torah*) and focused more on covenant renewal. In the New Testament, this feast day echoes the Jewish themes with the descent of the Holy Spirit to form the Christian community and to harvest the firstfruits of its universal mission.

COMMUNION ANTIPHON *(Acts 2:4, 11)*
They were all filled with the Holy Spirit / and spoke of the marvels of God, alleluia.

PRAYER AFTER COMMUNION
O God, who bestow heavenly gifts upon your Church,
safeguard, we pray, the grace you have given,
that the gift of the Holy Spirit poured out upon her
may retain all its force
and that this spiritual food
may gain her abundance of eternal redemption.
Through Christ our Lord. ***Amen.***

SOLEMN BLESSING: THE HOLY SPIRIT *(Optional, page 62)*

DISMISSAL *(page 57)*

Responding to the Word

The presence and power of God's Holy Spirit enabled the disciples to tell about Jesus.

When have I felt the Spirit's prompting to share my love for Jesus with others?

Paul reminds us that we have each been given gifts by the Holy Spirit.

What gift do I claim and how am I using it to benefit others?

Jesus reminds us that sharing God's Spirit enables the forgiveness of the sins that break down our relationships with God and others.

When have I felt the Spirit drawing me more deeply into relationships with others?

May 23

God is always with us

How do we understand the nature of our triune God? Today's readings were chosen with purpose to help us remember the God who saved the Hebrews from slavery in Egypt, who saved us from slavery to sin through Jesus Christ, and, yes, whose liberating Spirit we experience in 2027 through the Eucharist and through our faithfulness.

The nature of God can seem beyond our language and imagination. Perhaps the Trinity cannot best be understood through formulas, dogmas, or creeds. Matthew's Gospel suggests that the best way to know God is through *discipleship*. We are called to live in communal relationships of evangelical synodality in our societies, families, and communities of faith. Through our prayers, words, and actions for justice and peace, we continually make disciples of ourselves and thus proclaim the gospel—together.

St. Paul does not fear God's invitation to discipleship. A faith-filled life is not meant to resemble slavery. We are free to choose to become both children and heirs of God and "joint heirs with Christ." Living a loving discipleship provides the consolation that God will always be with us.

JOE GUNN

ENTRANCE ANTIPHON

Blest be God the Father, / and the Only Begotten Son of God, / and also the Holy Spirit, / for he has shown us his merciful love.

INTRODUCTORY RITES *(page 10)*

COLLECT

God our Father, who by sending into the world
the Word of truth and the Spirit of sanctification
made known to the human race your wondrous mystery,
grant us, we pray, that in professing the true faith,
we may acknowledge the Trinity of eternal glory
and adore your Unity, powerful in majesty.
Through our Lord Jesus Christ, your Son,
who lives and reigns with you in the unity of the Holy Spirit,
God, for ever and ever. ***Amen.***

FIRST READING *(Deuteronomy 4:32–34, 39–40)*

Moses said to the people: "Ask now of the days of old, before your time, ever since God created man upon the earth; ask from one end of the sky to the other: Did anything so great ever happen before? Was it ever heard of? Did a people ever hear the voice of God speaking from the midst of fire, as you did, and live? Or did any god venture to go and take a nation for himself from the midst of another nation, by testings, by signs and wonders, by war, with strong hand and outstretched arm, and by great terrors, all of which the LORD, your God, did for you in Egypt before your very eyes? This is why you must now know, and fix in your heart, that the LORD is God in the heavens above and on earth below, and that there is no other. You must keep his statutes and commandments that I enjoin on you today, that you and your children after you may prosper, and that you may have long life on the land which the LORD, your God, is giving you forever."

The word of the Lord. ***Thanks be to God.***

RESPONSORIAL PSALM *(Psalm 33:4-5, 6, 9, 18-19, 20, 22)*

℟. Blessed the people the Lord has chosen to be his own.

Upright is the word of the LORD,
and all his works are trustworthy.
He loves justice and right;
of the kindness of the LORD the earth is full. ℟.
By the word of the LORD the heavens were made;
by the breath of his mouth all their host.
For he spoke, and it was made;
he commanded, and it stood forth. ℟.
See, the eyes of the LORD are upon those who fear him,
upon those who hope for his kindness,
to deliver them from death
and preserve them in spite of famine. ℟.
Our soul waits for the LORD,
who is our help and our shield.
May your kindness, O LORD, be upon us
who have put our hope in you. ℟.

SECOND READING *(Romans 8:14-17)*

Brothers and sisters: Those who are led by the Spirit of God are sons of God. For you did not receive a spirit of slavery to fall back into fear, but you received a Spirit of adoption, through whom we cry, "Abba, Father!" The Spirit himself bears witness with our spirit that we are children of God, and if children, then heirs, heirs of God and joint heirs with Christ, if only we suffer with him so that we may also be glorified with him.

The word of the Lord. ***Thanks be to God.***

ALLELUIA *(See Revelation 1:8)*

Alleluia, alleluia. Glory to the Father, the Son, and the Holy Spirit; / to God who is, who was, and who is to come. ***Alleluia, alleluia.***

GOSPEL *(Matthew 28:16–20)*

A reading from the holy Gospel according to Matthew.

Glory to you, O Lord.

The eleven disciples went to Galilee, to the mountain to which Jesus had ordered them. When they all saw him, they worshiped, but they doubted. Then Jesus approached and said to them, "All power in heaven and on earth has been given to me. Go, therefore, and make disciples of all nations, **baptizing**+ them in the name of the Father, and of the Son, and of the Holy Spirit, teaching them to observe all that I have commanded you. And behold, I am with you always, until the end of the age."

The Gospel of the Lord. ***Praise to you, Lord Jesus Christ.***

PROFESSION OF FAITH *(page 13)*

PRAYER OF THE FAITHFUL

PREPARATION OF GIFTS *(page 16)*

PRAYER OVER THE OFFERINGS

Sanctify by the invocation of your name,
we pray, O Lord our God,
this oblation of our service,
and by it make of us an eternal offering to you.
Through Christ our Lord. ***Amen.***

PREFACE: THE MYSTERY OF THE MOST HOLY TRINITY

It is truly right and just, our duty and our salvation,
always and everywhere to give you thanks,
Lord, holy Father, almighty and eternal God.

For with your Only Begotten Son and the Holy Spirit
you are one God, one Lord:
not in the unity of a single person,
but in a Trinity of one substance.

For what you have revealed to us of your glory
we believe equally of your Son
and of the Holy Spirit,
so that, in the confessing of the true and eternal Godhead,
you might be adored in what is proper to each Person,
their unity in substance,
and their equality in majesty.

Taking a Closer Look

+ Baptizing Baptism means to immerse or wash in water and so becomes a natural sign for ritual purity or holiness. In Judaism, there were many ceremonial washings either in preparation for celebrating a ritual or as part of a cleansing right within a ritual. Thus John the Baptist uses a baptism of repentance (Mark 1:4) to symbolize one's desire to put off sinful ways and live as God wants. But for the Christian community, baptism replaced Jewish circumcision as the initiation ritual and sign of covenant belonging. This also meant that covenant membership was open to women and not just for the men who were circumcised.

For this is praised by Angels and Archangels,
Cherubim, too, and Seraphim,
who never cease to cry out each day,
as with one voice they acclaim:
Holy, holy, holy, Lord God of hosts... *(page 35)*

COMMUNION ANTIPHON *(Galatians 4:6)*
Since you are children of God, / God has sent into your hearts the Spirit of his Son, / the Spirit who cries out: Abba, Father.

PRAYER AFTER COMMUNION
May receiving this Sacrament, O Lord our God,
bring us health of body and soul,
as we confess your eternal holy Trinity and undivided Unity.
Through Christ our Lord. ***Amen.***

BLESSING & DISMISSAL *(page 56)* ⁜

Responding to the Word

Moses reviews the story of God's mighty deeds done for the covenant people.

➲ *What mighty deeds of God's loving power have been at work in my life?*

We share the same path as Jesus—through suffering and death into new life with God.

➲ *How have the little deaths I have experienced opened me up to new life?*

Jesus promises to be with us always.

➲ *Which experiences of Jesus' presence have been particularly important to me? Why?*

May 30

The ultimate sacrifice

A minister, recently converted to Catholicism, told this story. He had invited a former parishioner to a potluck at his new parish and she said to him, "You Catholics are always eating." He replied joyfully, "Yes, we even eat Jesus!"

Today's gospel leads us gently to the glory of the Eucharist. First, Jesus lets his disciples know something very special is about the happen when he tells them, "Go into the city." Then, during supper, he instructs them, "Take it; this is my Body," and he hands them the bread he has blessed.

He speaks once again, saying, "This is my Blood of the covenant," as he gives them the cup. The disciples recognize these as the words Moses used when he was offering his sacrifice of oxen. Except now, Jesus tells them, this is his Body and Blood. He is the sacrifice, and through this sacrifice Jesus promises new life "in the kingdom of God."

Our hearts are hungering for fulfillment, longing for the goodness that prepares us for eternal life with God. Jesus has made the ultimate sacrifice, so that we might be freed from all our sins. Yes, we do eat Jesus' body, so that with Christ we may live eternally. This is our miracle. We hunger for Christ; we need Christ. And here he is, in the Eucharist.

Liz Summers

ENTRANCE ANTIPHON *(Cf. Psalm 81 [80]:17)*
He fed them with the finest wheat / and satisfied them with honey from the rock.

INTRODUCTORY RITES *(page 10)*

COLLECT
O God, who in this wonderful Sacrament
have left us a memorial of your Passion,
grant us, we pray,
so to revere the sacred mysteries of your Body and Blood
that we may always experience in ourselves
the fruits of your redemption.
Who live and reign with God the Father
in the unity of the Holy Spirit,
God, for ever and ever. ***Amen.***

FIRST READING *(Exodus 24:3–8)*
When Moses came to the people and related all the words and ordinances of the LORD, they all answered with one voice, "We will do everything that the LORD has told us." Moses then wrote down all the words of the LORD and, rising early the next day, he erected at the foot of the mountain an altar and twelve pillars for the twelve tribes of Israel. Then, having sent certain young men of the Israelites to offer holocausts and sacrifice young bulls as peace offerings to the LORD, Moses took half of the blood and put it in large bowls; the other half he splashed on the altar. Taking the book of the covenant, he read it aloud to the people, who answered, "All that the LORD has said, we will heed and do." Then he took the blood and sprinkled it on the people, saying, "This is the blood of the covenant that the LORD has made with you in accordance with

all these words of his."

The word of the Lord. ***Thanks be to God.***

RESPONSORIAL PSALM *(Psalm 116:12-13, 15-16, 17-18)*

℟. I will take the cup of salvation, and call on the name of the Lord. *Or* **Alleluia.**

How shall I make a return to the LORD
for all the good he has done for me?
The cup of salvation I will take up,
and I will call upon the name of the LORD. ℟.
Precious in the eyes of the LORD
is the death of his faithful ones.
I am your servant, the son of your handmaid;
you have loosed my bonds. ℟.
To you will I offer sacrifice of thanksgiving,
and I will call upon the name of the LORD.
My vows to the LORD I will pay
in the presence of all his people. ℟.

SECOND READING *(Hebrews 9:11-15)*

Brothers and sisters: When Christ came as high priest of the good things that have come to be, passing through the greater and more perfect tabernacle not made by hands, that is, not belonging to this creation, he entered once for all into the sanctuary, not with the blood of goats and calves but with his own blood, thus obtaining eternal redemption. For if the blood of goats and bulls and the sprinkling of a heifer's ashes can sanctify those who are defiled so that their flesh is cleansed, how much more will the blood of Christ, who through the eternal Spirit offered himself unblemished to God, cleanse our consciences from dead works to worship the living God.

For this reason he is **mediator of a new covenant:** ✝ since a death has taken place for deliverance from transgressions under the first covenant, those who are called may receive the promised eternal inheritance.

The word of the Lord. ***Thanks be to God.***

SEQUENCE

The shorter version begins at the asterisks.

Laud, O Zion, your salvation,
Laud with hymns of exultation,
Christ, your king and shepherd true:

Bring him all the praise you know,
He is more than you bestow.
Never can you reach his due.

Special theme for glad thanksgiving
Is the quick'ning and the living
Bread today before you set:

From his hands of old partaken,
As we know, by faith unshaken,
Where the Twelve at supper met.

Full and clear ring out your chanting,
Joy nor sweetest grace be wanting,
From your heart let praises burst:

For today the feast is holden,
When the institution olden
Of that supper was rehearsed.

Here the new law's new oblation,

By the new king's revelation,
 Ends the form of ancient rite:

Now the new the old effaces,
Truth away the shadow chases,
 Light dispels the gloom of night.

What he did at supper seated,
Christ ordained to be repeated,
 His memorial ne'er to cease:

And his rule for guidance taking,
Bread and wine we hallow, making
 Thus our sacrifice of peace.

This the truth each Christian learns,
Bread into his flesh he turns,
 To his precious blood the wine:

Sight has fail'd, nor thought conceives,
But a dauntless faith believes,
 Resting on a pow'r divine.

Here beneath these signs are hidden
Priceless things to sense forbidden;
 Sign, not things are all we see:

Blood is poured and flesh is broken,
Yet in either wondrous token
 Christ entire we know to be.

Whoso of this food partakes,
Does not rend the Lord nor breaks;
 Christ is whole to all that tastes:

Thousands are, as one, receivers,
One, as thousands of believers,
  Eats of him who cannot waste.

Bad and good the feast are sharing,
Of what divers dooms preparing,
  Endless death, or endless life.

Life to these, to those damnation,
See how like participation
  Is with unlike issues rife.

When the sacrament is broken,
Doubt not, but believe 'tis spoken,
  That each sever'd outward token
    doth the very whole contain.

Nought the precious gift divides,
Breaking but the sign betides
  Jesus still the same abides,
    still unbroken does remain.

* * *

The shorter form of the sequence begins here.

Lo! the angel's food is given
To the pilgrim who has striven;
  See the children's bread from heaven,
    which on dogs may not be spent.

Truth the ancient types fulfilling,
Isaac bound, a victim willing,
Paschal lamb, its lifeblood spilling,
manna to the fathers sent.

Very bread, good shepherd, tend us,
Jesu, of your love befriend us,
You refresh us, you defend us,
Your eternal goodness send us
In the land of life to see.

You who all things can and know,
Who on earth such food bestow,
Grant us with your saints, though lowest,
Where the heav'nly feast you show,
Fellow heirs and guests to be. Amen. Alleluia.

ALLELUIA *(John 6:51)*
Alleluia, alleluia. I am the living bread that came down from heaven, / says the Lord; / whoever eats this bread will live forever. ***Alleluia, alleluia.***

GOSPEL *(Mark 14:12-16, 22-26)*
A reading from the holy Gospel according to Mark.
Glory to you, O Lord.
On the first day of the Feast of Unleavened Bread, when they sacrificed the Passover lamb, Jesus' disciples said to him, "Where do you want us to go and prepare for you to eat the Passover?" He sent two of his disciples and said to them, "Go into the city and a man will meet you, carrying a jar of water. Follow him. Wherever he enters, say to the master of the house,

'The Teacher says, "Where is my guest room where I may eat the Passover with my disciples?" ' Then he will show you a large upper room furnished and ready. Make the preparations for us there." The disciples then went off, entered the city, and found it just as he had told them; and they prepared the Passover.

While they were eating, he took bread, said the blessing, broke it, gave it to them, and said, "Take it; this is my body." Then he took a cup, gave thanks, and gave it to them, and they all drank from it. He said to them, "This is my blood of the covenant, which will be shed for many. Amen, I say to you, I shall not drink again the fruit of the vine until the day when I drink it new in the kingdom of God." Then, after singing a hymn, they went out to the Mount of Olives.

The Gospel of the Lord. ***Praise to you, Lord Jesus Christ.***

PROFESSION OF FAITH *(page 13)*

PRAYER OF THE FAITHFUL

PREPARATION OF GIFTS *(page 16)*

PRAYER OVER THE OFFERINGS

Grant your Church, O Lord, we pray,
the gifts of unity and peace,
whose signs are to be seen in mystery
in the offerings we here present.
Through Christ our Lord. ***Amen.***

PREFACE *(Most Holy Eucharist 1-2, pages 32-33)*

COMMUNION ANTIPHON *(John 6:57)*

Whoever eats my flesh and drinks my blood / remains in me and I in him, says the Lord.

TAKING A CLOSER LOOK

+ **Mediator of a new covenant** In the biblical social world, many relationships were between unequals in honor and status. The patron/lord/benefactor controlled some essential good (food, water, protection, etc.) that the client/servant/petitioner needed. So there was a great need for brokers/mediators to put clients in touch with the right benefactors. In religion, the priest acted as this mediator, putting the people into relationship with God—the divine benefactor—who gives everything necessary for eternal life. For Christians, Christ is this "priest-broker," who through his death and resurrection mediates our new covenant relationship with God.

PRAYER AFTER COMMUNION

Grant, O Lord, we pray,
that we may delight for all eternity
in that share in your divine life,
which is foreshadowed in the present age
by our reception of your precious Body and Blood.
Who live and reign for ever and ever. ***Amen.***

BLESSING & DISMISSAL *(page 56)*

Responding to the Word

The Israelites seal their covenant with blood and a promise to do all that God asks.

What covenant pledge might I make today to seal my relationship with God?

Jesus is the mediator between ourselves and God to deliver us from our sins.

What message would I wish Jesus to take to God for me today?

Jesus promised to be present in the bread and wine of our Eucharist.

How am I preparing each week to experience Jesus' eucharistic presence?

June 6

Our spiritual home in God

Today's gospel prompts us to consider the nature of home. Chaos reigns as Jesus returns to his hometown. The crowds don't give him space and inquisitors come from Jerusalem to falsely accuse him. His family is concerned about him, wondering if he is out of his mind. Some homecoming!

The episode concludes with his mother and brothers outside calling for him. In one of the more challenging Scriptures, Jesus seems to reject them by saying, "Who are my mother and my brothers?" But he goes on to explain: "Whoever does the will of God is my brother and sister and mother."

With these words, Jesus points us to a most profound sense of home. He is speaking about home as spiritual rather than social, home as a place of our deepest belonging. At our cores, we belong to God; our true homes are the places where we are aligned with God.

Our spiritual home in God is our destination. We are like Peter on the water with our eyes on Christ and the Prodigal Son returning to the house of his father. Beyond the noise and bustle of the crowds, beyond misunderstandings and social pressures, beyond family conflict, we are on our way home. Understanding home this way, work becomes prayer and life becomes pilgrimage.

LES MILLER

ENTRANCE ANTIPHON *(Cf. Psalm 27 (26): 1-2)*
The Lord is my light and my salvation; whom shall I fear? / The Lord is the stronghold of my life; whom should I dread? / When those who do evil draw near, they stumble and fall.

INTRODUCTORY RITES *(page 10)*

COLLECT
O God, from whom all good things come,
grant that we, who call on you in our need,
may at your prompting discern what is right,
and by your guidance do it.
Through our Lord Jesus Christ, your Son,
who lives and reigns with you in the unity of the Holy Spirit,
God, for ever and ever. ***Amen.***

FIRST READING *(Genesis 3:9-15)*
After the man, Adam, had eaten of the tree, the LORD God called to the man and asked him, "Where are you?" He answered, "I heard you in the garden; but I was afraid, because I was naked, so I hid myself." Then he asked, "Who told you that you were naked? You have you eaten, then, from the tree of which I had forbidden you to eat!" The man replied, "The woman whom you put here with me—she gave me fruit from the tree, and so I ate it." The LORD God then asked to the woman, "Why did you do such a thing?" The woman answered, "The serpent tricked me into it, so I ate it."

Then the LORD God said to the serpent:
"Because you have done this, you shall be banned
from all the animals
and from all the wild creatures;

on your belly shall you crawl,
and dirt you shall eat
all the days of your life.
I will put enmity between you and the woman,
and between your offspring and hers;
he will strike your head,
while you strike at his heel."
The word of the Lord. ***Thanks be to God.***

RESPONSORIAL PSALM *(Psalm 130:1-2,3-4,5-6,7-8)*

℟. With the Lord there is mercy, and fullness of redemption.

Out of the depths I cry to you, O LORD;
LORD, hear my voice!
Let your ears be attentive
to my voice in supplication. ℟.
If you, O LORD, mark iniquities,
LORD, who can stand?
But with you is forgiveness,
that you may be revered. ℟.
I trust in the LORD;
my soul trusts in his word.
More than sentinels wait for the dawn,
let Israel wait for the LORD. ℟.
For with the LORD is kindness
and with him is plenteous redemption
and he will redeem Israel
from all their iniquities. ℟.

SECOND READING *(2 Corinthians 4:13–5:1)*

Brothers and sisters: Since we have the same spirit of faith, according to what is written, *I believed, therefore I spoke*, we too believe and therefore we speak, knowing that the one who raised the Lord Jesus will raise us also with Jesus and place us with you in his presence. Everything indeed is for you, so that the grace bestowed in abundance on more and more people may cause the thanksgiving to overflow for the glory of God. Therefore, we are not discouraged; rather, although our outer self is wasting away, our inner self is being renewed day by day. For this momentary light affliction is producing us for an **eternal weight of glory**✝ beyond all comparison, as we look not to what is seen but to what is unseen; for what can is seen is transitory, but what is unseen is eternal. For we know that if our earthly dwelling, a tent, should be destroyed, we have a building from God, a dwelling not made with hands, eternal in heaven.

The word of the Lord. ***Thanks be to God.***

ALLELUIA *(John 12:31b–32)*

Alleluia, alleluia. Now the ruler of the world will be driven out, says the Lord; / and when I am lifted up from the earth, I will draw everyone to myself. ***Alleluia, alleluia.***

GOSPEL *(Mark 3:20–35)*

A reading from the holy Gospel according to Mark.
Glory to you, O Lord.

Jesus came with his disciples into the house. Again the crowd gathered, making it impossible for them even to eat. When his relatives heard of this they set out to seize him, for they said, "He is out of his mind." The scribes who had come from Jerusalem said, "He is possessed by Beelzebul," and "By the prince of demons he drives out demons."

Summoning them, he began to speak to them in parables, "How can Satan drive out Satan? If a kingdom is divided against itself, that kingdom cannot stand. And if a house is divided against itself, that house will not be able to stand. And if Satan has risen up against himself and is divided, he cannot stand; that is the end of him. But no one can enter a strong man's house and plunder his property unless he first ties up the strong man. Then he can plunder the house. Amen, I say to you, all sins and all blasphemies that people utter will be forgiven them. But whoever blasphemes against the Holy Spirit will never have forgiveness, but is guilty of an everlasting sin." For they had said, "He has an unclean spirit."

His mother and his brothers arrived. Standing outside they sent word to him and called him. A crowd seated around him told him, "Your mother and your brothers and your sisters are outside asking for you." But he said to them in reply, "Who are my mother and my brothers?" And looking at those seated in the circle he said, "Here are my mother and my brothers. For whoever does the will of God is my brother and sister and mother."

The Gospel of the Lord. ***Praise to you, Lord Jesus Christ.***

PROFESSION OF FAITH *(page 13)*

PRAYER OF THE FAITHFUL

PREPARATION OF GIFTS *(page 16)*

PRAYER OVER THE OFFERINGS

Look kindly upon our service, O Lord, we pray,
that what we offer
may be an acceptable oblation to you
and lead us to grow in charity.
Through Christ our Lord.

PREFACE *(Sundays in Ordinary Time, pages 28–32)*

TAKING A CLOSER LOOK

✝ **Eternal weight of glory** Paul, recognizing that the Church in Corinth was struggling, seeks to encourage the Corinthians. Following the teachings of the Church meant opening one's self to ridicule and suffering. Living the gospel was not easy. And it is still difficult. So Paul reminds these early Christians, and us, that we will have "grace in abundance" to such a degree that it is "beyond comparison." May we be encouraged in our difficulties, encouraged to live out our faith with an eye toward eternal life...a life of glory.

COMMUNION ANTIPHON *(Psalm 18 (17): 3)*
The Lord is my rock, my fortress, and my deliverer; / my God is my saving strength.

OR *(1 John 4: 16)*
God is love, and whoever abides in love / abides in God, and God in him.

PRAYER AFTER COMMUNION
May your healing work, O Lord,
free us, we pray, from doing evil
and lead us to what is right.
Through Christ our Lord.

BLESSING AND DISMISSAL *(page 56)*

Responding to the Word

Adam and Eve recognize that they have sinned, and that life will never be the same.

How often do I examine my conscience and return to the Lord?

God's grace often goes unseen by us in our everyday lives.

Am I in the habit of considering what is unseen?

Jesus tells us today that by doing the will of God, we are part of God's family.

What is the will of God for me in my life?

June 13

Deeply rooted in love

My favorite biking trails are those which lead through deeply wooded areas. From tiny saplings to stands of towering old growth, trees offer a feast for the senses and a lifting of the spirits. From ancient times, people have had a special relationship with trees. In our contemporary world, Indigenous voices and those of forest ecologists, among others, remind us of the critical importance of trees for the health of both humans and the planet.

Today's readings offer just a few among countless scriptural images of trees. What lessons can they teach us about our spiritual journey?

As the cedar sprig and the mustard seed grow abundantly large, so too can the smallest actions of ours have unforeseen impacts. Trees provide shade, shelter, and a home for many species; similarly, we too are called to reach out with openness and generosity to those in need. Even in the face of advancing age or other challenges, we can be fruitful and nurturing because, like the trees, we are wrapped in the powerful and providential love of God.

May the God of green and growing things keep us deeply rooted in love, so that we in turn can radiate God's compassion within not only the human community but the whole web of creation which is our common home.

■ Krystyna Higgins

ENTRANCE ANTIPHON *(Cf. Psalm 27 (26):7,9)*
O Lord, hear my voice, for I have called to you;
be my help. / Do not abandon or forsake me,
O God, my Savior!

INTRODUCTORY RITES *(page 10)*

COLLECT
O God, strength of those who hope in you,
graciously hear our pleas,
and, since without you mortal frailty can do nothing,
grant us always the help of your grace,
that in following your commands
we may please you by our resolve and our deeds.
Through our Lord Jesus Christ, your Son,
who lives and reigns with you in the unity of the Holy Spirit,
God, for ever and ever. ***Amen.***

FIRST READING *(Ezekiel 17:22-24)*
Thus says the Lord GOD:
I, too, will take from the crest of the cedar,
from its topmost branches tear off a tender shoot,
and plant it on a high and lofty mountain;
on the mountain heights of Israel I will plant it.
It shall put forth branches and bear fruit,
and become a majestic cedar.
Birds of every kind shall dwell beneath it,
every winged thing in the shade of its boughs.
And all the trees of the field shall know
that I, the LORD,
bring low the high tree,
lift high the lowly tree,

wither up the green tree,
and make the withered tree bloom.
As I, the LORD, have spoken, so will I do.
The word of the Lord. ***Thanks be to God.***

RESPONSORIAL PSALM *(Psalm 92:2-3, 13-14, 15-16)*

℟. Lord, it is good to give thanks to you.

It is good to give thanks to the LORD,
to sing praise to your name, Most High,
to proclaim your kindness at dawn
and your faithfulness throughout the night. ℟.
The just one shall flourish like the palm tree,
like a cedar of Lebanon shall he grow.
They that are planted in the house of the LORD
shall flourish in the courts of our God. ℟.
They shall bear fruit even in old age;
vigorous and sturdy shall they be,
declaring how just is the LORD,
my rock, in whom there is no wrong. ℟.

SECOND READING *(2 Corinthians 5:6-10)*

Brothers and sisters: We are always courageous, although we know that while we are at home in the body we are away from the Lord, for we walk by faith, not by sight. Yet we are courageous, and we would rather leave the body and go home to the Lord. Therefore, we aspire to please him, whether we are at home or away. For we must all appear before the judgment seat of Christ, so that each may receive recompense, according to what he did in the body, whether good or evil.

The word of the Lord. ***Thanks be to God.***

ALLELUIA

Alleluia, alleluia. The seed is the word of God, Christ is the sower. / All who come to him will live for ever. ***Alleluia, alleluia.***

GOSPEL *(Mark 4:26-34)*

A reading from the holy Gospel according to Mark.
Glory to you, O Lord.

Jesus said to the crowds: "This is how it is with the kingdom of God; it is as if a man were to scatter seed on the land and would sleep and rise night and day and through it all the seed would sprout and grow, he knows not how. Of its own accord the land yields fruit, first the blade, then the ear, then the full grain in the ear. And when the grain is ripe, he wields the sickle at once, for the harvest has come."

He said, "To what shall we compare the kingdom of God, or what **parable**✝ can we use for it? It is like a mustard seed that, when it is sown in the ground, is the smallest of all the seeds on the earth. But once it is sown, it springs up and becomes the largest of plants and puts forth large branches, so that the birds of the sky can dwell in its shade." With many such parables he spoke the word to them as they were able to understand it. Without parables he did not speak to them, but to his own disciples he explained everything in private.

The Gospel of the Lord. ***Praise to you, Lord Jesus Christ.***

PROFESSION OF FAITH *(page 13)*

PRAYER OF THE FAITHFUL

PREPARATION OF GIFTS *(page 16)*

PRAYER OVER THE OFFERINGS
O God, who in the offerings presented here
provide for the twofold needs of human nature,
nourishing us with food
and renewing us with your Sacrament,
grant, we pray,
that the sustenance they provide
may not fail us in body or in spirit.
Through Christ our Lord. ***Amen.***

PREFACE *(Sundays in Ordinary Time, pages 28–32)*

• TAKING A CLOSER LOOK •

✝ **Parable** A parable (from the Greek word *parabole*, to "throw together" things for comparison or illustration) is a short realistic story intended to encourage reflection by connecting the parable to our own life. Since one can connect the parable to various aspects of one's life or that of one's family or community, parables are open-ended in their application.

Parables were a common teaching device of the Jewish rabbis and important to Jesus in his teaching, because the only way we have to talk about what is unfamiliar to us (God's ruling presence or "kingdom") is in terms that are familiar to us (our everyday life and world). Thus, parables challenge the audience to think about their meaning and change their lives because of what they discover.

COMMUNION ANTIPHON *(Psalm27 [26]:4)*
There is one thing I ask of the Lord, only this do I seek: / to live in the house of the Lord all the days of my life.

Or *(John 17:11)*
Holy Father, keep in your name those you have given me, / that they may be one as we are one, says the Lord.

PRAYER AFTER COMMUNION
As this reception of your Holy Communion, O Lord,
foreshadows the union of the faithful in you,
so may it bring about unity in your Church.
Through Christ our Lord. ***Amen.***

BLESSING & DISMISSAL *(page 56)*

Responding to the Word

All on earth is under the rule of God, who can "bring low the high tree, lift high the lowly tree."

What situations in life make me forget how truly powerful God is?

Paul reminds us to look forward to an eternal life with God after we die.

How can this reminder change the way I live today?

The mustard seed can't grow until it is planted in the ground.

What opportunities do I have to sow the seed of God's word so that it can grow in others?

June 20

Jesus gives us his peace

Today's readings reflect a creation vibrant with divinity and relationship. Cameos of our spiritual history, they illustrate the increasing intimacy developing between God and humankind.

Out of a whirlwind, the disembodied voice of God challenges Job, one whose faith is unaffected despite intense suffering. The psalmist urges gratitude for a God whose love is shown in wondrous deeds. St. Paul offers a theological image of a world enlivened by the love of Christ. Each image, in its own way, seems distanced, impersonal.

In contrast, Mark's Gospel startles through a deceptively simple story that grounds us in the everyday. It has an immediacy that encourages us to see, hear, and feel. Asleep on a boat tossed about in stormy seas, Jesus is awakened by companions fearful for their safety and annoyed at his inattention. He commands the storm to be still. And in the ensuing peaceful calm, all hear an invitation to embrace transformation through relationship with him. This scene becomes a parable about discipleship.

In life, Jesus modeled peace as he resolved personal, societal, moral, and spiritual chaos; in death he gifted us his peace through the Spirit. As resurrection people we recall, receive, and exchange that peaceful blessing, here and now.

■ ELLA ALLEN

ENTRANCE ANTIPHON

(Cf. Psalm 28 [27]:8-9) The Lord is the strength of his people, / a saving refuge for the one he has anointed. / Save your people, Lord, and bless your heritage, / and govern them for ever.

INTRODUCTORY RITES *(page 10)*

COLLECT

Grant, O Lord,
that we may always revere and love your holy name,
for you never deprive of your guidance
those you set firm on the foundation of your love.
Through our Lord Jesus Christ, your Son,
who lives and reigns with you in the unity of the Holy Spirit,
God, for ever and ever. ***Amen.***

FIRST READING *(Job 38:1, 8-11)*

The Lord addressed Job out of the storm and said:
Who shut within doors the sea,
  when it burst forth from the womb;
when I made the clouds its garment
  and thick darkness its swaddling bands?
When I set limits for it
  and fastened the bar of its door,
and said: Thus far shall you come but no farther,
  and here shall your proud waves be stilled!
The word of the Lord. ***Thanks be to God.***

RESPONSORIAL PSALM *(Psalm 107:23-24, 25-26, 28-29, 30-31)*

℟. Give thanks to the Lord, his love is everlasting. *Or* **Alleluia.**

They who sailed the sea in ships,
trading on the deep waters,
these saw the works of the LORD
and his wonders in the abyss. ℟.
His command raised up a storm wind
which tossed its waves on high.
They mounted up to heaven; they sank to the depths;
their hearts melted away in their plight. ℟.
They cried to the LORD in their distress;
from their straits he rescued them,
he hushed the storm to a gentle breeze,
and the billows of the sea were stilled. ℟.
They rejoiced that they were calmed,
and he brought them to their desired haven.
Let them give thanks to the LORD for his kindness
and his wondrous deeds to the children of men. ℟.

SECOND READING *(2 Corinthians 5:14-17)*

Brothers and sisters: The love of Christ impels us, once we have come to the conviction that one died for all; therefore, all have died. He indeed died for all, so that those who live might no longer live for themselves but for him who for their sake died and was raised.

Consequently, from now on we regard no one according to the flesh; even if we once knew Christ according to the flesh, yet now we know him so no longer. So whoever is in Christ is **a new creation:** ✝ the old things have passed away; behold, new things have come.

The word of the Lord. ***Thanks be to God.***

ALLELUIA *(Luke 7:16)*
Alleluia, alleluia. A great prophet has risen in our midst, / God has visited his people. ***Alleluia, alleluia.***

GOSPEL *(Mark 4:35-41)*
A reading from the holy Gospel according to Mark.
Glory to you, O Lord.

On that day, as evening drew on, Jesus said to his disciples: "Let us cross to the other side." Leaving the crowd, they took Jesus with them in the boat just as he was. And other boats were with him. A violent squall came up and waves were breaking over the boat, so that it was already filling up. Jesus was in the stern, asleep on a cushion. They woke him and said to him, "Teacher, do you not care that we are perishing?" He woke up, rebuked the wind, and said to the sea, "Quiet! Be still!" The wind ceased and there was great calm. Then he asked them, "Why are you terrified? Do you not yet have faith?" They were filled with great awe and said to one another, "Who then is this whom even wind and sea obey?"

The Gospel of the Lord. ***Praise to you, Lord Jesus Christ.***

PROFESSION OF FAITH *(page 13)*

PRAYER OF THE FAITHFUL

PREPARATION OF GIFTS *(page 16)*

PRAYER OVER THE OFFERINGS

Receive, O Lord, the sacrifice of conciliation and praise
and grant that, cleansed by its action,
we may make offering of a heart pleasing to you.
Through Christ our Lord. ***Amen.***

PREFACE *(Sundays in Ordinary Time, pages 28–32)*

COMMUNION ANTIPHON

(Psalm 145 [144]:15) The eyes of all look to you, Lord, / and you give them their food in due season.

Or

(John 10:11, 15) I am the Good Shepherd, / and I lay down my life for my sheep, says the Lord.

TAKING A CLOSER LOOK

✝ **A new creation** Unlike ourselves, biblical people did not think the world was progressing, but rather always regressing. From the Garden of Eden onward, God's original vision for creation had steadily declined. But since God alone rules creation, the only way things could really be better was through a new creation by which God would re-order the world without sin, and everything would finally be perfect. Paul believed that God had begun this re-ordering in Jesus, and so a new creation had actually taken place. He also believed that the whole world would soon be transformed by God's power. We realize that this transformation did not happen as fast as Paul wanted but that it still continues even today.

PRAYER AFTER COMMUNION

Renewed and nourished
by the Sacred Body and Precious Blood of your Son,
we ask of your mercy, O Lord,
that what we celebrate with constant devotion
may be our sure pledge of redemption.
Through Christ our Lord. ***Amen.***

BLESSING & DISMISSAL *(page 56)* ⁜

Responding to the Word

God reminds Job that creation is under God's control.

What thanks might I give for God's gifts to me through nature?

Paul changes how he evaluates people now that he see them "in Christ."

How has the reality that each person is beloved by Christ changed the way I think of others?

Jesus calms a storm and calms the panicked disciples.

What "storms" in my life has Jesus helped me get through?

June 27

Faith over fear

Picture the scene. It's hot and noisy. A large crowd presses in on all sides trying to get closer to Jesus as Jairus elbows his way through. He's shouting. Pleading. Desperately begging for Jesus to come save his dying daughter. He knows Jesus can heal her. But he also knows that in this life-or-death situation, every second counts.

Jesus follows him but soon stops to discover who touched his cloak. Now imagine Jairus' panic at the delay. Imagine his heartbreak when he finally arrives home, only to discover that his daughter has passed away.

Prayer feels like this sometimes. Urgent. Desperate. Yet, seemingly met with silence or delay. In these difficult moments, it can be hard not to rage, doubt, or despair. Yet, those are the very times we need to ask the Holy Spirit for the strength to persevere in hope.

Jesus heals one daughter on the way to raise another, and through both encounters, Jesus' message for all of us is the same: have faith over fear.

Jesus asks us to entrust our loved ones to his timing, not ours. He invites us to push past the doubts that crowd our hearts and minds and to reach for him with total confidence. Do not give up. Do not fear. Just keep doing what you can to get closer to Jesus.

■ Caroline Pignat

ENTRANCE ANTIPHON *(Psalm 47 [46]:2)*
All peoples, clap your hands. / Cry to God with shouts of joy!

INTRODUCTORY RITES *(page 10)*

COLLECT
O God, who through the grace of adoption
chose us to be children of light,
grant, we pray,
that we may not be wrapped in the darkness of error
but always be seen to stand in the bright light of truth.
Through our Lord Jesus Christ, your Son,
who lives and reigns with you in the unity of the Holy Spirit,
God, for ever and ever. ***Amen.***

FIRST READING *(Wisdom 1:13-15; 2:23-24)*
God did not make death,
nor does he rejoice in the destruction of the living.
For he fashioned all things that they might have being;
and the creatures of the world are wholesome,
and there is not a destructive drug among them
nor any domain of the netherworld on earth,
for justice is undying.
For God formed man to be imperishable;
the image of his own nature he made him.
But by the envy of the devil, death entered the world,
and they who belong to his company experience it.
The word of the Lord. ***Thanks be to God.***

RESPONSORIAL PSALM *(Psalm 30:2, 4, 5-6, 11, 12, 13)*

℟. I will praise you, Lord, for you have rescued me.

I will extol you, O LORD, for you drew me clear
and did not let my enemies rejoice over me.
O LORD, you brought me up from the netherworld;
you preserved me from among those going down
into the pit. ℟.
Sing praise to the LORD, you his faithful ones,
and give thanks to his holy name.
For his anger lasts but a moment;
a lifetime, his good will.
At nightfall, weeping enters in,
but with the dawn, rejoicing. ℟.
Hear, O LORD, and have pity on me;
O LORD, be my helper.
You changed my mourning into dancing;
O LORD, my God, forever will I give you thanks. ℟.

SECOND READING *(2 Corinthians 8:7, 9, 13-15)*

Brothers and sisters: As you excel in every respect, in faith, discourse, knowledge, all earnestness, and in the love we have for you, may you excel in this gracious act also.

For you know the gracious act of our Lord Jesus Christ, that though he was rich, for your sake he became poor, so that by his poverty you might become rich. Not that others should have relief while you are burdened, but that as a matter of equality your abundance at the present time should supply their needs, so that their abundance may also supply your needs, that there may be equality. As it is written:

Whoever had much did not have more,
and whoever had little did not have less.
The word of the Lord. ***Thanks be to God.***

ALLELUIA *(See 2 Timothy 1:10)*

Alleluia, alleluia. Our Savior Jesus Christ destroyed death / and brought life to light through the Gospel. ***Alleluia, alleluia.***

GOSPEL *(Mark 5:21-43 or 5:21-24, 35b-43)*

For the shorter version, omit the indented part in brackets.

A reading from the holy Gospel according to Mark.
Glory to you, O Lord.

When Jesus had crossed again in the boat to the other side, a large crowd gathered around him, and he stayed close to the sea. One of the synagogue officials, named Jairus, came forward. Seeing him he fell at his feet and pleaded earnestly with him, saying, "My daughter is at the point of death. Please, come lay your hands on her that she may get well and live." He went off with him, and a large crowd followed him and pressed upon him.

[There was a woman afflicted with hemorrhages for twelve years. She had suffered greatly at the hands of many doctors and had spent all that she had. Yet she was not helped but only grew worse. She had heard about Jesus and came up behind him in the crowd and touched his cloak. She said, "If I but touch his clothes, I shall be cured." Immediately her flow of blood dried up. She felt in her body that she was healed of her affliction. Jesus, aware at once that power had gone out from him, turned around in the crowd and asked, "Who has touched my clothes?" But his disciples said to Jesus, "You see how the crowd is pressing upon you, and yet you ask, 'Who touched me?' " And he looked around to see who had done it.

The woman, realizing what had happened to her, approached in fear and trembling. She fell down before Jesus and told him the whole truth. He said to her, "Daughter, **your faith has saved you.** ✝ Go in peace and be cured of your affliction."]

While he was still speaking, people from the synagogue official's house arrived and said, "Your daughter has died; why trouble the teacher any longer?" Disregarding the message that was reported, Jesus said to the synagogue official, "Do not be afraid; just have faith." He did not allow anyone to accompany him inside except Peter, James, and John, the brother of James. When they arrived at the house of the synagogue official, he caught sight of a commotion, people weeping and wailing loudly. So he went in and said to them, "Why this commotion and weeping? The child is not dead but asleep." And they ridiculed him. Then he put them all out. He took along the child's father and mother and those who were with him and entered the room where the child was. He took the child by the hand and said to her, "*Talitha koum*," which means, "Little girl, I say to you, arise!" The girl, a child of twelve, arose immediately and walked around. At that they were utterly astounded. He gave strict orders that no one should know this and said that she should be given something to eat.

The Gospel of the Lord. ***Praise to you, Lord Jesus Christ.***

PROFESSION OF FAITH *(page 13)*

PRAYER OF THE FAITHFUL

PREPARATION OF GIFTS *(page 16)*

PRAYER OVER THE OFFERINGS

O God, who graciously accomplish
the effects of your mysteries,
grant, we pray,
that the deeds by which we serve you
may be worthy of these sacred gifts.
Through Christ our Lord. ***Amen.***

PREFACE *(Sundays in Ordinary Time, pages 28-32)*

COMMUNION ANTIPHON *(Cf. Psalm 103 [102]:1)*

Bless the Lord, O my soul, / and all within me, his holy name.

Or *(John 17:20-21)*

O Father, I pray for them, that they may be one in us, / that the world may believe that you have sent me, says the Lord.

TAKING A CLOSER LOOK

+ **Your faith has saved you** In Greek, the same word (*sodzo*) means both heal and save. Thus the gospel writers can use this word to join physical healing from illness or disease with spiritual healing from sin (whatever breaks down our relationship with God). Those who approach Jesus for bodily healing are also cleansed from spiritual sin and restored to relationship with God and the community. The outer healing alerts us to the inner reconciliation that happens when we commit ourselves in faith to a relationship with Jesus.

PRAYER AFTER COMMUNION

May this divine sacrifice we have offered and received
fill us with life, O Lord, we pray,
so that, bound to you in lasting charity,
we may bear fruit that lasts for ever.
Through Christ our Lord. ***Amen.***

BLESSING & DISMISSAL *(page 56)*

Responding to the Word

God created us for life and shared divine life with us.

When have I most felt God's life-giving power at work in me?

Paul urges us to imitate the way Christ shared his riches with us and share our own riches with those in need.

What might I do this week to help meet someone else's needs?

Jesus shows great concern for the sick child and helps her.

What might I do this week to help a child be more healthy or free?

July 4

Holiness in the ordinary

"You mean this could be God's path for me?" I still remember sitting with a friend 40 years ago, as her streaming tears mirrored the rain splashing on our parked car. She longed for holiness, but felt she had failed to achieve it and had to settle for an ordinary life. What she didn't see was the light shining from her union with God in her own "Nazareth"—holiness hidden in the ordinary. This joyous revelation opened her eyes to God's presence everywhere, as she now abides in God's love.

"What could possibly be said about her?" asked a nun in a little convent in France over a 100 years ago. A life of profound union with God was cloaked in ordinariness but burst out in dazzling light when St. Thérèse of Lisieux died at age 24.

Many in Jesus' hometown acknowledged his works of wisdom and power but could not see beyond his humanity to the divine light radiating from his very being. Even the thought was offensive to them. But the Lord came among us to unite heaven and earth, and God is in every atom, every breath, every person and place, whether humble or great. God is even in our ordinary, tarnished hearts. *Lord, open our eyes and hearts to see and receive you in our own Nazareth.*

■ Cheryl Ann Smith

ENTRANCE ANTIPHON *(Cf. Psalm 48 [47]:10-11)*
Your merciful love, O God, / we have received in the midst of your temple. / Your praise, O God, like your name, / reaches the ends of the earth; / your right hand is filled with saving justice.

INTRODUCTORY RITES *(page 10)*

COLLECT
O God, who in the abasement of your Son
have raised up a fallen world,
fill your faithful with holy joy,
for on those you have rescued from slavery to sin
you bestow eternal gladness.
Through our Lord Jesus Christ, your Son,
who lives and reigns with you in the unity of the Holy Spirit,
God, for ever and ever. ***Amen.***

FIRST READING *(Ezekiel 2:2-5)*
As the LORD spoke to me, the spirit entered into me and set me on my feet, and I heard the one who was speaking say to me: Son of man, I am sending you to the Israelites, rebels who have rebelled against me; they and their ancestors have revolted against me to this very day. Hard of face and obstinate of heart are they to whom I am sending you. But you shall say to them: Thus says the Lord GOD! And whether they heed or resist—for they are a rebellious house—they shall know that a prophet has been among them.

The word of the Lord. ***Thanks be to God.***

RESPONSORIAL PSALM *(Psalm 123:1-2, 2, 3-4)*

℟. Our eyes are fixed on the Lord, pleading for his mercy.

To you I lift up my eyes
who are enthroned in heaven—
as the eyes of servants
are on the hands of their masters. ℟.
As the eyes of a maid
are on the hands of her mistress,
so are our eyes on the LORD, our God,
till he have pity on us. ℟.
Have pity on us, O LORD, have pity on us,
for we are more than sated with contempt;
our souls are more than sated
with the mockery of the arrogant,
with the contempt of the proud. ℟.

SECOND READING *(2 Corinthians 12:7-10)*

Brothers and sisters: That I, Paul, might not become too elated, because of the abundance of the revelations, a thorn in the flesh was given to me, an angel of Satan, to beat me, to keep me from being too elated. Three times I begged the Lord about this, that it might leave me, but he said to me, "My grace is sufficient for you, for power is made perfect in weakness." I will rather boast most gladly of my weaknesses, in order that the power of Christ may dwell with me. Therefore, I am content with weaknesses, insults, hardships, persecutions, and constraints, for the sake of Christ; for when I am weak, then I am strong.

The word of the Lord. ***Thanks be to God.***

ALLELUIA *(See Luke 4:18)*
Alleluia, alleluia. The Spirit of the Lord is upon me / for he sent me to bring glad tidings to the poor. ***Alleluia, alleluia.***

GOSPEL *(Mark 6:1-6a)*
A reading from the holy Gospel according to Mark.
Glory to you, O Lord.

Jesus departed from there and came to his native place, accompanied by his disciples. When the sabbath came he began to teach in the synagogue, and many who heard him were astonished. They said, "Where did this man get all this? What kind of wisdom has been given him? What mighty deeds are wrought by his hands! Is he not the carpenter, the son of Mary, and the brother of James and Joses and Judas and Simon? And are not his sisters here with us?" And they took offense at him. Jesus said to them, "A **prophet**✝ is not without honor except in his native place and among his own kin and in his own house." So he was not able to perform any mighty deed there, apart from curing a few sick people by laying his hands on them. He was amazed at their lack of faith.

The Gospel of the Lord. ***Praise to you, Lord Jesus Christ.***

PROFESSION OF FAITH *(page 13)*

PRAYER OF THE FAITHFUL

PREPARATION OF GIFTS *(page 16)*

PRAYER OVER THE OFFERINGS

May this oblation dedicated to your name
purify us, O Lord,
and day by day bring our conduct
closer to the life of heaven.
Through Christ our Lord. ***Amen.***

PREFACE *(Sundays in Ordinary Time, pages 28–32)*

COMMUNION ANTIPHON

(Psalm 34 [33]:9) Taste and see that the Lord is good; / blessed the man who seeks refuge in him.

Or *(Matthew 11:28)*

Come to me, all who labor and are burdened, / and I will refresh you, says the Lord.

TAKING A CLOSER LOOK

+ **Prophet** Prophets are those who speak for or on behalf of God to the community. Their major task was not to foretell the future but to forth-tell God's presence in the events affecting their nation. In a world that did not clearly separate issues of religion and politics, the prophets reminded the kings that God was present and active in the political and social crises of the community. Like lobbyists for the rule of God, they demanded that courses of action in times of crisis must follow what God desires and not simply what is most expedient according to human political wisdom.

PRAYER AFTER COMMUNION

Grant, we pray, O Lord,
that, having been replenished by such great gifts,
we may gain the prize of salvation
and never cease to praise you.
Through Christ our Lord. ***Amen.***

BLESSING & DISMISSAL *(page 56)*

Responding to the Word

Ezekiel is commanded to prophesy even though his audience will be unreceptive.

What gives me the courage to go on when others are unreceptive to my witness?

Paul learns the hard way that his weakness is a showcase for God's strength.

When have my weaknesses been an unexpected source of blessing for me and others around me?

Jesus' neighbors were unreceptive because they could not see beyond their rigid stereotypes.

How might I be missing what Jesus is calling me to discover?

July 11

When called, trust in God

When I was 28 years old, despite having worked less than three years for a newspaper and with no theological education, I was hired as the editor of the *Western Catholic Reporter*. There was another good candidate, and I never learned why the committee chose me over him. I was green as grass, and it showed.

Today's readings are about the mystery of God choosing and sending the unworthy. The prophet Amos was a dresser of sycamore trees who had been critical of the social injustice in ancient Israel. The priest at the temple of Bethel scorned Amos, but Amos responded that God had called him, saying, "Go, prophesy to my people Israel."

The gospel is similar. Jesus had already chosen the Twelve, but now he sends them on a mission. They are to take no food or money, and to leave their backpacks at home. Their only advantage was that Jesus gave them power over unclean spirits. The apostles preached repentance, cast out demons, and cured the sick. The mission was a success.

The call is a mystery, and the success of the mission even more so. Success is a testimony to the power of God. Humans are weak, but the Spirit is strong. When called, trust in God. God will claim his victory through your feeble hands.

■ Glen Argan

ENTRANCE ANTIPHON *(Cf. Psalm 17 [16]:15)*
As for me, in justice I shall behold your face; /
I shall be filled with the vision of your glory.

INTRODUCTORY RITES *(page 10)*

COLLECT
O God, who show the light of your truth
to those who go astray,
so that they may return to the right path,
give all who for the faith they profess
are accounted Christians
the grace to reject whatever is contrary to the name of Christ
and to strive after all that does it honor.
Through our Lord Jesus Christ, your Son,
who lives and reigns with you in the unity of the Holy Spirit,
God, for ever and ever. ***Amen.***

FIRST READING *(Amos 7:12–15)*
Amaziah, priest of **Bethel,**✝ said to Amos, "Off with you, visionary, flee to the land of Judah! There earn your bread by prophesying, but never again prophesy in Bethel; for it is the king's sanctuary and a royal temple." Amos answered Amaziah, "I was no prophet, nor have I belonged to a company of prophets; I was a shepherd and a dresser of sycamores. The LORD took me from following the flock, and said to me, Go, prophesy to my people Israel."

The word of the Lord. ***Thanks be to God.***

RESPONSORIAL PSALM *(Psalm 85:9-10, 11-12, 13-14)*

℟. Lord, let us see your kindness and grant us your salvation.

I will hear what God proclaims;
 the LORD—for he proclaims peace.
Near indeed is his salvation to those who fear him,
 glory dwelling in our land. ℟.
Kindness and truth shall meet;
 justice and peace shall kiss.
Truth shall spring out of the earth,
 and justice shall look down from heaven. ℟.
The LORD himself will give his benefits;
 our land shall yield its increase.
Justice shall walk before him,
 and prepare the way of his steps. ℟.

SECOND READING *(Ephesians 1:3-14 or 1:3-10)*

The shorter version ends at the asterisks.

Blessed be the God and Father of our Lord Jesus Christ, who has blessed us in Christ with every spiritual blessing in the heavens, as he chose us in him, before the foundation of the world, to be holy and without blemish before him. In love he destined us for adoption to himself through Jesus Christ, in accord with the favor of his will, for the praise of the glory of his grace that he granted us in the beloved.

In him we have redemption by his blood, the forgiveness of transgressions, in accord with the riches of his grace that he lavished upon us. In all wisdom and insight, he has made known to us the mystery of his will in accord with his favor that he set forth in him as a plan for the fullness of times, to sum up all things in Christ, in heaven and on earth.

* * *

In him we were also chosen, destined in accord with the purpose of the One who accomplishes all things according to the intention of his will, so that we might exist for the praise of his glory, we who first hoped in Christ. In him you also, who have heard the word of truth, the gospel of your salvation, and have believed in him, were sealed with the promised Holy Spirit, which is the first installment of our inheritance toward redemption as God's possession, to the praise of his glory.

The word of the Lord. ***Thanks be to God.***

ALLELUIA *(See Ephesians 1:17-18)*

Alleluia, alleluia. May the Father of our Lord Jesus Christ / enlighten the eyes of our hearts, / that we may know what is the hope that / belongs to our call. ***Alleluia, alleluia.***

GOSPEL *(Mark 6:7-13)*

A reading from the holy Gospel according to Mark.

Glory to you, O Lord.

Jesus summoned the Twelve and began to send them out two by two and gave them authority over unclean spirits. He instructed them to take nothing for the journey but a walking stick—no food, no sack, no money in their belts. They were, however, to wear sandals but not a second tunic. He said to them, "Wherever you enter a house, stay there until you leave. Whatever place does not welcome you or listen to you, leave there and shake the dust off your feet in testimony against them." So they went off and preached repentance. The Twelve drove out many demons, and they anointed with oil many who were sick and cured them.

The Gospel of the Lord. ***Praise to you, Lord Jesus Christ.***

PROFESSION OF FAITH *(page 13)*

PRAYER OF THE FAITHFUL

PREPARATION OF GIFTS *(page 16)*

PRAYER OVER THE OFFERINGS

Look upon the offerings of the Church, O Lord,
as she makes her prayer to you,
and grant that, when consumed by those who believe,
they may bring ever greater holiness.
Through Christ our Lord. ***Amen.***

PREFACE *(Sundays in Ordinary Time, pages 28–32)*

TAKING A CLOSER LOOK

✝ **Bethel** Located about fourteen miles north of Jerusalem, Bethel (Hebrew, "house of God") was a sacred site dating back to the time of Abraham, who built an altar there (Genesis 12:8) and Jacob, who had his famous dream there of the ladder to heaven (Genesis 28:10-20). It was a place for worship, national assembly, and prophetic activity before these functions were taken over by Jerusalem and its temple under King David.

COMMUNION ANTIPHON *(Cf. Psalm 84 [83]:4-5)*
The sparrow finds a home, / and the swallow a nest for her young: / by your altars, O Lord of hosts, my King and my God. / Blessed are they who dwell in your house, / for ever singing your praise.

Or *(John 6:57)*
Whoever eats my flesh and drinks my blood / remains in me and I in him, says the Lord.

PRAYER AFTER COMMUNION
Having consumed these gifts, we pray, O Lord,
that, by our participation in this mystery,
its saving effects upon us may grow.
Through Christ our Lord. ***Amen.***

BLESSING & DISMISSAL *(page 56)*

Responding to the Word

Amos recounts how God came to him amidst his regular job and commissioned him to witness.

➡ *When has God's presence in my regular tasks prompted me to do something new?*

Paul reminds us that God has chosen us, adopted us, and lavished many gifts on us.

➡ *For which gifts am I especially thankful today?*

Jesus commissions the disciples to begin sharing in Christ's work.

➡ *To whom is Christ sending me now to bring his healing power?*

July 18

Rest with the Good Shepherd

I'm sure we have all encountered bad shepherds that have led us astray, leading us into danger and leaving us in a state of abandonment and fear. We might have also felt isolated and alone and have lost our sense of peace. When we draw close to the Lord and see him as the Divine Shepherd, we have no more fear. He is our peace, heals our wounds, and gives us access to the Father through the Holy Spirit.

Jesus invited his apostles to go with him to a deserted place to rest for a while. We all need rest, and he invites us to rest with him as well. He wants to fill that void, to be the shepherd who leads us, and to teach us many things, just like he did for the great crowd that followed him and his apostles when they needed rest the most. The gospel tells us that they didn't even have the time to sit and eat because they were so busy.

Today, may we respond to Jesus' invitation and rest with him awhile. He will remove your fear and fill you with his peace. The Lord also promises to appoint shepherds for us so that we "need no longer fear and tremble." In today's eucharistic celebration, we give thanks to the Lord for his good shepherds in our lives.

■ Sarah Escobar

ENTRANCE ANTIPHON *(Psalm 54 [53]:6, 8)*
See, I have God for my help. / The Lord sustains my soul. / I will sacrifice to you with willing heart, / and praise your name, O Lord, for it is good.

INTRODUCTORY RITES *(page 10)*

COLLECT
Show favor, O Lord, to your servants
and mercifully increase the gifts of your grace,
that, made fervent in hope, faith and charity,
they may be ever watchful in keeping your commands.
Through our Lord Jesus Christ, your Son,
who lives and reigns with you in the unity of the Holy Spirit,
God, for ever and ever. ***Amen.***

FIRST READING *(Jeremiah 23:1-6)*
Woe to the shepherds who mislead and scatter the flock of my pasture, says the LORD. Therefore, thus says the LORD, the God of Israel, against the shepherds who shepherd my people: You have scattered my sheep and driven them away. You have not cared for them, but I will take care to punish your evil deeds. I myself will gather the remnant of my flock from all the lands to which I have driven them and bring them back to their meadow; there they shall increase and multiply. I will appoint shepherds for them who will shepherd them so that they need no longer fear and tremble; and none shall be missing, says the LORD.

Behold, the days are coming, says the LORD,
  when I will raise up a righteous shoot to David;
as king he shall reign and govern wisely,
  he shall do what is just and right in the land.
In his days Judah shall be saved,

Israel shall dwell in security.
This is the name they give him:
"The LORD our justice."
The word of the Lord. ***Thanks be to God.***

RESPONSORIAL PSALM *(Psalm 23:1–3, 3–4, 5, 6)*

℟. The Lord is my shepherd; there is nothing I shall want.

The LORD is my shepherd; I shall not want.
In verdant pastures he gives me repose;
beside restful waters he leads me;
he refreshes my soul. **℟.**
He guides me in right paths
for his name's sake.
Even though I walk in the dark valley
I fear no evil; for you are at my side
with your rod and your staff
that give me courage. **℟.**
You spread the table before me
in the sight of my foes;
you anoint my head with oil;
my cup overflows. **℟.**
Only goodness and kindness follow me
all the days of my life;
and I shall dwell in the house of the LORD
for years to come. **℟.**

SECOND READING *(Ephesians 2:13–18)*

Brothers and sisters: In Christ Jesus you who once were far off have become near by the blood of Christ.

For he is our peace, he who made both one and broke down the dividing wall of enmity, through his flesh, abolishing the law with its commandments and legal claims, that he might create in himself one new person in place of the two, thus establishing peace, and might reconcile both with God, in one body, through the cross, putting that enmity to death by it. He came and preached peace to you who were far off and peace to those who were near, for through him we both have access in one Spirit to the Father.

The word of the Lord. ***Thanks be to God.***

ALLELUIA *(John 10:27)*

Alleluia, alleluia. My sheep hear my voice, says the Lord; /
I know them, and they follow me. ***Alleluia, alleluia.***

GOSPEL *(Mark 6:30–34)*

A reading from the holy Gospel according to Mark.
Glory to you, O Lord.

The apostles gathered together with Jesus and reported all they had done and taught. He said to them, "Come away by yourselves to a deserted place and rest a while." People were coming and going in great numbers, and they had no opportunity even to eat. So they went off in the boat by themselves to a deserted place. People saw them leaving and many came to know about it. They hastened there on foot from all the towns and arrived at the place before them.

When he disembarked and saw the vast crowd, his heart was moved with **pity**✝ for them, for they were like sheep without a shepherd; and he began to teach them many things.

The Gospel of the Lord. ***Praise to you, Lord Jesus Christ.***

PROFESSION OF FAITH *(page 13)*

PRAYER OF THE FAITHFUL

PREPARATION OF GIFTS *(page 16)*

PRAYER OVER THE OFFERINGS

O God, who in the one perfect sacrifice
brought to completion varied offerings of the law,
accept, we pray, this sacrifice from your faithful servants
and make it holy, as you blessed the gifts of Abel,
so that what each has offered to the honor of your majesty
may benefit the salvation of all.
Through Christ our Lord. ***Amen.***

PREFACE *(Sundays in Ordinary Time, pages 28–32)*

TAKING A CLOSER LOOK

+ **Pity** Pity, in its common modern sense of "to feel sorry for someone," is not a very good translation of what Jesus feels here. The Greek word is much closer to our sense of compassion, that is, a strong emotional reaction that is felt deep within in response to someone else's difficulty or suffering. This strong sense of compassion is the springboard that launches Jesus into action. Thus it echoes the divine compassion that prompted God to come down to deliver the people from their Egyptian oppressors (see Exodus 3:7).

COMMUNION ANTIPHON *(Psalm 111 [110]:4-5)*
The Lord, the gracious, the merciful, / has made a memorial of his wonders; / he gives food to those who fear him.

Or *(Revelation 3:20)*
Behold, I stand at the door and knock, says the Lord. / If anyone hears my voice and opens the door to me, / I will enter his house and dine with him, and he with me.

PRAYER AFTER COMMUNION
Graciously be present to your people, we pray, O Lord,
and lead those you have imbued with heavenly mysteries
to pass from former ways to newness of life.
Through Christ our Lord. ***Amen.***

BLESSING & DISMISSAL *(page 56)* ✣

Responding to the Word

God's example instructs us that we must have both justice and compassion.

What might I do today to be more just and compassionate toward others?

The Holy Spirit helps us to pray when we don't know how.

For what help with my prayer do I ask the Holy Spirit today?

Jesus tells us that God's presence (kingdom) often starts out very small but can grow very large.

How has my awareness of God grown recently?

July 25

God's love is abundant

Today's readings all speak of the abundant, profligate love of God the Father, a love that calls all of us to a rich and flourishing unity. God has so much love for us that it is literally teeming, filling baskets to overflowing.

Both the first reading and the gospel tell of feeding the multitude: God confounds human expectations about how we can take care of each other. When we rely on our own resources, we are limited. There likely won't be enough to go around. When we allow God to work through us, anything is possible.

Many of us have been fortunate enough to know this abundant and transformative love through our grandparents. When I had my first child, people looked at me strangely as I declared I could hardly wait to be a grandmother. What I saw in my daughter's grandparents made me eager to grow into that level of steady, assured, boundless love.

Today, on this Catholic World Day for Grandparents and the Elderly, let us pray with gratitude for all elders whose lives are a witness to the prodigal Father watching all of us with affection, joy, and pride as we too falter and stumble, wonder and yearn, and eat of the Bread of Life which sustains us in all ways.

■ Maureen Kinahan

ENTRANCE ANTIPHON *(Cf. Psalm 68 [67]:6-7, 36)*
God is in his holy place, / God who unites those who dwell in his house; / he himself gives might and strength to his people.

INTRODUCTORY RITES *(page 10)*

COLLECT
O God, protector of those who hope in you,
without whom nothing has firm foundation, nothing is holy,
bestow in abundance your mercy upon us
and grant that, with you as our ruler and guide,
we may use the good things that pass
in such a way as to hold fast even now
to those that ever endure.
Through our Lord Jesus Christ, your Son,
who lives and reigns with you in the unity of the Holy Spirit,
God, for ever and ever. ***Amen.***

FIRST READING *(2 Kings 4:42-44)*
A man came from Baal-shalishah bringing to Elisha, the man of God, twenty barley loaves made from the firstfruits, and fresh grain in the ear. Elisha said, "Give it to the people to eat." But his servant objected, "How can I set this before a hundred people?" Elisha insisted, "Give it to the people to eat." "For thus says the LORD, 'They shall eat and there shall be some left over.' " And when they had eaten, there was some left over, as the LORD had said.

The word of the Lord. ***Thanks be to God.***

RESPONSORIAL PSALM *(Psalm 145:10-11, 15-16, 17-18)*

℟. The hand of the Lord feeds us; he answers all our needs.

Let all your works give you thanks, O LORD,
 and let your faithful ones bless you.
Let them discourse of the glory of your kingdom
 and speak of your might. ℟.
The eyes of all look hopefully to you,
 and you give them their food in due season;
you open your hand
 and satisfy the desire of every living thing. ℟.
The LORD is just in all his ways
 and holy in all his works.
The LORD is near to all who call upon him,
 to all who call upon him in truth. ℟.

SECOND READING *(Ephesians 4:1-6)*

Brothers and sisters: I, a prisoner for the Lord, urge you to live in a manner worthy of the call you have received, with all humility and gentleness, with patience, bearing with one another through love, striving to preserve the unity of the spirit through the bond of peace: one body and one Spirit, as you were also called to the one hope of your call; one Lord, one faith, one baptism; one God and Father of all, who is over all and through all and in all.

The word of the Lord. ***Thanks be to God.***

ALLELUIA *(Luke 7:16)*

Alleluia, alleluia. A great prophet has risen in our midst. / God has visited his people. ***Alleluia, alleluia.***

GOSPEL *(John 6:1–15)*

A reading from the holy Gospel according to John.

Glory to you, O Lord.

Jesus went across the Sea of Galilee. A large crowd followed him, because they saw the signs he was performing on the sick. Jesus went up on the mountain, and there he sat down with his disciples. The Jewish feast of Passover was near. When Jesus raised his eyes and saw that a large crowd was coming to him, he said to Philip, "Where can we buy enough food for them to eat?" He said this to test him, because he himself knew what he was going to do. Philip answered him, "Two hundred days' wages worth of food would not be enough for each of them to have a little." One of his disciples, Andrew, the brother of Simon Peter, said to him, "There is a boy here who has five **barley loaves**✛ and two fish; but what good are these for so many?" Jesus said, "Have the people recline." Now there was a great deal of grass in that place. So the men reclined, about five thousand in number. Then Jesus took the loaves, gave thanks, and distributed them to those who were reclining, and also as much of the fish as they wanted. When they had had their fill, he said to his disciples, "Gather the fragments left over, so that nothing will be wasted." So they collected them, and filled twelve wicker baskets with fragments from the five barley loaves that had been more than they could eat. When the people saw the sign he had done, they said, "This is truly the Prophet, the one who is to come into the world." Since Jesus knew that they were going to come and carry him off to make him king, he withdrew again to the mountain alone.

The Gospel of the Lord. ***Praise to you, Lord Jesus Christ.***

PROFESSION OF FAITH *(page 13)*

PRAYER OF THE FAITHFUL

PREPARATION OF GIFTS *(page 16)*

PRAYER OVER THE OFFERINGS

Accept, O Lord, we pray, the offerings
which we bring from the abundance of your gifts,
that through the powerful working of your grace
these most sacred mysteries may sanctify our present way of life
and lead us to eternal gladness.
Through Christ our Lord. ***Amen.***

PREFACE *(Sundays in Ordinary Time, pages 28–32)*

TAKING A CLOSER LOOK

✛ **Barley loaves** Barley was one of the two main Palestinian grain crops, along with wheat. It was planted in the autumn and harvested in April, a month or so earlier than wheat. At the end of the harvest was the feast of Pentecost. The bread made from barley was coarser than wheat bread, and it was much more commonly used among the poorer people. Since barley was so important for the poor, any failure of the barley crop brought much hardship.

COMMUNION ANTIPHON *(Psalm 103 [102]: 2)*
Bless the Lord, O my soul, / and never forget all his benefits.

Or *(Matthew 5:7–8)*
Blessed are the merciful, for they shall receive mercy. / Blessed are the clean of heart, for they shall see God.

PRAYER AFTER COMMUNION
We have consumed, O Lord, this divine Sacrament,
the perpetual memorial of the Passion of your Son;
grant, we pray, that this gift,
which he himself gave us with love beyond all telling,
may profit us for salvation.
Through Christ our Lord. ***Amen.***

BLESSING & DISMISSAL *(page 56)* ⁜

RESPONDING TO THE WORD

Elisha is not worried that sharing will exhaust his resources.

When have I experienced someone else's gift of generosity after I have been generous with others?

Paul notes many ways in which we are united.

Which sign of unity is most important to me? Why?

Jesus' wondrous sharing of bread leaves everyone satisfied.

When has my sharing of the Eucharist left me feeling especially nourished?

August 1

Live in the present with the Lord

Recently I was asked to help prepare a memorial with someone whose dear friend had died. It required all my focus for quite a while. Afterward, I was aware that I had stopped checking the news—a good thing. It was a valuable lesson, for it's easy to become like the Israelites in the desert and focus on the past rather than being grateful for the present.

In the gospel, the disciples have been following Jesus—living in the present—and yet they ask for more signs. Do they not trust his words? Am I like them? Do I believe because I ate my fill or because I saw signs? Do I act on my knowledge, on my desire for Jesus, and cross the sea to look for him? In the readings today, I can almost see my own salvation history—times of learning, knowing, and wondering, and times of turning away and then turning back again.

Today's readings remind me of God's presence in my life, a gift that slips from view if I'm not careful. Thankfully I can rely on the experience and knowledge of others, and I too can be a reminder to them. We can be a true communion of saints, a eucharistic people, a grateful people.

■ Sr. Susan Kidd, CND

ENTRANCE ANTIPHON *(Psalm 70 [69]:2, 6)*
O God, come to my assistance; / O Lord, make haste to help me! / You are my rescuer, my help; / O Lord, do not delay.

INTRODUCTORY RITES *(page 10)*

COLLECT
Draw near to your servants, O Lord,
and answer their prayers with unceasing kindness,
that, for those who glory in you as their Creator and guide,
you may restore what you have created
and keep safe what you have restored.
Through our Lord Jesus Christ, your Son,
who lives and reigns with you in the unity of the Holy Spirit,
God, for ever and ever. ***Amen.***

FIRST READING *(Exodus 16:2-4, 12-15)*
The whole Israelite community grumbled against Moses and Aaron. The Israelites said to them, "Would that we had died at the LORD's hand in the land of Egypt, as we sat by our fleshpots and ate our fill of bread! But you had to lead us into this desert to make the whole community die of famine!"

Then the LORD said to Moses, "I will now rain down bread from heaven for you. Each day the people are to go out and gather their daily portion; thus will I test them, to see whether they follow my instructions or not.

"I have heard the grumbling of the Israelites. Tell them: In the evening twilight you shall eat flesh, and in the morning you shall have your fill of bread, so that you may know that I, the LORD, am your God."

In the evening quail came up and covered the camp. In the morning a dew lay all about the camp, and when the dew evaporated, there on the surface of the desert were fine flakes like hoarfrost on the ground. On seeing it, the Israelites asked one another, "What is this?" for they did not know what it was. But Moses told them, "This is the bread that the LORD has given you to eat."

The word of the Lord. ***Thanks be to God.***

RESPONSORIAL PSALM *(Psalm 78:3-4, 23-24, 25, 54)*

℟. The Lord gave them bread from heaven.

What we have heard and know,
and what our fathers have declared to us,
We will declare to the generation to come,
the glorious deeds of the LORD and his strength
and the wonders that he wrought. ℟.
He commanded the skies above
and opened the doors of heaven;
he rained manna upon them for food
and gave them heavenly bread. ℟.
Man ate the bread of angels,
food he sent them in abundance.
And he brought them to his holy land,
to the mountains his right hand had won. ℟.

SECOND READING *(Ephesians 4:17, 20-24)*

Brothers and sisters: I declare and testify in the Lord that you must no longer live as the Gentiles do, in the futility of their minds; that is not how you learned Christ, assuming that you have heard of him and were taught in him, as truth is in Jesus, that you should put away the old self of your former way of life, corrupted through deceitful desires, and be renewed in the spirit of your minds, and put on the new self, created in God's way in righteousness and holiness of truth.

The word of the Lord. ***Thanks be to God.***

ALLELUIA *(Matthew 4:4b)*

Alleluia, alleluia. One does not live on bread alone, / but on every word that comes forth from the mouth of God. ***Alleluia, alleluia.***

GOSPEL *(John 6:24-35)*

A reading from the holy Gospel according to John.
Glory to you, O Lord.

When the crowd saw that neither Jesus nor his disciples were there, they themselves got into boats and came to Capernaum looking for Jesus. And when they found him across the sea they said to him, "Rabbi, when did you get here?" Jesus answered them and said, "Amen, amen, I say to you, you are looking for me not because you saw **signs**✛ but because you ate the loaves and were filled. Do not work for food that perishes but for the food that endures for eternal life, which the Son of Man will give you. For on him the Father, God, has set his seal." So they said to him, "What can we do to accomplish the works of God?" Jesus answered and said to them, "This is the work of God, that you believe in the one he sent." So they said to him, "What sign can you do, that we may see and believe in you? What can you do? Our ancestors ate manna in the desert, as it is written:

He gave them bread from heaven to eat."

So Jesus said to them, "Amen, amen, I say to you, it was not Moses who gave the bread from heaven; my Father gives you the true bread from heaven. For the bread of God is that which comes down from heaven and gives life to the world."

So they said to him, "Sir, give us this bread always." Jesus said to them, "I am the bread of life; whoever comes to me will never hunger, and whoever believes in me will never thirst."

The Gospel of the Lord. ***Praise to you, Lord Jesus Christ.***

PROFESSION OF FAITH *(page 13)*

PRAYER OF THE FAITHFUL

PREPARATION OF GIFTS *(page 16)*

PRAYER OVER THE OFFERINGS

Graciously sanctify these gifts, O Lord, we pray,
and, accepting the oblation of this spiritual sacrifice,
make of us an eternal offering to you.
Through Christ our Lord. ***Amen.***

PREFACE *(Sundays in Ordinary Time, pages 28–32)*

TAKING A CLOSER LOOK

✝ **Signs** Although we use the word 'miracle' to describe these events, the biblical writers used the terms "deeds of power," "signs," and "wonders." These are God's actions to reorder our world from the domination of Satan and evil powers that frustrate God's plan for a covenant community. Jesus' deeds of power are directly related to his kingdom message. They are the first signs (his resurrection to new life will be the final sign) that God is re-ordering our world. Like Jesus' parables and meals, Jesus' cures, exorcisms, and resuscitations are signs of God's presence breaking into our world to change it forever.

COMMUNION ANTIPHON *(Wisdom 16:20)*
You have given us, O Lord, bread from heaven, / endowed with all delights and sweetness in every taste.

Or *(John 6:35)*
I am the bread of life, says the Lord; / whoever comes to me will not hunger / and whoever believes in me will not thirst.

PRAYER AFTER COMMUNION
Accompany with constant protection, O Lord,
those you renew with these heavenly gifts
and, in your never-failing care for them,
make them worthy of eternal redemption.
Through Christ our Lord. ***Amen.***

BLESSING & DISMISSAL *(page 56)* ⁜

Responding to the Word

God feeds the Israelites in the wilderness.

When has God provided for me in recent weeks?

Paul encourages us to adopt a new way of life modeled on Christ.

What might I do to be more like Christ today?

Jesus says he is the bread that gives us life.

How has Jesus nourished my life this week?

August 8

Christ, the Bread of Life

As a person with multiple food allergies, I must be alert in order to maintain my health and be nourished properly. For this, I need to have a deep understanding of my food choices while suppressing my cravings. Food is necessary for life, and sharing a meal is a pleasure, but for me it can also be dangerous and a burden.

In today's gospel, the people are struggling to understand the message Jesus communicated—that he came down from heaven. They feel they have enough information to make a judgment. Isn't he the son of Joseph and Mary? Similarly, we can be convinced of our knowledge or opinions, which can create problems in our families and communities. We fail when we rely solely on ourselves instead of feeding on the Living Bread, Jesus.

Are we like the people in today's gospel, trusting we know it all, or do we believe Jesus is the Bread of Life? The word Eucharist means "having given thanks." Are we a grateful people? Are we honestly striving to be like Jesus? Do we rely on him to nourish us, to save us with the living bread? Rather than suppressing our craving, let us rely on our deep understanding of Jesus as the Bread of Life and believe.

■ Ildiko O'Dacre

ENTRANCE ANTIPHON *(Cf. Psalm 74 [73]:20, 19, 22, 23)*
Look to your covenant, O Lord, / and forget not the life of your poor ones for ever. / Arise, O God, and defend your cause, / and forget not the cries of those who seek you.

INTRODUCTORY RITES *(page 10)*

COLLECT
Almighty ever-living God,
whom, taught by the Holy Spirit,
we dare to call our Father,
bring, we pray, to perfection in our hearts
the spirit of adoption as your sons and daughters,
that we may merit to enter into the inheritance
which you have promised.
Through our Lord Jesus Christ, your Son,
who lives and reigns with you in the unity of the Holy Spirit,
God, for ever and ever. ***Amen.***

FIRST READING *(1 Kings 19:4-8)*
Elijah went a day's journey into the desert, until he came to a broom tree and sat beneath it. He prayed for death, saying: "This is enough, O LORD! Take my life, for I am no better than my fathers." He lay down and fell asleep under the broom tree, but then an **angel**✝ touched him and ordered him to get up and eat. Elijah looked and there at his head was a hearth cake and a jug of water. After he ate and drank, he lay down again, but the angel of the LORD came back a second time, touched him, and ordered, "Get up and eat, else the journey will be too long for you!" He got up, ate, and drank;

then strengthened by that food, he walked forty days and forty nights to the mountain of God, Horeb.

The word of the Lord. ***Thanks be to God.***

RESPONSORIAL PSALM *(Psalm 34:2-3, 4-5, 6-7, 8-9)*

℟. Taste and see the goodness of the Lord.

I will bless the LORD at all times;
his praise shall be ever in my mouth.
Let my soul glory in the LORD;
the lowly will hear me and be glad. ℟.
Glorify the LORD with me,
let us together extol his name.
I sought the LORD, and he answered me
and delivered me from all my fears. ℟.
Look to him that you may be radiant with joy,
and your faces may not blush with shame.
When the afflicted man called out, the LORD heard,
and from all his distress he saved him. ℟.
The angel of the LORD encamps
around those who fear him and delivers them.
Taste and see how good the LORD is;
blessed the man who takes refuge in him. ℟.

SECOND READING *(Ephesians 4:30–5:2)*

Brothers and sisters: Do not grieve the Holy Spirit of God, with which you were sealed for the day of redemption. All bitterness, fury, anger, shouting, and reviling must be removed from you, along with all malice. And be kind to one another, compassionate, forgiving one another as God has forgiven you in Christ.

So be imitators of God, as beloved children, and live in love, as Christ loved us and handed himself over for us as a sacrificial

offering to God for a fragrant aroma.
The word of the Lord. ***Thanks be to God.***

ALLELUIA *(John 6:51)*
Alleluia, alleluia. I am the living bread that came down from heaven, says the Lord; / whoever eats this bread will live forever.
Alleluia, alleluia.

GOSPEL *(John 6:41-51)*
A reading from the holy Gospel according to John.
Glory to you, O Lord.

The Jews murmured about Jesus because he said, "I am the bread that came down from heaven," and they said, "Is this not Jesus, the son of Joseph? Do we not know his father and mother? Then how can he say, 'I have come down from heaven'?" Jesus answered and said to them, "Stop murmuring among yourselves. No one can come to me unless the Father who sent me draw him, and I will raise him on the last day. It is written in the prophets:

They shall all be taught by God.

Everyone who listens to my Father and learns from him comes to me. Not that anyone has seen the Father except the one who is from God; he has seen the Father. Amen, amen, I say to you, whoever believes has eternal life. I am the bread of life. Your ancestors ate the manna in the desert, but they died; this is the bread that comes down from heaven so that one may eat it and not die. I am the living bread that came down from heaven; whoever eats this bread will live forever; and the bread that I will give is my flesh for the life of the world."

The Gospel of the Lord. ***Praise to you, Lord Jesus Christ.***

PROFESSION OF FAITH *(page 13)*

PRAYER OF THE FAITHFUL

PREPARATION OF GIFTS *(page 16)*

PRAYER OVER THE OFFERINGS

Be pleased, O Lord, to accept the offerings of your Church,
for in your mercy you have given them to be offered
and by your power you transform them
into the mystery of our salvation.
Through Christ our Lord. ***Amen.***

PREFACE *(Sundays in Ordinary Time, pages 28–32)*

TAKING A CLOSER LOOK

✛ **Angel** An angel (Greek, *angelos*) was a spiritual messenger sent by God for a particular purpose. Sometimes angels conveyed information, while at other times they carried out God's judgment or punishment. Especially in the earlier books of the Old Testament, it is not always clear whether the angel of the Lord is the form that God takes to interact with humans or is actually a different being from God. By the New Testament time, angels were thought of as distinct spiritual beings whose task was to serve God by their heavenly worship and by sharing in God's struggle against evil.

COMMUNION ANTIPHON *(Psalm 147:12, 14)*
O Jerusalem, glorify the Lord, / who gives you your fill of finest wheat.

Or *(Cf. John 6:51)*
The bread that I will give, says the Lord, / is my flesh for the life of the world.

PRAYER AFTER COMMUNION
May the communion in your Sacrament
that we have consumed, save us, O Lord,
and confirm us in the light of your truth.
Through Christ our Lord. ***Amen.***

BLESSING & DISMISSAL *(page 56)*

Responding to the Word

Elijah was nourished by God when he thought his troubles were too great.

➔ *How has God strengthened me in times of trouble?*

Paul urges us to eliminate bitterness and grow in compassion.

➔ *What bitterness keeps me from being more compassionate toward someone?*

Jesus promises to nourish us with his life.

➔ *When has my participation in the Eucharist been especially life-giving?*

August 15

Willing instruments of God's grace

Today, we celebrate the assumption of Mary: God's lifting up of an ordinary woman with an extraordinary willingness to cooperate with grace. When she prays, "My soul proclaims the greatness of the Lord," she expresses deep understanding of and bold confidence in her connection to God.

Mary's assumption into heaven is a mystery. We do not know exactly how this happens—whether the assumed pass over death or experience resurrection before or without dying. The how is less important than the example of journeying in our humanity to toward new life in Christ—now and at the hour of our death.

Redemption is not about human power but about deep receptivity to what God is doing in the smallest and darkest places inside us. It takes courage and humility to let God work precisely where we are weak, small, and lowly— to imitate Mary's confidence that God is looking with favor on us, right now, exactly as we are.

Mary is a model in her openness to let God work in and through her life—and in her faith that such receptivity would be enough. May we follow her example in being willing instruments of God's grace, that we might make our own grace-filled journey through this life and into eternity with Jesus.

■ Leah Perrault

For the ***Mass during the Day,***
turn to page 497.

VIGIL MASS

ENTRANCE ANTIPHON
Glorious things are spoken of you, O Mary, / who today were exalted above the choirs of Angels / into eternal triumph with Christ.

INTRODUCTORY RITES *(page 10)*

COLLECT
O God, who, looking on the lowliness of the Blessed Virgin Mary,
raised her to this grace,
that your Only Begotten Son was born of her according
to the flesh
and that she was crowned this day with surpassing glory,
grant through her prayers,
that, saved by the mystery of your redemption,
we may merit to be exalted by you on high.
Through our Lord Jesus Christ, your Son,
who lives and reigns with you in the unity of the Holy Spirit,
God, for ever and ever. ***Amen.***

FIRST READING *(1 Chronicles 15:3–4, 15–16; 16:1–2)*
David assembled all Israel in Jerusalem to bring the ark of the LORD to the place which he had prepared for it. David also called together the sons of Aaron and the Levites.

The Levites bore the ark of God on their shoulders with poles, as Moses had ordained according to the word of the LORD.

David commanded the chiefs of the Levites to appoint their

kinsmen as chanters, to play on musical instruments, harps, lyres, and cymbals, to make a loud sound of rejoicing.

They brought in the ark of God and set it within the tent which David had pitched for it. Then they offered up burnt offerings and peace offerings to God. When David had finished offering up the burnt offerings and peace offerings, he blessed the people in the name of the LORD.

The word of the Lord. ***Thanks be to God.***

RESPONSORIAL PSALM *(Psalm 132:6-7, 9-10, 13-14)*

℟. Lord, go up to the place of your rest, you and the ark of your holiness.

Behold, we heard of it in Ephrathah;
we found it in the fields of Jaar.
Let us enter his dwelling,
let us worship at his footstool. ℟.
May your priests be clothed with justice;
let your faithful ones shout merrily for joy.
For the sake of David your servant,
reject not the plea of your anointed. ℟.
For the LORD has chosen Zion;
he prefers her for his dwelling.
"Zion is my resting place forever;
in her will I dwell, for I prefer her." ℟.

SECOND READING *(1 Corinthians 15:54b–57)*

Brothers and sisters: When that which is mortal clothes itself with immortality, then the word that is written shall come about:

Death is swallowed up in victory.
Where, O death, is your victory?
Where, O death, is your sting?

The sting of death is sin, and the power of sin is the law. But thanks be to God who gives us the victory through our Lord Jesus Christ.

The word of the Lord. ***Thanks be to God.***

ALLELUIA *(Luke 11:28)*

Alleluia, alleluia. Blessed are they who hear the word of God / and observe it. ***Alleluia, alleluia.***

GOSPEL *(Luke 11:27–28)*

A reading from the holy Gospel according to Luke.
Glory to you, O Lord.

While Jesus was speaking, a woman from the crowd called out and said to him, "Blessed is the womb that carried you and the breasts at which you nursed." He replied, "Rather, blessed are those who hear the word of God and observe it."

The Gospel of the Lord. ***Praise to you, Lord Jesus Christ.***

PROFESSION OF FAITH *(page 13)*

PRAYER OF THE FAITHFUL

PREPARATION OF GIFTS *(page 16)*

PRAYER OVER THE OFFERINGS

Receive, we pray, O Lord,
the sacrifice of conciliation and praise,
which we celebrate on the Assumption of the holy Mother of God,
that it may lead us to your pardon
and confirm us in perpetual thanksgiving.
Through Christ our Lord. ***Amen.***

PREFACE: THE GLORY OF MARY ASSUMED INTO HEAVEN *(page 501)*

COMMUNION ANTIPHON *(Luke 11: 27)*

Blessed is the womb of the Virgin Mary, / which bore the Son of the eternal Father

PRAYER AFTER COMMUNION

Having partaken of this heavenly table,
we beseech your mercy, Lord our God,
that we, who honor the Assumption of the Mother of God,
may be freed from every threat of harm.
Through Christ our Lord. ***Amen.***

SOLEMN BLESSING: THE BLESSED VIRGIN MARY *(Optional, page 62)*

DISMISSAL *(page 57)* ⁂

MASS DURING THE DAY

ENTRANCE ANTIPHON *(Cf. Revelation 12:1)*
A great sign appeared in heaven: / a woman clothed with the sun, and the moon beneath her feet, / and on her head a crown of twelve stars.

Or
Let us all rejoice in the Lord, / as we celebrate the feast day in honor of the Virgin Mary, / at whose Assumption the Angels rejoice / and praise the Son of God.

INTRODUCTORY RITES *(page 10)*

COLLECT
Almighty ever-living God,
who assumed the Immaculate Virgin Mary, the Mother of your Son,
body and soul into heavenly glory,
grant, we pray,
that, always attentive to the things that are above,
we may merit to be sharers of her glory.
Through our Lord Jesus Christ, your Son,
who lives and reigns with you in the unity of the Holy Spirit,
God, for ever and ever. ***Amen.***

FIRST READING *(Revelation 11:19a; 12:1-6a, 10ab)*
God's temple in heaven was opened, and the ark of his covenant could be seen in the temple.

A great sign appeared in the sky, a woman clothed with the sun, with the moon under her feet, and on her head a crown of twelve stars. She was with child and wailed aloud in pain as she labored to give birth. Then another sign appeared in the sky; it was a huge red dragon, with seven heads and ten horns, and on its heads were seven diadems. Its tail swept away a third of the stars in the sky and hurled them down to the earth. Then the dragon stood before the woman about to give birth, to devour her child when she gave birth. She gave birth to a son, a male child, destined to rule all the nations with an iron rod. Her child was caught up to God and his throne. The woman herself fled into the desert where she had a place prepared by God.

Then I heard a loud voice in heaven say:
"Now have salvation and power come,
and the Kingdom of our God
and the authority of his Anointed One."
The word of the Lord. ***Thanks be to God.***

RESPONSORIAL PSALM *(Psalm 45:10, 11, 12, 16)*

℟. The queen stands at your right hand, arrayed in gold.

The queen takes her place at your right hand in gold of Ophir. ℟.
Hear, O daughter, and see; turn your ear,
forget your people and your father's house. ℟.
So shall the king desire your beauty;
for he is your lord. ℟.
They are borne in with gladness and joy;
they enter the palace of the king. ℟.

SECOND READING *(1 Corinthians 15:20–27)*

Brothers and sisters: Christ has been raised from the dead, the **firstfruits**✝ of those who have fallen asleep. For since death came through man, the resurrection of the dead came also through man. For just as in Adam all die, so too in Christ shall all be brought to life, but each one in proper order: Christ the firstfruits; then, at his coming, those who belong to Christ; then comes the end, when he hands over the Kingdom to his God and Father, when he has destroyed every sovereignty and every authority and power. For he must reign until he has put all his enemies under his feet. The last enemy to be destroyed is death, for "he subjected everything under his feet."

The word of the Lord. ***Thanks be to God.***

ALLELUIA

Alleluia, alleluia. Mary is taken up to heaven; / a chorus of angels exults. ***Alleluia, alleluia.***

GOSPEL *(Luke 1:39–56)*

A reading from the holy Gospel according to Luke.
Glory to you, O Lord.

Mary set out and traveled to the hill country in haste to a town of Judah, where she entered the house of Zechariah and greeted Elizabeth. When Elizabeth heard Mary's greeting, the infant leaped in her womb, and Elizabeth, filled with the Holy Spirit, cried out in a loud voice and said, "Blessed are you among women, and blessed is the fruit of your womb. And how does this happen to me, that the mother of my Lord should come to me? For at the moment the sound of your greeting reached my ears, the infant in my womb leaped for joy. Blessed are you who believed that what was spoken to you by the Lord would be fulfilled."

And Mary said:
"My soul proclaims the greatness of the Lord;
my spirit rejoices in God my Savior
for he has looked with favor on his lowly servant.
From this day all generations will call me blessed:
the Almighty has done great things for me,
and holy is his Name.

He has mercy on those who fear him
in every generation.
He has shown the strength of his arm,
and has scattered the proud in their conceit.
He has cast down the mighty from their thrones,
and has lifted up the lowly.
He has filled the hungry with good things,
and the rich he has sent away empty.
He has come to the help of his servant Israel
for he has remembered his promise of mercy,
the promise he made to our fathers,
to Abraham and his children forever."

Mary remained with her about three months and then returned to her home.

The Gospel of the Lord. ***Praise to you, Lord Jesus Christ.***

PROFESSION OF FAITH *(page 13)*

PRAYER OF THE FAITHFUL

PREPARATION OF GIFTS *(page 16)*

PRAYER OVER THE OFFERINGS

May this oblation, our tribute of homage,
rise up to you, O Lord,
and, through the intercession of the most Blessed Virgin Mary,
whom you assumed into heaven,
may our hearts, aflame with the fire of love,
constantly long for you.
Through Christ our Lord. ***Amen.***

PREFACE: THE GLORY OF MARY ASSUMED INTO HEAVEN

It is truly right and just, our duty and our salvation,
always and everywhere to give you thanks,
Lord, holy Father, almighty and eternal God,
through Christ our Lord.

For today the Virgin Mother of God
was assumed into heaven
as the beginning and image
of your Church's coming to perfection
and a sign of sure hope and comfort to your pilgrim people;
rightly you would not allow her
to see the corruption of the tomb
since from her own body she marvelously brought forth
your incarnate Son, the Author of all life.

And so, in company with the choirs of Angels,
we praise you, and with joy we proclaim:
Holy, Holy, Holy Lord God of hosts... *(page 35)*

TAKING A CLOSER LOOK

✝ **Firstfruits** The firstfruits are the initial agricultural products and so represent the rest of the harvest. Like the firstborn son and first offspring of animals, they were considered sacred to God, the source of all good. The reason for their sacred character is not clearly indicated, but perhaps it was associated with the idea that in them God continued the process of creating new life, or perhaps they were a token of the people's need to thank God for the continuation of life. So if Christ is the firstfruits of the resurrection, then the new life that first appears in him will also be found in all those who share his life.

COMMUNION ANTIPHON *(Luke 1:48-49)*
All generations will call me blessed, / for he who is mighty has done great things for me.

PRAYER AFTER COMMUNION
Having received the Sacrament of salvation,
we ask you to grant, O Lord,
that, through the intercession of the Blessed Virgin Mary,
whom you assumed into heaven,
we may be brought to the glory of the resurrection.
Through Christ our Lord. ***Amen.***

SOLEMN BLESSING: THE BLESSED VIRGIN MARY *(Optional, page 62)*

DISMISSAL *(page 57)*

RESPONDING TO THE WORD

The woman and her child are a sign that God's power conquers evil.

How might I work to overcome evil in my life and be a sign of God's work?

Christ's resurrection and then Mary's assumption show God's life-giving power.

How has my growing relationship with Christ been stirring God's new life in me?

Mary's prayer reveals that she shares God's outlook and values.

To which word or phrase from Mary's prayer is my attention most drawn today?

August 22

Feed us, Lord

She sat on a smooth rock by the sea, watching the waves move in and out. The news she had received that morning still echoed in her heart. It was not what she had hoped for, and she was not sure how to face what came next. The wind brushed her cheek as she listened to the steady rhythm of the water and let its calm hold what she could not yet understand.

The disciples knew moments like this as well. When Jesus spoke of giving his flesh to eat, many turned away. The mystery was too deep and the words too difficult to accept. They could not yet see that he was speaking of a love so complete that it would offer itself as food for their journey, a love that would enter their weariness and become their life.

Then he asked, "Do you also want to leave?" It was not a challenge but an invitation to stay close, to receive, to trust that his life would become their strength.

She looked out at the sea once more. The waves continued to move with quiet faithfulness. In their rhythm she felt her heart begin to rest. She knew she needed that love, that presence, the Bread that gives life when words and strength fall short. In that stillness, she whispered, "Yes, Lord, feed me with yourself."

■ Caroline Dupuis

ENTRANCE ANTIPHON *(Cf. Psalm 86 [85]:1-3)*
Turn your ear, O Lord, and answer me; / save the servant who trusts in you, my God. / Have mercy on me, O Lord, for I cry to you all the day long.

INTRODUCTORY RITES *(page 10)*

COLLECT
O God, who cause the minds of the faithful
to unite in a single purpose,
grant your people to love what you command
and to desire what you promise,
that, amid the uncertainties of this world,
our hearts may be fixed on that place
where true gladness is found.
Through our Lord Jesus Christ, your Son,
who lives and reigns with you in the unity of the Holy Spirit,
God, for ever and ever. ***Amen.***

FIRST READING *(Joshua 24:1-2a, 15-17, 18b)*
Joshua gathered together all the tribes of Israel at Shechem, summoning their elders, their leaders, their judges, and their officers. When they stood in ranks before God, Joshua addressed all the people: "If it does not please you to serve the LORD, decide today whom you will serve, the gods your fathers served beyond the River or the gods of the Amorites in whose country you are now dwelling. As for me and my household, we will serve the LORD."

But the people answered, "Far be it from us to forsake the LORD for the service of other gods. For it was the LORD, our God, who brought us and our fathers up out of the land of Egypt, out of a state of slavery. He performed those great miracles before our very eyes and protected us along our entire journey and among the peoples through whom we passed. Therefore we also will serve the LORD, for he is our God."

The word of the Lord. ***Thanks be to God.***

RESPONSORIAL PSALM *(Psalm 34:2–3, 16–17, 18–19, 20–21)*

℟. Taste and see the goodness of the Lord.

I will bless the LORD at all times;
his praise shall be ever in my mouth.
Let my soul glory in the LORD;
the lowly will hear me and be glad. ℟.
The LORD has eyes for the just,
and ears for their cry.
The LORD confronts the evildoers,
to destroy remembrance of them from the earth. ℟.
When the just cry out, the LORD hears them,
and from all their distress he rescues them.
The LORD is close to the brokenhearted;
and those who are crushed in spirit he saves. ℟.
Many are the troubles of the just one,
but out of them all the LORD delivers him;
he watches over all his bones;
not one of them shall be broken. ℟.

SECOND READING *(Ephesians 5:21–32 or 5:2a, 25–32)*

The shorter version begins at the asterisks. The passage in brackets is only read in the short form.

Brothers and sisters: Be subordinate to one another out of reverence for Christ. **Wives should be subordinate to their husbands**✝ as to the Lord. For the husband is head of his wife just as Christ is head of the church, he himself the savior of the body. As the church is subordinate to Christ, so wives should be subordinate to their husbands in everything.

* * *

[Brothers and sisters: Live in love, as Christ loved us.]

Husbands, love your wives, ✝ even as Christ loved the church and handed himself over for her to sanctify her, cleansing her by the bath of water with the word, that he might present to himself the church in splendor, without spot or wrinkle or any such thing, that she might be holy and without blemish. So also husbands should love their wives as their own bodies. He who loves his wife loves himself. For no one hates his own flesh but rather nourishes and cherishes it, even as Christ does the church, because we are members of his body.

For this reason a man shall leave his father and his mother
and be joined to his wife,
and the two shall become one flesh.

This is a great mystery, but I speak in reference to Christ and the church.

The word of the Lord. ***Thanks be to God.***

ALLELUIA *(John 6:63, 68)*

Alleluia, alleluia. Your words, Lord, are Spirit and life; / you have the words of everlasting life. ***Alleluia, alleluia.***

GOSPEL *(John 6:60-69)*

A reading from the holy Gospel according to John.

Glory to you, O Lord.

Many of Jesus' disciples who were listening said, "This saying is hard; who can accept it?" Since Jesus knew that his disciples were murmuring about this, he said to them, "Does this shock you? What if you were to see the Son of Man ascending to where he was before? It is the spirit that gives life, while the flesh is of no avail. The words I have spoken to you are Spirit and life. But there are some of you who do not believe." Jesus knew from the beginning the ones who would not believe and the one who would betray him. And he said, "For this reason I have told you that no one can come to me unless it is granted him by my Father."

As a result of this, many of his disciples returned to their former way of life and no longer accompanied him. Jesus then said to the Twelve, "Do you also want to leave?" Simon Peter answered him, "Master, to whom shall we go? You have the words of eternal life. We have come to believe and are convinced that you are the Holy One of God."

The Gospel of the Lord. ***Praise to you, Lord Jesus Christ.***

PROFESSION OF FAITH *(page 13)*

PRAYER OF THE FAITHFUL

PREPARATION OF GIFTS *(page 16)*

PRAYER OVER THE OFFERINGS

O Lord, who gained for yourself a people by adoption

TAKING A CLOSER LOOK

✝ **Wives should be subordinate to their husbands/ Husbands, love your wives** In Paul's time, marriages were arranged by families, and their purpose was to increase the family's status or wealth and to continue the family through children. Paul's advice for women repeats what was already known about rightly ordered relationships in the household: women were expected to obey (be subordinate). For the men, however, Paul's advice is shocking and challenging. He requires them to love their wives (not necessarily part of the family marriage agreement!) with the self-sacrificing love that Christ had for the Church.

through the one sacrifice offered once for all,
bestow graciously on us, we pray,
the gifts of unity and peace in your Church.
Through Christ our Lord. ***Amen.***

PREFACE *(Sundays in Ordinary Time, pages 28–32)*

COMMUNION ANTIPHON *(Cf. Psalm 104 [103]:13–15)*
The earth is replete with the fruits of your work, O Lord; / you bring forth bread from the earth / and wine to cheer the heart.

Or *(Cf. John 6:54)*
Whoever eats my flesh and drinks my blood / has eternal life, says the Lord, / and I will raise him up on the last day.

PRAYER AFTER COMMUNION
Complete within us, O Lord, we pray,
the healing work of your mercy
and graciously perfect and sustain us,
so that in all things we may please you.
Through Christ our Lord. ***Amen.***

BLESSING & DISMISSAL *(page 56)* ✣

Responding to the Word

Joshua and the people renewed their commitment to God.

➡ *What can I do today to renew my commitment to God?*

Paul encourages us to live in love, creating the kind of community that God wants.

➡ *What loving thing can I do to help build God's community?*

Many people left Jesus because his message and lifestyle were too hard.

➡ *What parts of Jesus' message are hard for me to follow?*

August 29

Give heed

The first line of today's first reading offers us the theme of all the readings: give heed. Pay attention to the things we need to do. It is sometimes very difficult to know what we should say or do in any given situation. Aware of that, God offers us the framework of our faith. We are provided with instructions that are intended to guide us all along the way. We are called to be wise and discerning.

The foundation underneath all our decision-making is what is in our hearts. Jesus speaks clearly. It is not what goes into us that causes the challenges: it is "the things that come out from within." If we are to live as true *doers* of God's word, we must be aware of what is happening in our hearts. We must be attentive to God's voice. We must welcome God's word deep into our hearts so we can be transformed. St. James reminds us: it is "the word that has been planted in you and is able to save your souls."

The bedrock truth underneath this foundation? God loves us too much to lose us. We return to the beginning. With our best care-full attention, we heed God's instructions. Praying for God's blessing, we ask for the gift of a heart that is pure and undefiled.

■ Brenda Merk Hildebrand

ENTRANCE ANTIPHON *(Cf. Psalm 86 [85]:3, 5)*
Have mercy on me, O Lord, for I cry to you all the day long. / O Lord, you are good and forgiving, / full of mercy to all who call to you.

INTRODUCTORY RITES *(page 10)*

COLLECT
God of might, giver of every good gift,
put into our hearts the love of your name,
so that, by deepening our sense of reverence,
you may nurture in us what is good
and, by your watchful care,
keep safe what you have nurtured.
Through our Lord Jesus Christ, your Son,
who lives and reigns with you in the unity of the Holy Spirit,
God, for ever and ever. ***Amen.***

FIRST READING *(Deuteronomy 4:1-2, 6-8)*
Moses said to the people: "Now, Israel, hear the statutes and decrees which I am teaching you to observe, that you may live, and may enter in and take possession of the land which the LORD, the God of your fathers, is giving you. In your observance of the commandments of the LORD, your God, which I enjoin upon you, you shall not add to what I command you nor subtract from it. Observe them carefully, for thus will you give evidence of your wisdom and intelligence to the nations, who will hear of all these statutes and say, 'This great nation is truly a wise and intelligent people.' For what great nation is there that has gods so close to it as the LORD, our God, is to us whenever we call upon him? Or what great nation has statutes and decrees that are as just as this whole law which I

am setting before you today?"

The word of the Lord. ***Thanks be to God.***

RESPONSORIAL PSALM *(Psalm 15:2-3, 3-4, 4-5)*

℟. The one who does justice will live in the presence of the Lord.

Whoever walks blamelessly and does justice;
who thinks the truth in his heart
and slanders not with his tongue. ℟.
Who harms not his fellow man,
nor takes up a reproach against his neighbor;
by whom the reprobate is despised,
while he honors those who fear the LORD. ℟.
Who lends not his money at usury
and accepts no bribe against the innocent.
Whoever does these things
shall never be disturbed. ℟.

SECOND READING *(James 1:17-18, 21b-22, 27)*

Dearest brothers and sisters: All good giving and every perfect gift is from above, coming down from the Father of lights, with whom there is no alteration or shadow caused by change. He willed to give us birth by the word of truth that we may be a kind of firstfruits of his creatures.

Humbly welcome the word that has been planted in you and is able to save your souls.

Be doers of the word and not hearers only, deluding yourselves.

Religion that is pure and undefiled before God and the Father is this: to **care for orphans and widows**✝ in their affliction and to keep oneself unstained by the world.

The word of the Lord. ***Thanks be to God.***

ALLELUIA *(James 1:18)*
Alleluia, alleluia. The Father willed to give us birth by the word of truth / that we may be a kind of firstfruits of his creatures.
Alleluia, alleluia.

GOSPEL *(Mark 7:1-8, 14-15, 21-23)*
A reading from the holy Gospel according to Mark.
Glory to you, O Lord.

When the Pharisees with some scribes who had come from Jerusalem gathered around Jesus, they observed that some of his disciples ate their meals with unclean, that is, unwashed, hands.—For the Pharisees and, in fact, all Jews, do not eat without carefully washing their hands, keeping the tradition of the elders. And on coming from the marketplace they do not eat without purifying themselves. And there are many other things that they have traditionally observed, the purification of cups and jugs and kettles and beds.—So the Pharisees and scribes questioned him, "Why do your disciples not follow the tradition of the elders but instead eat a meal with unclean hands?" He responded, "Well did Isaiah prophesy about you hypocrites, as it is written:

This people honors me with their lips,
but their hearts are far from me;
in vain do they worship me,
teaching as doctrines human precepts.

You disregard God's commandment but cling to human tradition."

He summoned the crowd again and said to them, "Hear me, all of you, and understand. Nothing that enters one from outside can defile that person; but the things that come out from within are what defile.

"From within people, from their hearts, come evil thoughts, unchastity, theft, murder, adultery, greed, malice, deceit, licentiousness, envy, blasphemy, arrogance, folly. All these evils come from within and they defile."

The Gospel of the Lord. ***Praise to you, Lord Jesus Christ.***

PROFESSION OF FAITH *(page 13)*

PRAYER OF THE FAITHFUL

PREPARATION OF GIFTS *(page 16)*

PRAYER OVER THE OFFERINGS

May this sacred offering, O Lord,
confer on us always the blessing of salvation,
that what it celebrates in mystery
it may accomplish in power.
Through Christ our Lord. ***Amen.***

PREFACE *(Sundays in Ordinary Time, pages 28–32)*

TAKING A CLOSER LOOK

✝ **Care for orphans and widows** In the tightly structured society of biblical times, families had to rely on themselves and their relatives for protection and sustenance rather than on the legal system. Women and children were socially "located" in relation to their household, in particular to the head of the household (the father, husband, or master). Widows, orphans, and foreigners residing in the land who were not connected to a household were thus "dislocated" and vulnerable because they lacked a protective male. In Israel, God assumed the role of protector of widows and orphans and promised to take vengeance on those who would seek to exploit these vulnerable ones.

COMMUNION ANTIPHON *(Psalm 31 [30]:20)*
How great is the goodness, Lord, / that you keep for those who fear you.

Or *(Matthew 5:9–10)*
Blessed are the peacemakers, / for they shall be called children of God. / Blessed are they who are persecuted for the sake of righteousness, / for theirs is the Kingdom of Heaven.

PRAYER AFTER COMMUNION
Renewed by this bread from the heavenly table,
we beseech you, Lord,
that, being the food of charity,
it may confirm our hearts
and stir us to serve you in our neighbor.
Through Christ our Lord. ***Amen.***

BLESSING & DISMISSAL *(page 56)* ⁜

Responding to the Word

God's guidelines for the covenant people's behavior were not always easy to keep.

➔ *Which of God's commandments is particularly troublesome for me now?*

James tells us to be doers of the word and not hearers only.

➔ *When and for what reasons have I been an eager hearer but a reluctant doer?*

Jesus warns that the real roots of sin are our inner attitudes.

➔ *What attitude is giving me trouble lately and pushing me toward wrong actions?*

September 5

Ask the Lord to open our hearts

Hearing God's voice can be difficult in a noisy world. Our worries and preoccupations can occupy our thoughts and distract us, preventing us from isolating it and paying attention.

In today's gospel, Jesus restores a deaf man's hearing. Out of loving compassion, he takes the deaf man away from the crowd, gives him his full attention, and treats him with care. He not only opens his ears to hear physical sounds but also heals his soul, enabling him to hear God's voice.

At times, we may be spiritually deaf, unable to recognize God's voice in our lives and in the people we encounter. Jesus invites us to quiet ourselves, to pull ourselves away from the many cares and distractions of life, and to spend time alone with him in prayer. He may offer us a new understanding that calms our troubled hearts, or he may ask us to be more patient. If we humbly listen to him during these moments, he can heal us if we trust him and allow his love to enter our hearts.

Spending time in prayer, away from the noise of everyday life, can change our lives, as it changed the life of the deaf man. Let us ask the Lord to open our hearts—and ears—today to hear his voice and to joyfully share his love with others.

■ Nada Mazzei

ENTRANCE ANTIPHON *(Psalm 119 [118]:137, 124)*
You are just, O Lord, and your judgment is right; / treat your servant in accord with your merciful love.

INTRODUCTORY RITES *(page 10)*

COLLECT
O God, by whom we are redeemed and receive adoption,
look graciously upon your beloved sons and daughters,
that those who believe in Christ
may receive true freedom
and an everlasting inheritance.
Through our Lord Jesus Christ, your Son,
who lives and reigns with you in the unity of the Holy Spirit,
God, for ever and ever. ***Amen.***

FIRST READING *(Isaiah 35:4–7a)*
Thus says the LORD:
Say to those whose hearts are frightened:
Be strong, fear not!
Here is your God,
he comes with vindication;
with divine recompense
he comes to save you.
Then will the eyes of the blind be opened,
the ears of the deaf be cleared;
then will the lame leap like a stag,
then the tongue of the mute will sing.
Streams will burst forth in the desert,
and rivers in the steppe.
The burning sands will become pools,

and the thirsty ground, springs of water.
The word of the Lord. ***Thanks be to God.***

RESPONSORIAL PSALM *(Psalm 146:6-7, 8-9, 9-10)*

℟. Praise the Lord, my soul! *Or* **Alleluia.**

The God of Jacob keeps faith forever,
secures justice for the oppressed,
gives food to the hungry.
The LORD sets captives free. **℟.**
The LORD gives sight to the blind;
the LORD raises up those who were bowed down.
The LORD loves the just;
the LORD protects strangers. **℟.**
The fatherless and the widow the LORD sustains,
but the way of the wicked he thwarts.
The LORD shall reign forever;
your God, O Zion, through all generations. Alleluia. **℟.**

SECOND READING *(James 2:1-5)*

My brothers and sisters, show no partiality as you adhere to the faith in our glorious Lord Jesus Christ. For if a man with gold rings and fine clothes comes into your assembly, and a poor person in shabby clothes also comes in, and you pay attention to the one wearing the fine clothes and say, "Sit here, please," while you say to the poor one, "Stand there," or "Sit at my feet," have you not made distinctions among yourselves and become judges with evil designs?

Listen, my beloved brothers and sisters. Did not God choose those who are poor in the world to be rich in faith and heirs of the kingdom that he promised to those who love him?

The word of the Lord. ***Thanks be to God.***

ALLELUIA *(See Matthew 4:23)*
Alleluia, alleluia. Jesus proclaimed the Gospel of the kingdom / and cured every disease among the people. ***Alleluia, alleluia.***

GOSPEL *(Mark 7:31–37)*
A reading from the holy Gospel according to Mark.
Glory to you, O Lord.

Again Jesus left the district of Tyre and went by way of Sidon to the Sea of Galilee, into the district of the Decapolis. And people brought to him a deaf man who had a speech impediment and begged him to **lay his hand on him.** ✝ He took him off by himself away from the crowd. He put his finger into the man's ears and, spitting, touched his tongue; then he looked up to heaven and groaned, and said to him, "*Ephphatha*!"—that is, "Be opened!"—And immediately the man's ears were opened, his speech impediment was removed, and he spoke plainly. He ordered them not to tell anyone. But the more he ordered them not to, the more they proclaimed it. They were exceedingly astonished and they said, "He has done all things well. He makes the deaf hear and the mute speak."

The Gospel of the Lord. ***Praise to you, Lord Jesus Christ.***

PROFESSION OF FAITH *(page 13)*

PRAYER OF THE FAITHFUL

PREPARATION OF GIFTS *(page 16)*

PRAYER OVER THE OFFERINGS

O God, who give us the gift of true prayer and of peace,
graciously grant that, through this offering,
we may do fitting homage to your divine majesty
and, by partaking of the sacred mystery,
we may be faithfully united in mind and heart.
Through Christ our Lord. ***Amen.***

PREFACE *(Sundays in Ordinary Time, pages 28–32)*

COMMUNION ANTIPHON *(Cf. Psalm 42 [41]:2-3)*

Like the deer that yearns for running streams, / so my soul is yearning for you, my God; / my soul is thirsting for God, the living God.

Or *(John 8:12)*

I am the light of the world, says the Lord; / whoever follows me will not walk in darkness, / but will have the light of life.

TAKING A CLOSER LOOK

✝ **Lay his hand on him** The hand (especially the right hand) was a natural symbol for power and strength. Thus the laying on of hands signified the transfer of power or strength or holiness. It was part of the rituals for sacrifice, for the consecration of priests, and for conferring blessings. It also served as the medium for the transfer of spiritual and physical healing power from the healer to the one being healed. Although Jesus sometimes heals from a distance or merely by the power of his word, most often he transmits his healing power through his loving touch.

PRAYER AFTER COMMUNION

Grant that your faithful, O Lord,
whom you nourish and endow with life
through the food of your Word and heavenly Sacrament,
may so benefit from your beloved Son's great gifts
that we may merit an eternal share in his life.
Who lives and reigns for ever and ever. ***Amen.***

BLESSING & DISMISSAL *(page 56)*

Responding to the Word

Isaiah encourages us to "Be strong, fear not!" because God is with us.

When has God's presence helped to calm my fears?

James warns us not to be misled by outer appearances and misjudge the worth of others.

What leads me to overlook the hidden riches of the poor?

Jesus opens the ears of a man who is deaf.

What might Jesus be doing to open my ears so I can pay more attention to what God is trying to say to me?

September 12

SEP 12

Truly trusting God

It's comforting to know that God listens when we call and that he responds with compassion. He's a living presence close to us, steadying us when life feels uncertain, guiding us toward love and service. Whether we long for healing, justice, peace, or courage, we can bring our cares to him with confidence, trusting that he listens and cares for us.

Fully trusting in God this way does not, of course, remove the trials of life, but it assures us that we are never alone in them. Jesus drew strength from that unwavering trust in the Father. I've seen that quiet courage in the eyes of some dying patients I've visited in my volunteer work at the hospital, and I'm always inspired by it. Knowing that God suffers with them and sustains them at the very end gives them an inner peace like no other.

Truly trusting in God this much in our daily lives also inspires us to forgive, to care, and to reflect his love. This is how we know our faith is truly bearing fruit.

As we gather for this Eucharist, let's thank God for his love shown through Christ made present in bread and wine, for listening to us, for the gift of faith that strengthens us, and for the grace to let that faith shine in our lives.

EUGENE AUCOIN

ENTRANCE ANTIPHON *(Cf. Sirach 36:18)*
Give peace, O Lord, to those who wait for you, / that your prophets be found true. / Hear the prayers of your servant, / and of your people Israel.

INTRODUCTORY RITES *(page 10)*

COLLECT
Look upon us, O God,
Creator and ruler of all things,
and, that we may feel the working of your mercy,
grant that we may serve you with all our heart.
Through our Lord Jesus Christ, your Son,
who lives and reigns with you in the unity of the Holy Spirit,
God, for ever and ever. ***Amen.***

FIRST READING *(Isaiah 50:5-9a)*
The Lord GOD opens my ear that I may hear;
and I have not rebelled,
have not turned back.
I gave my back to those who beat me,
my cheeks to those who plucked my beard;
my face I did not shield
from buffets and spitting.

The Lord GOD is my help,
therefore I am not disgraced;
I have set my face like flint,
knowing that I shall not be put to shame.
He is near who upholds my right;
if anyone wishes to oppose me,
let us appear together.

Who disputes my right?
  Let that man confront me.
See, the Lord GOD is my help;
  who will prove me wrong?
The word of the Lord. ***Thanks be to God.***

RESPONSORIAL PSALM *(Psalm 116:1-2, 3-4, 5-6, 8-9)*

℟. I will walk before the Lord, in the land of the living.
  Or **Alleluia.**

I love the LORD because he has heard
  my voice in supplication,
Because he has inclined his ear to me
  the day I called. ℟.
The cords of death encompassed me;
  the snares of the netherworld seized upon me;
  I fell into distress and sorrow,
and I called upon the name of the LORD,
  "O LORD, save my life!" ℟.
Gracious is the LORD and just;
  yes, our God is merciful.
The LORD keeps the little ones;
  I was brought low, and he saved me. ℟.
For he has freed my soul from death,
  my eyes from tears, my feet from stumbling.
I shall walk before the LORD
  in the land of the living. ℟.

SECOND READING *(James 2:14-18)*

What good is it, my brothers and sisters, if someone says he has faith but does not have works? Can that faith save him? If a brother or sister has nothing to wear and has no food for the day, and one of you says to them, "Go in peace, keep warm, and eat well," but you do not give them the necessities of the body, what good is it? So also faith of itself, if it does not have works, is dead.

Indeed someone might say, "You have faith and I have works." Demonstrate your faith to me without works, and I will demonstrate my faith to you from my works.

The word of the Lord. ***Thanks be to God.***

ALLELUIA *(Galatians 6:14)*

Alleluia, alleluia. May I never boast except in the cross of our Lord / through which the world has been crucified to me and I to the world. ***Alleluia, alleluia.***

GOSPEL *(Mark 8:27-35)*

A reading from the holy Gospel according to Mark.

Glory to you, O Lord.

Jesus and his disciples set out for the villages of Caesarea Philippi. Along the way he asked his disciples, "Who do people say that I am?" They said in reply, "John the Baptist, others Elijah, still others one of the prophets." And he asked them, "But who do you say that I am?" Peter said to him in reply, "You are the Christ." Then he warned them not to tell anyone about him.

He began to teach them that the Son of Man must suffer greatly and be rejected by the elders, the chief priests, and the scribes, and be killed, and rise after three days. He spoke this openly. Then Peter took him aside and began to rebuke him. At this he turned around and, looking at his disciples, rebuked Peter and said, "Get behind me, **Satan.**✝ You are thinking not as God does, but as human beings do."

He summoned the crowd with his disciples and said to them,

"Whoever wishes to come after me must deny himself, take up his cross, and follow me. For whoever wishes to save his life will lose it, but whoever loses his life for my sake and that of the gospel will save it."

The Gospel of the Lord. ***Praise to you, Lord Jesus Christ.***

PROFESSION OF FAITH *(page 13)*

PRAYER OF THE FAITHFUL

PREPARATION OF GIFTS *(page 16)*

PRAYER OVER THE OFFERINGS

Look with favor on our supplications, O Lord,
and in your kindness accept these, your servants' offerings,
that what each has offered to the honor of your name
may serve the salvation of all.
Through Christ our Lord. ***Amen.***

PREFACE *(Sundays in Ordinary Time, pages 28–32)*

TAKING A CLOSER LOOK

+ **Satan** In the earlier books of the Bible (especially Job), the "satan" or accuser is a kind of legal prosecutor in the divine assembly who questions the sincerity of human faith. After the exile, as the Jews began to stress God as transcendent and supremely good, they found it difficult to account for evil in the world. Gradually, they developed the figure of Satan as an evil spirit who is subordinate but hostile to God, struggling with God for domination of the earth and tempting humans from following God's ways. Jesus' triumph over Satan encourages us to resist temptations that lead us away from being sons and daughters of God.

COMMUNION ANTIPHON *(Cf. Psalm 36 [35]:8)*
How precious is your mercy, O God! / The children of men seek shelter in the shadow of your wings.

Or *(Cf. 1 Corinthians 10:16)*
The chalice of blessing that we bless / is a communion in the Blood of Christ; / and the bread that we break / is a sharing in the Body of the Lord.

PRAYER AFTER COMMUNION
May the working of this heavenly gift, O Lord, we pray,
take possession of our minds and bodies,
so that its effects, and not our own desires,
may always prevail in us.
Through Christ our Lord. ***Amen.***

BLESSING & DISMISSAL *(page 56)*

Responding to the Word

God's servant must put up with hardship to do what God asks.

How do I respond to hardship and difficulties in living as God requires?

James knows that works are necessary to make faith relevant.

What works am I doing that show my desire to follow Christ more closely?

Jesus asks the disciples to tell him who they think he is.

How would I answer Jesus' question today?

September 19

Called to be servants of all

I recently watched a sci-fi film in which the alien protagonist is cast out and condemned to death, simply for being the weakest. Their alpha leader is the strongest and most ruthless; as such, he's deemed to be the greatest. Jesus' disciples are much like us and the film's characters, coming from a world that often equates greatness with fleeting qualities like strength, ability, beauty, popularity, or wealth. In today's gospel, Jesus flips that version of greatness upside down.

The passage starts with Jesus foreshadowing his death and resurrection. Given that Jesus, the Alpha (and Omega), lays down his life so that we may have eternal life, we see that greatness first involves the act of loving one another.

Next, Jesus instructs the disciples that the greatest is the one who is last and servant of all. Who does the "all" include? Only the strong? When Jesus teaches the disciples that they should welcome a child (one among the most vulnerable) as though they were welcoming him, Jesus shows that servanthood includes a special care for the weakest among us.

At Mass, we welcome the greatest in our midst, Jesus, who becomes present in such humble forms, the bread and wine. May the reception of our servant Lord today inspire us to a deeper love as servants of one another.

■ Alison Endrizzi

ENTRANCE ANTIPHON

I am the salvation of the people, says the Lord. / Should they cry to me in any distress, / will hear them, and I will be their Lord for ever.

INTRODUCTORY RITES *(page 10)*

COLLECT

O God, who founded all the commands of your sacred Law
upon love of you and of our neighbor,
grant that, by keeping your precepts,
we may merit to attain eternal life.
Through our Lord Jesus Christ, your Son,
who lives and reigns with you in the unity of the Holy Spirit,
God, for ever and ever. ***Amen.***

FIRST READING *(Wisdom 2:12, 17–20)*

The wicked say:
Let us beset the just one, because he is obnoxious to us;
he sets himself against our doings,
reproaches us for transgressions of the law
and charges us with violations of our training.
Let us see whether his words be true;
let us find out what will happen to him.
For if the just one be the son of God, God will defend him
and deliver him from the hand of his foes.
With revilement and torture let us put the just one to the test
that we may have proof of his gentleness
and try his patience.
Let us condemn him to a shameful death;
for according to his own words, God will take care of him.
The word of the Lord. ***Thanks be to God.***

RESPONSORIAL PSALM *(Psalm 54:3-4, 5, 6-8)*

℟. The Lord upholds my life.

O God, by your name save me,
and by your might defend my cause.
O God, hear my prayer;
hearken to the words of my mouth. ℟.
For the haughty men have risen up against me,
the ruthless seek my life;
they set not God before their eyes. ℟.
Behold, God is my helper;
the Lord sustains my life.
Freely will I offer you sacrifice;
I will praise your name, O LORD, for its goodness. ℟.

SECOND READING *(James 3:16–4:3)*

Beloved: Where jealousy and selfish ambition exist, there is disorder and every foul practice. But the wisdom from above is first of all pure, then peaceable, gentle, compliant, full of mercy and good fruits, without inconstancy or insincerity. And the fruit of righteousness is sown in peace for those who cultivate peace.

Where do the wars and where do the conflicts among you come from? Is it not from your passions that make war within your members? You covet but do not possess. You kill and envy but you cannot obtain; you fight and wage war. You do not possess because you do not ask. You ask but do not receive, because you ask wrongly, to spend it on your passions.

The word of the Lord. ***Thanks be to God.***

ALLELUIA *(See 2 Thessalonians 2:14)*

Alleluia, alleluia. God has called us through the Gospel / to possess the glory of our Lord Jesus Christ. ***Alleluia, alleluia.***

GOSPEL *(Mark 9:30-37)*

A reading from the holy Gospel according to Mark.
Glory to you, O Lord.

Jesus and his disciples left from there and began a journey through Galilee, but he did not wish anyone to know about it. He was teaching his disciples and telling them, "The Son of Man is to be handed over to men and they will kill him, and three days after his death the Son of Man will rise." But they did not understand the saying, and they were afraid to question him.

They came to Capernaum and, once inside the house, he began to ask them, "What were you arguing about on the way?" But they remained silent. They had been discussing among themselves on the way who was the greatest. Then he sat down, called the Twelve, and said to them, "If anyone wishes to be first, he shall be the last of all and the servant of all." Taking a **child,** + he placed it in the their midst, and putting his arms around it, he said to them, "Whoever receives one child such as this in my name, receives me; and whoever receives me, receives not me but the One who sent me."

The Gospel of the Lord. ***Praise to you, Lord Jesus Christ.***

PROFESSION OF FAITH *(page 13)*

PRAYER OF THE FAITHFUL

PREPARATION OF GIFTS *(page 16)*

PRAYER OVER THE OFFERINGS

Receive with favor, O Lord, we pray,
the offerings of your people,
that what they profess with devotion and faith
may be theirs through these heavenly mysteries.
Through Christ our Lord. ***Amen.***

PREFACE *(Sundays in Ordinary Time, pages 28–32)*

TAKING A CLOSER LOOK

+ **Child** A child had very little social status, yet required much attention from the parents to survive to maturity. Thus the child was a perfect illustration of Jesus' point that the disciples are to seek their greatness or high status in service to those who have the least status. We might note the curious translation that expresses the Greek term here for child as neuter gender, that is, it does not identify the child as a boy or girl but as an "it." To make his case even clearer, we might imagine Jesus bringing forth a young girl, whose social status was even lower than that of a boy.

COMMUNION ANTIPHON *(Psalm 119 [118]:4–5)*
You have laid down your precepts to be carefully kept; / may my ways be firm in keeping your statutes.

Or *(John 10:14)*
I am the Good Shepherd, says the Lord; / I know my sheep, and mine know me.

PRAYER AFTER COMMUNION
Graciously raise up, O Lord,
those you renew with this Sacrament,
that we may come to possess your redemption
both in mystery and in the manner of our life.
Through Christ our Lord. ***Amen.***

BLESSING & DISMISSAL *(page 56)*

Responding to the Word

The innocent person often suffers at the hands of the wicked.

When did my innocence not protect me from suffering?

James reminds us that our desires can often lead us away from God.

What desires are prominent in me now, and where are they leading me?

Jesus tells the disciples that their greatness will come only from service.

What service am I doing that would make Jesus happy?

September 26

Solidarity in Christ

"Unlikely companions." That's how I've described the people who came forward to help with a Catholic initiative in my area. From various Christian churches, they gave of their talents and resources to assist this distinctly Catholic venture. Recognizing the importance of the project, they were motivated out of their love of Jesus and their confidence in his work amongst other Christians. The example of unbelievers and those of different faith traditions who supported this endeavor was also staggering.

Encouraging and humbling to behold, this witness calls to mind today's gospel, wherein Jesus is asked about "someone driving out demons" in his name but who was not counted amongst Jesus' followers.

Within our world, and even amongst members of the Church, we see division and fragmentation. We divide people, even fellow believers, into categories of "us" and "them." However, the gospel orients us toward the source of all true unity, Jesus, who explains, "No one who performs a mighty deed in my name...can at the same time speak ill of me. For whoever is not against us is for us." During today's Eucharist, let us give thanks for examples of our solidarity in Christ. May we ask the Lord for authentic unity rooted in him, which begins with us.

Nicole Snook

ENTRANCE ANTIPHON *(Deuteronomy 3:31, 29, 30, 43, 42)*
All that you have done to us, O Lord, / you have done with true judgment, / for we have sinned against you / and not obeyed your commandments. / But give glory to your name / and deal with us according to the bounty of your mercy.

INTRODUCTORY RITES *(page 10)*

COLLECT
O God, who manifest your almighty power
above all by pardoning and showing mercy,
bestow, we pray, your grace abundantly upon us
and make those hastening to attain your promises
heirs to the treasures of heaven.
Through our Lord Jesus Christ, your Son,
who lives and reigns with you in the unity of the Holy Spirit,
God, for ever and ever. ***Amen.***

FIRST READING *(Numbers 11:25–29)*
The LORD came down in the cloud and spoke to Moses. Taking some of the spirit that was on Moses, the LORD bestowed it on the seventy elders; and as the spirit came to rest on them, they prophesied.

Now two men, one named Eldad and the other Medad, were not in the gathering but had been left in the camp. They too had been on the list, but had not gone out to the tent; yet the spirit came to rest on them also, and they prophesied in the camp. So, when a young man quickly told Moses, "Eldad and Medad are prophesying in the camp," Joshua, son of Nun, who from his youth had been Moses' aide, said, "Moses, my lord, stop them." But Moses answered him, "Are you jealous for my sake? Would that all the people of the LORD were prophets! Would that the

LORD might bestow his spirit on them all!"
The word of the Lord. ***Thanks be to God.***

RESPONSORIAL PSALM *(Psalm 19:8, 10, 12-13, 14)*

℟. The precepts of the Lord give joy to the heart.

The law of the LORD is perfect,
refreshing the soul;
the decree of the Lord is trustworthy,
giving wisdom to the simple. ℟.
The fear of the LORD is pure,
enduring forever;
the ordinances of the LORD are true,
all of them just. ℟.
Though your servant is careful of them,
very diligent in keeping them,
Yet who can detect failings?
Cleanse me from my unknown faults! ℟.
From wanton sin especially, restrain your servant;
let it not rule over me.
Then shall I be blameless and innocent
of serious sin. ℟.

SECOND READING *(James 5:1-6)*

Come now, you rich, weep and wail over your impending miseries. Your wealth has rotted away, your clothes have become moth-eaten, your gold and silver have corroded, and that corrosion will be a testimony against you; it will devour your flesh like a fire. You have stored up treasure for the last days. Behold, the wages you withheld from the workers who harvested your fields are crying aloud; and the cries of the harvesters have reached the ears of the Lord of hosts. You have lived on earth in luxury and pleasure; you have fattened your hearts for the day of slaughter. You have condemned; you have murdered the righteous one; he offers you no resistance.

The word of the Lord. ***Thanks be to God.***

ALLELUIA *(See John 17:17b, 17a)*

Alleluia, alleluia. Your word, O Lord, is truth; / consecrate us in the truth. ***Alleluia, alleluia.***

GOSPEL *(Mark 9:38–43, 45, 47–48)*

A reading from the holy Gospel according to Mark.

Glory to you, O Lord.

At that time, John said to Jesus, "Teacher, we saw someone driving out demons in your name, and we tried to prevent him because he does not follow us." Jesus replied, "Do not prevent him. There is no one who performs a mighty deed in my name who can at the same time speak ill of me. For whoever is not against us is for us. Anyone who gives you a cup of water to drink because you belong to Christ, amen, I say to you, will surely not lose his reward.

"Whoever causes one of these little ones who believe in me to sin, it would be better for him if a great millstone were put around his neck and he were thrown into the sea. If your hand causes you to sin, cut it off. It is better for you to enter into life maimed than with two hands to go into **Gehenna,**✛ into the unquenchable fire. And if your foot causes you to sin, cut if off. It is better for you to enter into life crippled than with two feet to be thrown into Gehenna. And if your eye causes you to sin, pluck it out. Better for you to enter into the kingdom of God with one eye than with two eyes to be thrown into Gehenna, where 'their worm does not die, and the fire is not quenched.'"

The Gospel of the Lord. ***Praise to you, Lord Jesus Christ.***

PROFESSION OF FAITH *(page 13)*

PRAYER OF THE FAITHFUL

PREPARATION OF GIFTS *(page 16)*

PRAYER OVER THE OFFERINGS

Grant us, O merciful God,
that this our offering may find acceptance with you
and that through it the wellspring of all blessing
may be laid open before us.
Through Christ our Lord. ***Amen.***

PREFACE *(Sundays in Ordinary Time, pages 28–32)*

Taking a Closer Look

✝ **Gehenna** Located west and south of Jerusalem, Gehenna (Hebrew, valley of Hinnom) divided the tribes of Judah and Benjamin. Some of the kings of Judah used its heights for idolatrous human sacrifices and so incurred God's wrath. Jeremiah cursed it and called it a place of fire and destruction. This association soon made it a synonym for the place of God's punishment of the wicked after death—hell. It was distinguished both from heaven or paradise, where the just received their reward, and from Hades, which was either the abode of all the dead or where the wicked wait until God's final judgment.

COMMUNION ANTIPHON *(Cf. Psalm 119 [118]:49-50)*
Remember your word to your servant, O Lord, / by which you have given me hope. / This is my comfort when I am brought low.

Or *(1 John 3:16)*
By this we came to know the love of God: / that Christ laid down his life for us; / so we ought to lay down our lives for one another.

PRAYER AFTER COMMUNION
May this heavenly mystery, O Lord,
restore us in mind and body,
that we may be coheirs in glory with Christ,
to whose suffering we are united
whenever we proclaim his Death.
Who lives and reigns for ever and ever. ***Amen.***

BLESSING & DISMISSAL *(page 56)*

Responding to the Word

God's Spirit can empower the most unlikely people.

What unlikely "prophet" surprised me by being someone from whom I learned much about God?

James reminds us that the pursuit of riches will ultimately not satisfy us.

When has my desire for riches drawn me away from a proper relationship with God or others?

Jesus reminds us that even small kindnesses done in his spirit will bring great rewards.

What small acts of kindness done to me do I recall and still appreciate very much?

October 3

God heals and restores

God is the author of marriage. He forms woman from man, bone of his bones and flesh of his flesh. Adam clings to Eve, his wife, and the two become one. The foundation of their union is their love of God and love for each other. When Adam and Eve later disobey God, sin enters their world. It creates enmity initially between the man and woman, a legacy felt millennia later. Overcome with shame and fear, Adam and Eve cover themselves and hide. The bond they shared with God and with each other has been wounded. But not irredeemably destroyed.

In the gospel, Jesus Christ is questioned about marriage and divorce. Speaking with authority, Jesus restores marriage to what it was in the beginning: "What God has joined together, no human being must separate." Marriage is a lifelong covenant, where the two become one. Their union is based on divine love. Jesus then shows mercy by welcoming little children into his arms, inviting us all to be merciful to the weakest.

May all Christians put God at the center of their marriages and families. Where there are pain and brokenness, he will heal and restore. Holy Family of Jesus, Mary, and Joseph, model of the Christian family, restorers of broken families—pray for us.

■ CONNOR BROWNRIGG

ENTRANCE ANTIPHON *(Cf. Esther 4:17)*
Within your will, O Lord, all things are established, / and there is none that can resist your will. / For you have made all things, the heaven and the earth, / and all that is held within the circle of heaven; / you are the Lord of all.

INTRODUCTORY RITES *(page 10)*

COLLECT
Almighty ever-living God,
who in the abundance of your kindness
surpass the merits and the desires of those who entreat you,
pour out your mercy upon us
to pardon what conscience dreads
and to give what prayer does not dare to ask.
Through our Lord Jesus Christ, your Son,
who lives and reigns with you in the unity of the Holy Spirit,
God, for ever and ever. ***Amen.***

FIRST READING *(Genesis 2:18-24)*
The LORD God said: "It is not good for the man to be alone. I will make a suitable partner for him." So the LORD God formed out of the ground various wild animals and various birds of the air, and he brought them to the man to see what he would call them; whatever the man called each of them would be its name. The man gave names to all the cattle, all the birds of the air, and all wild animals; but none proved to be the suitable partner for the man.

So the LORD God cast a deep sleep on the man, and while he was asleep, he took out one of his ribs and closed up its place with flesh. The LORD God then built up into a woman the rib that he had taken from the man. When he brought her to the man, the man said:

"This one, at last, is bone of my bones
and flesh of my flesh;
this one shall be called 'woman,'
for out of 'her man' this one has been taken."
That is why a man leaves his father and mother and clings to his wife, and the two of them become one flesh.

The word of the Lord. ***Thanks be to God.***

RESPONSORIAL PSALM *(Psalm 128:1-2, 3, 4-5, 6)*

℟ May the Lord bless us all the days of our lives.

Blessed are you who fear the LORD,
who walk in his ways!
For you shall eat the fruit of your handiwork;
blessed shall you be, and favored. ℟
Your wife shall be like a fruitful vine
in the recesses of your home,
your children like olive plants
around your table. ℟
Behold, thus is the man blessed
who fears the LORD.
The LORD bless you from Zion:
may you see the prosperity of Jerusalem
all the days of your life. ℟
May you see your children's children.
Peace be upon Israel! ℟

SECOND READING *(Hebrews 2:9-11)*

Brothers and sisters: He "for a little while" was made "lower than the angels," that by the grace of God he might taste death for everyone.

For it was fitting that he, for whom and through whom all

things exist, in bringing many children to glory, should make the leader to their salvation perfect through suffering. He who consecrates and those who are being consecrated all have one origin. Therefore, he is not ashamed to call them "brothers."

The word of the Lord. ***Thanks be to God.***

ALLELUIA *(1 John 4:12)*

Alleluia, alleluia. If we love one another, God remains in us / and his love is brought to perfection in us. ***Alleluia, alleluia.***

GOSPEL *(Mark 10:2–16 or 10:2–12)*

The short form ends at the asterisks.

A reading from the holy Gospel according to Mark.
Glory to you, O Lord.

The Pharisees approached Jesus and asked, "Is it lawful for a husband to **divorce**+ his wife?" They were testing him. He said to them in reply, "What did Moses command you?" They replied, "Moses permitted a husband to write a bill of divorce and dismiss her." But Jesus told them, "Because of the hardness of your hearts he wrote you this commandment. But from the beginning of creation, *God made them male and female. For this reason a man shall leave his father and mother and be joined to his wife, and the two shall become one flesh.* So they are no longer two but one flesh. Therefore what God has joined together, no human being must separate." In the house the disciples again questioned Jesus about this. He said to them, "Whoever divorces his wife and marries another commits adultery against her; and if she divorces her husband and marries another, she commits adultery."

* * *

And people were bringing children to him that he might

touch them, but the disciples rebuked them. When Jesus saw this he became indignant and said to them, "Let the children come to me; do not prevent them, for the kingdom of God belongs to such as these. Amen, I say to you, whoever does not accept the kingdom of God like a child will not enter it." Then he embraced them and blessed them, placing his hands on them.

The Gospel of the Lord. ***Praise to you, Lord Jesus Christ.***

PROFESSION OF FAITH *(page 13)*

PRAYER OF THE FAITHFUL

PREPARATION OF GIFTS *(page 16)*

PRAYER OVER THE OFFERINGS

Accept, O Lord, we pray,
the sacrifices instituted by your commands
and, through the sacred mysteries,
which we celebrate with dutiful service,

Taking a Closer Look

+ Divorce The particular meaning of divorce is directly related to the cultural customs of marriage. For ancient people, marriage was primarily an arrangement between families, without much emotional attachment between husband and wife. Dissolving a marriage did not mean the untangling of years of emotional commitment but rather the untangling of family alliances. In Judaism, only a husband could initiate divorce, which entailed sending the wife back to her family with her personal wealth (dowry) and forfeiting whatever compensation (bride price) he might have made to her family at the time of marriage.

graciously complete the sanctifying work
by which you are pleased to redeem us.
Through Christ our Lord. ***Amen.***

PREFACE *(Sundays in Ordinary Time, pages 28–32)*

COMMUNION ANTIPHON *(Lamentations 3:25)*
The Lord is good to those who hope in him, / to the soul that seeks him.

Or *(Cf. 1 Corinthians 10:17)*
Though many, we are one bread, one body, / for we all partake of the one Bread and one Chalice.

PRAYER AFTER COMMUNION
Grant us, almighty God,
that we may be refreshed and nourished
by the Sacrament which we have received,
so as to be transformed into what we consume.
Through Christ our Lord. ***Amen.***

BLESSING & DISMISSAL *(page 56)* ⁜

Responding to the Word

God saw that being alone is not good for humans.

➔ *What might I do this week to make sure that someone does not feel so alone?*

Jesus became "perfect" (or "complete") through suffering.

➔ *When did my suffering make me feel more complete or increase my compassion for others?*

God's desire is that marriage partners share a life-long commitment to one another.

➔ *What has made my commitments difficult to fulfill?*

October 10

With God, all things are possible

The crucial and consoling message in Mark's Gospel that all things are possible for God is often overshadowed by the ominous warning that earthly wealth can be a hurdle to eternal life. Gospel lessons about wealth and sharing run the gamut of the rich man's lack of concern for Lazarus, the poor widow who gave all she had to the temple treasury, and the rich young man who turned away from the advice about giving all to the poor. We are left to ponder if we are considered wealthy in God's eyes and how much of what we have should be shared with those less fortunate.

Referring to the poor as blessed, Jesus said that whatever we do for those in need, we do for him. Biblical and papal teachings champion love for the downtrodden, disempowered, and impoverished as a pillar of our Catholic faith. We can't fully embrace the Eucharist and the sacrifice Christ made for us while ignoring those in need around us.

Poverty comes in different forms, including those bereft of life's necessities, the marginalized and outcast, and those rich in earthly means but lacking in faith. Personal discretion dictates how much time and treasure we share with the poor while respecting the recipient's situation and dignity. It might seem an impossible balance but with God, all things are possible.

■ FRANK CAMPBELL

ENTRANCE ANTIPHON *(Psalm 130 [129]:3–4)*

If you, O Lord, should mark iniquities, / Lord, who could stand? / But with you is found forgiveness, / O God of Israel.

INTRODUCTORY RITES *(page 10)*

COLLECT

May your grace, O Lord, we pray,
at all times go before us and follow after
and make us always determined
to carry out good works.
Through our Lord Jesus Christ, your Son,
who lives and reigns with you in the unity of the Holy Spirit,
God, for ever and ever. ***Amen.***

FIRST READING *(Wisdom 7:7–11)*

I prayed, and prudence was given me;
I pleaded, and the spirit of **wisdom** ✝ came to me.
I preferred her to scepter and throne,
and deemed riches nothing in comparison with her,
nor did I liken any priceless gem to her;
because all gold, in view of her, is a little sand,
and before her, silver is to be accounted mire.
Beyond health and comeliness I loved her,
and I chose to have her rather than the light,
because the splendor of her never yields to sleep.
Yet all good things together came to me in her company,
and countless riches at her hands.
The word of the Lord. ***Thanks be to God.***

RESPONSORIAL PSALM *(Psalm 90:12-13, 14-15, 16-17)*

℟. Fill us with your love, O Lord, and we will sing for joy!

Teach us to number our days aright,
  that we may gain wisdom of heart.
Return, O LORD! How long?
  Have pity on your servants! **℟.**
Fill us at daybreak with your kindness,
  that we may shout for joy and gladness all our days.
Make us glad, for the days when you afflicted us,
  for the years when we saw evil. **℟.**
Let your work be seen by your servants
  and your glory by their children;
and may the gracious care of the LORD our God be ours;
  prosper the work of our hands for us!
  Prosper the work of our hands! **℟.**

SECOND READING *(Hebrews 4:12-13)*

Brothers and sisters: Indeed the word of God is living and effective, sharper than any two-edged sword, penetrating even between soul and spirit, joints and marrow, and able to discern reflections and thoughts of the heart. No creature is concealed from him, but everything is naked and exposed to the eyes of him to whom we must render an account.

The word of the Lord. ***Thanks be to God.***

ALLELUIA *(Matthew 5:3)*

Alleluia, alleluia. Blessed are the poor in spirit, / for theirs is the kingdom of heaven. ***Alleluia, alleluia.***

GOSPEL *(Mark 10:17–30 or 10:17–27)*
The shorter version ends at the asterisks.

A reading from the holy Gospel according to Mark.
Glory to you, O Lord.

As Jesus was setting out on a journey, a man ran up, knelt down before him, and asked him, "Good teacher, what must I do to inherit eternal life?" Jesus answered him, "Why do you call me good? No one is good but God alone. You know the commandments: *You shall not kill; you shall not commit adultery; you shall not steal; you shall not bear false witness; you shall not defraud; honor your father and your mother.*" He replied and said to him, "Teacher, all of these I have observed from my youth." Jesus, looking at him, loved him and said to him, "You are lacking in one thing. Go, sell what you have, and give to the poor and you will have treasure in heaven; then come, follow me." At that statement his face fell, and he went away sad, for he had many possessions.

Jesus looked around and said to his disciples, "How hard it is for those who have wealth to enter the kingdom of God!" The disciples were amazed at his words. So Jesus again said to them in reply, "Children, how hard it is to enter the kingdom of God! It is easier for a camel to pass through the eye of a needle than for one who is rich to enter the kingdom of God." They were exceedingly astonished and said among themselves, "Then who can be saved?" Jesus looked at them and said, "For human beings it is impossible, but not for God. All things are possible for God."

* * *

Peter began to say to him, "We have given up everything and followed you." Jesus said, "Amen, I say to you, there is no one who has given up house or brothers or sisters or mother or father or children or lands for my sake and for the sake of the gospel who will not receive a hundred times more now in this present age: houses and brothers and sisters and mothers and children and lands, with persecutions, and eternal life in the age to come."

The Gospel of the Lord. ***Praise to you, Lord Jesus Christ.***

PROFESSION OF FAITH *(page 13)*

PRAYER OF THE FAITHFUL

PREPARATION OF GIFTS *(page 16)*

PRAYER OVER THE OFFERINGS

Accept, O Lord, the prayers of your faithful
with the sacrificial offerings,
that, through these acts of devotedness,
we may pass over to the glory of heaven.
Through Christ our Lord. ***Amen.***

TAKING A CLOSER LOOK

+ **Wisdom** For the Jews, wisdom was the practical understanding of how the world and society worked, and so it helped people cope with the complexities of everyday life, especially sickness and suffering, death and disaster. Since wisdom did not rely on divine revelation but rather on practical human experience and observation of nature, it summarized the most helpful advice for responsible living, which the Jews shared with many ancient Near Eastern peoples. The Jews, though, sought to merge this secular tradition with the religious guidelines of their covenant instruction (Torah). Thus wisdom joined the pursuit of knowledge to the ordering of life in relation to God.

PREFACE *(Sundays in Ordinary Time, pages 28–32)*

COMMUNION ANTIPHON *(Cf. Psalm 34 [33]:11)*
The rich suffer want and go hungry, / but those who seek the Lord lack no blessing.

Or *(1 John 3:2)*
When the Lord appears, we shall be like him, / for we shall see him as he is.

PRAYER AFTER COMMUNION
We entreat your majesty most humbly, O Lord,
that, as you feed us with the nourishment
which comes from the most holy Body and Blood of your Son,
so you may make us sharers of his divine nature.
Who lives and reigns for ever and ever. ***Amen.***

BLESSING & DISMISSAL *(page 56)* ⁘

Responding to the Word

True wisdom can be more valuable to us than many material things.

What wisdom have I found most valuable for my daily guidance?

God's word can penetrate deep into our inner self and reveal things we might not want to see.

When has God's word in Scripture revealed surprising depths about myself and about God?

Jesus challenges the rich man to give up his riches and follow.

What riches of mine is Jesus asking me to give up in order to follow him more closely today?

October 17

Becoming servant leaders

In today's gospel, two of the apostles make an audacious request of Jesus, one which upsets all the other apostles. They want to sit with Jesus in heaven. How dare they ask Jesus for such special treatment! Jesus, however, clearly sees this tension as a "teaching moment" for them. He asks a few key questions to clarify the essential attitude of humility that we are all called to live. Jesus' response is rooted in the astounding truth that he did not come to be served but to serve.

Whatever authority we have, at home or work, in private or public, impacts all the important relationships we have, for better or worse. We typically see any misuse of authority more clearly in others than in ourselves. Our culture encourages us to live out of our ego and to seek pleasure, privilege, and power. Doing so can cause many problems and much pain. However, in today's gospel, Jesus invites his apostles and us to choose a different path.

At this Eucharist, let us ask for the grace to drink the cup of our own lives, with its delights and challenges. Let us also ask for the grace of humility so that we too can become servant leaders like Jesus. May we embrace the truth that to serve the good of others can be a source of joy for ourselves.

■ Joe Egan

ENTRANCE ANTIPHON *(Cf. Psalm 17 [16]:6, 8)*
To you I call; for you will surely heed me, O God; / turn your ear to me; hear my words. / Guard me as the apple of your eye; / in the shadow of your wings protect me.

INTRODUCTORY RITES *(page 10)*

COLLECT
Almighty ever-living God,
grant that we may always conform our will to yours
and serve your majesty in sincerity of heart.
Through our Lord Jesus Christ, your Son,
who lives and reigns with you in the unity of the Holy Spirit,
God, for ever and ever. ***Amen.***

FIRST READING *(Isaiah 53:10-11)*
The LORD was pleased
to crush him in infirmity.

If he gives his life as an offering for sin,
he shall see his descendants in a long life,
and the will of the LORD shall be accomplished through him.

Because of his affliction
he shall see the light in fullness of days;
through his suffering, my servant shall justify many,
and their guilt he shall bear.
The word of the Lord. ***Thanks be to God.***

RESPONSORIAL PSALM *(Psalm 33:4-5, 18-19, 20, 22)*
℟. Lord, let your mercy be on us, as we place our trust in you.

Upright is the word of the LORD,
and all his works are trustworthy.

He loves justice and right;
  of the kindness of the LORD the earth is full. ℟
See, the eyes of the LORD are upon those who fear him,
  upon those who hope for his kindness,
To deliver them from death
  and preserve them in spite of famine. ℟
Our soul waits for the LORD,
  who is our help and our shield.
May your kindness, O LORD, be upon us
  who have put our hope in you. ℟

SECOND READING *(Hebrews 4:14–16)*

Brothers and sisters: Since we have a great high priest who has passed through the heavens, Jesus, the Son of God, let us hold fast to our confession. For we do not have a high priest who is unable to sympathize with our weaknesses, but one who has similarly been tested in every way, yet without sin. So let us confidently approach the **throne of grace**✝ to receive mercy and to find grace for timely help.

The word of the Lord. ***Thanks be to God.***

ALLELUIA *(Mark 10:45)*

Alleluia, alleluia. The Son of Man came to serve / and to give his life as a ransom for many. ***Alleluia, alleluia.***

GOSPEL *(Mark 10:35–45 or 10:42–45)*

The shorter version begins at the asterisks.

A reading from the holy Gospel according to Mark.
Glory to you, O Lord.

James and John, the sons of Zebedee, came to Jesus and said to him, "Teacher, we want you to do for us whatever we ask of you." He replied, "What do you wish me to do for you?" They answered him, "Grant that in your glory we may sit one at your right and the other at your left." Jesus said to them, "You do not know what you are asking. Can you drink the cup that I drink or be baptized with the baptism with which I am baptized?" They said to him, "We can." Jesus said to them, "The cup that I drink, you will drink, and with the baptism with which I am baptized, you will be baptized; but to sit at my right or at my left is not mine to give but is for those for whom it has been prepared." When the ten heard this, they became indignant at James and John.

* * *

Jesus summoned them [the Twelve] and said to them, "You know that those who are recognized as rulers over the Gentiles lord it over them, and their great ones make their authority over them felt. But it shall not be so among you. Rather, whoever wishes to be great among you will be your servant; whoever wishes to be first among you will be the slave of all. For the Son of Man did not come to be served but to serve and to give his life as a ransom for many."

The Gospel of the Lord. ***Praise to you, Lord Jesus Christ.***

PROFESSION OF FAITH *(page 13)*

PRAYER OF THE FAITHFUL

PREPARATION OF GIFTS *(page 16)*

PRAYER OVER THE OFFERINGS

Grant us, Lord, we pray,
a sincere respect for your gifts,
that, through the purifying action of your grace,
we may be cleansed by the very mysteries we serve.
Through Christ our Lord. ***Amen.***

PREFACE *(Sundays in Ordinary Time, pages 28–32)*

COMMUNION ANTIPHON *(Cf. Psalm 33 [32]:18–19)*

Behold, the eyes of the Lord / are on those who fear him, / who hope in his merciful love, / to rescue their souls from death, / to keep them alive in famine.

Or *(Mark 10:45)*

The Son of Man has come / to give his life as a ransom for many.

Taking a Closer Look

✛ **Throne of grace** The throne of grace is the chair on which a wealthy patron or head of a household receives the petitioners seeking help. In the biblical world, everyone in one way or another depended on the resources held by the king or these wealthy patrons. So each morning these patrons would receive those who sought "favors" or "gifts" (Greek, *charis*). In the reading, the author pictures God in heaven, seated on a throne like a powerful king who is receiving petitioners. Like those who need help, we approach God as our merciful benefactor or gift-giver who will supply us with what we ask.

PRAYER AFTER COMMUNION

Grant, O Lord, we pray,
that, benefiting from participation in heavenly things,
we may be helped by what you give in this present age
and prepared for the gifts that are eternal.
Through Christ our Lord. ***Amen.***

BLESSING & DISMISSAL *(page 56)* ⁜

Responding to the Word

Through suffering, God's servant helps many others.

➔ *How has my suffering made me more ready to help others who suffer?*

Jesus knows our human weaknesses.

➔ *Which weakness do I want Jesus to help me with today?*

Jesus encourages us to become great through serving others.

➔ *What hidden service can I do for someone this week?*

October 24

Go forth with new vision!

"Master, I want to see." In that split second after Jesus asks him what he wants him to do, did Bartimaeus think about how profoundly his life would change? Living life as a blind beggar was not easy, but it was all he knew, and sometimes there is comfort in the familiar. At the end of the passage, we are told that rather than going home and rebuilding his life as a sighted person, Bartimaeus chose to follow the One who had opened his eyes. We can only imagine where that led. So yes, life as he knew it was never the same.

If we are honest, perhaps there are times when we would rather not have our eyes opened, especially if it means making some very real changes to the way we live. Seeing the needs of the poor and the marginalized right around us might challenge us to reconsider the way we spend our time or our money. Having our eyes opened to the reasons behind a damaged relationship might mean having to apologize or make amends. If we are open, we see things in a new light, through God's eyes, not our own.

Like Bartimaeus, we are invited to follow Christ in faith. Nourished by word and sacrament, may we go forth today with new vision, seeking his face in all we meet.

■ Teresa Whalen Lux

ENTRANCE ANTIPHON *(Cf. Psalm 105 [104]:3-4)*
Let the hearts that seek the Lord rejoice; / turn to the Lord and his strength; / constantly seek his face.

INTRODUCTORY RITES *(page 10)*

COLLECT
Almighty ever-living God,
increase our faith, hope and charity,
and make us love what you command,
so that we may merit what you promise.
Through our Lord Jesus Christ, your Son,
who lives and reigns with you in the unity of the Holy Spirit,
God, for ever and ever. ***Amen.***

FIRST READING *(Jeremiah 31:7-9)*
Thus says the LORD:
Shout with joy for Jacob,
exult at the head of the nations;
proclaim your praise and say:
The LORD has delivered his people,
the remnant of Israel.
Behold, I will bring them back
from the land of the north;
I will gather them from the ends of the world,
with the blind and the lame in their midst,
the mothers and those with child;
they shall return as an immense throng.
They departed in tears,
but I will console them and guide them;
I will lead them to brooks of water,
on a level road, so that none shall stumble.

For I am a father to Israel,
  Ephraim is my first-born.
The word of the Lord. ***Thanks be to God.***

RESPONSORIAL PSALM *(Psalm 126:1–2, 2–3, 4–5, 6)*

℟. The Lord has done great things for us; we are filled with joy.

When the LORD brought back the captives of Zion,
  we were like men dreaming.
Then our mouth was filled with laughter,
  and our tongue with rejoicing. ℟.
Then they said among the nations,
  "The LORD has done great things for them."
The LORD has done great things for us;
  we are glad indeed. ℟.
Restore our fortunes, O LORD,
  like the torrents in the southern desert.
Those that sow in tears
  shall reap rejoicing. ℟.
Although they go forth weeping,
  carrying the seed to be sown,
They shall come back rejoicing,
  carrying their sheaves. ℟.

SECOND READING *(Hebrews 5:1–6)*

Brothers and sisters: Every high priest is taken from among men and made their representative before God, to offer gifts and sacrifices for sins. He is able to deal patiently with the ignorant and erring, for he himself is beset by weakness and so, for this reason, must make sin offerings for himself as well as for the people. No one takes this honor upon himself but only when called by God, just as Aaron was. In the same way, it was not

Christ who glorified himself in becoming high priest, but rather the one who said to him:

You are my son:
this day I have begotten you;

just as he says in another place:

You are a priest forever
according to the order of Melchizedek.

The word of the Lord. ***Thanks be to God.***

ALLELUIA *(See 2 Timothy 1:10)*

Alleluia, alleluia. Our Savior Jesus Christ destroyed death / and brought life to light through the Gospel. ***Alleluia, alleluia.***

GOSPEL *(Mark 10:46–52)*

A reading from the holy Gospel according to Mark.

Glory to you, O Lord.

As Jesus was leaving Jericho with his disciples and a sizable crowd, Bartimaeus, a blind man, the son of Timaeus, sat by the roadside begging. On hearing that it was Jesus of Nazareth, he began to cry out and say, "Jesus, **son of David,** ✝ have pity on me." And many rebuked him, telling him to be silent. But he kept calling out all the more, "Son of David, have pity on me." Jesus stopped and said, "Call him." So they called the blind man, saying to him, "Take courage; get up, Jesus is calling you." He threw aside his cloak, sprang up, and came to Jesus. Jesus said to him in reply, "What do you want me to do for you?" The blind man replied to him, "Master, I want to see." Jesus told him, "Go your way; your faith has saved you." Immediately he received his sight and followed him on the way.

The Gospel of the Lord. ***Praise to you, Lord Jesus Christ.***

PROFESSION OF FAITH *(page 13)*

PRAYER OF THE FAITHFUL

PREPARATION OF GIFTS *(page 16)*

PRAYER OVER THE OFFERINGS

Look, we pray, O Lord,
on the offerings we make to your majesty,
that whatever is done by us in your service
may be directed above all to your glory.
Through Christ our Lord. ***Amen.***

PREFACE *(Sundays in Ordinary Time, pages 28–32)*

TAKING A CLOSER LOOK

✝ **Son of David** "Son of David" is a title indicating that the crowds recognize Jesus not only as an Israelite of the tribe of Judah (from which we get the word "Jew") but also of the royal bloodline of King David, who unified the twelve tribal peoples into a single kingdom around 1000 BC. The title reveals the crowd's hope that Jesus is indeed David's long-awaited successor, the one chosen and anointed (Hebrew, *messiah;* Greek, *christos*) by God to restore the Jewish nation into a kingdom dedicated to life with God.

COMMUNION ANTIPHON *(Cf. Psalm 20 [19]:6)*
We will ring out our joy at your saving help / and exult in the name of our God.

Or *(Ephesians 5:2)*
Christ loved us and gave himself up for us, / as a fragrant offering to God.

PRAYER AFTER COMMUNION
May your Sacraments, O Lord, we pray,
perfect in us what lies within them,
that what we now celebrate in signs
we may one day possess in truth.
Through Christ our Lord. ***Amen.***

BLESSING & DISMISSAL *(page 56)*

Responding to the Word

God promises to gather the people and end their suffering.

What signs of God's activity do I detect in the Church today?

Jesus is our representative before God.

What problem or need do I want Jesus to take before God today?

Jesus helps a blind man to see.

For what do I need Jesus' help to "see" more clearly about my life today?

October 31

Loving all our neighbors

Today's readings remind us of the simple message God has for us: God is love and all we are to do in exchange for the gift of his love is to love our neighbor. As is often the case with our faith, there is room for deeper reflection here. If we are to love others as ourselves, then we must start by loving ourselves. This love is not an exercise in vanity, but rather an appreciation for the good we see in ourselves or in others.

"Love the Lord, your God, with all your heart" brings to my mind the symbolic joining together of fingers in the shape of a heart to communicate this message. Elsewhere in the gospels Jesus is asked, "Who is my neighbor?" (He answers: the Good Samaritan.) It is tempting to limit our understanding of neighbor, yet in the Biblical sense the term is broader and meant to include everyone.

Today, let us give thanks for the blessings we have received from others throughout our lives. Let us pause and broaden our focus to include others not in our immediate vicinity—perhaps a former teacher, family friend, or even a stranger. Remembering the good in them will provide us with a hint of the joys to come when we can be reconciled with the One who is the author of all that is good.

■ John O'Brien

ENTRANCE ANTIPHON *(Cf. Psalm 38 [37]:22-23)*
Forsake me not, O Lord, my God; / be not far from me! / Make haste and come to my help, / O Lord, my strong salvation!

INTRODUCTORY RITES *(page 10)*

COLLECT
Almighty and merciful God,
by whose gift your faithful offer you
right and praiseworthy service,
grant, we pray,
that we may hasten without stumbling
to receive the things you have promised.
Through our Lord Jesus Christ, your Son,
who lives and reigns with you in the unity of the Holy Spirit,
God, for ever and ever. ***Amen.***

FIRST READING *(Deuteronomy 6:2-6)*
Moses spoke to the people, saying: "**Fear the Lord,** ✠ your God, and keep, throughout the days of your lives, all his statutes and commandments which I enjoin on you, and thus have long life. Hear then, Israel, and be careful to observe them, that you may grow and prosper the more, in keeping with the promise of the Lord, the God of your fathers, to give you a land flowing with milk and honey.

"Hear, O Israel! The Lord is our God, the Lord alone! Therefore, you shall love the Lord, your God, with all your heart, and with all your soul, and with all your strength. Take to heart these words which I enjoin on you today."

The word of the Lord. ***Thanks be to God.***

RESPONSORIAL PSALM *(Psalm 18:2-3, 3-4, 47, 51)*

℟. I love you, Lord, my strength.

I love you, O LORD, my strength,
O LORD, my rock, my fortress, my deliverer. ℟.
My God, my rock of refuge,
my shield, the horn of my salvation, my stronghold!
Praised be the LORD, I exclaim,
and I am safe from my enemies. ℟.
The LORD lives! And blessed be my rock!
Extolled be God my savior,
you who gave great victories to your king
and showed kindness to your anointed. ℟.

SECOND READING *(Hebrews 7:23-28)*

Brothers and sisters: The levitical priests were many because they were prevented by death from remaining in office, but Jesus, because he remains forever, has a priesthood that does not pass away. Therefore, he is always able to save those who approach God through him, since he lives forever to make intercession for them.

It was fitting that we should have such a high priest: holy, innocent, undefiled, separated from sinners, higher than the heavens. He has no need, as did the high priests, to offer sacrifice day after day, first for his own sins and then for those of the people; he did that once for all when he offered himself. For the law appoints men subject to weakness to be high priests, but the word of the oath, which was taken after the law, appoints a son, who has been made perfect forever.

The word of the Lord. ***Thanks be to God.***

ALLELUIA *(John 14:23)*
Alleluia, alleluia. Whoever loves me will keep my word, says the Lord; / and my Father will love him and we will come to him.
Alleluia, alleluia.

GOSPEL *(Mark 12:28b–34)*
A reading from the holy Gospel according to Mark.
Glory to you, O Lord.
One of the scribes came to Jesus and asked him, "Which is the first of all the commandments?" Jesus replied, "The first is this: *Hear, O Israel! The Lord our God is Lord alone! You shall love the Lord your God with all your heart, with all your soul, with all your mind, and with all your strength.* The second is this: *You shall love your neighbor as yourself.* There is no other commandment greater than these." The scribe said to him, "Well said, teacher. You are right in saying, 'He is One and there is no other than he.' And 'to love him with all your heart, with all your understanding, with all your strength, and to love your neighbor as yourself' is worth more than all burnt offerings and sacrifices." And when Jesus saw that he answered with understanding, he said to him, "You are not far from the kingdom of God." And no one dared to ask him any more questions.

The Gospel of the Lord. ***Praise to you, Lord Jesus Christ.***

PROFESSION OF FAITH *(page 13)*

PRAYER OF THE FAITHFUL

PREPARATION OF GIFTS *(page 16)*

PRAYER OVER THE OFFERINGS

May these sacrificial offerings, O Lord,
become for you a pure oblation,
and for us a holy outpouring of your mercy.
Through Christ our Lord. ***Amen.***

PREFACE *(Sundays in Ordinary Time, pages 28–32)*

COMMUNION ANTIPHON *(Cf. Psalm 16 [15]:11)*

You will show me the path of life, / the fullness of joy in your presence, O Lord.

Or *(John 6:58)*

Just as the living Father sent me / and I have life because of the Father, / so whoever feeds on me / shall have life because of me, says the Lord.

Taking a Closer Look

✝ **Fear the Lord** Fear of the Lord describes the reverent respect or awe that a person must have before God. Since God is so utterly different from anything created—awesome in power (almighty) and holiness—coming into God's presence always creates an apprehension about what might happen. Thus God often counsels the person, "Don't be afraid." Fear in God's presence thus changes to adoration. But it almost always carries an overtone of judgment because, when confronted by God's holiness, humans cannot help but recognize their distance from God (sinfulness). Fear of the Lord is also the beginning of wisdom for it is the experience of one's humble place in relation to God.

PRAYER AFTER COMMUNION

May the working of your power, O Lord,
increase in us, we pray,
so that, renewed by these heavenly Sacraments,
we may be prepared by your gift
for receiving what they promise.
Through Christ our Lord. ***Amen.***

BLESSING & DISMISSAL *(page 56)* ⁜

Responding to the Word

Moses encourages us to love God as completely as we can.

What can I do this week to strengthen my love for God?

Jesus is always able to save those who approach God through him.

What difficulty would I like Jesus to help me with today?

Jesus summarizes our task as loving God and our neighbor.

Which of these loves needs more attention in my life now?

November 1

NOV 1

Rejoice in all our saints

When people are asked, "Who have been the models of holiness and the greatest examples for your life?" the first response is often the popular saints—Francis of Assisi, Thérèse of Lisieux, and so forth. The likes of such great men and women grace the Church calendar throughout the year.

But when we start to think of the people whose lives and faith have inspired and nourished us, our thoughts might then turn to less well-known "saints": parents, grandparents, neighbors, community leaders, religious, and parish priests. Many of these have been wonderful examples for us and a strong influence on our lives. Some have already gone on to live with God.

Today is their day. On this solemn feast, we rejoice in all the saints who are now living with God, yet who may not be so well-known and celebrated as to have their own feast day. Today we particularly remember the saints of our own lives. We give thanks to God, and to these saints, for the grace they have been for us. And we hope to join their company one day.

■ MSGR. STEPHEN J. ROSSETTI

ENTRANCE ANTIPHON

Let us all rejoice in the Lord, / as we celebrate the feast day in honor of all the Saints, / at whose festival the Angels rejoice / and praise the Son of God.

INTRODUCTORY RITES *(page 10)*

COLLECT

Almighty ever-living God,
by whose gift we venerate in one celebration
the merits of all the Saints,
bestow on us, we pray,
through the prayers of so many intercessors,
an abundance of the reconciliation with you
for which we earnestly long.
Through our Lord Jesus Christ, your Son,
who lives and reigns with you in the unity of the Holy Spirit,
God, for ever and ever. ***Amen.***

FIRST READING *(Revelation 7:2–4, 9–14)*

I, John, saw another angel come up from the East, holding the seal of the living God. He cried out in a loud voice to the four angels who were given power to damage the land and the sea, "Do not damage the land or the sea or the trees until we put the seal on the foreheads of the servants of our God." I heard the number of those who had been marked with the seal, **one hundred and forty-four thousand**✝ marked from every tribe of the children of Israel.

After this I had a vision of a great multitude, which no one could count, from every nation, race, people, and tongue. They stood before the throne and before the Lamb, wearing white robes and holding palm branches in their hands. They cried out

in a loud voice:
"Salvation comes from our God, who is seated on the throne,
and from the Lamb."
All the angels stood around the throne and around the elders and the four living creatures. They prostrated themselves before the throne, worshiped God, and exclaimed:
"Amen. Blessing and glory, wisdom and thanksgiving,
honor, power, and might
be to our God forever and ever. Amen."
Then one of the elders spoke up and said to me, "Who are these wearing white robes, and where did they come from?" I said to him, "My lord, you are the one who knows." He said to me, "These are the ones who have survived the time of great distress; they have washed their robes and made them white in the Blood of the Lamb."
The word of the Lord. ***Thanks be to God.***

RESPONSORIAL PSALM *(Psalm 24:1bc-2, 3-4ab, 5-6)*

℟. Lord, this is the people that longs to see your face.

The LORD's are the earth and its fullness;
the world and those who dwell in it.
For he founded it upon the seas
and established it upon the rivers. **℟.**
Who can ascend the mountain of the LORD?
or who may stand in his holy place?
One whose hands are sinless, whose heart is clean,
who desires not what is vain. **℟.**
He shall receive a blessing from the LORD,
a reward from God his savior.
Such is the race that seeks him,
that seeks the face of the God of Jacob. **℟.**

SECOND READING *(1 John 3:1-3)*

Beloved: See what love the Father has bestowed on us that we may be called the children of God. Yet so we are. The reason the world does not know us is that it did not know him. Beloved, we are God's children now; what we shall be has not yet been revealed. We do know that when it is revealed we shall be like him, for we shall see him as he is. Everyone who has this hope based on him makes himself pure, as he is pure.

The word of the Lord. ***Thanks be to God.***

ALLELUIA *(Matthew 11:28)*

Alleluia, alleluia. Come to me, all you who labor and are burdened, / and I will give you rest, says the Lord. ***Alleluia, alleluia.***

GOSPEL *(Matthew 5:1-12a)*

A reading from the holy Gospel according to Matthew.
Glory to you, O Lord.

When Jesus saw the crowds, he went up the mountain, and after he had sat down, his disciples came to him. He began to teach them, saying:

"Blessed are the poor in spirit,
for theirs is the Kingdom of heaven.
Blessed are they who mourn,
for they will be comforted.
Blessed are the meek,
for they will inherit the land.
Blessed are they who hunger and thirst for righteousness,
for they will be satisfied.
Blessed are the merciful,
for they will be shown mercy.

Blessed are the clean of heart,
for they will see God.
Blessed are the peacemakers,
for they will be called children of God.
Blessed are they who are persecuted for the sake of righteousness,
for theirs is the Kingdom of heaven.

Blessed are you when they insult you and persecute you and utter every kind of evil against you falsely because of me. Rejoice and be glad, for your reward will be great in heaven."

The Gospel of the Lord. ***Praise to you, Lord Jesus Christ.***

PROFESSION OF FAITH *(page 13)*

PRAYER OF THE FAITHFUL

PREPARATION OF GIFTS *(page 16)*

PRAYER OVER THE OFFERINGS

May these offerings we bring in honor of all the Saints
be pleasing to you, O Lord,
and grant that, just as we believe the Saints
to be already assured of immortality,
so we may experience their concern for our salvation.
Through Christ our Lord. ***Amen.***

PREFACE: THE GLORY OF JERUSALEM, OUR MOTHER

It is truly right and just, our duty and our salvation,
always and everywhere to give you thanks,
Lord, holy Father, almighty and eternal God.

For today by your gift we celebrate the festival of your city,
the heavenly Jerusalem, our mother,

where the great array of our brothers and sisters
already gives you eternal praise.

Towards her, we eagerly hasten as pilgrims advancing by faith,
rejoicing in the glory bestowed upon those exalted members
of the Church
through whom you give us, in our frailty, both strength
and good example.

And so, we glorify you with the multitude of Saints and Angels,
as with one voice of praise we acclaim:
Holy, Holy, Holy Lord God of hosts... *(page 35)*

COMMUNION ANTIPHON *(Matthew 5:8-10)*
Blessed are the clean of heart, for they shall see God. / Blessed are the peacemakers, / for they shall be called children of God. / Blessed are they who are persecuted for the sake of righteousness, / for theirs is the Kingdom of Heaven.

Taking a Closer Look

+ One hundred and forty-four thousand

Although some Christian groups have taken this number as the actual count of those saved, it is evident both from the general way large numbers are used in the Bible and from what follows that this is a symbolic number. For people without sophisticated mathematics, large numbers are almost always symbolic, the way we say "million" or "zillion" for emphasis. In everyday life, counting to 144,000 of anything would be a major chore. The number means that an incredibly large number of Jews are saved. But this is not all the saved because there is an additional "great multitude" of non-Jews. This is John's way of saying that the number of those saved is innumerable.

PRAYER AFTER COMMUNION

As we adore you, O God, who alone are holy
and wonderful in all your Saints,
we implore your grace,
so that, coming to perfect holiness in the fullness of your love,
we may pass from this pilgrim table
to the banquet of our heavenly homeland.
Through Christ our Lord. ***Amen.***

SOLEMN BLESSING: ALL SAINTS *(Optional, page 63)*

DISMISSAL *(page 57)* ⁜

Responding to the Word

John has a heavenly vision of all the saints.

➔ *Which saints have been particularly helpful as examples for my Christian life?*

As God's children, we will be changed because we imitate God.

➔ *Which of God's characteristics can I try harder to imitate this week?*

Jesus' beatitudes describe the kind of behaviors that should characterize us as Christians.

➔ *Which beatitude is easiest (or hardest) for me to live by right now?*

November 7

Beware!

"Beware of the scribes," Jesus says. Because, once they "devour the houses of widows," they'll look to devour what we have? Or should we beware, lest we become like them? Lest we begin to justify casting aside widows, the poor, the marginalized—taking more while others have less and less? Jesus' words are a warning: it is frighteningly easy to become like the scribes.

We must also beware of believing Jesus meant only certain people of his own day. The word "scribes" represents all powerful people who abuse their power, seeking gain for themselves at the expense of others. Most of us have some degree of comfort, wealth, and power, even if it's small. We need to beware of our desire for more and the temptation to ignore the needy, which Jesus condemns.

We're tempted to think: beware of the widow and her example. Most of us would much rather be greeted with respect and have places of honor than give away everything we have. It's glaringly obvious: Jesus wants us to be like the widow, not like the scribes.

The gospel and the Eucharist call us to a radical generosity, a radical knowledge that all we have comes from God, a radical trust in and dependence on God. To give like the widow. To live like Jesus.

■ Dinah Simmons

ENTRANCE ANTIPHON *(Cf. Psalm 88 [87]:3)*
Let my prayer come into your presence. / Incline your ear to my cry for help, O Lord.

INTRODUCTORY RITES *(page 10)*

COLLECT
Almighty and merciful God,
graciously keep from us all adversity,
so that, unhindered in mind and body alike,
we may pursue in freedom of heart
the things that are yours.
Through our Lord Jesus Christ, your Son,
who lives and reigns with you in the unity of the Holy Spirit,
God, for ever and ever. ***Amen.***

FIRST READING *(1 Kings 17:10-16)*
In those days, Elijah the prophet went to Zarephath. As he arrived at the entrance of the city, a widow was gathering sticks there; he called out to her, "Please bring me a small cupful of water to drink." She left to get it, and he called out after her, "Please bring along a bit of bread." She answered, "As the LORD, your God, lives, I have nothing baked; there is only a handful of flour in my jar and a little oil in my jug. Just now I was collecting a couple of sticks, to go in and prepare something for myself and my son; when we have eaten it, we shall die." Elijah said to her, "Do not be afraid. Go and do as you propose. But first make me a little cake and bring it to me. Then you can prepare something for yourself and your son. For the LORD, the God of Israel, says, 'The jar of flour shall not go empty, nor the jug of oil run dry, until the day when the LORD sends rain upon the earth.' " She left and did as Elijah had said.

She was able to eat for a year, and he and her son as well; the jar of flour did not go empty, nor the jug of oil run dry, as the LORD had foretold through Elijah.

The word of the Lord. ***Thanks be to God.***

RESPONSORIAL PSALM *(Psalm 146:7, 8-9, 9-10)*

℟. Praise the Lord, my soul! *Or* **Alleluia.**

The LORD keeps faith forever,
secures justice for the oppressed,
gives food to the hungry.
The LORD sets captives free. ℟.
The LORD gives sight to the blind;
the LORD raises up those who were bowed down.
The LORD loves the just;
the LORD protects strangers. ℟.
The fatherless and the widow he sustains,
but the way of the wicked he thwarts.
The LORD shall reign forever;
your God, O Zion, through all generations. Alleluia. ℟.

SECOND READING *(Hebrews 9:24-28)*

Christ did not enter into a sanctuary made by hands, a copy of the true one, but heaven itself, that he might now appear before God on our behalf. Not that he might offer himself repeatedly, as the high priest enters each year into the sanctuary with blood that is not his own; if that were so, he would have had to suffer repeatedly from the foundation of the world. But now once for all he has appeared at the end of the ages to take away sin by his sacrifice. Just as it is appointed that human beings die once, and after this the judgment, so also Christ, offered once to take away the sins of many, will appear a second time, not to take away sin but to bring salvation to those who eagerly await him.

The word of the Lord. ***Thanks be to God.***

ALLELUIA *(Matthew 5:3)*

Alleluia, alleluia. Blessed are the poor in spirit, / for theirs is the kingdom of heaven. ***Alleluia, alleluia.***

GOSPEL *(Mark 12:38–44 or 12:41–44)*

The shorter version begins at the asterisks.

A reading from the holy Gospel according to Mark.
Glory to you, O Lord.

In the course of his teaching Jesus said to the crowds, "Beware of the scribes, who like to go around in long robes and accept greetings in the marketplaces, seats of honor in synagogues, and places of honor at banquets. They devour the houses of widows and, as a pretext, recite lengthy prayers. They will receive a very severe condemnation."

* * *

He [Jesus] sat down opposite **the treasury**✝ and observed how the crowd put money into the treasury. Many rich people put in large sums. A poor widow also came and put in two small coins worth a few cents. Calling his disciples to himself, he said to them, "Amen, I say to you, this poor widow put in more than all the other contributors to the treasury. For they have all contributed from their surplus wealth, but she, from her poverty, has contributed all she had, her whole livelihood."

The Gospel of the Lord. ***Praise to you, Lord Jesus Christ.***

PROFESSION OF FAITH *(page 13)*

PRAYER OF THE FAITHFUL

PREPARATION OF GIFTS *(page 16)*

PRAYER OVER THE OFFERINGS

Look with favor, we pray, O Lord,
upon the sacrificial gifts offered here,
that, celebrating in mystery the Passion of your Son,
we may honor it with loving devotion.
Through Christ our Lord. ***Amen.***

PREFACE *(Sundays in Ordinary Time, pages 28–32)*

Taking a Closer Look

✝ **The treasury** In the ancient world, the temple building and its surrounding area (sanctuary) were considered God's house. So the temple often included storerooms inaccessible to the public in which were kept not only the things needed for worship but also the money gathered for its upkeep. Each year, Jews throughout the world were required to contribute one half *shekel* (equivalent to about two days' wages) for the upkeep of the temple. In the Jerusalem temple sanctuary, there were thirteen different trumpet-shaped chests into which people put their specific types of contributions such as yearly taxes or bird offerings. It is likely into one of these chests that the widow put her contribution.

COMMUNION ANTIPHON *(Cf. Psalm 23 [22]:1-2)*
The Lord is my shepherd; there is nothing I shall want. / Fresh and green are the pastures where he gives me repose, / near restful waters he leads me.

Or *(Cf. Luke 24:35)*
The disciples recognized the Lord Jesus in the breaking of bread.

PRAYER AFTER COMMUNION
Nourished by this sacred gift, O Lord,
we give you thanks and beseech your mercy,
that, by the pouring forth of your Spirit,
the grace of integrity may endure
in those your heavenly power has entered.
Through Christ our Lord. ***Amen.***

BLESSING & DISMISSAL *(page 56)*

Responding to the Word

Small gifts sometimes reap unexpected rewards.

When has some small service of mine had unexpectedly good results?

Christ's self-sacrifice helped others come closer to God.

What sacrifice might I make this week to help someone else discover God's healing love?

Though the widow's gift was small, Jesus recognized that it was actually very generous.

What might I do this week to give more generously of my time, my treasure, and my talents?

November 14

Focus on God daily

In his book *Practicing the Presence of God* (a work recommended by Pope Leo XIV, by the way), Brother Lawrence (c. 1614-1691) shares much wisdom on how to respond to today's gospel about the end times: "We must keep our eyes fixed on God in all we say, do, or undertake." We might be forgiven for thinking we're living in these end times and for wondering where God is in all the world's upheaval—and how we can keep our eyes fixed on God in all we do.

Recognizing our need for God is a crucial first step. Focusing on God daily, moment by moment, helps us remain attentive, alert, and watchful—prayerfully discerning God's will, preparing ourselves, and stripping away all that is not of God. These practices anchor us in our journey and guard us against foolish prophecies, predictions, or fears.

As Catholics, we are lavishly blessed. Amid the unpredictability of life on earth, not only do we have a Savior, but our Church has given us practical tools to help us live these lofty ideals. Imagine how different the world would be if we all kept the Ten Commandments, faithfully attended Mass, went to confession regularly, and remained rooted in God's word and the sacraments. Not only would we be ready for the end times—we could change the world today.

■ Dorothy Pilarski

ENTRANCE ANTIPHON *(Jeremiah 29:11, 12, 14)*
The Lord said: I think thoughts of peace and not of affliction. / You will call upon me, and I will answer you, / and I will lead back your captives from every place.

INTRODUCTORY RITES *(page 10)*

COLLECT
Grant us, we pray, O Lord our God,
the constant gladness of being devoted to you,
for it is full and lasting happiness
to serve with constancy
the author of all that is good.
Through our Lord Jesus Christ, your Son,
who lives and reigns with you in the unity of the Holy Spirit,
God, for ever and ever. ***Amen.***

FIRST READING *(Daniel 12:1-3)*
In those days, I Daniel, heard this word of the Lord:
"At that time there shall arise
Michael, ✝ the great prince,
guardian of your people;
it shall be a time unsurpassed in distress
since nations began until that time.
At that time your people shall escape,
everyone who is found written in the book.

"Many of those who sleep in the dust of the earth shall awake;
some shall live forever,
others shall be an everlasting horror and disgrace.

"But the wise shall shine brightly
like the splendor of the firmament,
and those who lead the many to justice
shall be like the stars forever."
The word of the Lord. ***Thanks be to God.***

RESPONSORIAL PSALM *(Psalm 16:5, 8, 9-10, 11)*

℟. You are my inheritance, O Lord!

O LORD, my allotted portion and my cup,
you it is who hold fast my lot.
I set the LORD ever before me;
with him at my right hand I shall not be disturbed. ℟.
Therefore my heart is glad and my soul rejoices,
my body, too, abides in confidence;
because you will not abandon my soul to the netherworld,
nor will you suffer your faithful one to undergo corruption. ℟.
You will show me the path to life,
fullness of joys in your presence,
the delights at your right hand forever. ℟.

SECOND READING *(Hebrews 10:11-14, 18)*

Brothers and sisters: Every priest stands daily at his ministry, offering frequently those same sacrifices that can never take away sins. But this one offered one sacrifice for sins, and took his seat forever at the right hand of God; now he waits until his enemies are made his footstool. For by one offering he has made perfect forever those who are being consecrated.

Where there is forgiveness of these, there is no longer offering for sin.

The word of the Lord. ***Thanks be to God.***

ALLELUIA *(Luke 21:36)*
Alleluia, alleluia. Be vigilant at all times / and pray that you have the strength to stand before the Son of Man. ***Alleluia, alleluia.***

GOSPEL *(Mark 13:24-32)*
A reading from the holy Gospel according to Mark.
Glory to you, O Lord.

Jesus said to his disciples: "In those days after that tribulation
the sun will be darkened,
and the moon will not give its light,
and the stars will be falling from the sky,
and the powers in the heavens will be shaken.

"And then they will see 'the Son of Man coming in the clouds' with great power and glory, and then he will send out the angels and gather his elect from the four winds, from the end of the earth to the end of the sky.

"Learn a lesson from the fig tree. When its branch becomes tender and sprouts leaves, you know that summer is near. In the same way, when you see these things happening, know that he is near, at the gates. Amen, I say to you, this generation will not pass away until all these things have taken place. Heaven and earth will pass away, but my words will not pass away.

"But of that day or hour, no one knows, neither the angels in heaven, nor the Son, but only the Father."

The Gospel of the Lord. ***Praise to you, Lord Jesus Christ.***

PROFESSION OF FAITH *(page 13)*

PRAYER OF THE FAITHFUL

PREPARATION OF GIFTS *(page 16)*

PRAYER OVER THE OFFERINGS
Grant, O Lord, we pray,
that what we offer in the sight of your majesty
may obtain for us the grace of being devoted to you
and gain us the prize of everlasting happiness.
Through Christ our Lord. ***Amen.***

PREFACE *(Sundays in Ordinary Time, pages 28–32)*

TAKING A CLOSER LOOK

✝ **Michael** The ancient worldview considered heaven and earth as two separate and distinct realms (see Luke 16:26). Thus intermediaries (angels) were needed to bridge these two worlds. In the Bible there are three named angels who represent the primary roles of angels. Michael ("Who is like the Lord?") is a warrior against evil, "captain of the heavenly host" (Revelation 12:7-9), and special protector of Israel (Daniel 12:1) and of the Church. Gabriel ("God is mighty") is a messenger who announces the Messiah's coming (Daniel 9) and the births of John the Baptist and Jesus (Luke 1). Raphael ("God heals") serves as a guardian angel protecting Tobiah on his journey (Tobit 5-12).

COMMUNION ANTIPHON *(Psalm 73 [72]:28)*
To be near God is my happiness, / to place my hope in God the Lord.

Or *(Mark 11:23-24)*
Amen, I say to you: Whatever you ask in prayer, / believe that you will receive, / and it shall be given to you, says the Lord.

PRAYER AFTER COMMUNION
We have partaken of the gifts of this sacred mystery,
humbly imploring, O Lord,
that what your Son commanded us to do
in memory of him
may bring us growth in charity.
Through Christ our Lord. ***Amen.***

BLESSING & DISMISSAL *(page 56)*

Responding to the Word

God will reward those who "lead many to justice."

What might I do this week to help bring justice to some oppressive situation?

Jesus' self-sacrifice took away our sins, that is, it put us into the right relationship with God and others.

What in my relationships with God and others needs my attention most today?

Jesus prepares us for meeting God and the judgment that will happen.

What might I be most worried about if I faced God's judgment today? Why?

November 21

The absolute power of Christ

Pilate could hardly be satisfied with Jesus' response to his question, "Are you the King of the Jews?" Jesus knows that a straight answer here would confuse more than it would clarify. To say he *is* a king would mislead in one direction; to say he is *not* would mislead in another. Instead, Jesus challenges Pilate's false assumptions.

The solemnity of Christ the King is not a relic of medieval Europe, as one might innocently presume. It is a modern feast, instituted by Pius XI in 1925 as a response to the incipient totalitarian movements in 20th-century Europe.

Political ideologies are prone to overreach. And totalitarianism is always atheistic, whether officially or merely functionally. It cannot abide an authority beyond itself, something by which it might be judged. Its operative logic is raw power and its chosen ends can justify any means.

Today we celebrate that there is an absolute power in the universe. But it doesn't look at all like Pilate or any of his modern descendants imagine. Political authorities, in Pilate's world, have armies. They have the power of life and death. But this is not, in fact, ultimate power. Ultimate power is rooted in truth and love. And these cannot be put to death.

■ Brett Salkeld

ENTRANCE ANTIPHON *(Revelation 5:12; 1:6)*
How worthy is the Lamb who was slain, / to receive power and divinity, / and wisdom and strength and honor. / To him belong glory and power for ever and ever.

INTRODUCTORY RITES *(page 10)*

COLLECT
Almighty ever-living God,
whose will is to restore all things
in your beloved Son, the King of the universe,
grant, we pray,
that the whole creation, set free from slavery,
may render your majesty service
and ceaselessly proclaim your praise.
Through our Lord Jesus Christ, your Son,
who lives and reigns with you in the unity of the Holy Spirit,
God, for ever and ever. ***Amen.***

FIRST READING *(Daniel 7:13-14)*
As the visions during the night continued, I saw one like a Son of man coming,
on the clouds of heaven;
when he reached the Ancient One
and was presented before him,
the one like a Son of man received dominion, glory, and kingship;
all peoples, nations, and languages serve him.
His dominion is an everlasting dominion
that shall not be taken away,
his kingship shall not be destroyed.
The word of the Lord. ***Thanks be to God.***

RESPONSORIAL PSALM *(Psalm 93:1, 1-2, 5)*
℟. The Lord is king; he is robed in majesty.

The LORD is king, in splendor robed;
robed is the LORD and girt about with strength. ℟.
And he has made the world firm,
not to be moved.
Your throne stands firm from of old;
from everlasting you are, O LORD. ℟.
Your decrees are worthy of trust indeed;
holiness befits your house,
O LORD, for length of days. ℟.

SECOND READING *(Revelation 1:5-8)*
Jesus Christ is the faithful witness, the firstborn of the dead and ruler of the kings of the earth. To him who loves us and has freed us from our sins by his blood, who has made us into a kingdom, priests for his God and Father, to him be glory and power forever and ever. Amen.

Behold, he is coming amid the clouds,
and every eye will see him,
even those who pierced him.
All the peoples of the earth will lament him.
Yes. Amen.

"I am **the Alpha and the Omega,"** ✝ says the Lord God, "the one who is and who was and who is to come, the almighty."

The word of the Lord. ***Thanks be to God.***

ALLELUIA *(Mark 11:9, 10)*
Alleluia, alleluia. Blessed is he who comes in the name of the Lord! / Blessed is the kingdom of our father David that is to come! ***Alleluia, alleluia.***

GOSPEL *(John 18:33b-37)*

A reading from the holy Gospel according to John.
Glory to you, O Lord.

Pilate said to Jesus, "Are you the King of the Jews?" Jesus answered, "Do you say this on your own or have others told you about me?" Pilate answered, "I am not a Jew, am I? Your own nation and the chief priests handed you over to me. What have you done?" Jesus answered, "My kingdom does not belong to this world. If my kingdom did belong to this world, my attendants would be fighting to keep me from being handed over to the Jews. But as it is, my kingdom is not here." So Pilate said to him, "Then you are a king?" Jesus answered, "You say I am a king. For this I was born and for this I came into the world, to testify to the truth. Everyone who belongs to the truth listens to my voice."

The Gospel of the Lord. ***Praise to you, Lord Jesus Christ.***

PROFESSION OF FAITH *(page 13)*

PRAYER OF THE FAITHFUL

PREPARATION OF GIFTS *(page 16)*

PRAYER OVER THE OFFERINGS

As we offer you, O Lord, the sacrifice
by which the human race is reconciled to you,
we humbly pray
that your Son himself may bestow on all nations
the gifts of unity and peace.
Through Christ our Lord. ***Amen.***

PREFACE: CHRIST, KING OF THE UNIVERSE

It is truly right and just, our duty and our salvation,
always and everywhere to give you thanks,
Lord, holy Father, almighty and eternal God.

For you anointed your Only Begotten Son,
our Lord Jesus Christ, with the oil of gladness
as eternal Priest and King of all creation,
so that, by offering himself on the altar of the Cross
as a spotless sacrifice to bring us peace,
he might accomplish the mysteries of human redemption
and, making all created things subject to his rule,
he might present to the immensity of your majesty
an eternal and universal kingdom,
a kingdom of truth and life,
a kingdom of holiness and grace,
a kingdom of justice, love and peace.

TAKING A CLOSER LOOK

✝ **The Alpha and the Omega** Alpha (A) and omega (Ω) are the first and last letters of the Greek alphabet, the equivalent of our English A and Z, representing the beginning and ending ("from A to Z"). When applied to God they indicate that God's eternal existence spans the lesser extent of creation and human history. We decorate the Easter candle with these letters and bless it with the words, "Christ yesterday and today; the Beginning and the End; the Alpha; and the Omega. All time belongs to him; and all the ages. To him be glory and power; through every age and for ever. Amen."

And so, with Angels and Archangels,
with Thrones and Dominions,
and with all the hosts and Powers of heaven,
we sing the hymn of your glory,
as without end we acclaim:
Holy, Holy, Holy Lord God of hosts... *(page 35)*

COMMUNION ANTIPHON *(Psalm 29 [28]:10–11)*
The Lord sits as King for ever. / The Lord will bless his people with peace.

PRAYER AFTER COMMUNION
Having received the food of immortality,
we ask, O Lord,
that, glorying in obedience
to the commands of Christ, the King of the universe,
we may live with him eternally in his heavenly Kingdom.
Who lives and reigns for ever and ever. ***Amen.***

BLESSING & DISMISSAL *(page 56)* ⁘

Responding to the Word

Jesus has received rule over me and my life.

What do I most reluctantly give Jesus control over?

Jesus' love binds us into his kingdom community.

How has being part of the kingdom made a difference in my life?

Jesus says that those who belong to his kingdom listen to his voice.

What might I do to be more attentive to what Jesus is calling me to be and do?

Praying and Living the Eucharist

Praying with the Scriptures

The Bible's message is that God desires to be with us in our world for a relationship. God invites us into a relationship that will not end with death but will go on forever. Building and nurturing this relationship is what living with Christ is all about.

Each week our Sunday Scripture readings help us to deepen our relationship with Jesus. Through Scripture, we learn who God is and who we are. We also discover ways to grow in our relationship with God and with others. By reading, reflecting, and discussing the meaning of these readings, we find keys to imitating Jesus' example, making his vision and values our own and discovering what a relationship with God demands.

A EUCHARISTIC FORMAT: PATTERN FOR OUR SPIRITUALITY

In our Eucharist and also in our preparation for the Eucharist, we imitate Jesus' actions at the Last Supper—*take, bless, break, share*. Jesus' command to *do this in his memory* characterizes not just our worship but our very lives and mission as Christians.

Participating in the eucharistic liturgy and living eucharistic lives is our way of thanking Jesus and of celebrating and nurturing his continual presence with us, not only in church but in all the moments and situations of our daily lives. Through our deepening experience of Christ in word and sacrament, we announce and celebrate the good news of God's presence among us.

The elements of the simple eucharistic format—*take, bless, break, share*—provide a pattern that can assist us in our goal of praying and living the Eucharist.

» **TAKE** To "take" is to accept the reality of the moment, to open ourselves to God's presence and God's gifts as they present themselves to us. We take a few moments of quiet to become centered, prayerful, and attentive to God's presence.

» **BLESS** To "bless" is to acknowledge God's role in something—as in the biblical acclamation, *Bless the Lord, O my soul!* When we think of God's creation, how can we not give thanks and praise? The word "eucharist" actually comes from the Greek *eucharistia* ("thanksgiving").

» **BREAK** To "break" the bread of our lives is to be willing to break through to the deeper meaning of our experience. To do that, we explore Sacred Scripture, we think about the ways that God is speaking to us in the events of our lives, we reflect on the words of Jesus, we listen to the wisdom of the Church's teachings—we open ourselves to the voice of God as it whispers to us in our daily experiences. And we discover God's love and forgiveness in the midst of our own brokenness.

» **SHARE** Christian spirituality is not a narrowly focused "God and me" affair. Christians discover that "I" is never alone; "I" is always an "I *in Christ.*" And as one realizes his or her identity as a member of Christ's body, one discovers that the true "I" is really a "we."

We have been called into communion with God and with one another. Our own experience of Jesus leads us to ministry, to share the gifts that God has given us, and to bring the fruits of our prayer to others and to our world.

SAMPLE FORMAT FOR PERSONAL REFLECTION

» TAKE Find a quiet spot where you can read, reflect, and pray. If you wish to record your thoughts and experiences, have your prayer journal handy. Take a few moments of quiet to become prayerful and centered.

» BLESS Begin your reflection time with a prayer. You may wish to use a spontaneous prayer, the Collect for the coming Sunday, or one from the ***Treasury of Prayers*** (page 615).

» BREAK

- ***Read:*** Read the Scripture readings from the coming Sunday. Pause in silence to be attentive to God's message for you today.
- ***Reflect:*** Read the Sunday reflection found at the start of the coming Sunday.
- ***Respond:*** To explore the meaning of the readings, consider first the questions in the ***Responding to the Word*** at the end of each Sunday. If you wish to explore the readings further, choose one or more of the ***Basic Questions for Exploring Scripture*** (page 598).

After reflecting on the questions and writing down your answers in your prayer journal, if you wish, take some time to be quiet and attentive to Christ's presence with you—where he wants to dwell right now.

» SHARE Close with a spontaneous prayer, one chosen from the Mass for the coming Sunday, or one from the ***Treasury of Prayers*** (page 615).

Now you are better prepared to share the good news with others in the coming week!

Basic Questions for Exploring Scripture

There are several basic questions and some follow-up questions that we can use to explore any biblical reading. *(Note that not all of these questions are equally answered in every passage.)*

What does this text tell me about God? about Jesus? about the Holy Spirit?

• Does this confirm what I already know? • Is there something new here that I had not noticed before? • What does God want me to know or do?

What does God/Jesus/the Holy Spirit do in relation to us and our world?

• How is the divine presence and power revealed? • Why does God come to us? • What is required of us to do or not do?

What does this text tell me about myself?

• How am I like the person(s) in Scripture? • How would I respond if this happened to me? • How would I be changed if I did what the text says? • What challenged me to live out my faith more fully? • What surprised me the most about this passage? • What puzzled me the most? • What made me most comfortable? Why? • What made me most uncomfortable? Why?

What do I learn about the community that God desires?

• What does this text tell me about how to love God? • What does this text tell me about how to love others? • What guidelines for better community living does the passage offer?

The Practice of Lectio Divina

Lectio divina ("sacred reading") is a contemplative way of reading Sacred Scripture that has been part of the Christian tradition since the third century.

We may find it helpful to think of it as involving three "moments" or stages: reading, meditating, and praying.

READING

This *first moment* consists in our reading a short Scripture passage slowly, attentively, repeatedly—and aloud whenever possible. We may wish to choose the gospel reading for the coming Sunday and read it from the previous Monday all through the week.

Paying close attention to the story, and especially to the words themselves, we let ourselves *enjoy* the story and even grow to *love* the story and the very words in which it is told. When a word or phrase catches our attention, we may jot it down or simply stay with it for awhile to savor its message, allowing its fullness to penetrate our being.

MEDITATION

Reading leads us naturally to the *second moment*: meditation. Having settled on one section, phrase, or even a single word, we let its meaning unfold in our hearts.

Our meditation can take place as we sit in quiet prayer or as we perform the simple activities of our day. It may last an hour, a day, or over the course of a week.

During meditation, we may find ourselves focusing on the present: what does this text have to say about what is happening in my life or in the world around me now? Something in the text may jog a memory of an experience from our own lives. Or we may find that, when we return to our daily activities, some event or situation will unexpectedly bring us back to the text. In either case, the Holy Spirit may be trying to open up a dialogue with us!

PRAYER

Prayer, the *third moment*, also occurs naturally. This is not an intellectual exercise, but a dialogue with God. We respond authentically and spontaneously—as we would in a conversation with a close friend.

Our prayer may take four different forms:

- ***Thanksgiving:*** When the text reminds us of blessings and good things we have known, we praise and thank God.
- ***Repentance:*** When we become aware of wrong we have done or good we have failed to do, we humbly ask for forgiveness.
- ***Petition:*** When the text reminds us of our own needs or of the needs of others, we ask God for guidance and assistance.
- ***Contemplation:*** By grace, we may be led to a deeper moment of prayer in which we are no longer thanking or repenting or asking, but simply joyfully resting in God's presence, trustfully leaving ourselves in God's hands. This is called contemplative prayer.

I would like to recall and recommend the ancient tradition of ***lectio divina****: the diligent reading of Sacred Scripture accompanied by prayer brings about that intimate dialogue in which the person reading hears God who is speaking, and in praying, responds to God with trusting openness of heart. If it is effectively promoted, this practice will bring to the Church—I am convinced of it—a new spiritual springtime.*

POPE BENEDICT XVI

The Liturgical Calendar:
Unfolding the Mystery of Christ

One way the Church tells the story of God's saving activity is by its calendar. "Within the cycle of a year, she unfolds the whole mystery of Christ. Recalling thus the mysteries of redemption, the Church opens to the faithful the riches of her Lord's powers and mercies, so that they are in some way made present at all times, and the faithful are enabled to lay hold of them and become filled with saving grace" (Vatican II, *Constitution on the Sacred Liturgy*, #102). During this yearly cycle, we remember our story and deepen our understanding of its meaning for us.

The Church year is anchored by two segments: **Advent–Christmas–Epiphany** and **Lent–Holy Week–Easter**. **Pentecost** and the **Sundays in Ordinary Time** fill out the rest of the year. The overall pattern highlights the transitions from darkness to light to manifestation, and from promise to fulfillment to proclamation.

ADVENT, CHRISTMAS, AND EPIPHANY

Advent, the time of preparation for Christmas, begins on the fourth Sunday before Christmas. As December's darkness and short days permeate our lives, the Church proclaims that Christ comes as the light of the world. Christmas celebrates the mystery of God's incarnation—God-with-us as one of us in human flesh.

Christmas is followed by the Epiphany, celebrating the visit of the magi who traveled from afar to worship the babe in Bethlehem. They represent all the nations of the world searching for their savior. The revelation of God's light and the fulfillment of God's promise in Jesus lead to the proclamation of this good news. In the season after Epiphany, we share the news that God's love is available for every person, for all of creation!

LENT, HOLY WEEK, AND EASTER

The Church's greatest feast and most important rites were celebrated on Easter—the time of initiation, when new members would be baptized and emerge into a new life of fellowship. Today, the seasons of Lent and Easter retain this baptismal focus. Vatican II has renewed the ancient practice of initiation in its Rite of Christian Initiation for Adults (RCIA).

The forty days (excluding Sundays) of Lent recall Jesus' forty days in the wilderness prior to his public ministry. Lent is a time of inwardness, of spiritual discipline, and of growth. During Lent we seek out the shadows in our souls, inviting Christ's light to illumine them.

Lent concludes with Holy Week when we recall the last events of Jesus' life, beginning with his entry into Jerusalem (Passion or Palm Sunday). Then the most sacred Three Days (the Triduum) recall Jesus' Last Supper (Holy Thursday), his crucifixion and death (Good Friday), and his resurrection (Easter Vigil and Easter Day). Then, for fifty days, we bask in the joy of the resurrection and the promise of new life with God forever.

PENTECOST AND ORDINARY TIME

Witnesses are needed to guide others to discover the transforming presence of God. At Pentecost, the Holy Spirit descends on the disciples, uniting them as a community and giving them new tongues to proclaim the good news of God's triumph over death to the ends of the earth.

After Pentecost, we continue with Ordinary Time. It is "ordinary" not because it is common but because the Sundays are counted (they are "in order"). Each Sunday we follow Jesus and have the opportunity to move ever more deeply into sharing in his life, death, and resurrection.

As we attune ourselves to the rhythms of the Church's liturgical year, the mysteries of the Lord's life are made present, and our lives are sanctified by our participation.

Understanding the Lectionary

Since its beginning, the Church has gathered faithfully every Sunday to listen carefully to God's word. The Lectionary for Mass is the selection of the most important Bible readings for use at Mass. Through them the Church remembers and renews its relationship with God.

THE LECTIONARY'S ARRANGEMENT

The lectionary is not a chronological approach to reading the Bible, nor is it a book-by-book approach. Each week the gospel readings are closely linked to the seasons of the Church's life cycle, its liturgical calendar. In the first half of the Church year, we follow the major events of the life of Jesus, including his birth, death, resurrection, and the birth of the Church, and in the second half we study Jesus' actions and teachings.

In addition, the lectionary provides an opportunity to remember great persons in Church history on saints' days and to celebrate special events in the life of a parish, such as confirmation. Throughout the year, Scriptures have been chosen for their appropriateness for the occasions on which they are read.

THE EVOLUTION OF THE CURRENT LECTIONARY

From the time of the Council of Trent (1545-63), when the liturgy was fixed in the form that was familiar to all Catholics before Vatican II, the selection of lectionary readings consisted simply of a one-year cycle that included two Sunday readings, one from a New Testament letter or epistle and another from one of the gospels. The gospel readings were taken mostly from Matthew and Luke, with very few from Mark or John. The Old Testament was read only on Epiphany and during Holy Week.

The liturgical renewal of Vatican Council II (1962-65) directed that the "treasures of Scripture" be made more available so that the faithful would be fed on this richer fare. This momentous change reversed the previous limitation of Scripture by adding an additional reading that, for the first time in centuries, opened the riches of the Old Testament to the weekly Christian gathering (and the Acts of the Apostles during the Easter Season).

The new lectionary includes the following features:

- ***Three-year Cycle of Readings:*** The Sunday lectionary covers the most significant parts of the Old and New Testaments every three years. The three years, designated A, B, and C, always begin on the First Sunday of Advent. Each of the cycles focuses on one of the synoptic gospels. In Year A, Matthew is read; Year B, Mark; Year C, Luke. The Gospel of John is used during all three years on certain feast days, during Holy Week, and during the Easter season. Since the Gospel of Mark is so brief, the sixth chapter of John's gospel (on the Bread of Life) is read for five weeks of Year B.
- ***Four Readings Every Sunday:*** Each Sunday, four Scripture passages are assigned to be read: the first reading from the Old Testament (except during the Easter season), chosen to coincide thematically with the gospel; a responsorial psalm relating to the first reading or to the liturgical season; the second reading from the letters or other New Testament writings; and finally the gospel reading.
- ***The selected readings are about:***
  - **Christ,** so as to unfold the mystery of Christ's person and teachings over the cycle of the year (see Vatican II, *Constitution on the Sacred Liturgy* [CSL], #102)
  - **Salvation history,** in order to show the place of Christ in God's plan of salvation, thus connecting God's work with Israel (Old Testament) to God's work in Christ (New Testament) (CSL, #5)
  - **"The guiding principles of the Christian life"** (CSL, #52), to help people understand the Christian message and live it more fully in their everyday lives.

This Year's Scriptures:
The Gospel of Mark

In the three-year lectionary cycle, the Sunday gospel readings for Year B are drawn primarily from Mark's gospel, which is the shortest of the four gospels and the earliest to be written. Mark invented what we call a gospel, that is, a consecutive narrative account of Jesus' ministry, death, and resurrection.

MARK'S GOSPEL LIFE OF JESUS

Mark's great achievement was to shape the many things that Jesus said and did into a gospel life of Jesus. Mark gives Jesus' life a narrative shape beginning with his baptism or empowerment for ministry, his Galilean ministry of announcing and starting God's kingdom community with his chosen followers, and finally his journey from Galilee to Jerusalem where he is crucified and rises to new life. Mark also anchors Jesus' many sayings that were remembered by the Christian community into particular events and situations in his life story.

But the key to Mark's shaping of the gospel life of Jesus is discovered in its structure. He took the life of Jesus and shaped it into a proclamation of the good news of our salvation. In order to make the life of Jesus into a gospel life, nothing is more important than the ending.

THE GOOD NEWS OF NEW LIFE

Mark's gospel ends with the resurrection of Jesus, not with his death. Had the gospel ended with his death, there would have been no "good news" to proclaim but only a rehash of the old news that everybody dies.

But Mark's gospel proclaims that death only ends the earthly life of Jesus, not his relationship with God. The resurrection demonstrates that God's creative power to give life triumphs over evil's destructive desire to deal death. The good news is that what happens to Jesus in the middle of history will also happen to his followers (including us!) who dare to follow his way of relationship to God through death to new life.

As we hear, read, reflect, and pray about Mark's gospel this year, we will also discover how he shapes his gospel to proclaim who Christ is and to meet the special needs of his community.

A SUFFERING COMMUNITY

Mark's gospel was most likely written between 65 and 70 AD. During this period, for the first time in its history, the Christian community experienced government persecution. In Rome, Nero had blamed Christians for the terrible fire in the summer of the year 64. In Palestine, the Jews were carrying out a full scale rebellion against the Roman occupying forces, and Christians feared that they would be included in any punishments since the Romans did not differentiate between Jews and Christians at this time.

This time of suffering and persecution was thus a time of challenge. Would Christians give up their faith or keep it despite persecution or the threat of death? Mark's gospel is written to help answer these questions.

A SUFFERING CHRIST

Mark stresses that to understand the kind of Christ or Messiah that Jesus is, we must grasp the significance of his suffering, which occurs not only at the end of his life but accompanies him even during his ministry. Every attempt to understand Jesus apart from his suffering ends in misunderstanding. Jesus is misunderstood by his own family, rejected by the religious leaders and the people, and even abandoned by his own disciples. Feeling abandoned even by God his Father, Jesus dies alone on the cross.

The main thrust of Mark's gospel is to identify Jesus, "the Christ, the son of God" (1:1) as the Suffering Servant described by the prophet Isaiah (52:13–53:12). Throughout the first half of the gospel, Mark confirms the conventional Jewish expectations about the Messiah. Jesus appears as a prophetic teacher and lawgiver like Moses, a miracle worker like Elijah and a kingdom builder like David (although his kingdom is spiritual rather than political).

Mark then turns all of these tidy expectations on their head. Jesus is indeed the Messiah, but he "must suffer greatly and be rejected by the elders, the chief priests, and the scribes, and be killed, and rise after three days" (8:31). The rest of the gospel shows how the suffering Messiah fulfills God's plan for salvation.

Mark presents Jesus' passion as the great reversal of the common expectation that the Messiah would be a glorious king like David who would free the Jewish people from their oppressive Roman overlords. Jesus is indeed a king, but one who is crowned with thorns, mocked and beaten, and enthroned on a cross in humiliation with a sign indicating that he is "the King of the Jews." Mark's final picture of an abandoned Jesus dying alone outside the holy city challenges all the usual expectations about Jesus as a glorious and triumphant Messiah.

FOLLOWING CHRIST'S WAY TO GOD

Mark emphasizes that a Christian disciple is one who can take up his or her cross and follow Jesus on this way of suffering. He shows that any other claim to discipleship—for example, family ties, being one of the twelve apostles, personal knowledge of Jesus, or religious tradition—will always end in failure.

Although Mark offers Jesus as the model for Christians who are suffering and feel themselves abandoned by God, Mark offers no easy comfort. Jesus will not return miraculously to save us from our suffering. The only solution is to take up one's cross as Jesus did. For only by living through the suffering and death does resurrection follow. Suffering is not the end but the door to a new existence with God, who never abandons us.

Mark's invention of this new gospel form was immediately recognized as exactly what the Christian community needed. He gave Christians a new identity by showing both who Jesus was—the Christ who had to suffer—and who they were as his disciples—people who were called to take up their own cross and follow Jesus.

They were on the way, going up to Jerusalem, and Jesus went ahead of them. They were amazed, and those who followed were afraid. Taking the Twelve aside again, he began to tell them what was going to happen to him. "Behold, we are going up to Jerusalem, and the Son of Man will be handed over to the chief priests and the scribes, and they will condemn him to death and hand him over to the Gentiles who will mock him, spit upon him, scourge him, and put him to death, but after three days he will rise."

MARK 10:32-34

Liturgical and Devotional Prayer:
What's the Difference?

There are real differences between liturgical and devotional prayer, but they are linked; we need both, and both have the same goal: to help us grow in our life as Catholic disciples of our Lord. But just what are the major differences between these types of prayer? Here are a few central elements:

Liturgical prayer—officially, the celebration of the seven sacraments and the Liturgy of the Hours—is always primary. These celebrations are primary because these are the privileged ways we enter into Christ's paschal mystery (his life, death, and resurrection that bring life to the world) and learn to live this mystery in our own lives. While we are meant to pray these prayers in a deeply personal way, they are also always intended to link us to the whole Church at prayer. They belong to everybody, which is why the Church insists that individuals may not change them. Liturgical prayer *shapes us* into being ever more perfect members of the Body of Christ.

Devotional prayers, in the words of Vatican II's *Constitution on the Sacred Liturgy*, "should be so drawn up that they harmonize with the liturgical seasons, accord with the sacred liturgy, are in some fashion derived from it, and lead people to it, since the liturgy by its very nature far surpasses any of them" (#13). Devotions are meant to be prayed in a deeply personal way, and may or may not have a communal dimension. *We shape* these prayers to meet our personal prayer needs and encounter God in our daily lives, which in turn helps make us ready for full, conscious, and active participation in the liturgy. There are no required forms of devotional prayer—individuals are free to create or adopt and pray them as meets their needs, within the guidelines set by the Church.

What kind of guidelines? Along with the quote from the *Constitution on the Sacred Liturgy* given above, the Church advises, for example, that these devotions not be overly sentimental. They should not lead one into superstition or be based solely on legendary tales. They should not be added to the liturgy or preferred to liturgical prayer. People are free to pray them or not. They should help us relate emotionally—with the heart and not just the intellect—to the central mysteries of our faith. They should increase our yearning for liturgical prayer and help us pray the Mass deeply and reverently. And their ultimate aim should be the same as that of the liturgy: to say with St. Paul, "I live now, not I, but Christ lives in me" (Galatians 2:20).

Mass and Eucharistic Adoration provide an example of the difference between liturgical and devotional prayer. The Mass is the weekly or daily way we join ourselves to the dying and rising of the Lord. We gather through, with, and in Christ to offer thanks and praise to the Father and to be transformed by the Holy Spirit into the body and blood of Christ in our world—and to eat and drink of Christ's body and blood that we are, and are becoming.

Eucharistic Adoration (in the form of prayer before the tabernacle), on the other hand, is a wonderful way to pause in our busy lives, to step into the presence of God, and to marvel at the great mystery of love celebrated in the Eucharist, to thank God for it, and to pray about what it means to share in Christ's Body and Blood and be his disciples in the world around us.

Of the two, the Mass is always primary, because it is the action of our entering into the paschal mystery. Adoration is meant to strengthen our desire to participate in the Mass and to pray it more deeply, with our heart, mind, and soul. Because Adoration is derived from the eucharistic liturgy and meant to lead us back to the eucharistic liturgy, it has the same goal as the liturgy: to praise and thank God and to help us lead more Christ-like lives in all that we do.

Prayer is the source and origin of every upward journey toward God. Let us each, then, turn to prayer and say to our Lord God: "Lead me, O Lord, on your path, that I may walk in your truth."

— St. Bonaventure

Receiving Communion Outside Mass

In the celebration of the Eucharist we recognize the presence of Christ in the priest, in the word proclaimed, in the prayer and song of the assembly, and above all in the consecrated elements. Our eucharistic communion with Christ and one another is the living sign of our belonging to Jesus' kingdom community. So from its beginning, the Christian community has always made provision for those who are unable to be present to celebrate this eucharistic communion with Christ. The communion ritual outside of Mass mirrors the same four parts that give the Mass its structure: an introductory rite, a liturgy of the word, a liturgy of the Eucharist, and a concluding rite. You may wish to begin with the following prayers of preparation:

For the extraordinary minister of Holy Communion
O loving God, may your healing and nurturing presence be clearly evident in my whole being today: in my speaking and listening, in my attitude of compassion and understanding. Help me to communicate to those who are homebound the love and care of Christ and of our Christian community from whom I am sent. Let all that is in my mind, all that comes from my lips and from within my heart, reflect the greatness of your love. Amen.

For the communicant
This prayer may be said by the communicant, a family or household member, or the minister.

O loving and faithful God, you invite us to share in the eucharistic food, a sign of your commitment to be with us each day of our life's journey. Despite our personal limitations, you love us completely and nourish us with your divine life. Give us the strength we need to meet whatever challenges that we are now experiencing. Amen.

INTRODUCTORY RITE

May the blessing of God, the love of Christ,
the power of the Holy Spirit,
and the good wishes of our parish community be with you.
And with your spirit.

Use the Collect from any Sunday or from Holy Thursday (page 262).

LITURGY OF THE WORD

Jesus' words offer comfort in our time of need
and invite us to continue to be like Jesus
even in the difficult times of our lives.

Read aloud one of the Sunday Scripture readings from this missal or a reading from the suggestions below. After some time for quiet reflection, pray the Responsorial Psalm together and/or share one or two thoughts about the reading.

The following readings from this missal are also especially appropriate for a communion service.

Holy Thursday: Mass of the Lord's Supper, page 262
Feast of the Most Holy Body and Blood of Christ, page 420
Jesus, the bread of life (John 6:41-51), page 489
A spirit of wisdom (Ephesians 1:17-23), page 379
Come to me (Isaiah 55:1-11), page 144
The Holy Spirit is given to us (Romans 5:1-2, 5-8), page 206
God so loved the world (John 3:14-21), page 215
The loaves and fishes (John 6:1-15), page 477

RECEPTION OF THE EUCHARIST

The Lord's Prayer
Hearing God's word has drawn us together, and now we deepen our communion by sharing the body of Christ. To prepare ourselves for his coming, let us pray as he taught us: ***Our Father...***

Invitation to communion
This bread that we share is the body of Christ,
the sign of his endless love and the gift of himself
so that we may live with God now and forever.
Take and eat this bread with confidence that Jesus' presence in it
will nourish you, heal and strengthen you, and transform you from within.

As the bread is given, the minister says:
The Body of Christ. ***Amen.***

CONCLUDING RITE

After communion, allow time for quiet reflection to attend to Jesus' presence. You may wish to say a prayer such as the Anima Christi (page 624) or Psalm 23 (page 637).

Prayer after communion
Pray this prayer after communion or one from a Sunday:
Gracious God, you have nourished us with the bread that makes us one in Christ. Fill us with your Spirit, make us one in peace and love, and help us to bring your salvation and joy to those we meet today. We ask this through Christ our Lord. ***Amen.***

Conclude by sharing a sign of peace with one another.

A Treasury of Prayers

PRAYERS FROM THE BIBLE

The Lord's Prayer: found in Matthew 6:9-13 and in Luke 11:2-4, it is also used in our eucharistic liturgy (page 53)

Song of Moses: from Exodus 15 (page 307)

Paul's Prayers: from 1 Corinthians 1 (page 70), Ephesians 1 (page 379) and 1 Thessalonians 5 (page 89)

Canticle of Zechariah (Benedictus): *Luke 1:68-79*
Blessed be the Lord, the God of Israel;
  he has come to his people and set them free.
He has raised up for us a mighty savior,
  born of the house of his servant David.
Through his prophets he promised of old
  that he would save us from our enemies,
  from the hands of all who hate us.
He promised to show mercy to our fathers
  and to remember his holy covenant.
This was the oath he swore
  to our father Abraham: to set us free from the hands of our enemies,
  free to worship him without fear,
  holy and righteous in his sight all the days of our life.
You, my child, shall be called the prophet of the Most High,
  for you will go before the Lord to prepare his way,
  to give his people knowledge of salvation
  by the forgiveness of their sins.
In the tender compassion of our God

the dawn from on high shall break upon us,
to shine on those who dwell in darkness and the shadow of death,
and to guide our feet into the way of peace.

Canticle of Mary (Magnificat): *Luke 1:46-55*

My soul proclaims the greatness of the Lord,
my spirit rejoices in God my Savior
for he has looked with favor upon his lowly servant.
From this day all generations will call me blessed:
the Almighty has done great things for me,
and holy is his Name.
He has mercy on those who fear him in every generation.
He has shown the strength of his arm,
and has scattered the proud in their conceit.
He has cast down the mighty from their thrones,
and has lifted up the lowly.
He has filled the hungry with good things,
and the rich he has sent away empty.
He has come to the help of his servant Israel
for he has remembered his promise of mercy,
the promise he made to our fathers,
to Abraham and his children for ever.

The Song of Simeon: *Luke 2:29-32*

Lord, now let your servant go in peace;
your word has been fulfilled:
my own eyes have seen the salvation
which you have prepared in the sight of every people:
a light to reveal you to the nations
and the glory of your people Israel.

Paul's Blessing: *Ephesians 3:16-21*
May you be strengthened with power
through God's Spirit in your inner self.
May Christ dwell in your hearts through faith;
so that you, rooted and grounded in love, may have
strength to comprehend with all the holy ones
what is the breadth and length and height and depth,
and to know the love of Christ
that surpasses knowledge, so that you may be filled
with all the fullness of God.
Now to God, who by the power at work within us is able
to accomplish far more than all we ask or imagine,
be glory in the church and in Christ Jesus
to all generations, forever and ever. Amen.

TRADITIONAL PRAYERS FOR EUCHARISTIC ADORATION

The Divine Praises
Blessed be God.
Blessed be his holy name.
Blessed be Jesus Christ, true God and true man.
Blessed be the name of Jesus.
Blessed be his most Sacred Heart.
Blessed be his most Precious Blood.
Blessed be Jesus in the most holy sacrament of the altar.
Blessed be the Holy Spirit, the Paraclete.
Blessed be the great Mother of God, Mary most holy.
Blessed be her holy and immaculate conception.
Blessed be her glorious assumption.

Blessed be the name of Mary, Virgin and Mother.
Blessed be St. Joseph, her most chaste spouse.
Blessed be God in his angels and in his saints.

O Saving Host (O Salutaris Hostia) ***by St. Thomas Aquinas***
O saving Victim, opening wide
The gate of Heaven to us below;
Our foes press hard on every side;
Your aid supply; Your strength bestow.
To your great name be endless praise,
Immortal Godhead, One in Three.
O grant us endless length of days,
In our true native land with thee.
Amen.

Latin Text:
O salutaris Hostia,
Quae cæli pandis ostium:
Bella premunt hostilia,
Da robur, fer auxilium.
Uni trinoque Domino
Sit sempiterna gloria,
Qui vitam sine termino
Nobis donet in patria.
Amen.

Sing My Tongue (Pange Lingua Gloriosi) ***by St. Thomas Aquinas***

Sing, my tongue, the Savior's glory,
of his flesh the mystery sing;
of the blood, all price exceeding,
shed by our immortal King,
destined, for the world's redemption,
from a noble womb to spring.

Of a pure and spotless Virgin
born for us on earth below,
He, as Man, with us conversing,
stayed, the seeds of truth to sow;
then he closed in solemn order
wond'rously his Life of woe.

On the night of that Last Supper,
seated with his chosen band,
He, the Paschal Victim eating,
first fulfills the Law's command;
then as Food to his Apostles
gives himself with his own hand.

Word-made-Flesh, the bread of nature
by his Word to Flesh he turns;
wine into his Blood he changes;
what though sense no change discerns?
Only be the heart in earnest,
faith her lesson quickly learns.

Let us, therefore, bow and worship
such a wondrous Sacrament;
let the ancient law and custom
to a newer rite now yield;
let our faith supply conviction
where the senses tire and fail.

To the Father, unbegotten,
and the Sole-begotten Son,
be salvation, blessing, honor,
jubilation, pow'r, and praise;
to the One from both proceeding
equal glory and renown. Amen.

Latin Text:
Pange, lingua, gloriosi
Corporis mysterium,
Sanguinisque pretiosi,
quem in mundi pretium
fructus ventris generosi
Rex effudit Gentium.

Nobis datus, nobis natus
ex intacta Virgine,
et in mundo conversatus,
sparso verbi semine,
sui moras incolatus
miro clausit ordine.

In supremae nocte coenae
recumbens cum fratribus
observata lege plene
cibis in legalibus,
cibum turbae duodenae
se dat suis manibus.

Verbum caro, panem verum
verbo carnem efficit:
fitque sanguis Christi merum,
et si sensus deficit,
ad firmandum cor sincerum
sola fides sufficit.

Tantum ergo Sacramentum
veneremur cernui:
et antiquum documentum
novo cedat ritui:
praestet fides supplementum
sensuum defectui.

Genitori, Genitoque
laus et jubilatio,
salus, honor, virtus quoque
sit et benedictio:
Procedenti ab utroque
compar sit laudatio.
Amen. Alleluja.

PRAYERS FROM THE CHRISTIAN TRADITION

Glory be to the Father

Glory be to the Father,
    and to the Son,
    and to the Holy Spirit.
As it was in the beginning, is now,
    and ever shall be, world without end. Amen.

Hail, Holy Queen (Salve Regina)

Hail, holy Queen, mother of mercy,
our life, our sweetness and our hope.
To you do we cry, poor banished children of Eve;
to you do we send up our sighs,
mourning and weeping in this valley of tears.
Turn then, most gracious advocate,
your eyes of mercy toward us,
and after this, our exile, show unto us
the blessed fruit of your womb, Jesus.
O clement, O loving, O sweet Virgin Mary.

The Hail Mary

Hail Mary, full of grace, the Lord is with thee.
Blessed art thou among women
and blessed is the fruit of thy womb, Jesus.
Holy Mary, Mother of God, pray for us sinners,
now and at the hour of our death. Amen.

The Memorare

Remember, most gracious Virgin Mary,
that never was it known that anyone
who fled to your protection, implored your help,
and sought your intercession, was left unaided.
Inspired with this confidence, I fly to you,
O Virgin of virgins, my mother.
To you do I come; before you I stand,
sinful and sorrowful.
Mother of the Word Incarnate,
despise not my petitions
but in your mercy hear and answer me. Amen.

Anima Christi

Soul of Christ, be my sanctification;
Body of Christ, be my salvation;
Blood of Christ, fill all my veins;
Water of Christ's side, wash out my stains;
Passion of Christ, my comfort be;
O good Jesu, listen to me;
In Thy wounds I fain would hide;
Ne'er to be parted from Thy side;
Guard me, should the foe assail me;
Call me when my life shall fail me;
Bid me come to Thee above,
With Thy saints to sing Thy love,
World without end. Amen.
(Translation by St. John Henry Newman)

Act of Contrition
My God, I am sorry for my sins with all my heart.
In choosing to do wrong and failing to do good,
I have sinned against you
whom I should love above all things.
I firmly intend, with your help,
to do penance,
to sin no more,
and to avoid whatever leads me to sin.
Our Savior Jesus Christ suffered and died for us.
In his name, my God, have mercy. Amen.

Regina Caeli (Queen of Heaven)
O Queen of heaven, rejoice, alleluia!
For he whom you chose to bear, alleluia!
Is risen as he said, alleluia!
Pray for us to God, alleluia!
Rejoice and be glad, O Virgin Mary, alleluia!
For the Lord is truly risen, alleluia!

O God, by the resurrection of your Son, our Lord,
You were pleased to make glad the whole world;
grant, we beseech you, that through
the intercession of the Virgin Mary, his mother,
we may attain the joys of everlasting life,
through the same Christ our Lord. Amen.

The Angelus

The angel of the Lord declared unto Mary,
and she conceived of the Holy Spirit. *Hail Mary...*
Behold, the handmaid of the Lord;
be it done to me according to your word. *Hail Mary...*
And the word was made flesh,
and dwelt among us. *Hail Mary...*

Pray for us, O holy Mother of God;
that we may be made worthy of the promises of Christ.

Pour forth, we beseech you, O Lord,
your grace into our hearts
that we, to whom the incarnation of your Son
was made known by the message of an angel,
may by his passion and cross
be brought to the glory of his resurrection.
We ask this through the same Christ, our Lord. Amen.

THE ROSARY

Like the prayer beads that are used in many religious traditions, the rosary keeps our hands moving while our minds and hearts are meditating on the mysteries of Jesus' life, death, and resurrection. While using the rosary, we focus on twenty events or mysteries in the life and death of Jesus and reflect on how we share with Mary in the saving work of Christ today. Reading a related passage from the Bible helps to deepen meditation on a particular mystery. The Scripture citations given here are not exhaustive. Many other biblical texts are also be suitable for your prayerful reflection.

To pray the rosary:

- Begin the rosary at the crucifix, making the Sign of the Cross and praying the **Apostles' Creed**
- At the first large bead say the **Our Father**, then for the three beads pray the **Hail Mary** for each of the gifts of faith, hope, and love, then **Glory be to the Father.**
- For each mystery, begin with the **Our Father** (the single bead), then recite the **Hail Mary** ten times, and end with **Glory be to the Father**

The Five Joyful Mysteries
The Annunciation (Luke 1:26-38)
The Visitation (Luke 1:39-56)
The Nativity (Luke 2:1-20)
The Presentation (Luke 2:22-38)
The Finding in the Temple (Luke 2:41-52)

The Five Mysteries of Light
The Baptism in the Jordan (Matthew 3:13-17)
The Wedding at Cana (John 2:1-12)
The Proclamation of the Kingdom (Mark 1:14-15)
The Transfiguration (Luke 9:28-36)
The First Eucharist (Matthew 26:26-29)

The Five Sorrowful Mysteries
The Agony in the Garden (Matthew 26:36-56)
The Scourging at the Pillar (Matthew 27:20-26)
The Crowning with Thorns (Matthew 27:27-30)
The Carrying of the Cross (Matthew 27:31-33)
The Crucifixion (Matthew 27:34-60)

The Five Glorious Mysteries
The Resurrection (John 20:1-18)
The Ascension (Acts 1:9-11)
The Descent of the Holy Spirit (John 20:19-23)
The Assumption of Mary (John 11:26)
The Crowning of Mary (Philippians 2:1-11)

PRAYERS FROM THE SAINTS

Teach and strengthen us

Christ Jesus, we ask not that you would spare us affliction,
but that you will not abandon us in it.
When we encounter affliction,
teach us to see you in it as our sole comforter.
Let affliction strengthen our faith,
fortify our hope, and purify our love.
Grant us the grace to see how we can use
our affliction to your glory,
and to desire no other comforter but you,
our Savior, Strengthener, and Friend. Amen.
• ST. BERNADETTE SOUBIROUS (1844-1879)

Lord, make me an instrument of your peace

Lord, make me an instrument of your peace.
Where there is hatred, let me sow love;
where there is injury, pardon;
where there is doubt, faith;
where there is despair, hope;
where there is darkness, light;
and where there is sadness, joy.
Divine Master, grant that I may not so much seek
to be consoled as to console,
to be understood as to understand,
to be loved as to love.
For it is in giving that we receive,
in pardoning that we are pardoned,
and in dying that we are born to eternal life. Amen.
• INSPIRED BY ST. FRANCIS OF ASSISI (1181/82-1226)

To be like Jesus

O God, make us more like Jesus.
Help us to bear difficulty, pain, disappointment, sorrow,
knowing that in your perfect working and design
you can use such bitter experiences
to shape our characters
and make us more like our Lord.
We look with hope for that day
when we shall be wholly like Christ,
because we shall see him as he is. Amen.

• St. Ignatius of Antioch (d. 107)

Help me to seek you

Grant me, O Lord my God,
a mind to know you, a heart to seek you,
wisdom to find you, conduct pleasing to you,
faithful perseverance in waiting for you,
and a hope of finally embracing you. Amen.

• St. Thomas Aquinas (1225-1274)

May the angel of peace watch over us

May God the Father, who made us, bless us.
May God the Son send his healing among us.
May God the Holy Spirit move within us
and give us eyes to see with, ears to hear with,
and hands that your work might be done.
May we walk and preach the word of God to all.
May the angel of peace watch over us
and lead us at last by God's grace to the kingdom. Amen.

• St. Dominic (1170-1221)

May we serve others
Make us worthy, Lord,
to serve others throughout the world
who live and die in poverty and hunger.
Give them, through our hands,
this day their daily bread.
And by our understanding love,
give peace and joy. Amen.
• St. Teresa of Calcutta (1910-1997)

For generous service
Lord Jesus, teach me to be generous;
teach me to serve you as you deserve,
to give and not to count the cost,
to fight and not to heed the wounds,
to toil and not to seek for rest,
to labor and not to seek reward,
except that of knowing that I do your will. Amen.
• St. Ignatius Loyola (1491-1556)

Jesus, our Lover
Jesus Christ, the love that gives love.
You are higher than the highest star;
you are deeper than the deepest sea;
you cherish us as your own family;
you embrace us as your own spouse;
you rule over us as your own subjects;
you welcome us as your dearest friends.
Let all the world worship you! Amen.
• St. Hildegard of Bingen (1098-1179)

MORNING PRAYERS

Perfect and strengthen us

Almighty God, reveal to us what we do not know;
perfect in us what is lacking;
strengthen in us what we know;
and keep us faultless in your service,
through Jesus Christ our Lord. Amen.

• Pope St. Clement I of Rome (First Century)

Open and enlighten us

Jesus, open the eyes of my heart,
that I may hear your word and understand and do your will.
Open the eyes of my mind
to the understanding of your gospel teachings.
Speak to me the hidden and secret things of your wisdom.
Enlighten my mind and understanding
with the light of your knowledge,
not only to cherish those things that are written,
but to do them. Amen.

• St. John Chrysostom (347-407)

Help us to follow your will

O Lord, whose way is perfect,
help us, we pray, always to trust in your goodness;
that, walking with you in faith
and following you in all simplicity,
we may possess quiet and contented minds,
and cast all our care on you, because you care for us;
for the sake of Jesus Christ our Lord. Amen.

• Christina Rossetti (1830-1894)

EVENING PRAYERS

You are the One

Spirit of truth, you are the reward to the saints,
the comforter of souls, light in the darkness,
riches to the poor, treasure to lovers,
food for the hungry, comfort to the wanderer.
To sum up, you are the one in whom all treasures are contained. Amen.

• St. Mary Magdalene de'Pazzi (1566-1607)

Be with me

Alone with none but you, my God,
I journey on my way.
What need I fear, when you are near,
O King of night and day?
More safe am I within your hand
than if a host did round me stand.
Be a bright flame before me, a guiding star above me,
a smooth path beneath me, a kindly shepherd behind me,
today—tonight—and forever. Amen.

• St. Columba (521-597)

Be with us

Watch, dear Lord,
with those who wake, or watch, or weep tonight,
and give your angels charge over those who sleep.
Tend your sick ones, O Lord Jesus Christ.
Rest your weary ones. Bless your dying ones.
Soothe your suffering ones. Pity your afflicted ones.
Shield your joyous ones. And all for your love's sake. Amen.

• St. Augustine of Hippo (354-430)

LITANY OF THE MOST HOLY NAME OF JESUS

Lord, have mercy	*Lord, have mercy*
Christ, have mercy	*Christ, have mercy*
Lord, have mercy	*Lord, have mercy*
God our Father in heaven	*Have mercy on us*
God the Son, Redeemer of the world	*Have mercy on us*
God the Holy Spirit	*Have mercy on us*
Holy Trinity, one God	*Have mercy on us*
Jesus, Son of the living God	*Have mercy on us*
Jesus, splendor of the Father	*Have mercy on us*
Jesus, brightness of everlasting light	*Have mercy on us*
Jesus, king of glory	*Have mercy on us*
Jesus, dawn of justice	*Have mercy on us*
Jesus, Son of the Virgin Mary	*Have mercy on us*
Jesus, worthy of our love	*Have mercy on us*
Jesus, worthy of our wonder	*Have mercy on us*
Jesus, mighty God	*Have mercy on us*
Jesus, father of the world to come	*Have mercy on us*
Jesus, prince of peace	*Have mercy on us*
Jesus, all-powerful	*Have mercy on us*
Jesus, pattern of patience	*Have mercy on us*
Jesus, model of obedience	*Have mercy on us*
Jesus, gentle and humble of heart	*Have mercy on us*
Jesus, lover of chastity	*Have mercy on us*
Jesus, lover of us all	*Have mercy on us*
Jesus, God of peace	*Have mercy on us*
Jesus, author of life	*Have mercy on us*
Jesus, model of goodness	*Have mercy on us*

Jesus, seeker of souls *Have mercy on us*
Jesus, our God *Have mercy on us*
Jesus, our refuge *Have mercy on us*
Jesus, father of the poor *Have mercy on us*
Jesus, treasure of the faithful *Have mercy on us*
Jesus, Good Shepherd *Have mercy on us*
Jesus, the true light *Have mercy on us*
Jesus, eternal wisdom *Have mercy on us*
Jesus, infinite goodness *Have mercy on us*
Jesus, our way and our life *Have mercy on us*
Jesus, joy of angels *Have mercy on us*
Jesus, king of patriarchs *Have mercy on us*
Jesus, teacher of apostles *Have mercy on us*
Jesus, master of evangelists *Have mercy on us*
Jesus, courage of martyrs *Have mercy on us*
Jesus, light of confessors *Have mercy on us*
Jesus, purity of virgins *Have mercy on us*
Jesus, crown of all saints *Have mercy on us*

Lord, be merciful *Jesus, save your people*
From all evil *Jesus, save your people*
From every sin *Jesus, save your people*
From the snares of the devil *Jesus, save your people*
From your anger *Jesus, save your people*
From the spirit of infidelity *Jesus, save your people*
From everlasting death *Jesus, save your people*
From neglect of your Holy Spirit *Jesus, save your people*
By the mystery of your incarnation *Jesus, save your people*
By your birth *Jesus, save your people*
By your childhood *Jesus, save your people*

By your hidden life *Jesus, save your people*
By your public ministry *Jesus, save your people*
By your agony and crucifixion *Jesus, save your people*
By your abandonment *Jesus, save your people*
By your grief and sorrow *Jesus, save your people*
By your death and burial *Jesus, save your people*
By your rising to new life *Jesus, save your people*
By your return in glory to the Father *Jesus, save your people*
By your gift of the holy Eucharist *Jesus, save your people*
By your joy and glory *Jesus, save your people*

Christ, hear us *Christ, hear us*
Lord Jesus, hear our prayer *Lord Jesus, hear our prayer*
Lamb of God, you take away
the sins of the world *Have mercy on us*
Lamb of God, you take away
the sins of the world *Have mercy on us*
Lamb of God, you take away
the sins of the world *Have mercy on us*

Let us pray.

Lord, may we who honor the holy name of Jesus
enjoy his friendship in this life
and be filled with eternal joy
in the kingdom where he lives and reigns
for ever and ever. Amen.

PRAYERS FOR CEMETERY VISITS

Psalm 23: The Divine Shepherd

The Lord is my shepherd;
there is nothing I lack.
In green pastures he makes me lie down;
to still waters he leads me;
he restores my soul.
He guides me along right paths
for the sake of his name.
Even though I walk through the valley of the shadow of death,
I will fear no evil, for you are with me;
your rod and your staff comfort me.

You set a table before me
in front of my enemies;
You anoint my head with oil;
my cup overflows.
Indeed, goodness and mercy will pursue me
all the days of my life;
I will dwell in the house of the Lord
for endless days.

Prayer for the Dead

Receive in tranquility and peace, O Lord, the souls of your servants
who have departed this present life to come to you.
Grant them rest and place them in the habitations of light,
the abodes of blessed spirits.
Give them the life that will not age, good things that will not pass away,
delights that have no end, through Jesus Christ our Lord. Amen.
• St. Ignatius of Antioch

A Holy Rest

Lord, support us all the day long,
until the shadows lengthen and the evening comes,
and the busy world is hushed
and the fever of life is over
and our work is done.
Then in thy mercy grant us
a safe lodging, and a holy rest,
and peace at the last. Amen.
• St. John Henry Newman

A Wonderful Birth

Death is the ultimate grace
and the culmination of our Christian life.
It is not the end, as too many think,
but the beginning of a wonderful birth.
It marks not the end of a creature,
but their true development,
their full realization in love.
It fulfills our belonging in God's life,
removing the barriers that, here on Earth,
prevent us from enjoying life in God completely.
Death allows us to attend freely
to Love Eternal,
to be aware that Love gives itself to us
and to live in God forever...
When I think about my approaching death,
I say to myself,
"Good – soon I will see God!"
• Ven. Marthe Robin

Prayer for Eternal Rest (The Requiem Prayer)

Eternal rest grant unto them, O Lord,
and let perpetual light shine upon them.
May the souls of the faithful departed,
through the mercy of God, rest in peace. Amen.

De Profundis (Psalm 130)

Out of the depths I call to You, Lord;
    Lord, hear my cry.
May your ears be attentive
    to my cry for mercy.
If you, Lord, keep account of sins,
    Lord, who can stand?
But with you is forgiveness,
    and so you are revered.

I wait for the Lord;
    my soul waits
    and I hope for his word.
My soul looks for the Lord
    more than sentinels for daybreak.
More than sentinels wait for daybreak,
    let Israel hope in the Lord,
For with the Lord is mercy
    with him is plenteous redemption;
And he will redeem Israel
    from all its sins.

Pronunciation Guide for Biblical Words

Many biblical personal and place names are familiar to us and so offer little problem with their pronunciation. The following lists only unfamiliar names that might be difficult to pronounce. Words marked with an asterisk (*) in the readings are found in this pronunciation guide. The ***bold syllable*** *indicates the accent for the word.*

Amaziah (am-uh-**zai**-uh)
Arimathea (ehr-uh-muh-**thee**-uh)
Baal-shalishah (bay-uhl-**shuh**-lai-shuh)
Babylon (**bab**-i-lon)
Barabbas (bar-**ab**-ass)
Bartimaeus (bar-ti-**may**-us)
Bethany (**beth**-a-nee)
Bethphage (beth-**fa**-gay)
Bethsaida (beth-**sigh**-da)
Caesar (**see**-sar)
Caesarea (say-sa-**ree**-a)
Caiaphas (**keye**-a-fas)
Capernaum (ka-**per**-nah-um)
Cappadocia (kappa-**doe**-sha)
Cephas (**see**-fas)
Chaldeans (kal-**dee**-ans)
cherubim (**chair**-u-bim)
Cyrenian (sigh-**reen**-ee-an)
Decapolis (day-**cap**-o-lis)
Didymus (**did**-ee-mus)
Elamites (**ee**-la-mights)
Ephah (**ef**-ah)
Ephphatha (ef-**faf**-tha)
Ephraim (**ef**-ra-eem)
Gabbatha (**gab**-ba-tha)
Gehenna (ge-**hen**-na)
Gethsemane (geth-**sem**-an-ee)
Golgotha (**gol**-gaw-tha)
Horeb (**hoe**-reb)
hyssop (**hiss**-awp)
Jairus (**jeye**-rus)
Jericho (**jer**-i-ko)
Judean (jew-**dee**-an)
Kidron (**kid**-ron)
lema sabachthani (**lay**-ma sa-back-**than**-ee)
Levites (**Leev**-eyets)
Malchus (**mal**-kus)
Massah (**mass**-ah)
Medes (**meeds**)
Meribah (**mer**-i-bah)
Mesopotamia (messo-po-**tay**-mee-ah)
Midian (**mid**-ee-uhn)
Moriah (more-**eye**-ah)
Nazorean (naz-o-**ree**-an)
Nineveh (**nin**-e-va)
Pamphylia (pam-**fill**-ee-a)
Parthians (**par**-thee-ans)
Phrygia (**frige**-ee-a)
praetorium (pray-**tor**-ee-um)
Quirinius (kwe-**rin**-ee-us)
Salome (sa-**lo**-may)
Samaria (sa-**mare**-ee-a)
Sanhedrin (san-**heed**-ren)
Seba (**see**-bah)
Sheba (**shee**-ba)
Shechem (**shek**-em)
Sidon (**sigh**-don)
Siloam (**sill**-o-ahm)
Sychar (**si**-kar)
Tarshish (**tar**-sheesh)
Timaeus (ti-**may**-us)
Tyre (**tire**)
Yahweh-yireh (**yah**-way-**yi**-reh)
Zarephath (**zar**-eh-fafth)
Zechariah (zek-uh-**rahy**-uh)
Zion (**zeye**-on)